Political Change in the Arab Gulf States

Political Change in the Arab Gulf States

Stuck in Transition

edited by
Mary Ann Tétreault
Gwenn Okruhlik
Andrzej Kapiszewski

BOULDER
LONDON

Published in the United States of America in 2011 by
Lynne Rienner Publishers, Inc.
1800 30th Street, Boulder, Colorado 80301
www.rienner.com

and in the United Kingdom by
Lynne Rienner Publishers, Inc.
3 Henrietta Street, Covent Garden, London WC2E 8LU

Library of Congress Cataloging-in-Publication Data
Political change in the Arab Gulf States : stuck in transition /
Mary Ann Tétreault, Gwenn Okruhlik, and Andrzej Kapiszewski, editors.
p. cm.
Includes bibliographical references and index.
ISBN 978-1-58826-752-8 (hardcover : alk. paper)
1. Persian Gulf States—Politics and government. 2. Persian Gulf States—Politics and government—Case studies. 3. Democratization—Persian Gulf States. 4. Democratization—Persian Gulf States—Case studies. 5. Social change—Political aspects—Persian Gulf States. 6. Social change—Political aspects—Persian Gulf States—Case studies. 7. Saudi Arabia—Politics and government. 8. Democratization—Saudi Arabia. 9. Social change—Political aspects—Saudi Arabia.
I. Tétreault, Mary Ann, 1942– II. Okruhlik, Gwenn. III. Kapiszewski, Andrzej, 1948–
JQ1840.P65 2011
320.9536—dc22

2010032864

British Cataloguing in Publication Data
A Cataloguing in Publication record for this book
is available from the British Library.

Printed and bound in the United States of America

The paper used in this publication meets the requirements of the American National Standard for Permanence of Paper for Printed Library Materials Z39.48-1992.

5 4 3 2 1

To the memory of our beloved colleague
Andrzej Kapiszewski

Who set this project in motion,
Nourished its progress,
And imagined its fulfillment

We hope that our work reflects his passion for the Gulf region,
and that this final product is all he would have wished

Contents

Part 2 The Regional Context

Part 3 Conclusion

Acknowledgments

THIS VOLUME has taken a lot of time and hard work to put together, and I would like to express my appreciation to the people whose intelligence and good cheer made it possible to sustain the effort.

First on the list are the contributors. They revised and updated several times, always without complaining, as first Andrzej's death brought the proceedings to a complete halt for many months and then my own illness imposed another long hiatus. They responded carefully and imaginatively to comments from a new coeditor and from two very sharp external reviewers whose suggestions improved the individual chapters and the argument of the volume as a whole. I am grateful for their good humor and especially for the quality of their work.

I would also like to thank my student assistants at Trinity University for their stellar work on the manuscript: Caitlin Howell, Danny Hosein, Katherine Schmidt, Ragan Updegraff, Hunter Price, and Caitlin Dillon.

Special thanks go to Gwenn Okruhlik, who e-mailed immediately when she heard that I was ill to ask me what she could do to help. My request that she come on as coeditor was, I am sure, not what she expected when she made her offer. But Gwenn is a diplomat as well as a scholar, and she even managed to convince me that this was exactly the sort of thing she had in mind all along. She provided an excellent sounding board, worked closely with several chapter authors on their revisions, and took the lead in preparing the volume's concluding chapter.

Gwenn and I both want to thank Mohammed al-Ghanim for his invaluable research assistance. Mohammed brought his extensive transitions expertise to bear on our much-revised introduction, which incorporates substantial contributions from all three editors. In the process, he wore my tendency toward (unwarranted?) optimism down so much that, when the last edits on the introduction were finished, Gwenn observed that it seemed we were not so far apart on the subject of transitions in the Gulf after all.

Finally, we all thank Lynne Rienner, who stuck with this project through its many transitions. If I were Pope, I would beatify her. Yes, this is short of canonization, but beatification is probably as much as any normal person can stand. After all, if they make you a saint, people keep asking for things.

—Mary Ann Tétreault

Political Change in the Arab Gulf States

1

Twenty-First-Century Politics in the Arab Gulf States

Mary Ann Tétreault, Andrzej Kapiszewski, and Gwenn Okruhlik

THERE IS WIDESPREAD agreement that a deficit of freedom undermines human development.[1] There is less agreement about the connection between political and economic development, yet many believe that there is a dramatic gap between the levels of political freedom and economic development in Arab countries as compared to the rest of the world.[2] One often-cited indicator of the Arab states' failure to develop politically is that, with the exception of Iraq and Lebanon, none of the Arab-majority countries has a democratically elected government. Economic development also lags, surprisingly so in view of the region's oil resources. Labor productivity in these countries dropped between 1960 and 1990 while it soared elsewhere in the world, and it remains low for various reasons, including overemployment and labor importation in oil-exporting countries.[3] Even Africa outperformed the Arab region with regard to rates of economic growth during that time.

The contradictions embedded in these observations are products of creative and sometimes inappropriate aggregation as well as the tendency of analysts to consider too few "causes" when they examine "effects."[4] In an effort to disentangle assumptions from findings, in this volume we look at domestic politics in the seven Arab states that border the Gulf.

There is no better example of the disjunction between "what everybody knows" about the Arab world and the complex and multifaceted reality in this region than the monarchies of the Gulf. Saudi Arabia, Kuwait, Bahrain, Qatar, the United Arab Emirates (UAE), and Oman, the members of the Gulf Cooperation Council (GCC), enjoy relatively high incomes and, in consequence, their citizens enjoy relatively high standards of living. We show in this volume that, despite their "conservative" political systems, all six governments have carried out significant political and economic reforms. We also show, however, that, although civil rights and liberties are greater and citizens have more say in national politics now than they did a decade ago, there is no indication that any of these countries are launched on a "transition to democracy." Indeed, the complex politics of the GCC states offers an opportunity to test propositions about economic and political development—about transitions broadly conceived.

In Iraq as well as in the only non-Arab Gulf state, Iran, the picture offers little if anything more in the way of optimism about development and freedom, despite a popularly ratified constitution in Iraq and a postrevolution referendum that was used as a mandate to re-create Iran's constitution, although in a way that failed to elicit the same enthusiasm.[5] Despite hydrocarbon resources that rival those of their neighbors, both Iraq and Iran labor under the political and economic aftereffects of imperialist exploitation; violent revolutions to overthrow client governments; and, in the case of Iraq, invasion and war purportedly undertaken precisely to make it more democratic. Both continue to endure high levels of government corruption and repression. With regard to the rule of law, both have constitutions that, although differently flawed, contain provisions that undermine national unity and governmental accountability while the elections held under these organic laws are ambiguous with regard to their ability to produce stable and effective legitimate governments. Why do the Gulf states—and Middle Eastern states generally—seem to be exceptions to the third wave of democratization, a global political sea change that presumably was able to effect democratic transitions everywhere else in the world?[6] Indeed, the optimism that swept academic and policy communities in response to third-wave political openings in Latin America and Europe has given way to pessimism almost as deep.

Events seem to have overtaken theories that were cherished for their elegance, but proved to be wanting when it came to predicting the trajectory of politics in cases outside the regions that had served as the template of *transitology*, the study of transitions from authoritarian rule. In a recent article, Phillippe Schmitter, one of the founders of this analytical school, emphasizes that he and his research partners not only did not see themselves as the initiators of a new paradigm for understanding democratization in Latin America, but they also were unprepared for what Schmitter called "divine surprises" comprising the wave of democratization in Eastern Europe. Indeed, Schmitter asserts that stretching the "assumptions, concepts, hypotheses, and tentative conclusions" represented in that early work seemed at the outset to be "problematic" in the light of the divergence between the ideas it reflected and "most prevailing theories about 'really existing democracy.'"[7] We agree that the transition paradigm was carefully conceived and offered with many caveats, yet it often was inappropriately applied, in part as the result of the very real progress toward democracy made in states across the world, including some widely regarded as problematic at best.[8] The now highly criticized shortcomings of the transition paradigm[9] arise both from a problématique sited in the unique politics and history of Latin America and, perhaps especially, from wishful thinking on the part of those who embraced it so enthusiastically that they were convinced that the end of (authoritarian) history had arrived.[10]

In this volume, we consider recent political and economic openings and closures in the Arab Gulf states, an integral part of the Middle East, a region that transitologists generally agree is resistant to democratization. The substance and trajectories of political change play out in different ways in different places—there certainly is unevenness to this process within and across cases. This is as true among Arab Gulf states as it is between them and others. Kuwait is, in some ways, the Gulf's political outlier. In 1981, elections were held for a new National Assembly following five years of constitutionally illegal closure of the parliament by the regime. The prodemocracy movement that sought to end the second illegal closure culminated in 1990 when the ruler called for elections to an illegal advisory council that, ironically, took office just in time for the Iraqi invasion. During the occupation, prodemocracy activists pressured the ruler to agree to the restoration of the constitution should Kuwait be liberated, but it took additional pressure from coalition members after liberation to bring this about. Since then, democratization as a process continues to be three steps forward and at least two steps back, but what we emphasize here is that it is a process whose end point is yet to be determined.

Saudi Arabia and Oman are outliers on the other end of the spectrum. In Saudi Arabia, the centrality of the ruling family in national political life has been consolidated rather than diffused even under the guise of a "reform" agenda.[11] Social forces are vibrant, but have thus far been offset by the overwhelming power of the state. In the most understudied of all GCC states, Oman, discussions of reform are limited to expanding the scope of a partially elected Shura Council that has no defined scope or any legislative or advisory authority.[12] Its political future remains grim as decisionmaking continues to be dominated by the sultan and a tight cohort of advisers and individuals from the ruling family and their close associates.[13] In addition to being head of state, the sultan is prime minister as well as minister of foreign affairs, defense, and finance. But perhaps the most distinct threat to the future of Oman is the nexus between a somewhat totalitarian structure and the lack of an apparent successor to the Omani throne. While "succession crises" have occurred frequently in modern Gulf history, Oman is the only Gulf state that has no official heir to the throne.[14] Discussion of the country's political trajectory and future is therefore contentious at best (see Chapter 5).

Elsewhere in the Gulf, political opening proceeds at a snail's pace. Mediated by autocratic rulers, small steps are being taken. Yet even though many social and economic reforms have been instituted in these regimes, the fundamental distribution of political power remains unchanged in the Arab Gulf states. Why this is so is one of the questions we explore in this volume.

The events of the past decade have left most students of the Gulf, including the optimists, much more pessimistic than they were a decade ago about the prospects for democracy there and elsewhere in the Middle East in the near to medium term.[15] There are many reasons for the persistence of authoritarianism in the Middle East. They include the historical legacy of postcolonial/postimperial state-led development; indigenous social forces that were diminished if not crushed during the imperial era; and, in non-GCC states, the coercive capability of the state apparatus. Meanwhile, postimperial oil revenues from abroad lubricate the state bureaucracy and provide enviable—and envied—living standards to local populations. Even at the height of scholarly optimism, most analysts, including transitologists, omitted the Middle East from their lists of likely candidates for democratization.[16]

The size and reach of those oil revenues explain why rentier state theory is a common explanation for authoritarianism in the Middle East. Especially in oil-exporting states themselves, rentier income from labor remittances and service fees, foreign aid, and other external sources of income provide nontax income for states.[17] Oil exporters are sometimes characterized as political communities that live by the inverse of the slogan pushing the American colonies to revolt from Britain in the late eighteenth century; that is, they are regimes flying the banner of "no representation without taxation."[18] Rulers garner support from citizens or subjects by allocating resources to rather than extracting resources from them. (This is why they also are sometimes referred to as "allocation states," discussed below).[19] But payoffs to citizens are not the only source of state strength. Money also buys the means of coercion, supplying rentier states with resources to repress dissent.[20] Meanwhile, reliance on income generated by an enclave industry that creates little in the way of forward and backward economic linkages[21] retards societal diversification and, thereby, both the expansion and the effects of social changes with the potential to shift cultural norms and expectations. It also retards or sidelines economic changes that could reduce direct citizen dependence on the state.[22]

The omission of the Middle East from transitology wish lists of future democracies sparked Michael Ross's interest in testing rentier state theory in a global framework. He sought cases outside the community of oil-exporting countries and also outside the Middle East to determine whether and, if so, how and how much, high levels of mineral export earnings per se inhibit democratization.[23] A somewhat different take on the link between mineral wealth and democratic development appears in a look at substate units of a democratic country, explored by Ellis Goldberg, Erik Wibbels, and Eric Mvukiyehe, who found differences in institutional structures and praxis that helped explain variations in democratic practice among mineral-rich US states.[24] Ross concludes that oil and other forms of mineral wealth do reduce possibilities for democratization, in and out of the Middle East, and that all three causal mechanisms—allocation, repression, and low rates of social and cultural change—are implicated. Goldberg, Wibbles, and Mvukiyehe show that, even within the same federal nation-state, the quality of democracy in its constituent parts is shaped by mineral wealth. It is surprising that this finding holds up so well in places where mineral wealth is privately rather than state owned: "American state governments behaved (in collusion with private mineral firms) in much the same manner as international rentier states. . . . [The] combination of low taxes and extensive public outlays . . . seems to contribute to politicians' persistence in office."[25]

Rentier state theory notwithstanding, a minority among Middle East analysts interpreted the divine surprises that so startled Schmitter and his colleagues as holding out the possibility of transition from authoritarianism in the Middle East. Even in the Gulf monarchies, this perspective initially seemed justified as political openings began to appear, the most significant being the widely covered and discussed 1992 election in Kuwait.[26] A hopeful focus on the Middle East as a site of transitions was refashioned into a policy of interventionist regime change during the George W. Bush administration, when the US-led invasion of Iraq, and what had been predicted to be the modern equivalent of a splendid little war, was supposed to inaugurate a wave of political and economic reform in the region as a whole (see Chapter 11). Pressure from US policymakers on Middle East rulers, along with incentives in the form of free trade agreements, membership in the World Trade Organization, proposed cooperation with the European Union, and widespread public interest among citizens in several Gulf states, encouraged Gulf rulers to embrace the notion of reform.

The reforms they introduced were mostly cosmetic, however, designed to ease tension at pressure points, but not intended to transfer power from rulers to more broadly based institutions. For example, the Bush-era focus on women's rights and elections made it relatively easy for Gulf monarchs to comply with the letter of democratization while sidestepping more fundamental change. Indeed, the irony of *al islah* (reform) is that sometimes reforms serve to reassert the authority of ruling families.[27] In the months preceding the much-heralded Saudi Arabian municipal elections of 2005, for example, civil servants were warned that they would face disciplinary action, including loss of their jobs, if they criticized any government programs or state policies.[28] Women were excluded from suffrage. Some of the most articulate proponents of elections were arrested and jailed for the duration of the campaigning and voting. In the end, the government appointed fully half of each municipal council.[29] Under the guise of competitive elections, the ruling family had consolidated its power in political life.

Most of the reforms directed toward women are equally ambiguous. Women have long served as markers and counters in male-dominated conflicts between regimes and oppositions in the Middle East as elsewhere. The main contenders rarely care about women themselves, however, or what their political rights can or even might accomplish as independent variables in political equations. At best, like tribal voters, women are conceived by male citizens and by rulers as inherent supporters of the status quo, whether because of their essential conservatism or their situational subservience: they will vote simply as the men in their families direct.[30] The ease with which women's political participation was instituted in Bahrain, Oman, and Qatar—although not in Kuwait, whose parliament has real legislative authority—testifies to the assumption that election outcomes would not change if women were to vote. Yet some objected to women voting for the same reasons that they object to a woman driving, leaving the country without her husband's permission, or engaging in other behavior that men feel encroaches on their right to dominate women (see also Chapter 9).[31]

It is clear that elections are fraught with contradictions as indicators of democracy or even of democratization. They are easily manipulated from above (see Chapters 2 and 4), and frequently stolen outright by unscrupulous incumbents. Perhaps for this reason, elections appear to attract authoritarian rulers in search of methods to reduce external and internal pressure for reform, so much so that such regimes constitute a subcategory of authoritarianism. These competitive authoritarian regimes do not meet the minimum procedural standards for democracy because their elections are so heavily tainted, yet the possibility (and occasional actuality) that opposition members can turn incumbents out introduces an "inherent" tension in this strategy.[32]

Another approach to deflecting pressures for political reform is economic liberalization. Also a highly emphasized indicator of democratization by analysts of the George W. Bush era, economic liberalization addresses the third mechanism underlying the persistent authoritarianism investigated by Ross. Economic liberalization offers the prospect of transferring economic resources from the state to private actors. By adding to the wealth of existing economic elites, liberalization contributes to the construction of power centers able to compete to varying extents with state elites as directors of key aspects of the political economy.[33] Insofar as economic liberalization transfers resources directly to citizens, it can spark or add to the development of the class fractions and personal interests that modernization theorists,[34] among others,[35] thought would result in a flourishing civil society. Yet arguably the most successful exercises in post–World War II middle-class creation came in the Arab Gulf countries, and not as the result of foreign investment, but rather from wealth transfers and investment in human capital by rentier states.

Rivers of money, openings of various kinds, and the internal contradictions alluded to above have led to similarly peculiar outcomes in the regimes of the Arab Gulf states, with the exception of Iraq, which has moved on to a different, if related, set of transition problems, dilemmas, and possibilities. We see all seven of these states as being "in transition" in the sense that their systems of governance are much different from what they were fifty, or twenty-five, or even ten years ago. They have been transformed from tribal regimes into states with notable administrative capacity, increasingly coherent identities, and varying degrees of social, political, and economic inclusion among citizens. All of this occurred in the context of domestic and external pressures vastly more intrusive and influential than those experienced by most early developers.[36] The country case chapters in this volume indicate both the extent of this movement and the forces that keep it going. Yet even the most charitable interpretation of the politics of these actively changing states would not conclude that any is a "really existing democracy" as Schmitter defines it, and few would see them as embarked on a path toward democracy. Even so, they have moved, and sometimes in a progressive direction. Thus, we conclude that they are stuck in transition, states in motion each of whose multiple drivers is steering toward a different destination. There are more economic openings than explicitly political or social openings[37] but all of them are limited and engineered to minimize threats to the power of regimes.

Transitions Toward Democratization: From Authoritarianism or Within Authoritarianism?

We take a broad view of transition, seeing it simply as a process of structural change that alters the institutions and processes by which a political community is governed. We do this from what Mary Ann Tétreault and Mohammed Al-Ghanim call transitology's "original position";[38] that is, the assumption that the outcome or destination of transition is uncertain and, therefore, that it is premature to think of it as proceeding to democracy or anywhere else before a stable end point is reached.[39] Daniel Brumberg, in contrast, believes that the end point has been reached already. It is "the trap of liberalized autocracy," a sort of caldera into which regimes fall after having overcome initial resistance to reform. Once reforms have been effected—in different ways that usually derive from elite pacts—reformers find themselves confronted by insuperable obstacles to progressing further.[40]

Brumberg argues that such regimes are not in transition: they have arrived as liberalized autocracies, hybrid regimes that are functional and stable.

Like Brumberg, we see life in the caldera as active. Unlike him, we do not see it as stable. We regard the churning in the caldera as struggle in progress, and potentially capable of overcoming the reformers' one-down position (i.e., capable of pushing institutionalized political liberalization further). In consequence, although the events of the past decade leave most students of the Gulf—and the Middle East as a whole—pessimistic about the likelihood of continued real political opening,[41] we see the jury as still being out. There is movement—sometimes backward, sometimes forward—but movement nonetheless. Indeed, we hope that the current pessimism is as overstated as the earlier optimism.

During the optimistic era, US observers urging democratization were all too willing to interpret virtually any election, however "flawed," as evidence of transition in a country already deemed as being in transition (see Chapter 11). This infatuation with elections was communicated to the Gulf where the staging of elections for foreign and domestic consumption became an art form (see, especially, Chapter 2). In Iraq, elections follow timetables that are heavily influenced by external—usually US—political imperatives (see Chapter 3), and mostly domestic ones at that.[42] While we do not argue that elections are meaningless or unimportant, we do believe that they have to be seen as part of an elaborate dance engaging regime leaders and aspiring leaders, domestic forces pressing for liberalization, and external audiences whose good opinion Gulf governments seek to retain. Like Eric Bjornulund,[43] we believe that elections must be viewed holistically. Political dynamics can be understood only if we account for events prior to and after the actual vote.

Other approaches to explaining instances of significant political change focus on context, including personalities, movements, institutions, the overall environment, and the impact of particular events such as wars, economic collapses, or a massive public failure of the state.[44] From this "new institutionalist" perspective, political change is path dependent.[45] Its trajectory is influenced by existing institutions and enduring legacies from previous ones, the quality of leadership, and the impetus or constraint imposed by domestic and international political forces[46] and events. It is subject not only to derailment, but also to unplanned-for opportunities. This makes movements for democratization and government responses to them appear more like ad hoc reactions than the unfolding of a rational strategy,[47] a situation that may actually be the case.

The new institutionalist school also offers an explanation for regression and for the failure to seize an opportunity to initiate a transition that arguably would have served the interests of elites. An example of the first is the shift toward authoritarianism in Venezuela. Terry Karl foresaw it as one of several problematic effects of elite decisionmaking during the 1958 pacted transition because Communists were kept from the negotiating table. In consequence, the legitimate and, at that time, relatively moderate demands of workers received far less attention from the new regime than the inclusion of a strongly proworker party would have ensured.[48] A similar shortsightedness operated among Syrian elites in the 1960s, even among members of the same political party who lost—wasted?—an opportunity to move toward transition under a prime minister unusually willing to endure high political costs in the cause of national unity.[49] Arguments based on culture, institutions, and development trajectories are frequently used to delegitimate prospects for democratization in the Arab Middle East. Arguments focused on Islam as producing societies ideologically unsuited to support democracy remain common, as were similar arguments about Catholicism before the openings in Eastern Europe and Latin America. We suggest instead that religion can be and has been used to institutionalize repression, just as it has been used as a vehicle for attacking it.[50]

Institutions are more problematic. Political power struggles within ruling families loom large in negotiating institutional changes. Thus, institutional reforms were often instruments of intra-elite power games as much as they were attempts to modernize the state. As a result of these prior decisions, and even before there was strong path dependence via the rentier condition, patrimonial politics and struggles largely determined institutional design, and certain institutions continue to retain a "fiefdom" character.[51]

Historical memory in the Gulf monarchies incorporates elements of nationhood as well as tribalism.[52] Its shorter and more troubled history incorporating several divergent visions of a united Iraq[53] may explain part of the difficulty the Iraqi nation has faced putting itself back together as the third Gulf war since 1980 winds down. Indeed, institutions throughout the Gulf are contested and fragile. The tradition of *shura* (consultation), as opposed to separation of powers and rule of law, is used by Gulf rulers to argue that Arab or Islamic states have culturally embedded institutions that are more compatible with local values and customs than the constitutions, parliaments, and elections favored by prodemocracy forces. Like Christianity in the West, however, Islam is as often the handmaiden of autocratic rulers as a vehicle to challenge them.[54] Tribal organization and sectarian loyalties also are deployed to design constituencies and elections, and the institutions they produce (see Chapters 2, 4, 5, and 7). Constitutions have been overridden and rewritten as rulers attempt to force institutions to support their continued hold on power (see Chapter 2). Sites and processes of institutionalization may be incremental and multifocal; trade-offs are plenty. The challenges are daunting given the commanding heights and coercive capacities of authoritarian rulers.

The early transitions literature dealt with regime change in Latin

America and Eastern Europe. In both regions, the ability of authoritarian and totalitarian states to maintain control was substantially exhausted, politically and economically—unlike the contemporary situation in the Gulf states. The literature was written when rationalism was becoming the dominant ideological paradigm in political science and rested in part on the assumption that opening regimes politically, such as by increasing civil liberties and holding elections, no longer could be avoided. Despite the caution Schmitter and his colleagues urge, many early transitions did result in democratization, which often, although not always or entirely, was achieved.[55] In addition to political opening during this period, many states sought to stimulate their economies. They expanded trade and opened themselves to direct foreign investment; some made small moves toward domestic economic rationalization. Even authoritarian regimes in the Middle East saw an open door (*infitah*) as a possible route to growth.[56] At the same time, persistent economic difficulties increased the attraction of foregrounding domestic institutions that could be made to bear some of the responsibility should development remain elusive, even to states with no desire to democratize at all.[57] The concept of transition as a process of regime change and opening as an economic wedge that might initiate transition thus became intertwined.

Rethinking Transitions from Authoritarianism in the Gulf Context

As we stated at the outset of this chapter, whatever hopes existed for democratization in the Gulf have been substantially dashed by the appearance of competitive authoritarianism/electoral authoritarianism and other types of hybrid regimes. We suggest that they should be considered in the context of stickiness rather than as outright failures.

Transitions everywhere are anything but linear. They encompass progressive movement alongside retrograde movement and simple inertia, drifting along an already established pathway. The interesting questions include: Which factors contribute to what kind of outcome, and how do they do it? What do such openings and closures in political space look like? How are they felt and assessed? And perhaps most important, why do they happen and what do they accomplish? The Gulf's ruling families persist in the face of internal and external challenges. Is this manifestation of authoritarian resilience and opening different from persistent authoritarianism elsewhere?

Even cosmetic reforms may have unintended consequences. They raise expectations of further opening, limiting the ability of regimes to push back to square one as cheaply and unobtrusively as they might have done without them. Reforms also lay down structures such as elections and the popular mobilization that even sham elections necessitate. Alternatively, cosmetic reforms may provide cover for regimes that subsequently regress by undermining or crippling institutions and closing political space. We observe today in Saudi Arabia, Kuwait, Qatar, the UAE, Bahrain, and Oman substantial closure in terms of freedom of expression and assembly. The publication of newspapers is suspended, critics are arrested, blogs are blocked, and Internet cafes are monitored. Social and cultural gathering spaces are sites of contestation and, thus, frequently curtailed by the state. All of the countries considered here have "elastic" laws that prohibit such ambiguous things as criticism of ruling families; insults to Islam or human dignity; speech or writing that insults neighboring or friendly countries, threatens social stability, violates public order or morals, criticizes family values, or violates the security of the state or its public image.[58]

Although the cases under consideration are disparate, we also know that there is substantial emulation and political learning going on, and not only among regime actors.[59] Information sharing also supports cooperative behavior among domestic groups, just as it can trigger pushback from groups that see themselves as losing ground to rivals, as Jerzy Zdanowski shows in Chapter 7 on Saudi Arabia. Elections as sites of struggles over how institutions operate and for whose benefit are focal points of Gianluca Parolin's chapter on Bahrain and Mary Ann Tétreault's on Kuwait (Chapters 2 and 4, respectively). The results of elections may change the shape of the playing field along with the fortunes of aspiring leaders and their constituencies, as Juan Cole's examination of Shi'i politics in Iraq in Chapter 3 shows. Qatar's amirs have used liberalization to clothe their family coups in the garments of progress for some time, and Jill Crystal argues in Chapter 6 that even the establishment of Al-Jazeera was very much in Qatar's facade tradition. Yet as N. Janardhan shows in Chapter 10, enlarging Qatar's public sphere also provided a model for other new regional broadcasters whose clientele is somewhat different from Al-Jazeera's, not incidentally highlighting the station's differential treatment of its own rulers as compared to the way it treats others.

"Stuckness" is illustrated in different ways in J. E. Peterson's chapter on Oman, which suggests that top-down liberalization is virtually the only source of political opening—so far. Christian Koch presents a more active picture of liberalization in the UAE, but concludes that prosperity continues to dampen widespread enthusiasm for political power sharing there (Chapters 5 and 8, respectively). Perhaps the chapter that is most illustrative of the concatenation of elite and popular forces and their impact not only on women's rights but also on economic rationalization is Eleanor Doumato's take on the politics of women's rights (Chapter 9). Matteo Legrenzi's chapter on GCC security, and Mary Ann Tétreault's on US foreign policy, show the continuing influence of the United States in the Gulf, whether it is explicit, in the form of military transfers or direct pressure to democratize, or implicit, as illustrated by the shift from George W. Bush's push for democratization to Barack Obama's hands-off approach to the domestic politics of US allies (Chapters 12 and 11, respectively).

As these chapters also show, if we can say that the Arab Gulf states are stuck in transition from authoritarianism, we cannot say that they are stuck for the same reasons, in the same place, or facing in the same direction. The different tactics for navigating democratization pressures and expectations have, not surprisingly, produced different institutions, expectations, and civil society structures. Development trajectories also vary, and the relative vulnerability of the Gulf states to what we call internal *juxtapositions*, the results of trends initiated or amplified by past policies and events, may prove to be extensive (see Chapter 13). What we can say is that the main force for stuckness is virtually identical across all six Gulf monarchies and is struggling to emerge in Iraq. Like autocrats across time and space, rulers in the Gulf are unwilling to give up their positions on the commanding heights of their governments and societies. It is not that they tried in vain to democratize and were stymied at every step by resisting populations. Rather, it is that they have used the facade of reform to hide their determination to hold on to the power that they have—and even to extend it.

The chapters in this volume illustrate these main points. They show where democratization might be restarted and where a particular ruler's strategy has effectively used up the transition potential of a particular course of action.[60] Each chapter deals with pressures to democratize emanating from inside and out, how (much) rulers responded to them, and whether and how rulers got around them. The authors assess the degree of forward movement, inertia, and rollback that comprise the resilience that enables these regimes to come back again and again, in spite of popular efforts by citizens and encouragement from abroad to restart and nurture systemic change. They also identify juxtapositions in each society, ranging from demographic challenges to cultural politics, the ebb and flow of oil and gas income, and the strength and direction of momentum in their core constituencies that could strengthen or attenuate the ability of rulers to keep to their authoritarian ways.

Among the juxtapositions peculiar to the Arab Gulf states and few others is the potential of oil to complicate transitions and rollback. Comparisons between regions during the 1990s have noted superior rates of growth in Africa and Asia as compared to growth in the Arab Middle East. This difference reveals the acute dependence of oil-exporting states on economic externalities over which they have little control, chiefly oil prices, currency exchange rates, and stable consumer demand for hydrocarbons. During the 1990s, the Arab Gulf states labored under depressed oil prices.

Beginning with the new millennium and especially since the beginning of the Iraq War in March 2003, these burdens eased as oil prices soared. They returned in different forms as the result of the macroeconomic instability that accompanies hydrocarbon price inflation: rapidly rising consumer prices, the expansion of debt, and, in the most recent era of macroeconomic destabilization, the global economic collapse following the 2008 banking crisis. The Gulf oil exporters' external dependency has not altered significantly since the early days of their industries, despite income accruing to sovereign wealth funds, the expansion of private sectors whose businesses depend on demand from the state sector and its millions of employees supported by oil revenue, and changes in market structure that continue to enlarge the role of oil exporters in hydrocarbon markets downstream from production.

External dependency separates what Giacomo Luciani defines as production states, which depend on their domestic economies to generate employment and tax revenues, from allocation states, which rely on economic transfers from abroad to generate income for citizens and the state.[61] Although most of the literature on rentier states stresses the economic independence of governments from domestic populations that is conferred by oil revenues,[62] it underestimates the nature and strength of demands on them, especially during periods of low income, and the impact of these demands on state repression.[63] An example of juxtaposition par excellence, external dependency reduces the capacity of states to manage domestic conflict at the precise time at which domestic conflict is most likely to arise.[64] It also neglects the issue of strategic security addressed by Legrenzi in Chapter 12.

Other juxtapositions also stem from the oil wealth of the Arab Gulf states. Prosperity allowed governments to educate their populations and provide generous income, health care, and other forms of social support. Sadly, it also instituted a pattern of changed expectations and behavior such that the nation's dependency on external rents was echoed in popular dependency on state largesse to sustain extravagant lifestyles. This dependency is seen by analysts of the rentier state school as key to maintaining authoritarianism in the Middle East, not only in the oil-exporting states themselves, but also in neighboring labor-exporting states (like Egypt and Jordan) that send workers to the oil exporters, along with states that receive high levels of foreign aid and investment (again, like Egypt and Jordan). As we have noted, a closer look would show that these rulers, and probably Iraq's as well, are using facade reform as a tactic for holding on to power rather than as a strategy for peaceful transition to power sharing.

Although the strength and organization of civil societies also vary widely among the Arab Gulf states, it is arguably here that the greatest potential for pushing transition toward more open societies and polities lies. Of course, as we noted earlier, transition from and even within authoritarianism may (or may not) be a fact of life in some of these states. But even where it exists, its destination is far from clear. Under the right—or better, the wrong—conditions, populist authoritarianism such as in Egypt during the 1950s and 1960s, or Syria during the secession period, could result from failed management of juxtapositions.[65] Such juxtapositions thus constitute critical junctures in the possible transition from authoritarianism in the Arab states of the Gulf.

We turn now to the case studies to examine how and why these authoritarian regimes persist in the face of internal and external challenges, how they protect their centrality in political life even under the guise of reform, and the various forms in which authoritarian durability and resilience are manifest.

Notes

The authors would like to thank Mohammed al-Ghanim for his excellent research assistance during the final stages of preparing this chapter.

1. Among the most ethically and empirically grounded expressions of this perspective is Amartya Sen, *Development as Freedom* (New York: Anchor Books, 1999).

2. UNDP, *Arab Human Development Report 2002* (New York: United Nations, 2002), www.undp.org; and UNDP, *Arab Human Development Report 2003* (New York: United Nations, 2003), www.undp.org. The hierarchy among variables used to explain the persistence of authoritarianism in the Middle East varies. Some blame Islam for the lack of democracy in the Middle East—for example, Bernard Lewis, "Islam and Liberal Democracy," *Atlantic Monthly*, February 1993, pp. 89–94; M. Steven Fish, "Islam and Authoritarianism," *World Politics* 55, no. 1 (2002). Others point to oil revenues as a primary cause of authoritarianism—examples include Hazem Beblawi, "The Rentier State in the Arab World," in *The Arab State*, ed. Giacomo Luciani (Berkeley: University of California Press, 1990), pp. 85–98; Michael L. Ross, "Does Oil Hinder Democracy?" *World Politics* 53, no. 3 (2001): 325–361; and Terry Lynn Karl, *The Paradox of Plenty: Oil Booms and Petro-States* (Berkeley: University of California Press, 1997). The nomination of Arab culture as the greatest obstacle to democratization is the message of works like Hisham Donno, Daniela Donno, and Bruce Russett, "Islam, Authoritarianism, and Female Empowerment: What Are the Linkages?" *World Politics* 56, no. 4 (2004): 582–607.

3. See, for example, Syed Ali, *Dubai: Gilded Age* (New Haven: Yale University Press, 2010); John Chalcraft, "Monarchy, Migration, and Hegemony in the Arabian Peninsula," paper prepared for the Kuwait Programme in Globalization and Governance, London, June 2010; and Nader Fergany, "Aspects of Labor Migration and Unemployment in the Arab Region," Almishkat Center for Research, Cairo, www.mafhoum.com.

4. See Donno, Donno, and Russett, "Islam, Authoritarianism, and Female Empowerment."

5. The Iraqi constitution was submitted to voters in October 2005. For background about the ratification of Iran's postrevolution constitution, see Nikki Keddie, *Modern Iran: Roots and Results of Revolution* (New Haven: Yale University Press,

2003), pp. 246–249; and S. Waqar Hasib, "The Iranian Constitution: An Exercise in Contradictions," *Al-Nakhlah*, Spring 2004, www.fletcher.tufts.edu.

6. "Third wave" comes from Samuel P. Huntington, "Democracy's Third Wave," *Journal of Democracy* 2, no. 2 (1991): 12–34.

7. Phillippe C. Schmitter, "Twenty-Five Years, Fifteen Findings," *Journal of Democracy* 21, no. 1 (2010): 17.

8. Larry Diamond, "Thinking About Hybrid Regimes," *Journal of Democracy* 13, no. 2 (2002): 21–35.

9. See, for example, Thomas Carothers, "The End of the Transition Paradigm," *Journal of Democracy* 13, no. 1 (2002): 5–21.

10. See, for example, Francis Fukuyama, *The End of History and the Last Man* (London: HarperPerennial, 1993).

11. For more on the structural challenges to Saudi reform, see Madawi Al-Rasheed, *al-Saudiyyah wa ma'zaq al-islah al-siyasi fi al-qarn al-hadi wa-al-'ishrin* (London: Saqi, 2005).

12. Freedom House, *Freedom in the World—2009: Oman* (Washington, DC: Freedom House, July 16, 2009), www.unhcr.org.

13. Francis Owtram, *A Modern History of Oman: Formation of the State Since 1920* (London: I. B. Tauris, 2004), pp. 193–208.

14. For more on the upgrading of authoritarian rule in Oman's contemporary history, see Dahir Mas'ud, *al-Istimrārīya wa-al-taghyīr fi tajribat al-taḥdīth al-'Umānīyah, 1970–2005* (Beirut: Dar al-Farabi, 2008).

15. See, for example, Lisa Anderson, "Searching Where the Light Shines: Studying Democratization in the Middle East," *Annual Review of Political Science* 9 (2006): 189–214; Russell E. Lucas, *Institutions and the Politics of Survival in Jordan: Domestic Responses to External Challenges, 1988–2001* (Albany: SUNY Press, 2006); Marsha Pripstein Posusney and Michele Penner Angrist, eds., *Authoritarianism in the Middle East: Regimes and Resistance* (Boulder: Lynne Rienner, 2005); and Oliver Schlumberger, ed., *Debating Arab Authoritarianism: Dynamics and Durability in Nondemocratic Regimes* (Palo Alto, CA: Stanford University Press, 2007).

16. Oliver Schlumberger, "Arab Authoritarianism: Debating the Dynamics and Durability of Nondemocratic Regimes," in *Debating Arab Authoritarianism: Dynamics and Durability in Nondemocratic Regimes*, ed. Oliver Schlumberger (Palo Alto, CA: Stanford University Press, 2007), pp. 1–20.

17. Hossein Mahdavy, "The Patterns and Problems of Economic Development in Rentier States: The Case of Iran," in *Studies in the Economic History of the Middle East*, ed. M. A. Cook (London: Oxford University Press, 1970), pp. 428–467. This framework was taken up late by other scholars, such as Giacomo Luciani, ed., *The Arab State* (Berkeley: University of California Press, 1990).

18. For example, see Paul W. H. Aarts, "Oil, Money, and Participation: Kuwait's *Sonderweg* as a Rentier State," *Orient* 32, no. 2 (1991): 205–216. For a theoretical framework assessing Arab rentiers more generally, see Hazem Beblawi, "The Rentier State in the Arab World," pp. 85–98.

19. Giacomo Luciani, "Allocation vs. Production States: A Theoretical Framework," in *The Arab State*, ed. Giacomo Luciani (Berkeley: University of California Press, 1990), pp. 65–84. For a view of the devaluation of politics in much rentier analyses, see Gwenn Okruhlik, "Rentier Wealth, Unruly Law and the Rise of Political Opposition: The Political Economy of Oil States," *Comparative Politics* 31, no. 3 (1999): 295–315. Rentier states also foster opposition as a result of their political choices about how to distribute revenues.

20. Mark J. Gasiorowski, *U.S. Foreign Policy and the Shah: Building a Client State in Iran* (Ithaca: Cornell University Press, 1991).

21. Jane Jacobs, *Cities and the Wealth of Nations: Principles of Economic Life* (New York: Random House, 1984). Jacobs was an early critic of globalized industries, of which oil is the paradigmatic example.

22. Timothy W. Luke, "Dependent Development and the OPEC States: State Formation in Saudi Arabia and Iran Under the International Energy Regime," *Studies in Comparative International Development* 20, no. 1 (1985): 31–54; Luciani, "Allocation vs. Production States."

23. Michael L. Ross, "Does Oil Hinder Democracy?" pp. 325–361.

24. Ellis Goldberg, Erik Wibbels, and Eric Mvukiyehe, "Lessons from Strange Cases: Democracy, Development, and the Resource Curse in the U.S. States," *Comparative Political Studies* 41, nos. 4–5 (2008): 477–514.

25. Ibid., p. 506.

26. Mary Ann Tétreault, *Stories of Democracy: Politics and Society in Contemporary Kuwait* (New York: Columbia University Press, 2000); also Michael C. Hudson, "After the Gulf War: Prospects for Democratization in the Arab World," *Middle East Journal* 45, no. 3 (1991): 407–426; and Paul Aarts, "Democracy, Oil, and the Gulf War," *Third World Quarterly* 13, no. 3 (1992): 525–538.

27. Gwenn Okruhlik, "The Irony of Islah (Reform)," *Washington Quarterly* 28, no. 4 (2005): 153–170; Gwenn Okruhlik, "State Power, Religious Privilege, and Myths About Political Reform," in *Religion and Politics in Saudi Arabia: Wahhabism and the State*, eds. Mohammed Ayoob and Hasan Koselbalaban (Boulder: Lynne Rienner, 2009), pp. 91–107.

28. Hebah Saleh, "Saudi Warning to Critical Civil Servants Dents Hopes of Reform," *Financial Times*, September 16, 2004.

29. Pascal Menoret, *The Municipal Election in Saudi Arabia,* Arab Reform Initiative, December 27, 2005, http://arab-reform.net.

30. Mary Ann Tétreault, "A State of Two Minds: State Cultures, Women, and Politics in Kuwait," *International Journal of Middle East Studies* 33, no. 2 (2001): 203–220.

31. The point we make here is that what the rest of the Gulf is voting for is not a body that can claim a share of power or authority. Although people will vote as they choose (and perhaps not choose women for a while as also happened in Kuwait), whether women get to vote and run for office or not is less of an issue than whether any citizen gets a share of political power.

32. Quote from Steven Levitsky and Lucan A. Way, "Autocracy by Democratic Rules: The Dynamics of Competitive Authoritarianism in the Post–Cold War Era," paper prepared for the conference "Mapping the Great Zone: Clientelism and the Boundary Between Democratic and Democratizing," New York, April 2003, p. 2. See also Diamond, "Thinking About Hybrid Regimes"; Daniel Brumberg, "The Trap of Liberalized Autocracy," *Journal of Democracy* 13, no. 4 (2002): 56–68; Valerie J. Bunce and Sharon L. Wolchik, "Defeating Dictators: Electoral Change and Stability in Competitive Authoritarian Regimes," *World Politics* 62, no. 1 (2010): 43–86; and Steven Levitsky and Lucan A. Way, *Competitive Authoritarianism: Hybrid Regimes After the Cold War* (New York: Cambridge University Press, 2010).

33. Jonathan Nitzan, "Differential Accumulation: Toward a New Political Economy of Capital," *Review of International Political Economy* 2, no. 3 (1995): 446–515; and Jonathan Nitzan and Shimshon Bichler, *The Global Political Economy of Israel* (London: Pluto, 2002).

34. For example, see Daniel Lerner, *The Passing of Traditional Society: Modernizing the Middle East* (New York: Free Press, 1958).

35. Simon Bromley, *Rethinking Middle East Politics* (Austin: University of Texas Press, 1994).

36. Charles Tilly, "War Making and State Making as Organized Crime," in *Bringing the State Back In*, eds. Peter B. Evans, Dietrich Rueschemeyer, and Theda Skocpol (New York: Cambridge University Press, 1985), pp. 169–191.

37. See, for example, the articles in A. Ehteshami and S. Wright, ed., *Reform in the Middle East Oil Monarchies* (Reading: Ithaca, 2008).

38. This appears in Guillermo O'Donnell and Phillippe C. Schmitter, *Transitions from Authoritarian Rule: Tentative Conclusions About Uncertain Democracies* (Baltimore: Johns Hopkins University Press, 1986), p. 2.

39. Mary Ann Tétreault and Mohammed al-Ghanim, "Transitions *in* Authoritarianism: Political Reform in the Persian Gulf Reconsidered," paper prepared for annual meeting of the International Studies Association, Montreal, February 2011.

40. Daniel Brumberg, "The Trap of Liberalized Autocracy."

41. "Real political opening" is derived from Schmitter's "really existing democracies"; that is, it is a visible movement toward a situation in which state and society see themselves as democratic, other self-identified democracies recognize the regime as democratic, and the regime is classified as democratic by scholars and analysts; Schmitter, "Twenty-Five Years," p. 28. Thus, a real political opening must be stable—no regression, although a little backsliding might be expected—and recognized as a significant opening by the nation itself, by peer states, and by knowledgeable observers.

42. Ali A. Allawi, *The Occupation of Iraq: Winning the War, Losing the Peace* (New Haven: Yale University Press, 2008); also Chapter 3 in this volume.

43. Eric C. Bjornulund, *Beyond Free and Fair: Monitoring Elections and Building Democracy* (Washington, DC: Woodrow Wilson Center Press, 2004).

44. Terry Lynn Karl, "Petroleum and Political Pacts: The Transition to Democracy in Venezuela," *Latin American Research Review* 22, no. 1 (1987): 63–94; Maksim Kokushkin, "New Institutionalism and New Alternatives to Normative Positivism," paper presented at the annual meeting of the American Sociological Association, New York, August 2007; Doron Shultziner and Mary Ann Tétreault, "How Democratization Is Won Under Non-democratic Regimes: Emotion, Psychology, and Agency in the Kuwaiti Women's Rights Movement," paper presented at the annual meeting of the American Political Science Association, Washington, DC, August 2008.

45. Geraldo Munck and Carol Leff, "Modes of Transition and Democratization: South America and Eastern Europe in Comparative Perspective," *Comparative Politics* 29, no. 3 (1997): 343–362.

46. Karl, "Petroleum and Political Pacts"; John Foran, *The Future of Revolutions: Rethinking Radical Change in the Age of Globalization* (London: Zed, 2003).

47. Mohammed Al-Ghanim, "'Transitions to Nowhere?' Kuwait and the Challenge of Political Liberalization," paper presented at annual meeting of the Northeast Political Science Association, Philadelphia, November 2009.

48. Karl, "Petroleum and Political Pacts."

49. Steven Heydemann, *Authoritarianism in Syria: Institutions and Social Conflict, 1946–1970* (Ithaca: Cornell University Press, 1999); and Mohammed al-

Ghanim, "Republicanism and the Failure of Elite-Pacted Transitions in Syria, 1961–1963," unpublished manuscript, Georgetown University, Washington, DC, December 2009.

50. See Mary Ann Tétreault and Robert A. Denemark, eds., *Gods, Guns, and Globalization: Religious Resurgence and International Political Economy* (Boulder: Lynne Rienner, 2004); Gwenn Okruhlik, "Making Conversation Permissible: Islamism in Saudi Arabia," in *Islamic Activism: A Social Movement Theory Approach*, ed. Quintan Wiktorowicz (Bloomington: Indiana University Press, 2004), pp. 353–384; Gwenn Okruhlik, "Networks of Dissent: Islamism and Reform in Saudi Arabia," *Current History*, January 2002, pp. 22–28; and John Esposito, *The Islamic Threat: Myth or Reality* (Oxford: Oxford University Press, 1992).

51. See, for example, Steffen Hertog, "Shaping the Saudi State: Human Agency's Shifting Role in Rentier State Formation," *International Journal of Middle East Studies* 39, no. 4 (2007): 539–563.

52. The continuing conflict between contemporary attitudes and actions and the divergent historical memories of nations and tribes is captured by Anh Nga Longva, "Citizenship in the Gulf States: Conceptualization and Practice," in *Citizenship and the State in the Middle East*, eds. Nils A. Butenschön, Uri Davis, and M. Hassassian (Syracuse: Syracuse University Press, 2000), pp. 179–200.

53. Phoebe Marr, *The Modern History of Iraq* (Boulder: Westview, 1985).

54. Brumberg, "The Trap"; also Haya al-Mughni and Mary Ann Tétreault, "Gender, Citizenship, and Nationalism in Kuwait," *British Journal of Middle Eastern Studies* 22, nos. 1–2 (1995): 64–80.

55. Schmitter, "Twenty-Five Years." See also Diamond, "Hybrid Regimes"; and Levitsky and Way, "Autocracy by Democratic Rules."

56. See the first edition of Alan Richards and John Waterbury, *A Political Economy of the Middle East* (Boulder: Westview, 1990).

57. Bromley, *Rethinking Middle East Politics*; John Waterbury, "Democracy Without Democrats? The Potential for Political Liberalization in the Middle East," in *Democracy Without Democrats? The Renewal of Politics in the Muslim World*, ed. Ghassan Salamé (London: I. B. Tauris, 1994), pp. 23–47.

58. For more information about these and other examples, see the individual Country Reports for 2009 in US Department of State, "Human Rights Report," March 11, 2010, www.state.gov; and Reporters Without Borders, "Reporters Without Borders Updates Its Press Freedom Index," October 20, 2010, http://open.salon.com.

59. Steven Heydemann, "Upgrading Authoritarianism in the Arab World," Analysis Paper no. 13 (Washington, DC: Saban Center, October 2007); Levitsky and Way, "Competitive Authoritarianism."

60. Heydemann, "Upgrading Authoritarianism."

61. Luciani, "Allocation vs. Production States."

62. Karl, "Petroleum and Political Pacts." See also Ross, "Does Oil Hinder Democracy?"

63. Kirin Aziz Chaudhry, *The Price of Wealth: Economies and Institutions in the Middle East* (Ithaca: Cornell University Press, 1997); Shireen T. Hunter, "The Gulf Economic Crisis and Its Social and Political Consequences," *Middle East Journal* 40, no. 4 (1986): 593–613.

64. See also Brumberg, "The Trap."

65. Al-Ghanim, "Republicanism and the Failure of Elite-Pacted Transitions."

PART 1

Country Cases

2

Reweaving the Myth of Bahrain's Parliamentary Experience

Gianluca P. Parolin

SINCE HIS ACCESSION to the throne in 1999, Bahrain's ruler, Hamad bin 'Īssà Āl Khalīfah, has been weaving the story of his drive for political reform into a tapestry adorned with a row of pearls, the shiniest of which is the reinstatement of parliamentary life. As a result, Shaikh Hamad earned international praise and support for his efforts, and Bahrain became a favorite example of successful democratization processes in the region, especially to US policymakers.[1] The end of most overt violations of human, civil, and political rights, together with the adoption of a new constitution, coincided with the US democratization agenda in the Gulf and rehabilitated a regime in earnest need of foreign endorsement. At home, however, the opposition (which in Bahrain includes Shi'ites, who constitute a sizable majority of the Sunni-ruled country's population, secularists, and Arab nationalists) felt betrayed by the new constitution adopted in 2002 and assumed a critical stance toward the king's political reform. The opposition often references the 1973–1975 parliamentary experience as the golden age—however brief—of Bahrain's democracy.

The tiny island state finds itself in the midst of complex and contrasting external pressures. On the one hand, the United States (which keeps a naval base in the country) and the other Gulf Cooperation Council (GCC) governments back Bahrain's Sunni regime, although US administrations occasionally have asked for some degree of reform. On the other hand, Iran upholds the cause of its Shi'ite co-religionists through political and financial support of Shi'ite organizations and activities that are repeatedly denounced by the regime. From a different vantage point, some members of the British House of Lords, headed by Lord Avebury, champion the Bahraini opposition (both in its liberal and Shi'ite elements) while the UK government sides with its US counterpart in backing the regime.

Bahrain's regime has proven to be far more resilient than anticipated by many observers, both internal and external, who expected to see the system topple under the weight of an already large and growing demographic imbalance between the ruled Shi'ites, who make up two-thirds of the population, and the Sunni ruling family, the Āl Khalīfah, who came to the island from mainland Arabia in the late eighteenth century. The regime has been quite clever, though, in winning Western support by its compliance with formal democratic benchmarks. Overemphasizing formal indicators of democratization such as parliamentary activity, however, downplays behind-the-scenes political maneuvering while the apparent stability and underlying continuity of the regime conceal significant internal change. This ongoing transformation owes more to the regime's response to internal pressure than to external intervention.

In this chapter, I examine the contested and messy politics of Bahrain's constitution(s) and parliament(s) by analyzing the country's parliamentary structures and functions during the postindependence experiment (1973–1975) in the first legislature elected under the provisions of the 2002 constitution (2002–2006), and in the opposition's strategies after the 2006 election.

Comparing Bahrain's two parliamentary experiences, a large amount of evidence attests to the novelty of the 2002 legislature. Yet this testimony offers a blurred lens through which to compare the role played by the assembly in the past to the present constitutional experiments. The biases in such an approach can be found by comparing the actual exercise of legislative power allegedly vested in the new assembly against two yardsticks: the constitutional model and the 1973–1975 parliamentary experiment.

Estimates of legislative activity begin with an investigation of the political and legal conditions under which the legislature operates. The composition and political orientation of the 2002–2006 Chamber of Deputies (Majlis al-Nuwwāb), for instance, depended on factors like the opposition's election boycott that are not explicitly included in reports of the fall 2002 general election. Moreover, the opposition continues to criticize the chamber, demanding a return to the now heavily mythologized era of the 1973 constitution and its dissolved National Assembly. Yet a closer look at the 1973–1975 legislature shows just how far reality falls short of the myth, allowing us both to judge the novelty of the new institutions and to assess their democratizing potential. Actually, today's parliament is closer to the 1973–1975 legislature than to the myth for the simple reason that the real 1973–1975 experience was far from being a myth. Yet Bahrain's first parliamentary experience in 1973–1975 is reconstructed as a myth that is woven differently depending on the weaver. Every actor—mainly the opposition and the ruling family, but also external policymakers—contributes to the aura surrounding the historical memory of the country's first legislature. But each imagines it differently according to their own agenda without displaying the slightest interest in or attention to the actual 1973–1975 experience.

My purpose here is to deconstruct the myth of Bahrain's parliamentary experience, and consider the ends that this mythmaking really serves. I do so, first, by analyzing why and how the different actors reweave the story, comparing the mythology and the reality; and, second, by comparing the two constitutional frameworks with actual parliamentary politics in the two contexts, the litmus test being legislative activity. My primary argument is that focusing on the myth of the first parliament and recent legislative activities does not cast light on the core issues of democratization in the country. I demonstrate this with special emphasis on two large constituencies whose participation in public life is severely limited: Shiʿites and women.

Reweaving the Myth

Both the opposition and the ruling family have clear goals in mind when they look back at the parliamentary experiment of the mid-1970s. Domestically, to the opposition, it represents an unprecedented, unparalleled moment of open political debate while, to the ruling family, it is offered as evidence of its earlier attempts to instate a constitutional framework in Bahrain. External actors, however, favor reference to the 1973–1975 parliament both to underline the democratic tradition of the country and avoid the rejectionist claim that democracy is an imported, foreign idea.

Over the past decade, past and present stories, mythologies, and realities have been intensively and extensively reworked. One way to look at the reweaving phenomenon is to consider (1) the opposition mythology of 1973–1975 (reweaving from below), (2) the legal framework provided by the constitution (democratization and constitutionalism) along with the ruling family's manipulation (reweaving from above), and (3) international acclaim for Bahrain's democratization in spite of real exclusion (reweaving from afar).

As the story threads intertwine in the diachronic process of weaving, Bahrain's municipal and general elections can be seen as major confrontation points between the actors and their different agendas. The drive toward the broad political opening (*infirāj siyāsī*) promoted by the Amir Hamad bin ʿĪssà Āl Khalīfah accelerated smoothly from the commencement of the public debate in 2001 to the referendum on the National Action Charter (NAC).[2] It continued through the promulgation of the "new" constitution and the spring 2002 municipal elections. At the beginning, the opposition's support for the new course was wholehearted, a reflection of intensely hopeful expectations for the political future of the country.[3] Bahraini citizens in general were equally enthusiastic; turnout for the referendum to ratify the charter was extremely high (90.2 percent), and 98.4 percent of the votes were in favor of the charter. Both figures (i.e., the turnout and the votes in favor) demonstrated a strong public commitment to the amir's widely advertised policy of opening. At this point, the different actors' agendas seemed to coincide, and the reweavings from below, above, and afar appeared to produce a harmonious tapestry.

The Calm Before the Storm: The 2002 Municipal Elections

Municipal and legislative elections were announced on the same day that the amir promulgated the constitution (February 14, 2002). In a speech broadcast live on state-owned television, Shaikh Hamad told Bahrainis that the "amended Constitution" had been enacted. This constitution, presented by the amir as "the old 1973 Constitution as amended in 2002," needs, however, to be considered as a new constitution, both on formal and on substantive legal grounds since its adoption neither followed the amending procedure nor respected the popular will reflected in the referendum on the NAC. In the same speech, Shaikh Hamad discarded the title of amir and proclaimed himself king, declaring Bahrain to be a constitutional monarchy. He also announced an advance in the timing for both municipal and general elections, previously expected to be held no later than 2004. Shi'ite activists, secularists, and Arab nationalists were critical of what was touted as a new "egalitarian" bicameralism whose result was to give equal authority to the elected and the appointed houses of the legislature. The NAC had outlined an inegalitarian bicameralism under which the appointed house would have fewer legislative powers than the lower house.[4] Yet the opposition welcomed the accelerated election schedule, which had been one of its key demands.

Only the London-based Bahrain Freedom Movement (BFM) criticized the king's message openly. The BFM denounced the betrayal of popular expectations about the charter, which had been endorsed in previous official statements, and called the speech a constitutional putsch more alarming than the 1975 dissolution of parliament. Subsequently, the BFM pledged to "wage war by political means," aligning itself with other opposition groups in Bahrain that had announced their intention to use peaceful means to oppose policies they did not like.[5] The chief tactic chosen by the Bahraini opposition abroad (namely, the BFM) was to call for a boycott of the election, whereas the opposition in Bahrain did not take a clear position on the issue. Other political groups (mainly Sunni) backed the king and announced that they would put up candidates.

In spite of their brave words, opposition groups were soon overwhelmed by the subsequent flow of material benefits (*makramāt*) dispensed by the king.[6] Many had underestimated the impact of the new provisions of the constitution, but found it difficult to mobilize public dissent after the shower of amiri munificence. Consequently, the opposition decided to take part in the municipal elections held on May 9, 2002. Candidates backed by informal Shi'ite coalitions (as well as Sunni religious candidates) swept the results, but their participation in municipal elections linked to the king's "new course" weakened later claims that the entire system lacked legitimacy.

Various hypotheses have been offered to explain why religious figures and candidates supported by the religious establishment, Sunni and Shi'ites alike, dominated these local elections, winning nearly all fifty seats. Some say that because Bahrainis had had no locally elected representatives since the dissolution of the National Assembly in 1975, their historical tendency to look toward shaikhs, or other figures of religious authority, for guidance and arbitration remained intact. Others argue that secular candidates and groups had little time to prepare their platforms. Technically, the actual polling appears to have been carried out transparently and without major incidents. Shi'ite critics, however, accused the government of *gerrymandering*; that is, drawing election districts to get the results it preferred. This would explain why twenty-seven seats went to the Sunni ruling minority, but only twenty-three were won by representatives of the far larger Shi'ite majority, assuming that voters in both groups chose candidates along sectarian lines. The issue was later addressed by the king, who reallocated the number of seats across the districts to better reflect the size of the voting population in each, correcting the previous situation where districts with 500 voters and others with 12,000 voters each elected one representative.

As in the 1999 Qatari municipal balloting, no woman was elected. This seemed to disappoint the king. The election of a woman to a municipal council would have been a pearl of great value to decorate the fabric of his story about democratization in Bahrain. Turnout also was disappointing, with only 51.28 percent of the population voting in the first round. Among the reasons suggested were voter apathy and frustration with the redux of "old politics" after the constitutional announcement, in sharp contrast to the high figures registered in the referendum on the NAC just a year earlier.

Back to Confrontation: The 2002 General Elections

Political scenarios for the fall 2002 general elections remained confused and uncertain throughout the summer. In June, Shi'ite activists protested the government's decision to permit nationals of other GCC states to hold dual citizenship in Bahrain. They claimed that the measure was an attempt to alter Bahrain's demographic balance before the October election because Sunnis were the most likely among GCC citizens to accept the dual citizenship offer. On July 3, 2002, the government issued Decree 14/2002 on Political Rights,[7] barring (political) associations from taking part in the electoral campaign and, thereby, requiring all candidates to stand as independents. The measure was probably intended to prevent the opposition from openly campaigning as such and also to avoid having majority-minority dynamics in parliament. Two months later, the king rescinded some of these provisions, but he acted too late to allow opposition groups to reconsider their plan to boycott the election, while the ban on associations or societies (*jam'īyāt*) taking part was lifted only the day before candidates were permitted to begin filing. Shaikh Hamad also failed to meet the opposition's demand to strip the appointed house, the Consultative Council, of its legislative powers. As a result, the four main (political) associations—two Shi'ite groups, the al-Wifāq National Islamic Society (al-Wifāq) and the Islamic Action Society (IAS); one leftist group, the National Democratic Action Society (NDAS); and one pan-Arab nationalist group, the National Democratic Society (NDS)—declared a boycott of the October elections. They were strongly supported in their decision by the Bahraini opposition abroad, the BFM.[8]

These four associations, estimated to control some 70 percent of the electorate, decided that none of their members would even file for candidacy. Consequently, only 177 citizens ran for the forty seats in the Chamber of Deputies. In comparison, earlier municipal elections saw as many as 300 candidates running for fifty municipal council seats. There was little campaigning before the October 2002 election, and no major issues were raised in the party-free—and, in three cases, even contender-free–competition. Rather than the election, it was the conflict between the monarchy and the opposition that monopolized public attention.

On the eve of the election, the opposition expected that turnout would not rise above 25 to 30 percent. In response, the regime deployed a broad range of political devices to get Bahrainis to the polls. Critics charged that those measures were highly illegitimate, but the political confrontation became so crucial for the existence of the *dawlah* (in its whole etymological scope, from dynasty to state) and for the prevention of social unrest that all nonviolent means were regarded as acceptable by the regime. Bahrainis were inundated with large-scale displays of national symbols (flags, emblems, electoral hallmarks) in the streets, public offices, malls, and newspapers. State-owned television repeatedly broadcast addresses to the citizenry by the king, along with images of the king himself and the royal family waving the Bahraini flag, and played patriotic songs encouraging the people to go to the polls. Meanwhile, local media were banned from reporting the boycotters' position: opposition figures were allowed to state their reasons for boycotting the elections, but they could not campaign for a boycott per se.[9] General polling stations where voters from any district could cast ballots without risk of peer pressure were set up. Public employees and members of the armed forces were required to report to their superiors showing polling receipts for their entire families. A last-minute stipulation required that voters' passports be stamped with the electoral seal, creating major concern for citizens who feared being denied visas, passport renewals, and perhaps other forms of retaliation if they were to boycott the election.

On election day, October 24, 2002, the atmosphere at the polling stations appeared surreal to the Western spectator, although it might have seemed quite normal to Kuwaitis. Candidates, disregarding regulations on campaigning passed months earlier, set up booths in front of polling stations and handed out homemade food, *diwaniyya* style. Citizens came and went from polling centers, but pictures showing long lines and crowded halls recorded exceptions, not the norm. Polling stations were plastered with flags, electoral hallmarks, and portraits of the king, the crown prince (Walī al-'ahd), and the prime minister. The festive spirit projected by the media was deceptive, but the open environment allowed international observers and delegates from the four boycotting associations to enter polling stations and monitor the voting without interference.

When it became clear that turnout would reach and even exceed 50 percent, the regime kicked off celebrations that lasted a whole week. The official newspaper, *al-Ayyām*, proclaimed: "Bahrain sides with democracy: Participation exceeded expectations . . . and attained 53.2 percent."[10] This highly significant headline presents the unambiguous choice of the Bahraini people at the same time that it acknowledges that the regime was aware that its confrontation with the opposition was risky. On the front page, there were only three additional articles: one by the prime minister ("Triumph of Siding with Popular Will"),[11] another directly below it about those who did not participate ("al-Wifāq and al-'Amal: We Will Cooperate with the Representatives [of Parliament (*sic*)]"),[12]—an apparent bid for reconciliation—and the third reporting Washington's imprimatur ("Washington: Elections Free and Correct, and We Support Reforms").[13] The "victory" of the regime was celebrated for days in the press, complete with expressions of satisfaction from public authorities and private companies in the form of advertisements addressed to the king, the crown prince, and the prime minister, each featuring their portraits.

No one contested the reported turnout statistics notwithstanding the low hum of discontent coming from the official headquarters of the boycotting associations. Criticism focused on the strategies through which the ruling family had persuaded citizens to cast their ballots. No significant claim of fraud was put forward, showing how little confidence the opposition had in state institutions (including the judiciary), and perhaps also acknowledging its own poor choice of strategy.

Runoffs were held one week later (October 31, 2002). The overall result was that the boycott had ensured Sunni control of parliament. Twenty-seven seats were won by Sunnis, fourteen of whom were Islamists, about half each from the fundamentalist salafi movement and from the Muslim Brotherhood. Two liberal Sunnis were elected, and the remaining Sunni representatives were independents.[14] Shi'ite representation consisted of two Shi'ite Islamists from the Islamic League Association (considered to be close to the government), one liberal, and ten independents. Women failed again to win a seat, but two of the eight female contestants made it to the runoffs.

Shaikh Khalīfah, prime minister of Bahrain for over thirty years, submitted his resignation to the king on November 10, 2002, but the new government—assembled prior to the beginning of the first legislative session on December 14, 2002—was led once again by Shaikh Khalīfah. Eighteen members of the former government were reappointed (among them nine members of the Āl Khalīfah family), and key ministerial positions remained unchanged, although some portfolios were variously split and merged, and six new members were added, bringing the number of ministers to twenty-four. Among the most notable appointments were Majīd bin Muhsin al-'Alawī, a prominent, formerly London-based government critic who embraced the king's reform efforts, and 'Abdal-Hussayn bin 'Alī Mirzà, director general of the state-owned oil company, Bahrain Petroleum Company (BAPCO), and the first Bahraini of Iranian origin to be appointed a minister. The opposition criticized what it called a mere government reshuffle, saying that Bahrainis had expected real change. Yet although the government remained essentially the same and essentially conservative, the Majlis al-Shūrà—the upper house, appointed by the king in mid-November—did evince greater plurality: six women were appointed, including Alice Sam'ān, an Iraqi Christian. Ibrāhīm Dawūd Nūnū, a Jew, was also appointed, and a Shi'ite, Faysal al-Mūsawī, was named council chairman.[15]

Deconstructing the Myth

The Constitutional Framework: From the 1973 Constitution to the 2002 Constitution

Bicameralism is both the main raison d'être of the political conflict between the regime and the opposition, and one of the few new features of the 2002 constitution. The parliament under the 1973 constitution was monocameral, following the model that had inspired it: the liberal 1962 constitution of Kuwait, which continues to be held up as a model compromise between

Western liberal constitutional doctrine and Arab-Islamic tradition. The institutional idea behind the Kuwaiti constitution was that constitutional monarchy, the Western archetype, had to be adapted to the different legal environment[16] of the Gulf states. In Kuwait, as later in Bahrain, the monarch's powers were to be limited by a partly elected[17] National Assembly, chiefly through the exercise of legislative powers.[18]

Bahrain's old parliament, the National Assembly (al-Majlis al-Watanī), was originally composed of thirty deputies plus cabinet ministers serving ex officio.[19] No law could be promulgated unless it was passed by the National Assembly and ratified by the amir.[20] The dramatic dissolution of the National Assembly in 1975, however, did not follow the procedure set by paragraph 2 of Article 65:

> In the event of dissolution, elections for the new Assembly shall be held within a period not exceeding two months from the date of dissolution. If the elections are not held within the said period, the dissolved Assembly shall be restored to its full constitutional authority and shall meet immediately as if the dissolution had not taken place.

Kuwait also experienced two extraconstitutional dissolutions (1976–1981 and 1986–1992), but both were temporary. Bahrain's National Assembly was never reinstated because Amr Amīrī 4/1975 also suspended the provisions of Bahrain's constitution providing for the election of a new parliament.[21]

When Shaikh Hamad started his reform drive in 1999, he encountered problems amending the existing constitution,[22] which required that the dissolved National Assembly authorize any amendment. Article 104 expressly required that "any amendment to the Constitution be passed by a majority vote of two-thirds of the members constituting the Assembly and ratified by the Amir." This issue was not resolved directly, but rather was bypassed by the outcome of the popular referendum on the NAC.

Section Five of the NAC, titled "Parliamentary Life," is the centerpiece of the reweaving of Bahrain's parliamentary story. It opened with: "Bahrain has experienced direct democracy ever since Āl Khalīfah assumed the responsibility of Government." It explained, through an "authoritative argument,"[23] the ruler's determination to install a bicameral system by asserting that many deep-rooted democracies are bicameral.[24] It also declared that this would proceed according to the principle of *shura*, a basic Islamic principle of the government system in Bahrain. Even if the NAC reflected a degree of vagueness, it indicated clearly that the country would move toward a form of inegalitarian bicameralism favoring the elected house:

> It is in the interest of the state of Bahrain to adopt a bicameral system whereby the legislature will consist of two chambers, namely one that is

> constituted through free, direct elections whose mandate will be to enact laws, and a second one that would have people with experience and expertise who would give advice as necessary.[25]

The same words were repeated in the final Outlook section, where the two constitutional amendments were outlined. The king wove the 1973–1975 parliamentary experience—without ever explicitly referring to it—into a tapestry depicting the "direct democracy" that Bahrain would have experienced "ever since Āl Khalīfah assumed the responsibility of Government." This plan for reweaving from above was accepted both below and afar because the result seemed to suit everyone, but it soon turned out that the three sets of weavers were not working on the same picture.

Opposition groups welcomed the long-delayed acceptance of their thirty-year call for representation while the 2001 referendum's overwhelming success confirmed popular support. Official statements by different members of the ruling family confirmed its willingness to implement the charter as soon as possible.[26] Possible concerns about the new bicameralism (*nizām al-majlisayn*) were submerged beneath the most frequently recurring trope justifying the parliamentary system to be established in Bahrain: the British parliament. Then, in a sensational coup de théâtre, Shaikh Hamad, on February 14, 2002, declared himself king of Bahrain. Reversing the trajectory toward constitutional monarchy followed by Britain, he promulgated a new constitution that negated the system of inegalitarian bicameralism envisioned and expected by Bahrainis.

Section Three of the new constitution establishes the National Assembly as a compound body consisting of two chambers: the Consultative Council (Majlis al-Shura) and the Chamber of Deputies (Majlis al-Nuwwāb).[27] The members of the Consultative Council are appointed by royal order (*amr malakī*) while only the members of the Chamber of Deputies are directly elected by secret ballot. The shift in power from elected representatives to members appointed by the king is set out in Article 70, which states that "no law shall be promulgated unless approved by both the Consultative Council and the Chamber of Deputies, or the National Assembly as the situation demands, and ratified by the King." This provision effectively gives the Consultative Council a veto over bills approved by the Chamber of Deputies (Articles 82–84). If the two chambers differ twice over any bill, the entire National Assembly must convene in joint session to discuss the clauses in dispute. For the bill to be accepted, a majority of members must be present and are required to approve it (Article 85). Since each *majlis* has forty members, deputies alone cannot overcome the appointed chamber's veto, even if all were to vote to override it.[28] The king's appointees therefore hold an almost automatic majority in any dispute. Opposition groups immediately called for the repeal of these provisions, but amending the bicameral system is expressly forbidden by Article 120(c). Sections (a) and (b) of the same article forbid the amendment of Article 2—"The religion of the State is Islam. The Islamic Sharia is a principal source for legislation. The official language is Arabic," Article 120(a); and "the constitutional monarchy and the principle of inherited rule in Bahrain, as well as the principles of freedom and equality established in the Constitution," Article 120(b).[29]

The authority of deputies to change the composition of the government through procedures such as no-confidence votes also is limited. Under present constitutional provisions, a two-thirds vote by deputies may force individual ministers to submit their resignations (Article 66), but deputies may not vote on the performance of the prime minister. The Chamber of Deputies can, by a two-thirds majority, attest that it cannot cooperate with the prime minister and, by a subsequent two-thirds majority in the National Assembly (i.e., the elected and the appointed houses together), send the matter to the king for a decision "either by relieving the Prime Minister of his post and appointing a new Government, or by dissolving the Chamber of Deputies" (Article 67).[30] Suffice it to say that it is highly unlikely that the house appointed by the king would vote against the prime minister, making it easy to predict the results of such a no-confidence vote.

The parliament created by the 2002 constitution lacks other essential characteristics of institutional autonomy. First, it cannot regulate its own procedures, as the rushed approval of the bylaws of both chambers by decree-law (Marsūm bi-Qānūn) showed in the summer of 2002.[31] Autonomy in judging titles of membership as well as in ratifying electoral results is largely absent as well. The status of members is vitally limited by serious restrictions on parliamentary immunity[32] while other typical functions of parliaments also are sharply narrowed. For instance, the power to make appointments to certain positions in state agencies, as well as having a formally autonomous role in policymaking and authority to check the executive or the judiciary, are absent.[33]

Constraints on Parliament's Legislative Activity Under the 2002 Constitution

The exercise of legislative powers brings up a host of issues, especially when it comes to the role of the executive in legislative activity. One of the final lines of the NAC states: "laws shall be enacted as prescribed in detail by the Constitution and in congruence with constitutional norms and traditions followed in deep-rooted democracies."[34] Bahrain's executive, however, is awarded legislative powers well beyond the "norms and traditions followed in deep-rooted democracies."

Numerous examples illustrate this supremacy of the executive over the legislature, in breach of the principle of separation of powers. First, there is no *domaine réservé* for the law and, thus, the executive can legislate in all areas not covered by the law (until a law is enacted). The basic principle of the rule of law, formally established in Article 39 of the 2002 constitution, contains no provision regulating the relationship between laws and administrative decrees. Second, the executive can legislate in any case of "emergency." But what constitutes an emergency is interpreted quite broadly while the parliamentary control after the fact is reduced to a minimum or even avoided. Emergency legislation in the form of decree-laws can be issued by the king provided that they do not contravene the constitution:

> Such decrees must be referred to both the Consultative Council and the Chamber of Deputies within one month from their promulgation if the two chambers are in session, or within a month of the first meeting of each of the two new chambers in the event of dissolution, or if the legislative term has ended. If the decrees are not so referred, their legal force shall abate retrospectively without a need to issue a relevant ruling. If decrees are referred to but not confirmed by both chambers, their legal force shall also abate retrospectively. (Article 38, paragraph 2)

The constitution does not set a deadline for the chambers' approval, however.[35] A decree—if submitted to the chambers in time—could continue to produce legal effects as long as the chambers do not vote against it. Third, all legislation introduced by the executive before the convening of the National Assembly is considered to be fully in force and binding. Article 121 stipulates that "all laws, decree-laws, decrees, statutes, orders, edicts and circulars that have been issued and are in force prior to the first meeting convened by the National Assembly remain proper and valid, unless amended or rescinded in accordance with the regulations prescribed in this Constitution."[36] Fourth, emergency legislation introduced by the executive cannot be amended and can be rejected only by a qualified majority. Both chambers' bylaws stipulate that consideration of decree-laws enjoys priority (Article 122 of Decree-Law 54/2002, Article 121 of Decree-Law 55/2002), but prohibit amending them (Article 123 of Decree-Law 54/2002, Article 122 of Decree-Law 55/2002). The chamber can express only approval or rejection, and rejection requires an absolute majority (Article 124 of Decree-Law 54/2002, Article 123 of Decree-Law 55/2002).[37] Fifth, on economic or financial matters, there is a very short deadline for the legislature to consider the executive's emergency legislation, after which such legislation is fully in force and binding. This important restriction of the rule of law occurs in Article 87, which allows a decree (*marsūm lahu quwwat al-qānūn*) to bypass the procedure set out in Article 38 if the National Assembly does not reach a decision within fifteen days on a bill regulating economic or financial matters.[38]

These constraints explain some apparent anomalies in the legislative activity of the new bicameral legislature. Despite the thirty-year absence of parliament, during their first year, the two chambers passed few bills.[39] Half of the eight measures approved in the first session were ratifications of international agreements;[40] two dealt with bonds,[41] and one authorized the state's general budget for the 2003 and 2004 fiscal years.[42] The only piece of legislation suggesting a minimum exercise of legislative initiative was Law 7/2003 (June 14, 2003) on commercial secrets (*al-asrār al-tijārīyah*), even though the World Intellectual Property Organization (WIPO) guidelines were quite comprehensive and specific. The number of approved bills increased slightly in subsequent sessions, but "legislative productivity" remained low.[43] In 2004, for instance, the government forwarded forty-seven draft laws to parliament but, at the end of the year, all were still pending, notwithstanding the king's periodic calls urging the assembly to speed up the country's reform program by passing legislation more swiftly.

Elsewhere, a timid attempt to assert the principle of accountability was visible in the 2004 parliamentary discussion of the losses suffered by the Pension Fund and the General Organization for Social Insurance. The parliamentary committee investigating these two social security agencies submitted a lengthy report to the house accusing three ministers of mismanagement, but all the accused were cleared after questioning even though the evidence against them seemed substantial. The government intervened by approving a plan to restructure and reform the two social security funds.

Was It Any Different Under the 1973 Constitution?

This brief overview of the current parliamentary system in Bahrain supports the idea that the opposition's demands for a return to the constitutional experiment of the 1970s could have some validity. Although the only prime minister that the country has known since independence asserts that "Bahrain's pioneering parliamentary experience is a model to be followed, particularly in terms of the relations between the executive and the legislative branches for the benefit of the nation," legitimate doubts remain with regard to separation of powers.[44] Thus, when ʻAlī Rabīʻah, a former member of the 1973 National Assembly and a prominent figure in the NDAS, declared that "the people's impression is that this institution is incapable of representing their hopes and ambitions, or passing laws, or exercising check and balance [*sic*] on the Government,"[45] he brought important elements into the discussion even though—and perhaps especially because—he attributed his own views to a larger public.

In challenging the current system, however, the opposition relies on a highly mythologized history of the 1973–1975 parliamentary experience. From beneath the tapestry, the opposition reweaves the single, slender thread that the regime implicitly employed as evidence of the democratic tradition of the country, established "ever since Āl Khalīfah assumed the responsibility of Government." Considering it more closely, the activity of that short-lived National Assembly reveals several misconceptions. The first legislative session (December 16, 1973, through June 30, 1974) is usually described as "not exceptionally eventful,"[46] and "characterized by trial and error."[47] In fifty-four meetings, the National Assembly dealt with procedural matters and discussed its bylaws. Only two bills were passed,[48] and three decree-laws approved.[49] The National Assembly held fifty meetings in the second session (October 23, 1974, through June 23, 1975) but, rather than working to institutionalize parliamentary life, the debates gradually became rancorous and openly hostile. In this session, nine bills were passed and five decree-laws approved. During its entire eighteen months of existence, the National Assembly itself did not draft a single law. Most of its meetings were devoted to discussing bills drafted by the government, and considering petitions from individuals and groups. The government treated the National Assembly's legislative role as little more than advisory, and the "confrontational attitude and tactics of the Left" eased this task by diverting its attention from legislation to polemics.[50]

Most of today's deficiencies were foreshadowed in that earlier parliament. In addition to the 1973 parliament's inadequate legislative performance, the regime apparently never contemplated that this body would demand any degree of real accountability. In reference to the 1973 opposition, John Peterson observes that, "rather than seeking conciliation or a modus vivendi, thereby gradually gaining acceptance of the principle of accountability, the opposition insisted on confrontation with the regime and its representatives."[51] That observation continues to be valid for the 2002 legislature.

One remarkable difference between the 1973 and the 2002 assemblies lies in the role of the opposition as an outside actor. Indeed, this is one of the main accomplishments of the 2002 election boycott. The boycott brought political discourse out of its institutional home or, rather, left it outside. That is because, in the 2002 parliament, the opposition (which made up the quasi-totality of the country's political arena) was not represented.[52] The confrontation between the ruling family and the opposition ended in strengthening the family's position as it fought, prevailed, and then ruled on its own terms. Yet the grounds of that victory are not clear. Did citizens vote because they were threatened, won over by royal liberality, or swayed by propaganda? Or did some voters among the 53.4 percent of Bahrainis who went to the polls in 2002 think that having a weak—maybe even a "toothless"[53]—parliament would be better than not having a parliament at all? The ultimate underlying question was: Is it better to live under a suspended liberal constitution or under a limited constitution actually in force? The regime's moderate attitude toward the boycotters,[54] the technical "fairness" of the election (i.e., of the casting and counting of votes), and the massive propaganda campaign seem to have persuaded the citizenry toward the second alternative. Some in the opposition who had backed the boycott began to worry that their fellow citizens regarded them as people who had "betrayed their country."[55]

Technically transparent polling is not—and was not—equivalent to a fair election. While the casting and counting of votes were technically transparent, the environment itself was biased. There was no significant claim of fraud in the 2002 Bahraini election, and international observers confirmed that voting procedures were correct and impartial, but there was plenty of evidence to back up the assertion that the regime exerted a heavy influence on the electoral process. The purpose was not to "win": manipulating electoral results was unnecessary because candidates from the opposition did not even run. Indeed, every candidate—simply by running—was demonstrating his or her loyalty to the regime. Yet even though official statistics were consistent with voter turnout, there was interference in the electoral process.

Demographic manipulation is the key device applied in Bahrain to create and manage loyal bases that the regime can rely on, along with the temporary extension of voting rights to other GCC citizens.[56] Just as in Kuwait, grants of citizenship[57] as well as broad naturalization policies[58] dramatically transformed and continue to alter Bahrain's sociopolitical geography. Demographic manipulation is an extreme measure, resorted to when a pro-regime result cannot be accomplished through gerrymandering alone. Citizenship is thus becoming the key device to ensure the regime's political support and institutional resilience.[59]

Due to the boycott, a large section of Bahraini society was not represented or, at least, was highly underrepresented in the 2002 parliament. If, on the contrary, the opposition had participated in the election, would the role of the Bahraini parliament have changed? If we view Bahrain from the perspective of other democratic transitions in the region, we could consider the roles envisioned for parliaments in such confrontational contexts. Abdo Baaklini, Guilain Denoeux, and Robert Springborg argue that Arab parliaments can play a fundamental role in democratic transitions by (1) improving society's ability to express political demands and to follow and influence debates on public policy issues, (2) enhancing the political system's capacity to process and satisfy societal demands, (3) helping to legitimate government decisions, (4) providing channels through which the actions of the executive branch can be subjected to oversight, and (5) contributing to the regulation and management of political conflict.[60] If Bahrain was indeed undergoing democratic transition, this was happening without the positive accomplishments anticipated from Arab parliaments because the 2002 Bahraini National Assembly lacked basic representation of the country's main political groups, an unavoidable by-product of the electoral boycott.

In late 2005, the four opposition associations declared that they would not boycott the 2006 election for members of the lower house, marking a clear change of strategy. This followed a year of sharp political confrontation between the government and the Islamist bloc in parliament, and between the government and the opposition conducted informally outside parliament in the traditional way. Earlier in 2005, an important piece of legislation for the country's political life was introduced after having been discussed in parliament, where the opposition had no representation. This highly controversial bill dealt with political associations (*Qānūn al-jam'īyāt al-siyāsīyah*) and imposed restrictions on their establishment, funding, and activities. Political associations, for example, cannot be established on class, sectarian, ethnic, geographic, or occupational grounds (Article 4, paragraph 4). They should not aim at creating semimilitary or military auxiliaries (Article 4, paragraph 5). The financial resources of political associations should come from membership dues, contributions, and revenues from their investments in the country as directed by their internal regulations (Article 14, paragraph 1). A political association may not accept any contribution, advantage, or benefit from any foreigner, foreign entity, or international organization (Article 14, paragraph 2). The law directs the minister of justice to refer any association violating the provisions of Bahrain's constitution, the Law on Political Associations, or any other Bahraini law to the High Court. The minister can also ask the court to freeze the activities of the violating association for three months. During that time, the association can correct the violation or remove what is causing it (Article 22) or ask the court to dissolve the association, liquidate its assets, and decide who is entitled to those assets if the association is found to be in grave violation (Article 23). Six associations expressed their opposition to the bill after it was endorsed by both chambers of parliament; they had been waiting for the final text, and had not been able to obtain much information from parliament, where they had no representative. At that point, they could only ask the king not to ratify it, which they did, but the king ignored their plea and ratified and promulgated the bill as Law 26/2005 (July 23, 2005).

Moving Away from the Myth: A New General Election Strategy

Four years after the boycott, the opposition determined to change its strategy and try to work within the system. The main opposition group, al-Wifāq, decided to register under the Law on Political Associations (Law 26/2005) and comply with its restrictive rules. The registration caused a rift in al-Wifāq between the leadership and Hasan Mushayma' and others opposing the decision, but the leadership persisted. It filed an application and, in December, the minister of justice issued a decision that accepted the registration (Minister of Justice Decision 38/2005). As a result, Hasan Mushayma' pulled out of al-Wifāq and founded Harakat Haqq, a movement that preferred to operate unlicensed and therefore unrestrained. Al-Wifāq and Harakat Haqq also disagreed on the stance toward the 2006 municipal and legislative elections. Al-Wifāq chose to compete and suffered many defectors to Harakat Haqq over this issue. Moreover, al-Wifāq reached a tacit agreement with the government and filed candidacies only in districts where it had strong support; that is, only in Shi'ite-majority districts that showed a more conciliatory attitude toward the regime. Filing candidacies only in Shi'ite-majority districts meant al-Wifāq could gain sizable representation while allowing the government to maintain a comfortable number of seats without engaging in sharp, open-ended electoral contests.

In the run-up to the elections, a former government adviser, Salāh al-Bandar, disclosed documents revealing a Sunni plot—allegedly hatched by the minister of state for cabinet affairs and head of the High Electoral Committee, Ahmad bin 'Atīyat Allah Āl Khalifah, to rig the elections against Bahraini Shi'ites.[61] The "Bandar-gate" scandal stirred sectarian tension only a few weeks ahead of the November balloting. State authorities reacted by blocking access to websites and blogs covering the issue.[62]

On election day, November 25, 2006, voter turnout was significantly higher than in the previous election (72 percent to 53 percent). Al-Wifāq swept most of the seats it contested, but its liberal allies lost a few crucial seats in the first round and in the runoffs held on December 2, 2006. Three liberal candidates from the al-Wifāq coalition lost due to the contribution of out-of-district votes (i.e., votes cast in general polling centers). According to the Bahrain Human Rights Society, which the government had charged with monitoring the election, these out-of-district votes provided "circumstantial evidence" to support charges that pro-regime Sunnis had used fraud, enabling them to win a majority of seats in parliament.[63] In the case of the opposition candidate 'Abd al-Rahmān al-Nu'aymī, for instance, preliminary results from the district showed him leading by 741 votes, but late-counted ballots from general polling centers went mainly to his opponent (1,450 to 330). The final results gave the proregime abū al-Fath 3,890 votes and al-Nu'aymī 3,484 votes. The ballots of approximately 8,000 floating voters cast at ten general polling centers tipped the balance in the tightest races.[64] Final results gave the al-Wifāq coalition seventeen seats; twenty-three seats went to the conservative, progovernment al-Asālah, al-Minbar, and to independents.

The king appointed the new upper house (Consultative Council) on December 5, 2006. He picked mostly liberals to offset the victory of religious conservatives in the lower house (Chamber of Deputies), but Sunnis were a majority in the appointed house too.[65] A new government was formed on December 11, 2006. Shaikh Khalīfah bin Salmān Āl Khalīfah was reappointed prime minister but, for the first time in Bahrain's history, one of his three deputy prime ministers was a Shi'ite, Jawād bin Sālim al-'Urayd, and another Shi'ite, Nizār bin Sādiq al-Bahārinah, was named minister of state for foreign affairs.

Newly elected lawmakers were sworn in on December 20, 2006, but the transformation of the al-Wifāq coalition from an opposition movement to a parliamentary bloc was not smooth. Leaders of al-Wifāq claim to have positively affected government policies, especially on public housing and unemployment, but the group found it difficult to adjust to the system on the one hand, and deal with relentless criticism from the breakaway Harakat Haqq on the other.[66] A major conflict arose over the 1 percent income tax designed to fund unemployment benefits and imposed by Decree-Law 78/2006. The king had issued the decree while parliament was not in session, and therefore—according to Article 38 of the constitution—the decree had to be submitted to the new parliament to be ratified. Al-Wifāq voted in favor, misjudging the impact of the law on its own constituency. Harakat Haqq organized large street demonstrations and intense blogging activities, proving that Al-Wifāq's Shi'ite constituency saw in Harakat Haqq's active protests a better political alternative.[67] When Shaikh 'Issà Qāsim, the country's top Shi'ite cleric, declared the tax levied on all public and private sector salaries un-Islamic, al-Wifāq tried to pull back, but only obtained a 15 percent increase in public sector salaries (Council of Ministers Decision 15/2007 of March 7, 2007).

On May 8, 2007, the Chamber of Deputies voted against a public investigation of the Bandar-gate scandal, revealing a major drawback to the working-within-the-system strategy. Constituents voiced their dismay over al-Wifāq's failure to fulfull pledges during the campaign. The bloc's leader, Shaikh 'Alī Salmān, said in October 2007 that he was considering resigning from parliament "because I feel that I can serve more effectively from the outside."[68] In the end, however, he did not resign.

The 2010 municipal and general elections were preceded by a round of arrests of Shi'ite activists accused of plotting to overthrow the Sunni regime. The first round of the 2010 elections was held on October 23, and voter turnout slightly decreased to 67 percent. Votes cast in general polling centers tended to favor progovernment non-Islamist candidates. Al-Wifāq won all its eighteen seats in the first round, increasing its parliamentary group by one unit, while al-Asālah and al-Minbar suffered a major setback. In the runoffs, held on October 30, the two liberal NDAS candidates were defeated both in the local and the general polling centers, even though out-of-constituency votes played a more significant role in the contest of District 4 of the Central

Province (231 votes were added to the 2,835 of the NDAS candidate Munīrah Fakhrū, whereas 893 votes were added to the 3,004 of independent candidate ʻIssá al-Qādī). On the day after the runoffs, Shaikh Khalīfah resigned as prime minister, but was immediately re-appointed.

Missing Threads in the Continuous Reweaving: Shi'ites and Women

Formal compliance with legal democratic standards provided the Bahraini regime with a high degree of apparent legitimacy. On the one hand, instating a parliament and holding general elections won the monarchy commendations on the international stage while its opponents were dismissed as rabble-rousers. On the other hand, the absence of important segments of the Bahraini polity from the Chamber of Deputies as a result of the electoral boycott to protest against the limited powers of the lower house channeled politics into the familiar indirect regime-opposition dynamics that have dominated Bahrain's political history: petitions and street demonstrations followed by arrests.[69]

The first elected legislature under the 2002 constitution failed to represent the largest segment of Bahraini society, the Shiʻites, who make up two-thirds of the entire population. The Sunni ruling family, the Āl Khalīfah, keeps control through mobilizing allied Sunni tribes coming from mainland Arabia where the Āl Khalīfah themselves originated. The ruling family is reluctant to accept Shiʻites as participants in power sharing, and the question of Shiʻites is often posed in terms of loyalty (*walāʼ*).[70] Bahraini Shiʻites are frequently criticized by the regime for sympathizing with co-religionists in the region, and reproached for seeking religious and political guidance from Iraqi or Iranian clerics. Bahraini Shiʻites acknowledge that in the eighteenth century they opposed the Āl Khalīfah conquest of the island, but they also want to be acknowledged as the ones who "gave the power to the Āl Khalīfah" in 1970, when they backed the rule of the Āl Khalīfah in an informal UN referendum.[71]

It was the regime's recurring abuses and its steady resistance to power sharing that drove Bahraini Shiʻites into opposition. At a rally in December 2005, activists called for a new referendum under the UN aegis, a clear sign of disaffection from the regime.[72] Some analysts caution that a new uprising (intifada) should not be ruled out as Shiʻites observe that their brethren in other Arab countries like Iraq, Lebanon, and Syria have risen in status.[73]

On the international level, empowerment of Bahraini Shiʻites contradicts elements of US policy in the area and is seen by the United States as possibly being prejudicial to its interests in Bahrain, the home of its Fifth Fleet. Shiʻite unrest in Bahrain might even have played a role in the choice of Qatar instead of Bahrain for the US headquarters during the Iraq War, although no official reason was given. The fall of the Iraqi regime opened new horizons for Shi'ites in the Gulf, and raised a number of issues for the Shi'ites of Bahrain. Although it is unclear what the new Iraqi regime will look like after US forces leave, it seems highly unlikely that Shi'ites will be cut out of the political scene as they were under Saddam Hussein's rule. The political involvement of Iraqi Shi'ites sets an example for their co-religionists in Bahrain. Both are mainly Arab Shi'ites in nonhomogeneous societies and both were barred from the political arena for a long time. From the Bahraini perspective, turning to Iraqi Shi'ite clerics for guidance counters some of the risks of being accused of disloyalty for seeking religious and political guides in Iran, which the monarchy views with suspicion. The Iranian parliament formally renounced territorial claims over Bahrain in 1970 but, in the summer of 2007, an editorial by the managing director of the conservative Iranian daily *Kayhān*, Hosein Sharī'atmadārī (appointed by Iran's supreme leader Grand Ayatollah Khomeini), renewed Iran's territorial claims in the Gulf. The editorial sparked considerable political and diplomatic tension throughout the region, especially the statement that "public opinion in Bahrain, an Iranian territory (*khāk-e Īrān*), is in favor of reunification with the native land."[74] The potential diplomatic row was defused by Iran's foreign minister, Manouchehr Mottakī, who, in a press conference during his visit in Bahrain, dismissed the editorial as "a personal view of the author."[75] In early 2009 this simmering diplomatic row broke out even more harshly in response to declarations by 'Alī Akbar Nāteq-Nūrī, former interior minister of the Islamic Republic of Iran and member of the Expediency Council at the time of the episode, that Bahrain used to be Iran's fourteenth province and had a representative in the Iranian parliament.[76] This statement reminded many of Saddam's declarations before the invasion of Kuwait. Sādeq Mahsūlī, then Iranian interior minister, had to pay a special visit to Bahrain to ease the tension between the two countries. One of the reasons adduced for the self-proclamation of Shaikh Hamad as "king" in 2002 was precisely to highlight the independence of Bahrain as a kingdom, not "just" an emirate or an Iranian province. In the context of problematic regional relations, the benefits in terms of the country's international position must have overshadowed the political consequences of adopting a title for which Islam has a profound aversion.

Bahraini Shi'ites are underrepresented throughout the government's apparatus. They are informally but systematically barred from the Ministries of Interior and Defense, and are virtually absent in the court system both as judges and public prosecutors. Due to heavy gerrymandering, politically motivated naturalizations, and their own electoral boycott, Shi'ites are a minority in the elected house of parliament, where twenty-seven of the forty seats were occupied by Sunni deputies after the 2002 election. Even after the 2006 election, Shi'ites remained a minority with only seventeen seats in the lower house and half the membership of the upper house.

Bahrain's political and institutional system also falls short of expectations with regard to women, whether Sunni or Shi'ite. Political activism among Bahraini women is severely jeopardized by both the regime and religious leaders, notwithstanding that women have been granted full voting rights. The 2002 boycott smoothed the path to parliament for conservative religious figures who capitalized on making up the largest bloc in the lower house by promoting legislation extending gender discrimination. Consequently, the social, professional, and political role of women was curtailed, rather than enhanced, while segregation of the sexes also was institutionalized by the establishment of a separate university for women.[77] The government was no more sympathetic to the women's cause than the Islamists.[78] In mid-January 2006, the Ministry of Social Development approved the bylaws of the Bahraini Women's Federation (*alād al-nisā'ī al-bahraynī*), but deleted the provision stating that "the direction of the Federation endeavors [to promote the] participation of women in the political life in an effective way."[79]

The impact of Bahraini women activists remains unclear. In the 2006 polls, only one woman, Latīfah al-Qa'ūd, was elected to the lower house, but she ran unopposed in District 6 of the Southern Province. By contrast, in District 4 of the Central Province, Munīrah Fakhrū, a Sunni of the al-Wifāq coalition with the best chances among all the sixteen female candidates, did not make it to the runoff thanks to out-of-district ballots. In addition to their traditional call for full citizenship rights for women, activists are seeking reform of personal status courts (family courts) and the codification of family law in order to remove delicate issues (such as inheritance, divorce, and child custody) from unsupervised adjudication by clerics. Indeed, the public prosecutor brought charges against some activists in the Women's Petition Committee (like Ghadah Jamshīr) for writing articles and petitions advocating the systematization of personal status law and its adjudication. Amnesty International mobilized international support for Ghadah Jamshīr; this campaign, together with the petitions submitted to the UN Secretary-General for the self-determination of the Bahraini people, has aggravated domestic politics. New international pressures on the Bahraini regime could also originate from the fact that political arrests and physical coercion during interrogations have been resumed.[80]

The government's abrupt decision to speed up the adoption of a family law stirred renewed political animosity. On the eve of Bahrain's National Day in December 2008, the government approved and submitted to parliament for discussion a draft family law for both Sunni and Shi'ite Bahrainis. The small secular opposition (along with women's rights activists) favors the implementation of a family law. The Shi'ite opposition rejects the idea of a common Sunni-Shi'ite family law, and opposes secular legislation for confessional family law, just like nonopposition conservative religious Sunni groups (namely, al-Asālah).[81] In early 2009, the regime decided to tackle the issue of a codified family law for Sunnis first, and the parliament thus approved the first part of the family law (i.e., the part governing family law for Sunnis). When voting on the bill in the lower house, al-Wifāq deputies walked out of the chamber, showing their outright dismissal of positive law and institutions in lieu of religious law and institutions in the area of family law. By its actions, al-Wifāq also warned the government against adopting the second part (i.e., a section of the family law for Shi'ites). The king promulgated the Sunni family law in late May (Law 19/2009, *Qānūn ahkām al-usrah–al qism al-awwal*).

Although reform initiatives and democratization campaigns in Bahrain have fulfilled some formal international criteria, they fail to adequately address core issues of the Bahraini polity, such as the participation of Shi'ites and women in public life. These are the two most relevant threads absent from the various reweavings of the tapestry of Bahrain's political life. The regime weaves its portion from above, incorporating pearls but carefully leaving out Shi'ites and women. The opposition weaves its confrontational tapestry from below, following a conservative religious pattern with little or no sympathy for women's causes. External actors are inconsistent weavers while Shi'ites and women are threads that are not to be found in the sewing baskets of neighboring GCC countries. The Shi'ite thread is nonetheless heavily used by Bahrain's larger neighbor to the east, whereas both threads occasionally appear in Western baskets but are incorporated with prudence, usually one at a time.

As in other instances of democratization in the Gulf where civil society is engaged and alert, large sectors of the Bahraini polity seem quite determined to pursue full citizenship and good governance. The capacity of the actual constitutional system to convey these principles and transform them into institutions will be mainly measured against the yardstick of parliamentary life. In such a process, reweaving the myth of the 1973–1975 parliamentary experience appears crucial for the insertion of new threads and pearls for a more satisfactory result.

Notes

1. In his 2005 State of the Union speech, delivered on February 2, US president George W. Bush quoted Bahrain as a case of "hopeful reform [that] is already taking hold" in the Middle East. See George W. Bush, "State of the Union Address," February 2, 2005, www.whitehouse.gov (April 27, 2006).

2. The legal status of the National Action Charter as a constitutional document

is quite uncertain. See Gianluca P. Parolin, "L'evoluzione istituzionale delle monarchie del Golfo tra modernità e tradizione: Il caso del Bahrein," *Diritto Pubblico Comparato ed Europeo* 1 (2003): 59–80; and Gianluca P. Parolin, "Generations of Gulf Constitutions: Paths and Perspectives," in *Constitutional Reform and Political Participation in the Gulf*, eds. Abdulhadi Khalaf and Giacomo Luciani (Dubai: Gulf Research Center, 2006), pp. 51–87.

3. Taking a closer look at Bahrain's political arena, we can see that over the past five years public authorities have been steadily approving applications to form nongovernmental organizations. The process of legalizing (political) associations started in September 2001 with the approval of the National Democratic Action Society (NDAS; *Jam'īyah al-'amal al-watanī al-dīmuqrātī*). Among authorized associations, the al-Wifāq National Islamic Society (*Jam'īyah al-wifāq al-watanī al-islāmīyah*) emerged as the main opposition group, comprising key Shi'ite figures.

4. Parolin, "L'evoluzione istituzionale delle monarchie del Golfo tra modernità e tradizione," pp. 75–77.

5. A significant stand was assumed by leading dissident shaikh 'Abd al-Amīr al-Jamrī. See Habib Trabelsi, "Bahraini Opposition Turns Against King's 'Imposed' Reforms," Agence France Press, February 24, 2006.

6. *Makramāt malakīyah* ("royal liberalities") were a key feature of the general amiri design. See 'Abdulhādī Khalaf, *Binā' al-dawlah fī 'l-Bahrayn: al-Muhimmah ghayr al-munjazah* (Beirut: Dar al-Kunūz al-Adabīyah, 2000). Listing of major *makramāt* can be found (in Arabic only) on the Bahrain government's website at www.bahrain.gov.bh (February 16, 2006) in the section "Mamlakat al-Bahrayn," just after the national anthem, the constitution, its explanatory notes, and the NAC.

7. Marsūm bi-Qānūn 14/2002 (July 3, 2002), *bi-sha'n mubāsharat al-huqūq al-siyāsīyah* (Decree-Law 14/2002 on the practice of political rights), later modified by Marsūm bi-Qānūn 35/2002 (October 8, 2002), *bi-ta'dīl Marsūm bi-Qānūn 14/2002* (Decree-Law 35/2002 amending Decree-Law 14/2002).

8. In a statement published on September 3, 2002, the BFM declared that elections would bring new corruption because the elected members could not alter the political course and would consolidate the "one-party-rule phenomenon." Therefore, the BFM believed that "the right response is to boycott these ill-fated elections and call[ed] upon the people of Bahrain to continue their peaceful struggle to restore the 1973 Constitution and bring stability, civil and political rights, justice and freedom of expression to the country." See *Voice of Bahrain* at www.vob.org (September 30, 2002).

9. 'Abdulhādī Khalaf, "Bahrain's Election: Just What the King Ordered," *Voice of Bahrain,* no. 130, October 4, 2002.

10. "al-Bahrayn tantasir li-l-dīmuqrātīyah: al-Mushārakah fāqat al-tawaqqu'āt .. wa-haqqaqat 53.2 %," *al-Ayyām* (Manama), October 25, 2002.

11. "Intisār li-l-irādah al-sha'bīyah," *al-Ayyām* (Manama), October 25, 2002.

12. "al-Wifāq wa-l-'Amal: Sanata'āwun ma'a nuwwāb al-barlamān," *al-Ayyām* (Manama), October 25, 2002.

13. "Wāshintun: al-Intikhābāt hurrah wa-nazīhah wa-nad'am al-islāhāt," *al-Ayyām* (Manama), October 25, 2002.

14. As a result, state-owned media spoke of three parties: the salafi, al-Ikhwān, and the independents.

15. Most data in this section were supplemented with the Economist Intelligence Unit periodical reports for March, June, September, and December 2002.

16. The idea of legal environment was not yet developed in the early work of Giorgio Lombardi, *Premesse al corso di diritto pubblico comparato: Problemi di*

metodo (Milano: Giuffré, 1986). But later reflections on the character of comparative public law brought him to conceptualize this basic factor for the understanding of the circulation of legal models.

17. Ministers are members ex officio according to Article 80, clause 2, of the 1962 Kuwaiti constitution.

18. Articles 51 and 79 of the 1962 Kuwaiti constitution.

19. Article 43 of the 1973 Bahrain constitution.

20. Article 42 of the 1973 Bahrain constitution.

21. Interestingly, Amr Amīrī 4/1975 was adopted on the same day of Marsūm Amīrī 14/1975 (August 26, 1975) carrying the dissolution of the National Assembly.

22. Parolin, "L'evoluzione istituzionale delle monarchie del Golfo tra modernità e tradizione," pp. 72–73.

23. On the *argumentum quoad auctoritatem*, Lombardi, *Premesse al corso di diritto pubblico comparato*, p. 102.

24. The concept of bicameralism in the NAC is poorly conceived. The charter affirms that "one chamber represents the whole gamut of ideas and views on current affairs as reflected by popular representatives from all brackets whereas the other chamber serves as a forum of experts and expertise."

25. National Action Charter, chapter 5.

26. The opposition openly asked Shaikh Hamad to give his final word on the nature of the bicameral system and the implementation of other ambiguous NAC provisions ahead of the referendum. On February 7, 2001, Shaikh Hamad signed what is known as "the document of clergy," pledging that only the elected chamber would be vested with legislative powers, that the 1973 constitution would have superiority over the National Charter, and that constitutional amendments would be governed by the mechanism set out in Article 104. See 'Alī Rabī'ah, "The Constitutional Crisis in Bahrain," speech delivered in the House of Lords on August 22, 2003, *Voice of Bahrain* 4, no. 140 (October 2003).

27. Article 51 of the 2002 Bahraini constitution.

28. In February 1976, the Chamber of Deputies voted 26 to 5 against endorsing the sale of a US$500 million government Eurobond (which had already taken place) on the grounds that the loan paid interest, which is prohibited under Islamic law (Bahrain has the highest concentration of Islamic financial institutions in the world), and also because part of the loan was to be used for the construction of Bahrain's Formula One racetrack and a tourism project, both of which are venues where alcohol is likely to be consumed. The Consultative Council approved the bill and sent it back to the Chamber of Deputies, which reversed its rejection 19 to 15 in March. The bill is now Law 1/2003 (April 2, 2003).

29. Deputies are effectively barred from amending the constitution because each proposal—which must be requested by fifteen deputies or councillors—has to be referred to the relevant committee. And if the chamber sees fit to accept the proposal, it must be referred to the government to formulate it as a draft amendment to the constitution. A two-thirds majority of members in each house is required for an amendment to pass.

30. The 1973 dissolution was caused precisely because the prime minister declared that he was not willing to cooperate with *al-Majlis al-Watanī*.

31. *Marsūm bi-Qānūn* (Decree-Laws) 54/2002 and 55/2002 (October 23, 2002). Major amendments to the chamber's bylaws were proposed by the deputies to the government on October 8, 2003. 'Amr Barakāt, the chamber's legal adviser, said that "based on the regulations, the government has a period of two parliamentary sessions to give a reply." After the government's approval, the chamber could dis-

cuss the final charter and pass it with a majority vote. The charter would then be sent to the Consultative Council, where a specialized committee would discuss the proposal. The *Bahrain Tribune* (Manama), October 9, 2003.

32. See Article 89 of the 2002 constitution.

33. Designation to appointive offices refers to the appointment of heads of public offices (from the prime minister down, according to the government system) through (1) presentation of candidatures, (2) election, or (3) approval of appointments. Parliaments also play a significant role in policy setting or control over governments, especially if they can remove the executive with a no-confidence vote (according to majority-minority parliamentary forces). Sometimes parliaments are even called to ratify appointments of judges in order to check the choice of the executives.

34. National Action Charter, Final Outlook, Second: "The Legislature."

35. Article 38, paragraph 2, of the 2002 constitution does not differ from the 1973 version.

36. Under this provision, the government issued a striking amount of significant decree-laws in the summer of 2002. Among them was the widely criticized Decree-Law 56/2002. See ʻAbdallah al-Shamlāwī, *Qirā'ah fī 'l-Marsūm bi-Qānūn raqam 56/2002*, September 2, 2002, www.aldemokrati.org (June 20, 2003).

37. New bylaws bring (restrictive) clarity to earlier National Assembly bylaws of Law 4/1974 (July 6, 1974) stipulating that "there is no rejection if not by absolute majority of members present" (*illā bi-l-aghlabīyah al-mutlaqah li-l-aʻdā' al-hādirīn*) in Article 98.

38. Article 87 of the 2002 constitution states:

> Every bill that regulates economic or financial matters, and the Government requests its urgent consideration, shall first be submitted to the Chamber of Deputies so that it takes a decision on it within fifteen days. When that period elapses, the bill is presented to the Consultative Council with the opinion of the Chamber of Deputies if there is such an opinion, so that the Consultative Council decides on it within a further period of fifteen days. If the two Chambers should disagree on the bill in question, the matter is referred to the National Assembly for a vote on it within fifteen days. If the National Assembly does not reach a decision on it within that period, the King may issue the bill as a decree that has the force of a law.

39. During the first session, which began on December 14, 2002, the chamber held thirty sessions—twenty-one ordinary and nine extraordinary. The permanent committees held 122 meetings: the Legislative and Legal Affairs Committee, 25; the Financial and Economic Affairs Committee, 34; the Foreign, Defence and National Security Affairs Committee, 19; the Public Services Committee, 21; and the Public Utilities and Environment Committee, 23. The chamber formed four temporary panels to tackle the draft in response to the royal opening speech, draft in response to the government program, the unemployment folder, and petitions and complaints. Two investigative committees were also set up in relation to the naturalization process and the financial situation of the Pension Fund and the General Organization for Social Insurance. During the first session, the government submitted eighteen bills, and members initiated fifty-one proposals, nineteen proposed laws, and thirty-four questions to ministers on issues of public interest. Shortly after the National Assembly went into recess, King Hamad's donation of BD 10,000 (about US$26,500) to every deputy drew severe criticism from the opposition, through the *al-Wasat* newspaper. Under pressure, the Royal Court minister, Shaikh Khālid bin Ahmad Āl Khalīfah, on behalf of the king issued a state-

ment saying that the payment was made to compensate for campaign expenses. Some decided to return the funds (all the members of al-Minbar al-Islāmī Sunni group); some kept the money.

40. Law 2/2003 (April 4, 2003) amending some provisions of Decree-Law 6/1987 on the treatment of citizens of GCC states in relation to economic activities in Bahrain; Law 4/2003 (April 7, 2003) carrying ratification of a commercial agreement with the al-Sandūq al-kuwaytī li-l-tanmiyah al-iqtisādīyah al-'arabīyah (Kuwaiti Fund for Arab Economic Development); Law 5/2003 (April 7, 2003) carrying ratification of the regulations of Law of the Agricultural Chambers in GCC states; and Law 8/2003 (June 14, 2003) carrying ratification of the regulations of the Veterinary Chambers in GCC states.

41. Law 1/2003 (April 2, 2003) for loans of US$500 million to issue government bonds, and Law 3/2003 (April 7, 2003) amending some provisions of Decree-Law 15/1977 on the issue of development bonds.

42. Law 6/2003 (June 2, 2003).

43. Statistics are out also for the second and third sessions; during the second session (2003–2004), nineteen laws were approved, and fifty-seven during the third session (2004–2005). See Bahrain Chamber of Deputies, www.nuwab.gov.bh (in Arabic, accessed February 16, 2006).

44. *al-Ayyām* (Manama), July 15, 2003 (at the end of the first session of parliamentary activity).

45. 'Alī Rabī'ah, interviewed by the author, Bahrain, October 2002.

46. Emile Nakhleh, *Bahrain: Political Development and Stability* (Lanham, MD: Lexington Books, 1976), p. 169.

47. John E. Peterson, *The Arab Gulf States: Steps Towards Political Participation* (New York: Praeger, 1988), p. 75.

48. Law 2/1974 (March 12, 1974) carrying ratification of the agreement for the Arab society for the construction and restoration of ships; and Law 5/1974 (July 8, 1974) amending the general state budget for the financial year 1974 issued by Decree-Law 22/1973.

49. One of the three decree-laws approved was Law 4/1974 (July 6, 1974), containing the bylaws of the National Assembly.

50. See Peterson, *The Arab Gulf States*, pp. 75–78.

51. Ibid., p. 79.

52. On March 2, 2003, the four groups that boycotted parliamentary elections were joined by two other groups to form an alliance based on a "charter of unity" with the key demand of reinstating the 1973 constitution. The two new groups are the former communist Democratic Forum Society (two seats in the Chamber of Deputies) and the Nationalist Islamic Society, a Sunni *jam'īyah* (association). See *al-Hayāh* (London), March 3, 2003.

53. Rabī'ah interview.

54. Even after turnout data showing the regime's victory were made public, ruling family speakers kept affirming that boycotting was a democratic choice.

55. Munīrah Fakhrū, interviewed by the author, Bahrain, October 24, 2002. The interview was conducted at the boycotters' headquarters when turnout data were broadcast.

56. See the Zallaq affair; Hassan Mushaime, "On Political Naturalization," speech delivered in the House of Lords on August 22, 2003, *Voice of Bahrain* 4, no. 140 (October 2003).

57. The beneficiaries of the grants of citizenship seldom—if ever—comply with the strict rules of the Bahraini nationality legislation regarding ordinary or special naturalization.

58. See the al-Dawsarī tribe affair, unveiled by the opposition; *al-Ayyām* (Manama), September 1, 2003.

59. The issue of "political naturalization" in Bahrain is addressed in Gianluca P. Parolin, *Citizenship in the Arab World* (Amsterdam: Amsterdam University Press, 2009), pp. 116–117.

60. See Abdo Baaklini, Guilain Denoeux, and Robert Springborg, *Legislative Politics in the Arab World: The Resurgence of Democratic Institutions* (Boulder: Lynne Rienner, 1999), p. 47.

61. The full 216-page report (in Arabic) can be downloaded from www.bahrainrights.org (October 18, 2007).

62. Reporters Without Borders, October 27, 2006.

63. Associated Press, December 4, 2006.

64. See Munīrah Fakhrū's case; Agence France Presse, November 29, 2006.

65. Members of al-Wifāq are commonly counted by the monarchy among Islamists.

66. Jane Kinninmont, "Bahrain: Assessing al-Wefaq's Parliamentary Experiment," *Arab Reform Bulletin* 5, no. 8 (2007), www.carnegieendowment.org.

67. The Decree-Law 78/2006 (November 22, 2006) on unemployment benefits (*bi-sha'n al-ta'mīn didd al-ta'attul*) was approved by the Chamber of Deputies on March 6, 2007, and by the Consultative Council on March 19, 2007. It came into force six months from the date it was issued, and a decision of the finance minister regulated its enactment (Finance Minister Decision 19/2007 [June 25, 2007]).

68. "[W]a-jahdī khārij al-majlis yumkin an yakūn akthar fa'idah" (*al-Wasat* [Manama], October 8, 2007).

69. A new arena for political debate is the Web. The most popular website is www.bahrainonline.org, whose blogger, 'Alī 'Abd al-Imām, finds himself in and out of prison on charges such as contempt of the king and spreading false news that always seem to be pending. The website provides a free space to promote political actions, organize rallies, or post speeches that would not be published elsewhere. For instance, 'Abd al-Hādī al-Khawājah's speech that caused him to be arrested and the Bahrain Center for Human Rights to be closed in 2004 was posted only on 'Alī 'Abd al-Imām's blog.

70. In late 2005, Bahrain launched a program for "the strengthening of loyalty to the nation" and "the Bahraini identity pride"; *al-Sharq al-Awsat* (London), December 30, 2005. Interestingly, the woman in charge of the Project for the Development of the National Strategy for Youth (Mashrū' tatwīr al-istrātījīyah al-watanīyah li-l-shabāb) and head of the "loyalty program" is Amal al-Dawsarī, a member of a Sunni allied family of the Āl Khalīfah. The naturalization of a large number of al-Dawsarī tribesmen (who carried Saudi passports) in 2003 brought up the issue of political naturalizations in the country.

71. The UN referendum was not performed by the casting of ballots, but through interviews with Bahrain's prominent personalities carried out by the UN personal representative Vittorio Winspeare Guicciardi, who entered the country on March 30, 1970. On May 11, 1970, he submitted his report (no. 9772) to the UN Security Council stating: "The Bahrainis I met were virtually unanimous in wanting a fully independent sovereign state. The great majority added that this should be an Arab state." The report was ratified later in May 1970 by the two houses of the Iranian parliament; Iran was claiming Bahrain as its fourteenth province and even had a seat reserved for Bahrain in the National Assembly. See UN Security Council Doc. S/9772 (April 30, 1970).

72. The rally took place at the Manama International Airport on December 25, 2005. Twelve demonstrators were put in jail, and were later convicted and sentenced

to two years in prison. See *al-Hayāh* (London), February 7, 2006. Politicians and activists gathered at the airport after they heard the news that Bahraini authorities were detaining and questioning a senior cleric, Ayatollah Mohammad al-Sanad, who had signed the petition for self-determination addressed to the UN Secretary-General.

73. See 'Abdallāh al-'Atībī's interview with Ibrāhīm Sharīf, the NDAS president; *Ibrāhīm: Mā yahduth fī 'l-Bahrayn mazīj min al-idtihād al-tabaqī wa-l-tā'ifī* [Ibrāhīm: What Happens in Bahrain Is a Combination of Class and Sectarian Oppression], December 16, 2005, www.aldemokrati.com.

74. See *Kayhān* (Tehran), July 7, 2007.

75. See "Iran, Bahrain Reject Newspaper's Province Claim," Reuters, July 15, 2007.

76. See *al-Hayāh* (London), February/March 2009.

77. See *Akhbār al-Khalīj* (Manama), July 20, 2005.

78. The appointment in June 2008 of the first Jewish woman ambassador of the kingdom to the United States, Hudà Nūnū, should not be read—or at least not only—in terms of advancement of women's rights in the country; *al-Sharq al-Awsat* (London), April 25, 2006. She presented her credentials on July 28, 2008.

79. *Sa'ī idārat al-ittihād li-ishrāk al-mar'ah al-bahraynīyah bi-sūrah fā'ilah fī 'l-hayāt al-siyāsīyah.*

80. Especially in February and May 2007. On the revival of physical coercion during interrogations after December 2007, see the full eighty-nine-page report, Human Rights Watch, *Torture Redux*, February 2010, www.hrw.org (April 22, 2010).

81. See *al-Sharq al-Awsat* (London), December 15, 2008.

3

Shi'ite Parties and the Democratic Process in Iraq

Juan R. I. Cole

SHI'ITE RELIGIOUS PARTIES have dominated the landscape in post-Baath Iraq, especially in the country's south. Iraq's secular middle class, once among the most vital in the Arab world, has contracted enormously thanks to war and exile, and its remnants have little popular support anywhere in the country. In contrast, parties seeking to implement Islamic law and reinforce Islamic norms of behavior received widespread and consistent popular support, visible in the January 31, 2005, interim national parliamentary election, the provincial elections held in January 2005, the election for the full-term parliament held on December 15, 2005, and the provincial elections of January 2008.

Among Shi'ites, the United Iraqi Alliance (UIA), comprising three large religious parties and nearly a dozen smaller ones, did best in the two parliamentary elections held in 2005. Its major components were the al-Da'wa Party, the Supreme Council for Islamic Revolution in Iraq (SCIRI), and independents from the Sadr movement. The Sadr movement, having largely sat out the January 2005 election, joined the UIA for the contested December 15 election that year. In contrast, al-Da'wa and SCIRI actively campaigned under the UIA banner both times. At the provincial level, they sought seats as parts of ad hoc lists. In December 2005, this coalition of Shi'ite religious parties again emerged as the largest bloc in the national legislature, winning the prerogative of putting forward the prime minister in both governments. The same religious parties were victorious in the provinces in 2009, although there was a shift in the electorate from some religious parties toward others.

From these three major elections, a stable party system emerged with relatively little voter volatility. In particular, ethnic and religious loyalties showed great persistence. This development came as a surprise to the US architects of the Iraq War, many of whom initially hoped to install the expatriate financier Ahmad Chalabi in power; later, others fixed their hopes on the ex-Baathist Iyad Allawi. Either plan would have required that Iraqi voters be willing to switch political allegiances lightly. What are the reasons for the lack of voter volatility? Among the common theoretical explanations for party stability are that it is a consequence of the deep historical roots of the major parties, or that it results from a relatively small number of parties.[1] Do these explanations hold for Iraq?

Established Parties in Iraq

Political scientists argue that voter volatility is limited when parties have strong historical roots, thus "closing off the electoral marketplace, narrowing the range of viable alternatives and socializing voters to embrace established partisan identities."[2] Iraq was completely dominated by the Baath Party in the period from 1968 through 2003, and may have looked to outsiders as though it was a one-party state. In fact, however, the Baath Party faced strong challenges over decades from parties that managed to operate underground or in the interstices of Baghdad's often tenuous grip on power. Here, I survey the main Shi'ite parties whose historical roots extend deep into Iraq's past.

Modern Iraq is made up of Shi'ite Arabs in the south, Sunni Arabs in the center north, and Kurds and Turkmen in the farther north. The Shi'ites are about 60 percent of the population, with the Kurds and Sunni Arabs about 17 percent each. The Shi'ite branch of Islam developed from early tendencies that focused on devotion to the family of the Prophet Muhammad, and a conviction that only his blood relatives should lead the Muslim community after his death. Shi'ites are a minority among Muslims, making up only 10 percent of the wider Muslim world. But they constitute some 90 percent of Iran's population, and are also a majority in Iraq and Bahrain. They are probably a plurality in Lebanon, making up about 40 percent of the population.

Iraqi tribes began converting to Shi'ite Islam late in the eighteenth century, and the conversion proceeded apace for more than a hundred years.[3] The Shi'a remained the poorest community in the country, however, and were dominated by Sunni Arab political, landholding, and commercial elites (although a handful of Shi'ites were large landowners, entrepreneurs, and politicians). The Shi'ite community remained disproportionately rural until the mid-twentieth century.[4] In 1961, large numbers of Shi'ites began settling in Revolution City, a new, northeastern suburb of Baghdad founded by military dictator Abdul Karim Qasim. This complex attracted so many rural

Shi'ite immigrants that, by the turn of the twenty-first century, it comprised nearly half of Baghdad and some 10 percent of the population of the entire country.

Initially in the 1960s, Revolution City was a hotbed of Communism. It only appears to have turned to Shi'ite religious parties from the 1970s, as the Baath Party pursued a deliberate policy of disproportionately rewarding Sunni Arab supporters with state resources. That is, the Baath Party, with its Tikriti clique at the top, impelled other religious and ethnic groups to mobilize to pressure the state for a greater share of resources.

The high unemployment characteristic of this slum created social dysfunctions, and the adoption of fundamentalist religion by youth in the 1990s and after has parallels in the popularity of the Nation of Islam in ghetto neighborhoods in the United States. Fundamentalism has the advantage of structuring time, providing discipline, and creating realistic goals for social action. Unlike the more cosmopolitan Shi'ite movements based in the nice areas of Baghdad (such as Karrada and Kazimiya) or in Najaf, those in Sadr City tended toward nativism and their exponents lived and died in Iraq, lacking the resources to go abroad.

Da'wa

The first modern Shi'ite religious party in Iraq that went beyond representing community interests to devising strategies about a Shi'ite state was al-Da'wa.[5] Founded around 1957, it aimed at combating Marxism and secular Arab Baathism by developing a modern Shi'ite ideology. The party began as an attempt by committed religious Shi'ites to find a modern political vehicle for the aspirations of Shi'ite youth. Many were moving to the cities, becoming better educated, and increasingly being attracted to secular groups such as the Communist Party of Iraq or the Baath Socialist Party (an Arab nationalist party).

The year 1958 was notable for the overthrow of the pro-British constitutional monarchy in Iraq and the killing of the pro-Western prime minister Nuri al-Said. This prompted a reconsideration among a number of political trends with regard to what kind of government would be best for Iraq. Mohammad Baqir al-Sadr, a Da'wa leader and theorist of Islamic government, believed in consultative government and wanted some sort of elected parliament.[6] He rejected the idea that the government needed to be made up of clerics or that the clergy should have any special political perquisites. Al-Sadr not only put forward a theory of the Islamic state, but also sketched out what he thought an Islamic economy should look like. In his view, an Islamic economy would consist of both a public and a private sector. Even in the private sector, the Islamic system would work to stop exploitation of the poor and curb overweening greed among capitalists.

Resources would be distributed fairly. Finance capital and loan interest would be abandoned in favor of wealth generated by productive labor.[7] The Da'wa Party spread like wildfire, and the 1960s and 1970s are remembered as its golden age.

The governments in power from 1958 through 1968 in Iraq were dominated by the military and imbued with an ideology of Arab nationalism. The opposition Da'wa Party partook of the general anti-Western, anticolonial mood of the 1960s. After a failed attempt in 1963, the Baath Socialist Party came to power in a 1968 coup and it began to crack down on the Da'wa, seeing it as a danger to national unity and a rival for power. The Da'wa Party was organized into secret cells to protect its members, but this careful approach did not prevent occasional arrests of activists by the regime during the 1970s.

In 1977, massive Shi'ite demonstrations broke out, especially in the slums of east Baghdad. These were probably in part led by Da'wa organizers. This populist violence shook the Baathist regime, which had alienated Shi'ites by its aggressive secularism (it had opened liquor stores in the holy city of Najaf) and by its tendency to favor the Sunni Arab minority. During 1978–1979, the cleric Ruhollah Khomeini led a revolution against the modernizing, secular Shah of Iran, the success of which greatly alarmed the Baath leadership.

Iraqi strongman Saddam Hussein, who came to power in a 1979 coup, cracked down on the al-Da'wa Party. He had Mohammad Baqir al-Sadr hanged in 1980, and killed many other al-Da'wa activists. He made even belonging to the al-Da'wa Party a capital offense. Some prominent members of the party fled abroad, mostly to London or Tehran. Others went underground to lead secret lives inside Iraq. Al-Da'wa extended its network of secret cells, many apparently in Nasiriyah and Basra. Nevertheless, Saddam's secret police managed to penetrate many of those cells and to arrest, torture, and kill al-Da'wa operatives. The majority of the bodies found in mass graves in the south of the country since 2003 belonged to Shi'ites whose al-Da'wa Party membership had been discovered.

Meanwhile, exiled Iraqis organized for an eventual return to their country. Hundreds of thousands, most of them Shi'ites, congregated in Iran. The al-Da'wa Party initially joined the umbrella group, SCIRI, in 1982, but withdrew two years later because its lay leaders wanted to preserve al-Da'wa's independence, no easy task in Ayatollah Khomeini's Tehran of the 1980s. Those Da'wa leaders who had been trained as clerics (a minority) tended to accept Khomeini's theory of clerical rule and wished to place the party at his service. The fight between the two factions went on throughout the 1980s and 1990s. In Lebanon and Syria, expatriate Da'wa leaders turned radical, and some were involved in forming Hezbollah in Lebanon. Among the leaders of the Damascus organization was Nuri Kamil Abu al-Mahasin, a man from a prominent political family who adopted Jawad al-Maliki as his nom de guerre. When he returned to Iraq in 2003, he proved willing to cooperate with the United States under these changed circumstances and consequently rose high in the new system, eventually becoming Iraq's prime minister in May 2006.

The al-Da'wa Party faction based in London was led by physicians and attorneys and displayed a more lay cast all along. Among its leaders was Ibrahim Ja'fari. Born in Karbala in 1947, he trained as a physician in Mosul and joined the al-Da'wa Party in the late 1960s. He faced persecution and brief bouts of imprisonment after the Baath Party came to power in 1968. In 1980 he fled to Iran, where he is likely to have been one of the lay leaders who opposed the idea of dissolving the party into Khomeinism. Ja'fari lived in Tehran until 1989, when he moved to London. The London al-Da'wa cooperated with the US invasion of Iraq in spring of 2003 and was rewarded with key positions on the US-appointed Interim Governing Council. Ja'fari himself emerged as an important figure in that body, which positioned him as candidate for prime minister in February 2005.

SCIRI

SCIRI was founded with the encouragement of Ayatollah Ruhollah Khomeini in 1982, by Iraqi expatriate Shi'ite activists who had fled to Tehran after Saddam executed Mohammad Baqir al-Sadr and made al-Da'wa Party membership punishable by death.[8] In 1984, the group came to be headed by Mohammad Baqir al-Hakim, the elder son of the former spiritual leader of Shi'ism in Najaf, Grand Ayatollah Muhsin al-Hakim (d. 1971). Mohammad Baqir's younger brother, Abdul Aziz al-Hakim, devoted himself to developing a paramilitary capability for SCIRI, initially called the Badr Brigade. It grew to become the Badr Corps, with some 10,000 to 15,000 trained men under arms by the late 1990s, many drilled by the Iranian Revolutionary Guard. Throughout the 1980s and 1990s, they slipped into Iraq to carry out attacks on Baath officials and facilities. Iraqi leaders fought fiercely among themselves during their exile in Tehran. Some maintain that, at one point, the al-Da'wa Party-in-exile had plotted the assassination of SCIRI leader Mohammad Baqir al-Hakim.

Meanwhile, in London, Iraqi politician and banker Ahmad Chalabi formed a new umbrella group, the Iraqi National Congress (INC). Chalabi had been forced to flee Jordan in 1989, when he was indicted for embezzling some US$300 million from his Petra Bank. He was later convicted in absentia. Chalabi nevertheless managed to convince the US Central Intelligence Agency to back him in setting up the INC, which, during its heyday, comprised nineteen London-based expatriate political parties. These included Kurds, Sunni Arabs, and both secular and religious Shi'ite factions. For a time, both the London branch of al-Da'wa and SCIRI in Iraq belonged to the INC.[9]

In 1995, the al-Da'wa Party withdrew from the INC to protest the stance of the Kurds who wanted Iraq to develop into a loose federation on the Swiss model. The al-Da'wa Party, in contrast, desired a vigorous central government. In the mid-1990s, Chalabi's INC faced additional debilitating crises. First, in 1994–1996, the two major Kurdish factions fell to infighting between themselves, resulting in a virtual civil war in northern Iraq. Then in March 1995, an attempted uprising launched by Chalabi from Kurdistan, with the aim of moving south into Arab Iraq to challenge the regime, proved a miserable failure. The plan had depended on officers defecting and urban masses rising up, but nothing of the sort took place. Chalabi and his revolutionaries had to flee the country for Europe. The INC was in the wilderness but, when George W. Bush was elected president of the United States in 2000, Chalabi's friends among the neoconservative intellectuals were given key roles in the Pentagon. There, they used their positions to promote Chalabi, who was able to draw SCIRI back into meetings of expatriate Iraqi politicians aiming to cooperate with US secretary of defense Donald Rumsfeld in overthrowing Saddam. SCIRI representatives were even invited to Washington in summer 2002, despite the criticism of al-Hakim that this step provoked in Iran. Among the major components of the INC, only the two large Kurdish parties and the Supreme Council had significant grassroots inside Iraq.

Sadrism

The third large political tendency among Iraqi Shi'ites in the 1990s was the Sadr II movement, which grew up around the cleric Mohammad Mohammad Sadiq al-Sadr. He was related to the theorist of the al-Da'wa Party, Mohammad Baqir al-Sadr,[10] and in consequence was known as "Sadr the Second."

In the Usuli school of Shi'ite Islam that predominates in Iraq and Iran, each lay believer is obliged to choose a spiritual and legal mentor (Ar. *marja'* or source, i.e., of authority) from among the trained religious jurisprudents to whom he will look as a guide to the practice of religious law and ritual. This guide, or Object of Emulation, is typically a leading clergyman who has written a book of ritual practice called a manual (*Risalah*). The most popular and respected of these figures, most often the leading cleric resident in the holy city of Najaf, can rise to become a Grand Ayatollah and the highest Object of Emulation in the Shi'ite world (at least outside Iran itself). This position was held by Muhsin al-Hakim until his death in 1971, when he was succeeded by Abul-Qasim Khu'i (Khoei).[11]

The last two years of Khu'i's long life coincided with the Iraqi invasion of Kuwait, the US-led counterattack that forced Baath troops back out, and a Shi'ite uprising in the south of the country in March and April of 1991. The leadership of the uprising was provided by SCIRI, which had sent in agents from Iran. At the same time, the two Kurdistan parties rebelled in the north, and sixteen of Iraq's eighteen provinces threw off Baath Party rule. Although that uprising was called forth by then president George H. W. Bush, he did nothing to support it and allowed Saddam's helicopter gunships to crush it. The terrified Baath military killed an estimated 60,000 people in putting down the rebellion while Baath secret police made some 200 senior clergymen disappear from the holy cities of Najaf and Karbala.[12]

A year later, in 1992, al-Khu'i died and, after a while, was succeeded by his longtime protégé, Ali Sistani. Sistani was born in 1930 in Mashhad, in eastern Iran, and studied in the late 1940s with the leading cleric, Husayn Burujerdi. Sistani belonged to the quietist school of Shi'ism, which holds that clerics should not get too directly involved in governmental affairs. He had substantial disagreements with Khomeini's doctrine of the "guardianship of the jurisprudent" in politics (i.e., direct clerical rule).

Sistani's main competitor for authority from about the mid-1990s was Mohammad Sadiq al-Sadr. Al-Sadr advertised himself as advocating a "third way" between Khomeini's theocracy and Sistani's quietism. On most key issues he appears to have been closer to Khomeini, with whom he studied in the 1970s while the latter was in Najaf. Al-Sadr set up a new organization among poor Shi'ites in east Baghdad, Kufa, Basra, and the shrine cities of Najaf and Karbala. Although the Baath Party attempted to monitor all important developments in Iraqi society, it was unable to penetrate the poor Shi'ite neighborhoods effectively.

Al-Sadr demonstrated that it was possible to organize Shi'ites even under Saddam's nose, especially deep in Baghdad's labyrinthine slums and in the rural south. He urged his followers to defy Saddam by gathering for Friday prayers in storefront mosques (the Baathist dictator had not wanted large numbers of Shi'ites congregating anywhere). He organized informal courts and discouraged Shi'ites from taking legal cases to the secular Baathist courts. His teachings were imbued with a Puritanism that condemned most forms of entertainment, including films, and demanded veiling for all women. He forbade his followers to wear clothing manufactured in the United States. At his rallies, crowds chanted "Death to Israel, Death to America."

Al-Sadr's defiance of Saddam cost him dearly. In January of 1999, secret police came to him in Najaf and warned him to cease his antiregime activities. He refused and, mounting the pulpit, compared Saddam to a medieval tyrant who oppressed Shi'ites. In mid-February 1999, he was gunned down as he was driving home with his two elder sons. The Shi'ites living in the slums of east Baghdad, Basra, and many other southern neighborhoods came out to protest and riot, and were brutally repressed.

Al-Sadr was succeeded by two figures. His young son, Muqtada, went underground and kept his father's organization alive as the Sadr II Bloc (Jama'at al-Sadr al-Thani). An older disciple, who broke with Muqtada, the cleric Muhammad Ya'qubi, developed his own following, which he called the Virtuous (*al-fudala'*).[13] For the next four years these two leaders kept the Sadr movement alive from hiding places and safe houses, with Muqtada's cadres especially active in east Baghdad and Ya'qubi's in the southern port city of Basra.

After Saddam

All three major Shi'ite factions had been organizing for the overthrow of Saddam and the installation of a Shi'ite Islamic republic in Iraq throughout the 1980s and 1990s. When the United States deposed Saddam Hussein on April 9, 2003, the Shi'ite religious parties were suddenly liberated to organize for a takeover of the country. SCIRI rushed back to Iraq, with Abdul Aziz al-Hakim arriving in April. His older brother, Mohammad Baqir al-Hakim, arrived in early May and addressed some 10,000 Shi'ites gathered in a stadium in Basra. SCIRI's Badr Corps likewise also came back to Iraq.[14] Both SCIRI and Badr opened political offices in Shi'ite neighborhoods throughout the country, drawing on the base of relations they had established with local populations during their guerrilla activities against the regime, and also attracting new adherents. SCIRI established a powerful position in the southern port city of Basra, population 1.2 million, and went out from there to proselytize in surrounding villages.

SCIRI was given a seat on the Interim Governing Council appointed by US civil administrator Paul Bremer in July of 2003. The group generally cooperated with US officials although theirs was clearly a marriage of convenience. Then, on August 29, 2003, guerrillas detonated a huge car bomb in Najaf as Mohammad Baqir al-Hakim emerged from the mosque at the shrine of Ali, killing him along with over eighty others.[15] His younger brother, Abdul Aziz al-Hakim, succeeded him as the leader of SCIRI and took the party's seat on the Interim Governing Council.

The Shi'ite religious parties had chafed under Baathist secularism and were now determined to crush it. Abdul Aziz al-Hakim attempted in late December 2003 to enact *sharia* or Islamic law in Iraq with regard to personal status law (marriage, divorce, alimony, inheritance, and so forth). Al-Hakim initially got a majority on the Interim Governing Council, but secular Shi'ite physician Raja' al-Khuza'i, a prominent female member of the Interim Governing Council, led a charge to overturn the *sharia* decree. She succeeded, although her victory only postponed the debate until an elected parliament could take it up again.

The al-Da'wa Party also took advantage of the new freedom to organize and spread its influence. The party organized in Nasiriyah, Karbala, and Samawah in the south. But al-Da'wa had split into several factions during the Saddam period, and was unable to reunite. Abd al-Karim al-Anizi led one faction, the Islamic al-Da'wa-Iraq Organization, whereas Ja'fari continued to head up the branch of the party influenced by its London exile. Ja'fari joined in the attempt to impose Islamic law in personal status matters in January–February of 2004 while he was serving on the US-appointed Interim Governing Council. When the United States engineered a transition to an interim government in June of 2004, he agreed to serve as one of two vice presidents in the government of secularist ex-Baathist Allawi, who became prime minister.

Unlike SCIRI and al-Da'wa, the Sadr movement for the most part refused to cooperate with the United States. It may also be that SCIRI had made its own cooperation with the United States dependent on its snubbing of the Sadrists. Muqtada al-Sadr, the young son of the martyred Sadiq al-Sadr, began calling for an immediate US withdrawal from Iraq in April of 2003. He and his followers staged frequent demonstrations, ranging in size from a few hundred to a few thousand persons, on an average of every other week, in Baghdad and elsewhere in the south.

In the summer of 2003, Muqtada began to assemble a formal militia. His movement was spreading and becoming increasingly influential outside its old base of east Baghdad, now called Sadr City in honor of Sadiq al-Sadr. Most of the Marsh Arabs, southern tribes displaced by Saddam's draining of Iraq's extensive southern wetlands, were pushed into slums in Amara and elsewhere in the south. Nearly all of them went over to Muqtada al-Sadr. By the spring of 2004, there was a Sadrist majority on the governing council of Maysan Province, whose capital is Amara. The Mahdi Army's paramilitary activities appear to have been funded illicitly, by the black market sale of Iraqi antiquities to foreign buyers, gasoline smuggling, and similar activities.

In early April 2004, the US administration of Iraq suddenly announced that it wanted Muqtada al-Sadr "dead or alive" and then attempted to arrest him. Although Muqtada had been spreading his influence and organizing a militia, his men had seldom come into conflict with US troops. Why the United States suddenly decided to come after him remains a mystery but, in any case, they vastly underestimated him. Muqtada launched an uprising throughout the south to demonstrate that he could not so easily be destroyed. His militiamen, the Mahdi Army, took control of most of the country, capturing police and even army outposts in Sadr City, Nasiriyah, Kut, Amara, Najaf, and elsewhere in the south.[16]

The US military soon found its lines of supply and communications to the south cut off, and it lost control of the capital, Baghdad. After two months of hard fighting, however, it forced the Mahdi Army to back down and impelled Muqtada al-Sadr to seek a truce. Fighting broke out again in Najaf in August 2004 over the reassertion of control by the Mahdi Army over that central holy city. The fighting devastated the old city and threatened the holiest site for Shi'ites, the sacred tomb of Ali, the son-in-law and cousin of the Prophet, whom Shi'ites consider the true successor of Muhammad. A standoff at the shrine was averted by Grand Ayatollah Sistani, who called for a national march of civilians on Najaf in late August.[17] This Gandhian tactic succeeded in ending the fighting, and allowed Muqtada al-Sadr and his key lieutenants to escape. The two lessons of the US battles with the Mahdi Army were that the militiamen could be militarily defeated in hard urban combat given enough time, but that the United States could never hope either to finish them off altogether or to win politically against Muqtada.

The three major Shi'ite political movements each sought sectional advantage. A spiritual figure proved the most important advocate of pan-Shi'ite interests. Sistani intervened to shape post-Saddam Iraqi politics in key ways, often coming into conflict with the United States and always winning when he did. In late June 2003, Sistani issued a fatwa or ruling that it would be illegitimate for the United States to appoint a committee to draft a new Iraqi constitution, as Bremer had planned to do. Sistani insisted that only an elected body could represent the will of the Iraqi people. Bremer attempted to dismiss Sistani's intervention, but found that even his own Shi'ite appointees on the Interim Governing Council supported the Grand Ayatollah.

In the autumn of 2003, as the US administration of the country collapsed in the face of continued Shi'ite mobilization in the south and a growing guerrilla war in the Sunni Arab areas, Bremer flew back to Washington to seek the beginnings of an exit strategy. He returned to negotiate a November 15 agreement with the Interim Governing Council that called for elections in May 2004, after which the United States would devolve sovereignty onto an Iraqi government. The electorate, however, would not be the Iraqi public. Voting was to be restricted to members of the provincial governing councils that the United States and the United Kingdom had massaged into being.[18] Using its own personnel or a private contractor, the Coalition Provisional Authority (CPA) had called small meetings of roughly 150 local notables in each of the eighteen provinces to select members for a provincial governing council.

Sistani responded with a fatwa condemning the proposed caucus elections as completely undemocratic. He insisted on open, one-person, one-vote elections, along with UN involvement in Iraq's transition to sovereignty.[19] Sistani ultimately got his open elections, but they were postponed by the George W. Bush administration until January 30, 2005, rather than being held in May 2004 as planned. This move probably reflected a fear on Bush's part that the Iraqi elections had become unpredictable and might hurt him in the US presidential campaign. Until the elections could be held, UN special envoy Lakhdar Brahimi and the United States appointed an interim government, headed by longtime expatriate politician, physician, and ex-Baathist Allawi, which took power when Bremer slipped out of Iraq on June 28.[20] Allawi was known as a tough guy. On behalf of the US Central Intelligence Agency, he had for a decade attempted, although without success, to organize defecting Baathist officers to overthrow Saddam. He was backed by the United States as an alternative to the religious leaders.

The United States and Carina Perelli, head of the UN Electoral Assistance Mission to Iraq, adopted a proportional representation system based on party lists to organize elections in Iraq. This meant that parliamentary elections would be held on a nationwide basis, with no local districts. The system adopted may have been devised to reward parties that appealed to constituencies across the country, but it was open to being gamed by other, more exclusive strategies.

Because Iraqis are 60 percent Shi'ite, Grand Ayatollah Sistani and the people around him concluded that an alternative winning strategy would be to convince most Shi'ites to vote for a single coalition list that included all major Shi'ite religious parties, rather than splitting their vote. His envoys succeeded in persuading both the al-Da'wa Party and the Islamic al-Da'wa-Iraq Organization to join, along SCIRI and the Badr Corps (now the Badr Organization, a group with political ambitions of its own). Small parties such as those of the Faili or Shi'ite Kurds, the Turkmen, and some secular-leaning groups like Chalabi's INC also joined in. Two major groups did not join the coalition formally. One was the Sadr movement (although some thirty independents with loyalties either to Muqtada al-Sadr or to Ayatollah Ya'qubi of Fadilah were on the UIA list). The other was the secularist National Iraqi List of Allawi, an ethnic Shi'ite. Sistani then issued a fatwa urging Iraqi Shi'ites to vote for the UIA.[21]

The Ja'fari Government

In the elections for representatives to national and provincial legislatures held on January 30, 2005, Sistani's strategy was vindicated. When the proportional calculations were finally completed, using the reapportionment variation of the Hare method (which awards otherwise "wasted" votes cast for small parties that do not meet the threshold for being seated to the larger parties that do), the electoral commission announced that the UIA had won

140 seats in the 275-member National Assembly, or 51 percent. Allawi's secular list received only forty seats, or 14.5 percent. The Kurds had adopted the same strategy as Sistani for their groups, putting together the Kurdistan Alliance list that garnered seventy-five seats, or 27 percent. Few Sunni Arabs voted, which, in accordance with the proportional system that the United Nations had adopted for Iraq, magnified the effects of Shi'ite and Kurdish votes. Iraqi national politics had broken down along ethnic or subnational lines.[22]

The UIA strategy had greatly reduced the number of discrete political parties by creating a pan-Shi'ite coalition. Not only had the religious Shi'ite parties swept to power, but Sistani's grand alliance also served as a magnet to attract some small Shi'ite independent groups even after the election. Thus, the Cadres and Chosen Party of Sadrists gained three seats (although Muqtada al-Sadr had renounced involvement in the election, they had run on the grounds that he had not forbidden it). The Turkmen National Front won three seats and the Islamic Action Organization won two. After the election, all three joined the UIA coalition, bringing its total to 148 seats, nearly 54 percent of the National Assembly, thereby ensuring that its choice for prime minister would prevail. Although the UIA needed a partner to form a government, which requires a two-thirds majority, the alliance would be able to legislate and set parliamentary rules virtually on its own, since those required only a simple majority.[23] The Shi'ites' religious coalition made an alliance of convenience with the Kurdistan Alliance, with Jalal Talabani of the Patriotic Union of Kurdistan becoming president. For all practical purposes, Iraq was dominated by two large political parties. Over time, the unity of the UIA umbrella organization would be challenged by disagreements over policy and by factionalism, but it held together through 2008. Because the Kurds feel isolated and fear Arab dominance, their Kurdistan Alliance appears likely to be more long-lived.

At the provincial level, the Shi'ite parties ran independently from one another or cobbled together ad hoc lists. The Supreme Council for Islamic Revolution in Iraq dominated the lists that won control of the provincial governments in nine of the eighteen provinces in the country, including Baghdad. SCIRI dominance of the sacred shrine cities of Najaf and Karbala increased the party's prestige and allowed it to infiltrate the Badr Corps into local police departments. The wealthy shopkeepers and merchants of these two cities valued the sort of order and Islamic legitimacy that SCIRI brought, and dreamed of getting rich from a revived Iranian pilgrimage trade. Overall, Shi'ite lists won eleven of the eighteen provinces. Sadrists won Maysan. In the deep south, where Basra's governing council consisted of forty-one seats, the Supreme Council won twenty of them. But its rival in the province, the Virtue (Fadilah) Party, put together a coalition of the other twenty-one and so was able to dominate the council. The Virtue Party had been founded in April 2003, by Ayatollah Muhammad Ya'qubi, disciple of Grand Ayatollah Muhammad Sadiq al-Sadr. Ya'qubi disapproved of Muqtada al-Sadr and so founded his own Sadrist organization, which proved more popular in Basra than did Muqtada's Sadr II Bloc.

Provincial elections also were conducted on the list system, but which groups were listed in the coalitions differed from province to province. Surprisingly, candidates from the al-Da'wa Party did not run well at the provincial level in 2005, and failed to win a plurality in any of the provincial assemblies. The long decades of Baath repression had greatly weakened both of the main factions of the party, the London-based Islamic Da'wa Party of Ibrahim Ja'fari, and the Da'wa-Iraq Organization of 'Abd al-Karim 'Anizi. In contrast, SCIRI was able to capitalize on its popularity along the routes it had traveled when it infiltrated Baathist Iraq to strike at officials and facilities. These "rat lines" ran through Basra in the south and Baqubah in the northeast. Right from May 2003, SCIRI canvassers had begun establishing local party offices, offering patronage (probably funneled in some part from Iran), and gaining the loyalty of Iraqi voters in the small towns and villages of the south.

Perhaps precisely because SCIRI had done so well at the provincial level, the victorious UIA put forward Da'wa Party leader Ibrahim Ja'fari as prime minister at the federal level, and he was appointed to form a government by the three-person presidential council. It took Ja'fari three months to put together a cabinet able to win approval in the parliament. His government was sworn in at an early May 2005 ceremony.

In accordance with Sistani's fatwa, the major charge of the new government was to draft a permanent constitution. A wholly unrealistic deadline of August 15 was imposed by the United States, and it proved impossible to meet. The drafting committee in parliament was headed by Shi'ite cleric Humam Hammudi of SCIRI, and SCIRI appears to have dominated the deliberations, along with the Kurdistan Alliance. The constitution produced by this process was full of internal contradictions and also contained over fifty articles that required parliament to specify their content by statute later on. The transitional administrative law crafted jointly by the Bremer administration and the Interim Governing Council, neither of them elected bodies, formed the skeleton of the permanent constitution, which retained articles guaranteeing civil liberties such as freedom of speech, publication, and conscience. But the constitution also stated that Islam would be the religion of state, that parliament could pass no civil legislation that contravened the established laws of Islam, and that Muslim clerics were suitable appointees to civil court benches. Shi'ite deputies attempted to insert clauses establishing a body to review legislation for any contradictions with Islam and bestowing special status on the Shi'ite religious establishment in Najaf. This language was removed when the

United States and the representatives of the other ethnic groups strongly objected.

The most controversial provisions of the new constitution touched on the character of Iraq's new federalism. The woefully outnumbered Sunni Arabs rejected federalism altogether, preferring a French-style central government. The constitution produced the opposite: a central government that was much weaker, and provinces much stronger, than those of Switzerland. It recognized the Kurdistan regional confederacy, which had melded the provinces of Dohuk, Irbil, and Sulaymaniyyah into a single administration with its own parliament, prime minister, and president. The constitution exempted the regional confederacy from any federal laws it found inconvenient, and provided for the formation of further provincial confederacies. 'Abd al-'Aziz al-Hakim of the Supreme Council pushed openly for this measure, which would allow the nine southern Shi'ite provinces to join together into a superprovince.[24] The constitution also provided that provinces or regional confederacies could retain all profits from future natural resource finds in their territory, thereby denying them to the federal government in Baghdad. Sunni Arabs had no significant proven petroleum reserves in their provinces, so this provision effectively deprived them of a fair share of the income from future discoveries in the Shi'ite or Kurdish areas. The Sunni Arabs decisively rejected the new constitution, which had been drafted under circumstances that gave them little voice in it.[25]

Sunni Arabs were, ironically enough, politicized by the unwanted constitution foisted upon them. For the first time, they began registering to vote and collaborating on strategies for using the ballot box in their struggle. They knew that, if three provinces rejected the constitution by a two-thirds margin, it would fail. On October 15, the constitution was rejected in three provinces where Sunnis formed a majority, but in only two did they vote it down by a two-thirds majority. Sunnis were unable to defeat the constitution because in Ninevah, the third province, the vote was only 55 percent against. In contrast, even though Grand Ayatollah Sistani declined to ask Shi'ites to vote for the constitution, the UIA strongly backed it and an overwhelming majority of Shi'ites supported it in the referendum.[26]

Having come uncomfortably close to losing the referendum on the constitution, and facing a strong challenge by the National Iraqi List headed by former interim prime minister Allawi, the Shi'ite religious parties were prodded into taking measures to ensure that they would repeat their January victory. The UIA, headed by 'Abd al-'Aziz al-Hakim, brought in both major Sadrist groups. It gave the Muqtada al-Sadr faction thirty seats, and apportioned fifteen to the Virtue Party. Because the actual allocation of seats would be determined by list-based elections within provinces, these pledges were an effective commitment to adjust the final results. For Muqtada al-Sadr to agree to have his movement actively contest elections he already had declared were being held "under the shadow of occupation" represented a remarkable turnabout. The addition of the Sadr II Bloc changed the internal dynamics of the UIA significantly, reducing the dominance of the Supreme Council and giving the Da'wa Party a new internal ally. The Da'wa Party was given twenty-four seats, apparently because of its poor showing in the provincial elections the previous January. SCIRI also had thirty seats. The rest of the seats won by the list were filled by members of smaller parties and UIA independents. Sistani was annoyed by the failure of the Ja'fari government to provide security or services, and declined to endorse the UIA in the December 15 elections.

But this time, the Sunni Arabs were determined to vote. Three Sunni religious parties made a coalition, the Iraqi Accord Front. A secular Arab nationalist party, the National Dialogue Front, also ran. In this election, the eighteen Iraqi provinces were treated as electoral districts. Because most Iraqi provinces have a strong ethnic or religious coloration, this decision reinforced the tendency of ethnic groups to vote for parties that represented them. I was told by journalists at the time that analysts from the major neoconservative think tanks in Washington, DC, had thought that the election would reveal substantial voter volatility and expected that Allawi's National Iraqi List would win. Michael Rubin of the American Enterprise Institute told National Public Radio that he believed Sunni tribesmen would vote for Allawi.[27] Allawi had been appointed caretaker prime minister and had all the advantages of incumbency, including substantial television time and the ability to direct government money to potential constituencies. In fact, however, the December 2005 election was characterized by relatively low voter volatility.

Voters in principle had a choice of many party lists, but realistically there were only four or five significant contenders. These included the UIA, the Kurdistan Alliance, the Iraqi Accord Front, and the National Iraqi List. Ironically, it was Allawi's secular party that showed the most volatility, declining from 14 percent of seats to only 9 percent. The Kurdistan Alliance retained its voters. The Iraqi Accord Front did best among Sunni Arabs, winning forty-four seats, and the National Dialogue Front took eleven. Shi'ites voted overwhelmingly for the United Iraqi Alliance, which won 128 seats out of 275. Two winners from the Risaliyyun Party who were loyal to Muqtada al-Sadr joined the UIA, giving it a total of 130, or 47 percent, short of an absolute majority on its own. The failure to win a majority derived from the new, province-based electoral districts that guaranteed the Sunni Arab provinces greater representation. That is, it was a side effect of a different system of proportionality in the election rules rather than a sign of voter volatility. The determination of all parties to form a government of national unity, however, made this consideration less important than it might have been had the UIA sought to rule alone.

Because it was the largest single party, under the constitution the president was obliged to ask the UIA to form a government, but the UIA proved unable to choose a prime minister by consensus. It held an internal party vote to decide between the two leading candidates, Ibrahim Ja'fari of the Da'wa Party and 'Adil 'Abd al-Mahdi of the Supreme Council. The UIA had 130 potential votes, but one member of parliament (a Sadrist) arrived too late to cast a ballot and two members of SCIRI abstained. Of the remaining 127 votes, 64 went to Ja'fari, mainly from Da'wa and the Sadr II Bloc, and the rest from a few UIA independents. 'Adil 'Abd al-Mahdi garnered sixty-three votes from SCIRI and Virtue Party MPs, and from other independents.[28]

Ja'fari, however, proved unacceptable to the United States, the Kurdistan Alliance, and the two main Sunni parties, the Iraqi Accord Front and the National Dialogue Front. The Sunni Arabs believed he was implicated in the rise of Shi'ite death squads based in Interior Ministry special police commando units that targeted Sunnis. The death squad issue exploded after the February 20 destruction of the Shi'ite Askariyyah Shrine at Samarra by Sunni Arab guerrillas and the subsequent Shi'ite attacks on Sunnis. Ja'fari angered the Kurds by flying to Ankara to discuss with the Turkish government how to curb Kurdish autonomy and the creeping annexation of Kirkuk Province by the Kurdistan regional confederacy. Given that his charge was to form a government of national unity, this opposition was fatal to his bid to continue as prime minister. Ja'fari appeared also to have lost the confidence of Sistani. He was replaced by another old-time Da'wa Party leader, Nuri "Jawad" Abu al-Mahasin "al-Maliki." Al-Maliki pledged to address burning issues of militias engaged in sectarian attacks and ethnic cleansing as well as the spoils system that had grown up in the ministries and provincial administrations whereby the winners were able to pack the bureaucracy with members of their party.[29] Al-Maliki angered the Virtue Party by refusing to give it the Ministry of Petroleum. In response, the party withdrew from his coalition and reduced its cooperation with the central government to ensure the timely exporting of petroleum from Basra, which it dominates. Al-Maliki managed to form a government by June 8, when he finally appointed the heads of the Interior and Defense Ministries.[30] Al-Maliki suffered serious reversals at the cabinet level in 2007, as the Sunni Arab Iraqi Accord Front withdrew from his government in protest against the large number of Sunni Arabs being held without charges by the US military. Likewise, the Sadr II Bloc deserted him because he declined to break with the George W. Bush administration and call for a timetable for US troop withdrawal. The small National Iraqi List of Allawi also withdrew.

By summer 2008, however, al-Maliki had made enough compromises to entice the Iraqi Accord Front back into his cabinet.[31] In spring of 2008, he launched several military attacks on the Mahdi Army, in Basra, Nasiriyyah, and Sadr City. Despite initial setbacks, the new Iraqi army ultimately prevailed and improved the security situation. In November of 2008, al-Maliki managed to push through parliament a controversial security agreement with the United States. The agreement set 2011 as a deadline for all US troops to be out of the country and returned substantial sovereignty to the Iraqi state. This victory was widely seen as strengthening his hand.[32]

In January of 2009, new provincial elections, which had been long postponed, were finally held. The outcome largely confirmed the thesis that Iraqi Shi'ites in particular have demonstrated remarkably little voter volatility since 2003. What volatility was on display largely affected the relative distribution of power among the parties that once made up the old UIA, which had collapsed in 2008. Thus, Da'wa's stock rose. It won 38 percent of the vote in Baghdad and 35 percent in Basra. It received nearly a quarter of the vote in two rural Shi'ite provinces, Dhi Qar and Qadisiyyah. Elsewhere in the Shi'ite south, its proportion of the vote ranged from 8 percent to 16 percent. The Islamic Supreme Council of Iraq did relatively poorly, receiving between 5 percent and 15 percent in the Shi'ite-majority provinces. The Sadrists did not formally run, but generally backed a reform party that stood proxy for them, and did even worse than ISCI in most provinces. (ISCI is the new acronym for SCIRI. The Supreme Council for Islamic Revolution in Iraq dropped the word "Revolution" from its name in 2006. After that, it was known as the Islamic Supreme Council of Iraq, or ISCI.) Yet the majority of seats on the provincial councils in the Shi'ite south went to parties and individuals who earlier had belonged to the UIA (i.e., religious parties supporting a vaguely defined Islamic state). Because no one party received a majority on these councils, the victors were impelled to cobble together ruling coalitions in each one. Such coalitions resemble the old UIA, though Da'wa was now the leading party and ISCI was in a subordinate position. The US press often spoke of Da'wa as more "secular" than ISCI, but they were being inexact. It is a fundamentalist Shi'ite party that ultimately has a theocratic platform, though it is less clerical and less closely tied to Tehran than ISCI. In Karbala, an ex-Baathist technocrat won 13 percent of the vote, which some took to demonstrate a shift of the electorate, even in the shrine cities, toward secular candidates. But religious parties and Shi'ite independents still formed the provincial government. A referendum held in Basra on forming a regional government for Shi'ites on the model of the Kurdish one produced a resounding rejection from Shi'ite voters who appear to have been persuaded by al-Maliki and Da'wa that a strong, united, centralized Iraq offered them more benefits than a soft partition did. The Sunni Arabs did not participate in provincial elections in 2005, so the 2009 results are difficult to interpret with regard to voter volatility, though Iraqis did vote for more secular candidates than in the December 2005 parliamentary elections.[33]

The March 2010 parliamentary elections again showed no significant voter volatility among Shi'ites and Kurds. The major Shi'ite religious parties gained nearly a majority in parliament and, by May, appeared ready to ally with one another again. It is true that Da'wa and the Sadrists saw gains and some other parties shrank, but the general picture did not change dramatically. Only the Sunni Arabs, politically adrift since the fall of the Baath Party, showed real volatility as voters, with perhaps 85 percent voting for the secular, cross-sectarian Iraqiya list of Allawi (formerly known as the National Iraqi List).

Conclusion

The US overthrow of Saddam Hussein did not, as Washington had hoped, allow the United States to shape postwar Iraq virtually without opposition. Initially, the neoconservatives in the Pentagon had hoped to install Chalabi as a soft dictator while retaining authority over Iraqi policy on the economy and foreign affairs. Some of them later placed their hopes in Allawi, the ex-Baathist Shi'ite secularist with ties to the US Central Intelligence Agency and the old Baath officer corps. But the preexisting Shi'ite parties had fought Saddam for many years from their Iranian and western outposts and from grassroots organizations inside Iraq. Loyalty to these movements had developed strong roots over a long period in the Shi'ite south, and they were the beneficiaries of moral and institutional support from Ayatollah Sistani. Sistani used his moral authority to force the United States to allow open elections and to leave the crafting of the constitution to the elected assembly. He also cobbled together the United Iraqi Alliance, the coalition of religious Shi'ite parties that dominated the new parliament.

The Shi'ites benefited in their quest for political unity from the unity among their religious leaders, the four Grand Ayatollahs of Najaf, with Grand Ayatollah Sistani as the most prominent and authoritative. Sistani had the sort of authority that allowed him to convince the various Shi'ite political parties to form the United Iraqi Alliance in the fall of 2004, so as to contest the parliamentary elections from a position of strength and avoid splitting the Shi'ite vote. Sistani's endorsement of the UIA virtually ensured that it would win a majority in parliament in the January 30 election. The UIA, and especially the Supreme Council, also benefitted from the support of wealthy merchants and shopkeepers from cities such as Najaf and Karbala. They were aware that the United States was attempting to install a secular government headed by Washington favorites such as Chalabi and Allawi. They also remained afraid of a Sunni Arab or Baathist political resurgence. They realized that only a unified front such as the UIA could hope to outmaneuver a figure such as Allawi, who dreamed of allying with the Kurds and the Sunni Arabs to form a coalition that might gain a majority in parliament. Competition with secularists, Kurds, and, more recently, Sunni Arabs was a powerful incentive to maintain intra-Shi'ite unity.

The United States had not intended to install a government led by the Supreme Council for Islamic Revolution in Iraq and the al-Da'wa Party in Baghdad, but that was the ultimate result of their intervention. The subsequent victory of the UIA and its partner, the Kurdistan Alliance, in the December 2005 parliamentary election showed that, again contrary to US expectations, the new political landscape of Iraq was characterized by low voter volatility and substantial stability. Volatility was limited by the small number of party coalitions, by their virtual monopoly over ethnic and religious constituencies, and by their long historical grassroots in those communities. Stability was reinforced by the fact that the three main political coalitions were strongly ethnic in coloration, limiting the ability of voters to switch since few Shi'ites would have wanted to vote for the Kurdistan Alliance or the Sunni religious Iraqi Accord Front.

The best political strategist turned out to be an elderly cleric. By forming the UIA coalition, Sistani greatly reduced the number of parties plausibly contesting significant numbers of seats in parliament. That move reduced the choices for Shi'ites, who could have voted for Allawi's secular National Iraqi List in December of 2005, but chose not to do so. Allawi's list had no historical roots, except to the extent that it could be seen as a reform of the Baathist secularism that had appealed to some urban, middle-class Shi'ite constituencies in the old days. But those roots also tainted it with unpleasant connotations for Shi'ites who had suffered at the hands of the Baath Party. Although Shi'ites had a wider range of choices in the provincial elections of 2009, they nevertheless gave a disproportionate share of their votes to the religious parties.

The victory of the religious Shi'ite majority in Iraqi national politics disturbed the mostly Sunni Kurds less than might have been expected because they viewed the Iraqi nation as a fig leaf for their own autonomist ambitions. The Kurds insisted that their local law would take precedence over any national Iraqi laws that they found unacceptable. The constitution, the drafting of which they had dominated with US support, granted 100 percent ownership of newly discovered natural resources, such as oil and gas, to the regional confederacies rather than to the central government. Officials of the Kurdistan federal region were quick to begin issuing visas and inviting Western petroleum companies to carry out exploration. They did not even bother to alert Baghdad to these initiatives. Kurds concentrated their efforts in parliament on seeing that the Iraqi constitution continued to recognize their semiautonomous status and to guarantee that they would be able to hold a referendum in Kirkuk Province on whether its inhabitants wished to accede to the Kurdistan regional confederacy.

The emergence of a relatively united and hegemonic Shi'ite religious bloc in the central government and in the southern provinces proved more of a challenge to the Sunni Arab population than to the Kurds. Unlike the Kurds, the Sunni Arabs remained committed to a strong, centralized government over all of Iraq. Yet in a democratic Iraq with few checks and balances, such a government would always be dominated by the Shi'ite majority, which the Sunni Arabs found unacceptable. The Sunni Arab politicians rejected the whole notion of new provincial confederacies, although they were willing to allow the Kurdistan federal region to retain its prerogatives.

If Iraq were to be dominated by three ethnically based confederacies, however, the Sunni Arab unit would lack oil or gas resources while the Kurdish and Shi'ite confederacies would have such sources of wealth. The Sunni Arabs realized that a move to confederacies was a recipe for impoverishing them given that their territory was relatively resource-poor. Before the fall of 2005, only a minority of Sunni Arabs seemed comfortable participating in the new political process. Most constituted a dissident opposition to the new order or, at the very least, they declined to cooperate with it. Some Sunni Arabs actively engaged in guerrilla war against the new national regime. Beginning in the autumn of 2005, however, more Sunni Arabs became willing to play parliamentary politics, and violent guerrilla groups lost favor. The Sunni Arab defeat on the constitution that fall, along with the decision by some US military officers in the summer of 2006 to begin putting Sunni Arab guerrillas on a US payroll if they would switch sides, repositioned the Sunni Arabs. The Sunni fundamentalists voted into parliament in December 2005 remained relatively anti-American, but they also had substantial disagreements with the Shi'ite-dominated central government. The Awakening Councils, equally uncomfortable with the Shi'ite government, had allied with the United States against radical fundamentalists. Relatively secular Arab nationalist parties, and the tribally oriented Awakening Councils, did well in the 2009 provincial elections, but those sentiments were probably strong all along and had been obscured by Sunnis' reluctance to participate in elections under conditions of occupation.

The aspiration of the Kurds for autonomy if not complete independence from Iraq can only have been strengthened by the rise to national power of the Shi'ite religious parties. The policies of the central government are anathema to most Kurds, who tend to be secular or traditionalist in outlook and who are, after all, mostly Sunnis. The Sunni Arabs continued to have difficulty accepting that the new Iraq would be ruled by Shi'ite religious parties deeply influenced by an Iranian ayatollah, though most of them began in the fall of 2007 to turn toward political opposition, while the guerrilla movements declined somewhat. Consequently, Iraq's relatively stable political coalitions and lack of voter volatility are unlikely to lead to national stability, in part because stable electoral loyalties coincided with a hardening of ethnic and religious political identities and a refusal to seek grand bargains. A major shift of the electorate toward national parties that could incorporate several ethnic and religious communities would be a superior strategy for increasing national unity. In the period from 2003 to 2009, such a tectonic shift in voter orientation was rare.

Notes

1. Margit Tavits, "The Development of Stable Party Support: Electoral Dynamics in Post-Communist Europe," *American Journal of Political Science* 49, no. 2 (2005): 283–298.

2. Kenneth M. Roberts and Erik Wibbels, "Party Systems and Electoral Volatility in Latin America: A Test of Economic, Institutional, and Structural Explanations," *American Political Science Review* 93, no. 3 (September 1999): 575–590, quote on p. 578; cited in Tavits, "The Development of Stable Party Support," p. 286.

3. Yitzhak Nakash, "The Conversion of Iraq's Tribes to Shi'ism," *International Journal of Middle East Studies* 26, no. 3 (1994): 443–463.

4. Meir Litvak, *Shi'ite Scholars of Nineteenth Century Iraq* (Cambridge: Cambridge University Press, 1998); Yitzhak Nakash, *The Shi'is of Iraq* (Princeton: Princeton University Press, 1994); Juan Cole, *Sacred Space and Holy War: The Politics, Culture, and History of Shi'ite Islam* (London: I. B. Tauris, 2002).

5. Salah al-Khursan, *Hizb al-Da'wa al-Islamiyyah: Haqa'iq wa watha'iq* [The Islamic Da'wa Party: Facts and Documents] (Damascus: al-Mu'assassa al-'Arabiyya li'l-Dirasat wa'l-Buhuth al-Istratijiyya, 1999); Abdul Halim Ruhaimi, "The Da'wa Islamic Party," in *Ayatollahs, Sufis, and Ideologues*, ed. Faleh 'Abd al-Jabar (London: Saqi, 2002), pp. 149–161; Keiko Sakai, "Modernity and Tradition in the Islamic Movements in Iraq," *Arab Studies Quarterly* 23, no. 1 (2001): 37–52; Mahan Abedin, "Dossier: Hezb al-Daawa al-Islamiyya (Islamic Call Party)," *Middle East Intelligence Bulletin* (June 2003); Hanna Batatu, "Shi'ite Organizations in Iraq: Al-Da'wah al-Islamiyah and al-Mujahidin," in *Shi'ism and Social Protest*, eds. Juan R. I. Cole and Nikki R. Keddie (New Haven: Yale University Press, 1986), pp. 179–200; Joyce N. Wiley, *The Islamic Movement of Iraqi Shi'ites* (Boulder: Lynne Rienner, 1992).

6. Talib Aziz, "The Political Theory of Muhammad Baqir Sadr," in *Ayatollahs, Sufis, and Ideologues,* ed. Abd al-Jabbar, pp. 231–244; Chibli Mallat, *The Renewal of Islamic Law: Muhammad Baqer al-Sadr, Najaf, and the Shi'i International* (Cambridge: Cambridge University Press, 1993).

7. Taleb M. Aziz, "The Role of Muhammad Baqir al-Sadr in Shi'i Political Activism in Iraq from 1958 to 1980," *International Journal of Middle East Studies* 25, no. 2 (1993): 207–222; Taleb M. Aziz, "An Islamic Perspective of Political Economy: The Views of (Late) Muhammad Baqir al-Sadr," *Al-Tawhid Islamic Journal* (Qom) 10, no. 1 (1993), www.al-islam.org.

8. Mukhtar al-Asadi, *Al-Taqsir al-Kabir bayna al-Salah wa al-Islah* [Mere Passive Goodness Falls Far Short of Active Reform] (Beirut: Dar al-Furat, 2001); Juan Cole, "Marriage mal assorti entre les radicaux chiites irakiens et les Etats-Unis," *Le Monde Diplomatique* (July 2003), www.monde-diplomatique.fr.

9. Kenneth Katzman, "Iraq's Opposition Movements," Congressional Research Service Issue Brief, March 26, 1998, http://www.fas.org/.

10. Juan Cole, "The United States and Shi'ite Religious Factions in Post-Ba'thist Iraq," *Middle East Journal* 57, no. 4 (2003): 543–566; Nir Rosen, *In the Belly of the Green Bird* (New York: Free Press, 2006).

11. Linda Walbridge, "The Counterreformation: Becoming a Marja' in the Modern World," in *The Most Learned of the Shi'a: The Institution of the Marja' Taqlid*, ed. L. Walbridge (New York: Oxford University Press, 2001), pp. 237–244.

12. Faleh Abd al-Jabar, "Why the Uprisings Failed," *Middle East Report*, no. 176 (1992): 2–14.

13. Cole, "The United States and Shi'ite Religious Factions in Post-Ba'thist Iraq."

14. Juan Cole, "Shi'a Militias in Iraqi Politics," in *Iraq: Preventing a New Generation of Conflict*, eds. Markus E. Bouillon, David M. Malone, and Ben Roswell (Boulder: Lynne Rienner, 2007), pp. 109–123.

15. "Hilah Sayyarah Shabihah bi Sayyarat al-Hakim istukhdimat fi Ightiyalihi dakhil al-Masjid," *al-Sharq al-Awsat*, August 30, 2003.

16. Juan Cole, "Portrait of a Rebellion: Shi'ite Insurgency in Iraq Bedevils U.S.," *In These Times*, May 24, 2004, www.inthesetimes.com.

17. Reidar Vissar, "Sistani, the United States and Politics in Iraq: From Quietism to Machiavellianism?" NUPI Paper no. 700 (Oslo: Norwegian Institute of International Affairs, March 2006), http://historiae.org.

18. Larry Diamond, *Squandered Victory: The American Occupation and the Bungled Effort to Bring Democracy to Iraq* (New York: Holt, 2005), pp. 50–52, 78–87.

19. "Fatwa for Anthony Shadid" [in Arabic], www.sistani.org/, reported in Anthony Shadid and Rajiv Chandrasekaran, "Cleric Renews Call for Iraq Elections," *Washington Post*, November 29, 2003.

20. Juan Cole, "The New and Improved Iraq," *In These Times*, June 22, 2004, www.inthesetimes.com.

21. "Mutahaddith bi Ism al-Sistani: al-Marja' al-A'la yad'amu la'ihat al-I'tilaf al-'Iraqi al-Muwahhid," *al-Sharq al-Awsat*, January 17, 2005.

22. Juan Cole, "The Rise of Religious and Ethnic Mass Politics in Iraq," in *Religion and Nationalism in Iraq: A Comparative Perspective*, eds. David Little and Donald K. Swearer (Cambridge, MA: Center for the Study of the World Religions/Harvard University Press, 2006), pp. 43–62.

23. "Tahran tudhakkir washinton bi 'ta'awun' fi al-Iraq," *al-Hayat*, February 18, 2005; Juan Cole, "UIA Will Hold Secret Ballot," Informed Comment, February 22, 2005, www.juancole.com.

24. "Al-Hakim: Yajib an yakun li al-Shi'ah Iqlimuhum fi Junub al-'Iraq," *al-Sharq al-Awsat*, August 12, 2005.

25. Juan Cole, "The Iraqi Constitution DOA?" *Salon*, August 26, 2005, http://dir.salon.com.

26. "Najah al-istifta' 'ala Muswadat al-Dustur al-'Iraqi," Middle East Online, October 25, 2005, www.middle-east-online.com.

27. "Michael Rubin on the Sunni Vote in Iraq's Elections," National Public Radio, December 14, 2005.

28. "Fawz al-Ja'fari . . . ," *al-Zaman*, February 13, 2006.

29. Juan Cole, "Saving Iraq: Mission Impossible," *Salon*, May 11, 2006, http://www.salon.com.

30. "Inshiqaq fi Kutlat 'al-Tawafuq' . . . Hukumat al-Maliki ghayr al-Muktamalah tanal Thiqat al-Barlaman," *al-Hayat*, May 21, 2006.

31. "Sunnis Rejoin Iraqi Cabinet," Aljazeera.net, July 19, 2008, http://english.aljazeera.net.

32. Joseph Krauss, "US Troops Pact a Coup for Iraq's Maliki: Analysts," Agence France Presse Zawya (UAE), November 27, 2008, www.zawya.com.

33. "Intikhabat al-'Iraq," *al-Sharq al-Awsat*, February 6, 2009, www.aawsat.com; Stephen Farrell, "Election: Preliminary Results," *New York Times*, February 5, 2009.

4

Bottom-Up Democratization in Kuwait

Mary Ann Tétreault

TOP-DOWN LIBERALIZATION may be the standard in the Arab monarchies, but reform in Kuwait has taken a divergent path. Without the acquiescence of the ruling family, nonviolent reform in Kuwait would be impossible. But the ruling family of Kuwait is not particularly interested in reform. Reform has occurred in Kuwait only when bottom-up pressure was vigorously applied. Citizens created the first Kuwaiti parliament and constitution in 1938, an experiment that ended in violence when the ruler closed it down. Citizen activism supported the writing and adoption of the 1962 constitution after Kuwait's special relationship to Britain was ended in 1961, marking a peaceful transition toward representative government and the rule of law.[1] Although some nations in the Middle East might well be described as lacking in "organized popular enthusiasm for democratic reform,"[2] Kuwait is not among them. In this chapter, I argue that Kuwait is, indeed, exceptional in this regard, and that it is so because of its unusual civil society. *Civil society* refers to the complex of values, practices, and institutions that operate in and between the family and the state. An ambiguous frontier between private and public life, civil society is envisioned as the cradle of political dissent and democratic institutions.[3] Whether civil society exists or not in the Arab world is a matter of debate. Some argue that the family rarely offers an oasis of privacy to individuals while public spaces are arenas for "symbolic display" rather than spaces for "collective political action . . . [or] discourse that addresses common concerns."[4] Halim Barakat, who is sympathetic to the traditional vision of the Arab family, and Hisham Sharabi, who is not, agree that family is the place where children are taught to accept hierarchy and a structure that legitimates both private and state violence.[5] The Arab state is portrayed as defective, authoritarian,[6] and little more than a corrupt conduit for the exchange of natural resources and "unearned" income between state elites and foreign customers.[7] There are varying amounts of truth in these essentializing depictions, each embedded in a problématique that limits its range to a particular space at a particular time. But even together, they are not the whole story. If they were, how could anything change?

The concept of indigenous democratization in the Middle East is greatly neglected in academic and popular literature because most analysts believe it does not exist.[8] Progressive change, if it is noticed at all, seldom is seen in its entirety; even when it is noticed, the credit for it is usually misapplied.[9] Here, I argue that political development in Kuwait is analogous to political development elsewhere. It requires free spaces for mobilization, including, at the least, an absence of systematic external constraints and, at best, attractive models to be indigenized and improved upon.[10] It proceeds through the gradual accumulation of large and small victories in struggles for power and autonomy between rulers and subjects or citizens. These struggles become more complex as new groups find their voices and join ongoing national dialogues, and as institutional changes alter the terrain of struggles to make successful repression by the state more difficult to achieve.[11] Democratization depends especially on the broadening of civil society to include middle-class citizens of all kinds, educated persons brimming with expectations of a better life that will include not simply a higher economic standard of living, but also individual autonomy and social esteem—recognition.[12]

Kuwait is a "traditional" Arab society governed by an autocratic regime that benefits from the economics of dynastic monarchies and rentier states.[13] Its notably lively civil society has deep domestic roots and cosmopolitan branches reaching well beyond its formal borders.[14] Whether the regime or civil society influences politics more depends on the situation, in large part because the regime tends to be more reactive than proactive[15] while citizens tend to mobilize around specific issues or in response to what they perceive as violations of the social contract between Kuwaitis and their rulers. Among the issues that I address here are the May 2005 amendment of the election law to include women as citizens with full political rights, and the Orange Movement to change electoral districting. Seen by some as the gift of a Western-influenced, autocratic state, the May 2005 achievement of women's rights was actually the outcome of four decades of strong, grassroots politics that included, especially toward the end, artful mobilization of the foreign press. Although Kuwaiti women themselves were far from united on this issue, even the activities of women's rights opponents went a long way toward normalizing women's political participation. The 2006 Orange Movement, which included a number of activists from the successful women's rights campaign, employed similar tactics to press for significant changes in the electoral law. External actors were insignificant in the achievements of the Orange Movement, which were built on the breadth of its popular, visible, and highly enthusiastic support inside Kuwait.

Institutional Roots of Modern Civil Society in Kuwait

From its organization in the 1750s until the accession of Mubarak Al-Sabah in 1896 via Kuwait's one and only coup, the ruling family originally chosen by leading merchants governed within the parameters that the merchants had established. Whether merchants encouraged Mubarak (1896–1915) to overthrow his brother Mohammad or not, Mubarak was determined afterward to curb merchant power and reign as an autocrat.[16] This was possible because Mubarak's income from family date gardens in Iraq and the secret subventions he received from the Ottoman and British empires negated the merchants' fiscal leverage. *Rentierism* in Kuwait thus preceded the discovery and exploitation of oil and gas while Mubarak's precocious economic neoconservatism established a fifty-year tradition that forced Kuwaiti merchants to organize and provide whatever public and social services they desired at their own expense.

Mubarak was succeeded by two sons, Jaber (1915–1917) and Salim (1917–1921), both more accommodating than their father. Their successor, Ahmad al-Jaber (1921–1950), was another authoritarian. As part of his campaign to be named the new amir, he agreed to govern with the advice of a council, but abandoned the council after he took power and could afford to ignore demands from below. In 1938–1939 a small, well-organized movement to implant a council with legislative power at the center of Kuwait's governing structure succeeded in electing two prototypical representative assemblies that wrote Kuwait's first constitution and passed progressive legislation. But when the second assembly "intruded" into foreign affairs, it added the enmity of the resident British colonial official to the ire of the ruler. Ahmad al-Jaber disbanded it by force and those members who did not flee the country were arrested and jailed. Even though it was short-lived, however, this assertion of authority by civil society laid down principles of governance that encouraged Kuwaitis to think of themselves as a people with a democratic history.[17]

Ahmad al-Jaber's successor, Abdullah al-Salim (1950–1965), had been his rival in 1921. Being passed over then may have prompted Abdullah al-Salim to cultivate his own links to Kuwaiti merchants. During the turbulent era of the 1938–1939 parliament, he was the main intermediary between the constitutionalists and the amir. Following Ahmad al-Jaber's death in January 1950, Abdullah al-Salim was selected to succeed him despite initial British opposition, and he presided over Kuwait's transition to independence from Britain in 1961. He was responsible for institutional innovations that continue to underpin the vigor of Kuwaiti civil society, such as Kuwait's liberal constitution that promised equal rights to all Kuwaiti citizens and a wide array of civil rights and liberties. The constitution also provided for an elected representative assembly with real legislative authority. Although the parliament and many civil liberties were suspended unconstitutionally twice (1976–1981 and 1986–1992), the 1962 constitution remains a political lodestone. Popular demands for its restoration during the long periods of suspension enjoyed such legitimacy that the regime was forced to accede to citizen pressures, although not without making institutional changes intended to mute the constitution's democratic potential.

Civil Society at the Grassroots Level

A second innovation marked a break from Ahmad al-Jaber's policy of retaining virtually all of Kuwait's oil income for himself and his family. Abdullah al-Salim gave oil money to family members too, but he also spent lavishly on measures that improved standards of living in the larger society.[18] He launched ambitious programs to inject oil revenues into the private economy as rapidly as possible. The Land Acquisition Program, under which the government bought land from citizens, ended up transferring the bulk of what was spent to merchants and ruling family members whose insider knowledge had stimulated a rash of claims to desirable properties just in time to cash in.[19] Despite such inequities, however, substantial benefits accrued to the population as a whole. Family allowances for government employees and subsidies for basic foods supplemented family incomes while housing and utilities, including telephone service, were provided at low or no cost. Free health care and public education were provided and both girls and boys were required to attend school.

The outcomes of these social policies were mixed but, in conjunction with the political spaces opened by the constitution, one result was a profound democratization of Kuwaiti life. Higher incomes, better health, rising levels of education, and international travel created a new Kuwaiti middle class. It was not an investing bourgeoisie like the merchant elite (although a few families did achieve that status), but rather a group of prosperous, if wage-dependent, families that resemble middle-class populations in developed countries, including in their aspirations. Kuwaitis founded scores of professional and voluntary associations, many monopolized by merchant-class citizens but others that were more broadly representative. Aided by the amir's drastic redrawing of electoral constituencies prior to the 1981 election to reduce the political weight of urban-based groups like merchants and Arab nationalists,[20] Kuwait's "new men" ran for parliament after having cut their political teeth competing for positions on the boards of local cooperatives.[21] Many were religious activists whose political fortunes were aided by the ruling family, which, in the late 1970s, saw Islamists as a counterweight to the political power of liberals and Arab nationalists.[22] The newly drawn election districts boosted representation from the "outlying areas," suburbs and towns located beyond the geographic and social boundaries defining the urban core, and they also imported "tribal" populations into urban constituencies.[23] Tribal elements thereby entered constitutional politics, but how extensively allegiance to the tribe has been translated into allegiance to the state is an open question.[24]

Lingering Inequity: Kuwaiti Women

Social policy failed to compensate entirely for the decision by Kuwait's parliament to approve an electoral law banning women from participation as voters or candidates. For more than forty years, suffragists and the parliament struggled over whether to rescind this measure. Demands for rights by organized feminists were usually met with equally spirited resistance by parliamentary majorities.[25] Occasionally, however, the women's rights drama moved forward. The remarkable performances of women in and outside Kuwait during the Iraqi occupation undercut arguments against women's rights based on their supposed inadequacies as political actors.[26] The burden of the protests by opponents of women's rights then moved further into the realm of religion, an increasingly shaky justification for the denial of political rights given the growing number of Muslim countries in which women already voted and held elected office. A breakthrough occurred in May 1999 when the amir dismissed the parliament and, for the first time, did so according to constitutional rules mandating new elections within sixty days. A week later, one among the sixty-three interim decrees issued during the suspension conferred full political rights on Kuwaiti women; to become law, however, such amiri decrees must be ratified by the next parliament. As the history of the women's rights movement predicted, the amiri decree was defeated in mid-November 1999. One week later, an identical parliamentary measure introduced to remove the taint of government pressure also failed, although by a smaller margin.

The formal defeat of the women's rights proposal in the parliament masked significant forward movement with regard to social support and organization. Islamist women, already prominent among prosuffrage activists, mobilized further in response to the 1999 amiri decree. The conservative Federation of Kuwaiti Women's Associations revived its Women's Political Committee while longtime liberal activist Nouria al-Sadani established Kuwaiti Women of the Twenty-First Century to do grassroots mobilization. Lulua al-Mullah of the Women's Cultural and Social Society and

Fatma al-Abdaly of the Women's Issues Committee continued their long lobbying campaigns. Women's organizations were so energized that an organization called the Voluntary Working Group was formed by liberal attorney Badriya al-Awadi and two Islamist activists, Khawla al-Attiqi and Khadija al-Mahmeed, just to coordinate the efforts of all the groups working for the decree's passage in the National Assembly.[27]

Kuwaiti women could be described as left behind in their own country because of their political exclusion. But on measures from education to employment to public presence, until the turn of the century they were the vanguard among Gulf women. After women had achieved prominence in public life throughout much of the Gulf and the rest of the Middle East, Kuwait began to look less progressive. Women have voted since 1963 in Iran, since 1967 in the socialist People's Democratic Republic of Yemen (since 1970 in the "traditional" Yemen Arab Republic), and since 1980 in Iraq. The last straw for Kuwaiti suffragists was the inclusion of women's political rights among twenty-first-century political openings in other Gulf monarchies.[28] Kuwaitis used to pride themselves on being the most politically progressive nation in the Gulf, but this claim was difficult to make with a straight face once the only two countries on the Arabian Peninsula that both held elections and denied political rights to women turned out to be Kuwait and Saudi Arabia.[29]

Equally important in changing the tone of the debate was the refusal of Kuwaiti women to continue arguing that they had "earned" political rights. Claims that women should have political rights in recognition of their contributions to family, society, and economy or, after 1991, because of their exemplary efforts on their country's behalf during the Iraqi occupation were quietly dropped. Women revised their strategies, especially after the 2003 election[30] when it looked as though lobbying parliament was unlikely to get Kuwaiti feminists very far. Attention shifted to lobbying the government and particularly the prime minister. The tone of their arguments shifted to emphasize citizenship, entitlement, and national pride.[31] As the T-shirts worn by pro–women's rights demonstrators proclaimed, "Women are Kuwaitis, too."

The energy displayed by the government on women's behalf in 2005 was the most surprising change. After the amir announced his decree in May 1999, no one in the government tried to get parliamentary candidates to support it. Many candidates spoke against the women's rights measure during the campaign, and did not change their positions after they were elected. The new government made no discernable effort to line up supporters among the winners whether they had taken a position or not. When the measure finally came to a vote in November, feminists were angry and disappointed, but not surprised by the outcome.

In 2005, debates on women's rights in parliament seemed at first to be shaping up as the same old story, but with an altered cast of characters. In July 2003, Shaikh Sabah al-Ahmad, a latter-day supporter of women's rights, was named prime minister.[32] The opportunity for him to show leadership on the issue appeared in April 2005 when a mean-spirited measure allowing women to vote and run only for municipal-level offices was passed on its first reading. Pressed by activists who issued a series of press releases declaring that denial of women's political rights was a violation of their human rights,[33] he responded to the activists' suggestion that he take the initiative on the measure when a parliamentary technicality opened a new way forward. This occurred when the bill came up for the second and final reading on May 2 and was defeated on the floor. Because twenty-nine members had abstained, this constituted a lack of a quorum, which put the bill back on the table for consideration two weeks later.

When that day arrived, the government surprised everyone by introducing a new proposal granting women full political rights that invoked an "order for urgency," allowing it to become law in a single session. To supersede the parliament's bill limiting women's political participation to the municipality was audacious; to couple it with the order for urgency was inspired because it eliminated the opportunity for opponents to mobilize public protests to keep the antisuffrage coalition in line between the first and second readings. The debate went on for hours. Opponents offered amendments, and Islamists did manage to attach an ambiguous provision requiring female participants in elections to abide by Islamic law. But at the end of the (very long) day, those opposing women's rights failed when "independents" from tribal areas joined liberals, Shi'a, and the cabinet to pass the bill. Independents had been wooed with promised increases in pension payments and salaries for government workers and probably also with direct bribes.[34] Four weeks later, the first woman was appointed to the cabinet. Political scientist Ma'souma al-Mubarak took her place as planning minister and ex officio member of the parliament despite loud complaints on the floor of the National Assembly from Sunni Islamists and other unreconstructed members of parliament.

Old and New Political Spaces

Just as it would be incorrect to conclude that political rights for Kuwaiti women resulted merely from government largesse, we should not conclude that other reforms were top-down affairs. Progressive activists, many working through voluntary associations, labored for years to combat Kuwait's social divisions. In December 2004, they overcame status quo forces when Kuwaiti economists chose Rola Dashti to head their national professional association. Rola Dashti, the first woman to chair a mixed-gender organization in Kuwait, is a Shi'a, a business owner, and a women's rights activist.

Rola Dashti's assertions of her rights included her practice of hosting *diwaniyyas* (salons) in her home where women come to discuss politics, business, and other matters of interest just as men do at their *diwaniyyas*. Suad al-Humaidi held *diwaniyyas* in the 1970s, and Rasha Al-Sabah, a cousin of the emir, has hosted mixed-gender *diwaniyyas* for years, but Rola Dashti's gatherings were primarily middle-class and were designed to mirror their male counterparts as spaces in which to mobilize support for Rola Dashti's political projects.

Diwaniyyas are the quintessential institution of Kuwaiti civil society. Thought to have their beginnings in evening seafront conversations among merchants and fishermen, *diwaniyyas* today are (usually) weekly meetings that take place in private homes or nearby, privately owned halls. Regular attendance by a core of family, friends, and associates develops intimacy among the group based on discussions that literally go on for years. *Diwaniyyas* occupy a special political space because their location in the home insulates them from state intervention.[35] Although these protected spaces were breached to some degree during the prodemocracy movement in 1989–1990, their relative security was integral to sustaining the grassroots efforts that helped bring both periods of constitutional suspension to a close.

From the beginning of Kuwait's constitutional life, *diwaniyyas* were favored locations for political campaigning. Candidates' campaign headquarters were informally referred to as *diwaniyyas*. Campaign rallies were held in the large courtyards of the homes of wealthy Kuwaitis who made private rooms available to women for observing speeches on closed-circuit television. Kuwaitis could be reasonably, if not entirely, secure criticizing their government in these spaces while state intrusion into them, such as occurred several times during the prodemocracy movement, increased popular support for political activists.[36]

Boys begin attending *diwaniyyas* with their fathers, where they become familiar with the alliances, opinions, and folkways of the men in their families' social circles.[37] Expected to listen more than talk, some are bored by the slow rhythms of *diwaniyya* conversation. Others are stung to find themselves the target of jokes reflecting the tellers' envy of their education or disdain for their Western ways. Some parents encourage their children to absorb *diwaniyya* culture by setting up tents where they can entertain their own friends, but Kuwaiti youth also see opportunity costs in attending *diwaniyyas*, which take up precious afterschool or afterwork time that could be spent going online or socializing outside the range of their families' watchful eyes. New media are opening spaces for politics and social activism in Kuwait that appeal especially to youth.

This evolution began with the advent of regional satellite television and the different kinds of TV news it brought into Kuwaiti homes. Unlike state channels whose news programs tend to focus on state visits and the doings of the amir, or Western outlets whose stories confine people of the Middle East to subordinate roles, Al-Jazeera and its emulators broadcast news and commentary about the region, from the region, to the region.[38] Freewheeling talk and call-in shows give residents the opportunity to comment on leaders and policies and trade barbs with program hosts and guests. Coverage is pointed enough to cause governments to ban some stations' reporters; the Al-Jazeera bureau in Kuwait was shut down in June 1999 and November 2002. Satellite television stations now find themselves competing with new local stations in Kuwait and elsewhere throughout the Gulf, and with public affairs programming broadcast on state channels.

Communication via mobile telephone and the Internet is another revolutionary addition to political space in Kuwait. As I mention below, the train of events leading to the May 2006 dismissal of parliament was sped on its way by text-messaging, which kept activists connected during this period. Websites, listservs, and e-mail offer a range of opportunities to keep in touch with like-minded persons around the world. Jihadist organizations recruit and proselytize on the Web, and coordinate their operations via e-mail.[39] Perfectly respectable political groups and candidates also have websites, along with local commentators like attorney and later parliamentary candidate Mohammad al-Jassem, whose blog postings often are picked up by conventional news sources.[40] A combination of blogs and *diwaniyyas* were primary sources of inside information during the amiri transition in January 2006, and they helped to rally support for the Orange Movement later that year as described below.[41] Some of the most critical political blogs run by Kuwaitis have their home base outside the country, in political spaces where government officials have a more difficult time closing them down.

Another media innovation was a product of the 2006 election, which I discuss further in the next section. This took the form of broadcasts of videotapes of candidate forums, speeches, and debates transmitted from abroad via private satellite stations back into Kuwait. The videos were shot by members of the Alliance, a two-year-old umbrella group coordinating the reform efforts of several civil society organizations. Many featured speakers were critical of the government and prominent in the movement for redistricting. The information minister tried to shut these satellite broadcasts down, arguing that they did not cover all the candidates equally and, therefore, were biased—the same reason that was previously given for why state-owned electronic media did not cover campaign events. The government put pressure on ArabSat, the broadcaster, to stop carrying the programs. When ArabSat complied, the Alliance shifted its broadcasts to HotBird, a service fewer Kuwaitis subscribe to, while blogs like KuwaitJunior posted links offering streaming video for those without TV access.

Kuwait's Amazing Year

Civil society, especially the activism of young Kuwaitis, played a crucial part in the tumultuous events of 2006, which included two political crises and two elections that foreshadowed the next steps for expanding citizens' rights. The first political crisis concluded with an intricate double transition among amirs that took place in January. The deteriorating health of the crown prince, Shaikh Sa'ad al-Abdullah, had provoked ruling family quarrels over the succession. By the autumn of 2005, the acrimony was sharp enough to penetrate the public press. The ensuing scandal hardened the positions of the contenders, yet, after the amir Jabir al-Ahmad died in January with nothing resolved, other domestic institutions rose to the occasion. When the expected clash between the two feuding branches of the Al Sabah family, the al-Salims and al-Jabirs, broke out over whether Shaikh Ahmad al-Jaber's designated successor, Shaikh Sa'ad, should be replaced, the speaker of the parliament, Jasim al-Khorafy, intervened promptly to forestall its most deleterious effects.

Both Jasim Khorafy and the prime minister, Shaikh Sabah, hoped to avoid having to depose Shaikh Sa'ad formally, which would have invited comparisons between his condition and that of Ahmad al-Jaber during his last years as amir. They slowed the proceedings of the parliament and cabinet to a crawl, but resistance from Shaikh Sa'ad's immediate family prevented his letter of resignation from arriving at the National Assembly in time to avoid a vote to relieve him of his duties as amir and transfer his responsibilities to Shaikh Sabah. Later, the cabinet named Shaikh Sabah as the next amir. These decisions followed procedures outlined in Kuwait's constitution and were managed with dignity in spite of the unseemly behavior of a few. As a result, Shaikh Sabah's investiture took place amidst a wave of good feeling unlikely to have arisen without the speaker's deft, constitutionally guided intervention. The era of good feeling did not last, however. A second crisis that barely registered on the world's radar screen prompted another parliamentary dissolution in May and an unscheduled national election in June.

Kuwaiti political elites were caught off guard by a sudden upsurge of popular protest against corruption in elections. The electoral system imposed in 1981 by the late Jabir al-Ahmad had simplified vote-buying and other forms of election interference because the districts were small and could be manipulated in scores of small ways without drawing too much unwanted attention or running up huge expenditures. This made the 1981 system a prime target of reformers.[42] The ruling family had kept these dissidents at bay for years but, in the spring of 2006, about a dozen Kuwaiti twenty-somethings, men and women, decided to make redistricting a project, and organized a series of demonstrations in favor of a five-district plan.

The first "We want five" (*nabiha khamza*)[43] event coincided with a scheduled cabinet meeting. Text-messages were forwarded to friends of friends, and about 200 demonstrators wearing orange T-shirts and waving orange flags showed up in front of the Sayf Palace, startling ministers as they drove in to their meeting and again as they came out. "The prime minister waved to us," one activist reported. "And we heard in diwaniyyas that they kept asking why was everyone wearing orange."[44] Press coverage and word of mouth ensured that news of the demonstration would spread, sparking another rally the following week where more than 500 people gathered. The organizers scheduled a third demonstration for the following week, precipitating the crisis that brought down the government.

The morning after the third rally, the demonstrators entered the National Assembly to place orange leaflets on the desks of cabinet ministers and MPs, and then took seats in the gallery. The government introduced a ten-district proposal drawn either so ineptly or so cleverly that it seemed designed to trigger the antagonism it quickly provoked. When proredistricting MPs resisted the ploy, a cabinet member proposed forwarding the plan to the Constitutional Court, but this was seen as a delaying tactic. As soon as the roll call indicated that the ten-district proposal would have the support of the cabinet, all twenty-nine proponents of five districts rose and left the building, leaving the session without a quorum.

When demonstrators converged on the National Assembly building on the following morning, they found it surrounded by police and special forces dressed in riot gear and armed with batons. MPs came outside to stand with the protesters, but their parliamentary immunity did not protect them from being pushed back from the gate by the armed men admitted to the grounds by the speaker. In the scuffle, at least one demonstrator was struck with a baton and knocked to the ground. Some MPs threatened to interpellate (question) the prime minister and another rally was held outside the National Assembly building that night.[45] Two days later at another rally, several MPs pledged openly to question the prime minister in the parliament.[46] But the amir dissolved the body on May 21, and called for new elections to be held on June 29.

The unexpected parliamentary election was the second election in Kuwait during 2006. An April municipal by-election in Salmiyya was the first. Two women and ten men competed for a single seat (five candidates dropped out by election day). The first woman to declare and run for election in Kuwait was Jenan Boushehri, a thirty-two-year-old engineer; the second was Khaledeh al-Khader, a physician, who entered the race very late. Both women are Shi'a, who constitute a large minority in the district. Khaledeh al-Khader was assertive, making it clear that she expected support from first-time women voters. Jenan Boushehri took a different tack, running as a professional with experience germane to the concerns of the municipal council. In her *hijab* and with her quiet voice, she projected modesty and competence. She refused to campaign at men's *diwaniyyas*, but she spoke at several mixed-gender forums sponsored by voluntary associations exploring the consequences of women's entry into politics in Kuwait. She also held a mixed-gender meeting in a campaign tent.[47] Jenan Boushehri and her campaign chair consulted with respected women and men in her district, asking for their help and, not incidentally, giving them a stake in her success.[48] When the votes were counted, Jenan Boushehri came in a strong second, behind the man from the dominant tribe in the Salmiyya district who had been expected to win all along. Jenan Boushehri's strategy—to let her sex speak for itself while she ran as a competent and respectable member of her professional and religious faith communities—is likely to have attracted support from voters who otherwise might not have voted for a woman, but decided to cast their ballots for a candidate whose appeal went beyond gender to other issues. Although Jenan Boushehri lost the election, her strong showing augured well for women running for national office.

The national election was far less straightforward, however, presenting a complex dilemma to newly empowered Kuwaiti women. Coming a year earlier than they had expected, only a handful among the politically prominent decided to enter the race. All the female candidates were hampered by a campaign environment in which the many issues they had advocated for years were overshadowed by the anticorruption drive—and by corruption itself, some aimed at female voters.[49] Feminist observers were not surprised that male politicians throughout the campaign concentrated on corruption, with some naming names. Yet in a campaign noteworthy for media innovations that disseminated such criticism widely, most female candidates eschewed personal attacks to emphasize their own issues: the financial problems of divorcées, widows, and children, and the unequal treatment of women married to non-Kuwaitis, all the result of gendered state policies regarding entitlements and nationality, economic issues such as youth unemployment and the lack of planning for Kuwait's posthydrocarbon future, and poorly functioning state services such as health care and public education. It is true that these issues were overshadowed by popular revulsion at government corruption. But the election issue dilemma was more complex than a simple opposition between anticorruption and women's issues or deepening democracy.

This second quandary grew out of decisions made by the Alliance with regard to incumbents and challengers who had signed on to the reform agenda. The Alliance pledged active support to candidates who supported redistricting and the fight against corruption, regardless of their other leanings. This occasionally made strange bedfellows among candidates and liberal Orange activists. "Al-Muslem, an Islamist MP, had a seminar at Kuwait

University," one told me when I interviewed him in June 2006. "I was there. I told him, 'One of my goals is to bring you down.' Now I am [working] for him." Al-Muslem won as did other Islamists who "went Orange" in large numbers after the demonstrations at the parliament had revealed the popular appeal of the anticorruption campaign.

Women didn't sign on to the anticorruption program because they were not welcome.

> Everyone had a perception that a woman would not get more than 200 or 300 votes. So we would lose. They put their eggs in the basket of the candidates they thought would bring votes. . . . I look at it that the election was about two things, curbing corruption OR deepening democracy. In practicality, under the circumstances, it was not a normal election so we want to fight corruption at the same moment that women were entering the political process. The priority was not deepening democracy but fighting corruption. This corruption was already in process, vote buying and also a coalition among the corrupt.
>
> There is always vote buying. In 2006 it was unusual. The corrupted person usually does not mind where the second vote goes—it is your choice. The political groups also usually try to get at least one vote. The second vote, OK, it is your choice. So you always have the second vote floating. When I was running, I expected to pick up a lot of these second votes, where I would have a chance to win.[50]

In the 2006 election, many "second votes" were not "your choice" because Alliance members had brokered across political groups so that second votes from members of one group would go to a candidate from another group who also had pledged to support the Alliance program. When the corrupt candidates saw what the Alliance was doing, they did the same thing—buying one vote for themselves and the second for another corrupt candidate who agreed to make the same arrangement with the people from whom he was buying votes. There were no floating votes from either of these groups, cutting into the number of potential second votes for women.

Wait Until Next Time

The all-male 2006 parliament promptly passed legislation reorganizing the twenty-five election districts into five. Aspiring candidates of both sexes began to plan for their 2010 campaigns, but they were foiled again by the amir's reaction to this fractious parliament. The 2006 parliament, like its predecessor, used its right to interpellate cabinet ministers not only to check bad behavior by the government, but also to make political and ideological points. At first, the ruler managed to hold on to his serenity, even in the face of two interpellations of ruling family cabinet members. The first provoked the fall of the government when minister of health Shaikh Ahmad al-Abdullah Al-Sabah was accused of mismanagement and incompetence. He was interpellated on February 19, 2007, and the government resigned on March 4, having tried and failed to line up enough votes to save him.[51]

The second concerned the minister of energy, Shaikh Ali al-Jarrah Al-Sabah, who was appointed to the first cabinet formed after the 2006 election. He replaced Shaikh Ahmad al-Fahad Al-Sabah, widely believed to be among the most corrupt members of the ruling family.[52] In an interview published in the Kuwaiti daily *Al-Qabas*, Ali al-Jarrah unwisely revealed that another former oil minister, Shaikh Ali al-Khalifah Al-Sabah, "is my master and . . . I consult him occasionally on oil issues."[53] Ali al-Khalifah, who also had left the oil ministry under a cloud, is believed in Kuwait (and confirmed indirectly by a British jurist) of having been involved in a multi-million-dollar embezzlement from the government oil tanker company during the Iraqi occupation of Kuwait.[54]

No one thought that Ali al-Jarrah was corrupt before the publication of the *Al-Qabas* interview, but his comments touched a nerve among reformers, and launched a parliamentary investigation that uncovered a number of questionable activities, including his own possible involvement in the tanker company embezzlement through his position at the time as head of the Burgan Bank.[55] Contrary to the usual scenario, the minister did not resign before the interpellation. He chose instead to face hours of harsh questioning from parliamentarians, some armed with incriminating photographs of varying relevance to the accusations against him. Although Ali al-Jarrah started out with support from some Islamists in the parliament, the photographs of his cronies engaged in compromising acts projected on a large screen during the questioning may have kept them from speaking out on his behalf. Following an interpellation, there is a two-week period during which members can reflect on what they heard and saw—and become the targets of lobbying and bribery attempts—before they take a formal vote of confidence on a minister's performance. In this case, Ali al-Jarrah's position seemed hopeless and he resigned before the vote was taken. He was subsequently given a position that approximated the one he had vacated, but without cabinet rank.

Both the pattern of interpellations and their outcomes show the gap between the aspirations of civil society and the responses of the government and of the elected parliament. Following liberation, Kuwaiti civil society was livelier than it had been since 1938, when the first parliament thought it could reform the regime almost single-handedly. The population is far more mobilized now than it was before women received the vote, and the stunning electoral success of the Orange Movement raised expectations that the 2006 parliament would continue the campaign to reduce corruption and improve the effectiveness of governance.[56] These expectations were not met.

Following the 2006 election, the amir did remove the two cabinet members most closely associated with corrupt practices in the government, Shaikh Ahmad al-Fahad and Mohammad Sharrar. But he also created protected spaces for family members and cronies who are democratically ejected from ministerial posts: consolation appointments. The greater went to Ahmad al-Fahad, who became the head of state security without portfolio. His actual power is reflected in the widespread belief that he hired thugs to disrupt an Orange Movement gathering in an attempt to channel demonstrators into the arms of the police and thereby discredit their whole campaign, as described above. It also can be measured in the ease with which he resumed a formal position in government. He now serves as the deputy prime minister for economic affairs, holds in addition two positions as minister of state (for development and for housing), and retains a state security position.

Women in government also proved disappointing. The new education minister, Nouria al-Subeih, met the expectations of her feminist constituency by refusing to change her wardrobe for legislative sessions. Reactions when she was sworn in without *hijab* were more vociferous than those that had greeted a veiled Ma'souma Mubarak, but Nouria's disdain for her Islamist opponents may have sharpened their interest in cutting her down to size. And before the year was out, they found their opportunity. In January 2008, Nouria faced a vote of confidence after an interpellation triggered by news of illicit sexual behavior among low-level university employees. To ensure that she would retain her position, she agreed to a more rigorous enforcement of the gender segregation law that had been adopted in 1996 at Kuwait University, and to extend enforcement to private universities and high schools. Her decision appalled the women who had rejoiced in her appointment and prompted civil libertarian MP Ali al-Rashed to submit a bill to rescind gender segregation in all Kuwaiti universities. Ali's brave stand triggered a death threat.[57]

Parliament remained at the center of other contentious issues. In March 2008, sectarian ill will exploded in reaction to Shi'i Kuwaitis engaging in public mourning of the assassination death of Imad Mughniya. Charged with belonging to a secret Kuwaiti branch of Hezbollah bent on overturning the regime, Shi'i activists, including two former members of parliament, were arrested while two serving members were the subjects of a parliamentary inquiry.[58] In addition to the upheaval in parliament, incendiary charges were made in television broadcasts over two stations owned by a faction of the ruling family who used the occasion to try to reverse its political eclipse. On March 17, the cabinet resigned. Two days later the amir, rumored to have been surprised at the mass resignations, suspended the parliament once again, guaranteeing that the first election under the new five-district plan would take place far earlier than anyone had imagined, and under conditions of social and political turmoil. According to former US ambassador to Kuwait Skip Gnehm, one Kuwaiti told him that "we've become the Italians of the Gulf."[59]

Elections and Civil Society

The 2008 election was held in a tense and divided country. Technical preparations for the new system had not been matched by changes in other institutions.[60] The government did decide to crack down on violators of a 1998 amendment to the election law making tribal primaries illegal, one that had not been enforced consistently before. Tribal primaries select a limited number of candidates that all the members of the tribe are supposed to vote for in the general election. This limits vote scattering, thereby improving the chances that a member of the tribe will be able to bring back benefits for his constituents. The first tribal primaries were run in 1975; they became more widespread after the 1981 redistricting that gave the tribes and tribal culture a more prominent place in Kuwaiti public life.[61]

The five new districts, each electing ten members, were envisioned as a template for expanding direct representation of political minorities. Each voter would have only four votes, limiting the power of any one political group or trend to sweep an entire district. The tribes feared losing their post-1981 clout under the new system. They began holding meetings shortly after the closure of the parliament to organize and hold primary elections, but were surprised when police arrested tribal leaders, searched their offices and homes, and confiscated their papers and computers for evidence. Most of those arrested were soon released, but the names of scores of people implicated in the illegal elections were referred to the public prosecutor and a few were detained for a short period. Tribe members attacked police stations where their leaders were held, throwing stones and breaking windows; the police responded with tear gas, a level of violence on both sides unprecedented in Kuwaiti elections.[62] Despite arrests and altercations, most of the large tribes managed to select their nominees,[63] but small tribes found themselves shut out during the preelection maneuvering. Several were so desperate that their shaikhs approached at least one urban candidate in District 2, asking for cash in exchange for votes.[64]

Women also found themselves shut out although their overall position had improved over 2006. One woman, Aseel al-Awadhi, was invited to join a slate of three Alliance candidates in District 3, all of whom lost. Aseel came in eleventh in her district, however, ahead of both of her male colleagues, one of whom was a former MP.[65] Other female candidates also garnered significant vote totals, not enough to beat Islamist and tribal candidates who swept the election, but more than sufficient to cause voters who claimed afterward that they had not voted for any women because they thought a woman could not win to say they would think differently next time.[66] In April 2009, another confrontation between the amir and the parliament centered on multiple threats to interpellate ministers, including an attempt to question the prime minister, led to the third dissolution in a little over three years and a new parliamentary election on May 16, 2009. Four years to the day following the passage of legislation guaranteeing political rights for women, four women were elected to seats and a fifth attracted more than 6,500 votes in a tribal constituency.[67]

Among the other significant outcomes of that election was the shift away from group affiliation (political groups are informal substitutes for political parties, illegal in Kuwait) both by candidates declining to run as representatives of a group and by voters who opted for independents in higher than usual numbers. The smaller influence of political groups could have been another facet of the voters' desire to elect a parliament sufficiently different from its predecessors that it would take a new tack on policy. Rightly or wrongly, members of political groups are seen as less flexible than independents and more likely to follow a party line. Given a level of disgust so high that it kept many citizens from going to the polls at all, which was also reflected in the defeat of several incumbents in the still-illegal but not-suppressed-this-time tribal primaries, voters seemed to be looking for people they thought would exercise individual judgment on the critical issues facing Kuwait. Interestingly, the four female parliamentarians have attracted both criticism and praise for their moderate positions as legislators. Critics complain that they have not made the major changes expected from women in such positions: "they are just like the others." But those who praise them disagree. One close observer pointed out that all four were educated persons who were thoughtful speakers and committed to the proposition that parliamentary government could work. But they are not in the vanguard of those advocating change.

This judgment seems fair in the context of the next large face-off between the government and parliament over interpellation. This time, the target was the prime minister, who was accused of "financial irregularities" in the running of his office, a euphemism for bribery. The amir already had accepted the interpellation of other ruling family members, but an interpellation of the prime minister marked a gigantic step toward accountability that many feared the regime was not ready to take. As he did during the amiri transition, Speaker Jasim al-Khorafy mediated the clash between the National Assembly and the ruling family, announcing shortly before Prime Minister Nasir al-Mohammed al-Sabah agreed to be questioned that thirty out of the fifty elected members of parliament had signed a statement supporting him.[68] The interpellation of the prime minister took place on December 8, 2009, behind closed doors, and the vote of confidence occurred on December 16, when only thirteen members voted against him and one member abstained.

Significantly, all four women supported the prime minister in what might be termed a *Marbury* v. *Madison* moment in the Kuwaiti parliament. In the historic 1803 case before the US Supreme Court that established the precedent of judicial review, the Court decided that the magistrate appointed by outgoing president John Adams was not entitled to receive his commission from the incoming administration because part of the act authorizing judicial appointments was unconstitutional.[69] In this way, the immediate political goal of the new chief executive was fulfilled while, in exchange, the Court took the opportunity to create a precedent enlarging its own institutional power. In the Kuwaiti case, the parliament gave up any satisfaction it might have received from ousting a disliked prime minister in exchange for a precedent allowing prime ministers to be questioned by the parliament and, perhaps at some future time, voted out of office. Strategic decisions frequently incur such short-run losses, but lay down structures with significant potential to limit the authority of powerful opposing institutions in the future.

The wisdom of *Marbury* moments in Kuwait today is questioned by strong democrats who see such acquiescence as a sign of weakness, a lack of nerve, or a desire to hold on to their current positions rather than as a strategic investment. One longtime democratic activist commented in May 2010 that, if the amir were to close the parliament illegally, that is, without calling for new elections within sixty days, his decision might be welcomed at first by a national trend to associate failures in governance with the National Assembly rather than the amir and his ministers. But she was confident that, as they had before, Kuwaitis would mobilize to fight this coup against their constitution and, perhaps, this time succeed in pushing beyond political stalemate toward real democratization at last.

Conclusion

The Kuwaiti experience demonstrates the inadequacy of definitions that equate political opening with elections. Competitive elections[70] are democratic instruments, but they are not sufficient by themselves to constitute a democratic polity. The example of tribal primaries seems to argue for the legalization of political parties with authority to trim lists of aspirants and mobilize effective voting blocs, yet the 2009 election recommends caution. As they did in 2008, the large tribes managed to mobilize effective blocs despite the criminalization of their primaries, but candidates from religious groups found that religious solidarity was not so effective in cobbling successful pluralities together. Indeed, tribalism is Kuwait's shadow government, an informal system that operates side by side with governance structures and procedures laid out in the constitution and the laws.[71] Both are led by the chief tribe, the Al Sabah. Although tribalism is inherently exclusionary, the tribes have managed to organize an effective institution for rationalizing elections, something no other political force in Kuwait has accomplished. It is at least arguable that tribal representatives are the most coherent and consistent members of the parliamentary opposition and, perhaps, the least vulnerable to regime manipulation.

The amir's strategy of calling election after election, with the effect of alienating Kuwaiti voters, depressing voter turnout, and delegitimating the entire electoral enterprise and the parliament it produces, shows how elections become instruments of authoritarianism.[72] As Russell Lucas found in Jordan, elections can elide issues, aggravate social divisions, and confirm executive autocracy rather than beat it back.[73] From this vantage point, the parliament's *Marbury* moment appears as an act of statesmanship that established a liberal precedent whose utility and effectiveness are likely to be tested in the near future.

In the two instances I have described in this chapter, where Kuwaitis applied broadly based popular pressure on the regime to extend political rights, it is the extent of the popular pressure and its visibility that seem to have been most effective. The fight for women's rights benefited greatly from mobilizing supporters outside as well as inside Kuwait, confirming the observation that progressive political change is a product of triangulation whose third leg is external pressure.[74] Yet the assembly of youth from all over the country in front of the parliament—and their campouts on the median when demonstrations lasted for more than one day—show that highly focused movements entirely rooted in domestic politics can also be effective. Both demonstrate the regime's vulnerability to broadly based, highly public, civil society action.

No doubt in response, ruling family members are taking advantage of new press laws to create personal media empires, little Berlusconis amassing constituencies to support their own projects, as happened in the 2008 Mughniya fracas. Violent attacks on police stations during the 2008 election campaign also elicited a prompt response when the government's attempt to halt tribal primaries was itself halted. Attacks on elections by the regime are signs of the strength of democratizing forces in Kuwait, but they demonstrate as well the vulnerability of elections to strategic sabotage from above and outbursts of rage from below.

In its *Marbury* moment, the parliament reached toward Immanuel Kant's distinction between republics, which he praised for their representative governments and the separation of powers necessary to ensure the rule of law, and democracies, which he criticized for fusing legislative and executive power, thereby making the rule of law impossible.[75] Not surprisingly, the regime is reaching in the opposite direction. In an April 2010 interview in Germany, the amir asserted that the constitution should be changed because it fused executive and legislative power.[76] But what he was really criticizing were checks and balances: despite his words, the interview clearly reflected his distaste for power sharing, accountability, and the rule of law.

The amir's challenge to the constitution and the parliament promises a more difficult time for Kuwait politically as popular forces are mobilized by factions in the ruling family to advance their personal goals. Whether by intention or merely as an epiphenomenon of the family power struggle, the conflict could crush the only representative assembly in the Gulf with actual legislative authority. Fought in the press and, to an alarming degree in the context of Kuwait's generally nonviolent society, in the streets, this assault on representative institutions is unlikely to have a happy ending. Given its history, it is hard to imagine that Kuwait would turn into another Qatar or United Arab Emirates, where affluence still seems adequate enough compensation for most unmet desires for political participation (see Chapters 6 and 8). Yet to move peacefully toward a system based on the rule of law requires vigilant, well-organized, broadly based social movements; a representative institution whose members are nimble enough to stay at least one step ahead of the authoritarians in charge; and an external environment alert to the implications of rising restrictions on civil liberties and barely veiled threats to opposition actions conveyed through foreign media. Without them, Kuwait is unlikely to break out of the authoritarian trap in which it is enmeshed so it can find the path to a durable democratic future.

Notes

Research for this chapter was funded by the National Science Foundation (grant 0527339), "AOC: Collaborative Research: The Dissent/Repression Nexus in the Middle East." I would like to thank Mohammed al-Ghanim and Michael Herb for their advice on earlier drafts.

1. Mary Ann Tétreault, *Stories of Democracy: Politics and Society in Contemporary Kuwait* (New York: Columbia University Press, 2000).

2. Michelle P. Angrist, "The Outlook for Authoritarianism," in *Authoritarianism in the Middle East: Regimes and Resistance*, eds. Marsha P. Posusney and Michelle P. Angrist (Boulder: Lynne Rienner, 2005), p. 227.

3. John Keane, ed., *Civil Society and the State* (London: Verso, 1988). With regard to the Middle East in particular, see Nils Butenshøn, Uri Davis, and M. Hassassian, eds., *Citizenship and the State in the Middle East: Approaches and Applications* (Syracuse: Syracuse University Press, 2000); and Augustus Richard Norton, *Civil Society in the Middle East* (Boston: Brill Academic, 2005). Suad Joseph also visualizes civil society as coming between family and state, but looks at all three as permeated by patriarchal tribalism. See Suad Joseph,"Gendering Citizenship in the Middle East," in *Gender and Citizenship in the Middle East*, ed. Suad Joseph (Syracuse: Syracuse University Press, 2000), pp. 3–30.

4. Nazih N. Ayoubi, *Over-Stating the Arab State: Politics and Society in the Middle East* (London: I. B. Tauris, 1999), pp. 430–440.

5. Halim Barakat, *The Arab World: Society, Culture, and State* (Berkeley: University of California Press, 1993); Hisham Sharabi, *Neopatriarchy: A Theory of Distorted Change in Arab Societies* (New York: Oxford University Press, 1988).

6. For example, Jill Crystal, "Authoritarianism and Its Adversaries in the Arab World," *World Politics* 46, no. 2 (1994): 262–289; Ghassan Salamé, ed., *Democracy Without Democrats: The Renewal of Politics in the Muslim World* (London: I. B. Tauris, 1994).

7. Hazem Beblawi, "The Rentier State in the Arab World," in *The Arab State*, ed. Giacomo Luciani (Berkeley: University of California Press, 1990), pp. 85–98; Giacomo Luciani, "Allocation vs. Production States: A Theoretical Framework," in *The Arab State*, ed. Giacomo Luciani (Berkeley: University of California Press, 1990), pp. 65–84.

8. For example, see Lisa Anderson, "Searching Where the Light Shines: Studying Democratization in the Middle East," *Annual Review of Political Science* 9 (2006): 189–214.

9. I make this argument in Mary Ann Tétreault, "Kuwait's *Annus Mirabilis*," Merip Online, September 7, 2006, www.merip.org (September 11, 2007). Among the noteworthy exceptions to scholarly tendencies to treat democratization in the Arab world superficially is the work of Michael Herb. See, for example, Michael Herb, "Princes and Parliaments in the Arab World," *Middle East Journal* 58, no. 3 (2004): 1–8; and Michael Herb, "Taxation and Representation," *Studies in Comparative International Development* 38, no. 3 (2003): 3–31.

10. John Foran, ed., *Theorizing Revolutions* (New York: Routledge, 1997), especially the final chapter by Foran. Although reform is a far cry from revolution, it is similarly vulnerable to external constraints.

11. See the discussion of "endogenous democratization" in Carles Boix and Susan C. Stokes, "Endogenous Democratization," *World Politics* 55, no. 4 (2003): 517–549.

12. Doron Shultziner, "Struggles of Recognition: The Psychological Causes of Democratization," PhD diss., University of Oxford, 2007, chap. 8.

13. Jill Crystal, *Oil and Politics in the Gulf: Rulers and Merchants in Kuwait and Qatar* (New York: Cambridge University Press, 1990); Michael Herb, *All in the Family: Absolutism, Revolution, and Democracy in the Middle Eastern Monarchies* (Albany: SUNY Press, 1999).

14. Haya al-Mughni and Mary Ann Tétreault, "Engagement in the Public Sphere: Women and the Press in Kuwait," in *Women and the Media in the Middle East*, ed. Naomi Sakr (London: I. B. Tauris, 2004), pp. 120–137; Ghanim al-Najjar, "Human Rights in a Crisis Situation: The Case of Kuwait After Occupation," *Human Rights Quarterly* 23, no. 1 (2001): 188–209; Tétreault, *Stories of Democracy*; Deborah Wheeler, *The Internet in the Middle East: Global Expectations/Local Imaginations in Kuwait* (Albany: SUNY Press, 2005); "Civic Society," *Weekly Diwaniya*, July 3, 2007, www.facebook.com/group.php?gid=2399521688.

15. Mohammed al-Ghanim, "'Transitions to Nowhere?' Kuwait and the Challenge of Political Liberalization," unpublished paper, May 2009.

16. Accounts of Mubarak's precoup links to urban merchants and tribal leaders vary. Contemporary British observers reported Mubarak and the merchants to be virtual allies in the overthrow of Mohammad. Later analysts attribute the main impetus for the coup to Mubarak, although there is disagreement about his motives. See Tétreault, *Stories of Democracy*, pp. 37–39.

17. Crystal, *Oil and Politics in the Gulf*, p. 58.

18. Crystal, *Oil and Politics in the Gulf*; Tétreault, *Stories of Democracy.*

19. Ghanim Hamid al-Najjar, "Decision-Making Process in Kuwait: The Land Acquisition Policy as a Case Study," PhD diss., University of Exeter, 1984; also prodemocracy activist Abdullah Nibari, interviewed by the author, Kuwait, March and May 1990.

20. Shafeeq Ghabra, "Kuwait and the Dynamics of Socio-economic Change," *Middle East Journal* 51, no. 3 (1997): 358–372. This was part of the settlement ending the 1976–1981 parliamentary suspension. See also Nicolas Gavrielides, "Tribal Democracy: The Anatomy of Parliamentary Elections in Kuwait," in *Elections in the Middle East: Implications of Recent Trends*, ed. Lynda Layne (Boulder: Westview, 1987), pp. 153–223; and Tétreault, *Stories of Democracy*, pp. 107–110. Political scientist Mohammed al-Ghanim argues that Arab nationalism was the primary target of redistricting, rather than merchants as such; Mohammed al-Ghanim, personal communication with the author, May 2010.

21. Neil Hicks and Ghanim al-Najjar, "The Utility of Tradition: Civil Society in Kuwait," in *Civil Society in the Middle East*, ed. Augustus Richard Norton (New York: Brill, 1995), pp. 188–213.

22. Haya al-Mughni, *Women in Kuwait: The Politics of Gender*, 2nd ed. (London: Saqi, 2001); also Haya al-Mughni and Mary Ann Tétreault, "Gender, Citizenship, and Nationalism in Kuwait," *British Journal of Middle Eastern Studies* 22, nos. 1–2 (1995): 64–80.

23. Gavrielides, "Tribal Democracy"; see also Anh Nga Longva, "Citizenship in the Gulf: Conceptualization and Practice," in *Citizenship and the State in the Middle East: Approaches and Applications*, eds. Nils A. Butenschön, Uri Davis, and Manuel Hassassian (Syracuse: Syracuse University Press, 2000), pp. 179–197. "Tribal" refers to recently settled former bedouins. Longva argues that many identify more closely with their clans than with the nation as a whole.

24. Longva, "Citizenship in the Gulf"; see also Mary Ann Tétreault and Mohammed al-Ghanim, "Transitions *in* Authoritarianism: Political Reform in the Persian Gulf Reconsidered," paper prepared for annual meeting of the International Studies Association, Montreal, February 2011.

25. Haya al-Mughni, *Women in Kuwait: The Politics of Gender*, 2nd ed. (London: Saqi, 2001); Mary Ann Tétreault, "Kuwait's Parliament Considers Women's Rights, Again," Middle East Report Online, September 2, 2004, www.merip.org (October 20, 2005).

26. Al-Mughni, *Women in Kuwait*; Mary Ann Tétreault, "Divided Communities of Memory: Diasporas Come Home," in *The Muslim Diaspora: Gender, Culture, and Identity*, ed. Haideh Moghissi (London: Routledge, 2006), pp. 81–98.

27. Haya al-Mughni, "Women's Movements and the Autonomy of Civil Society in Kuwait," in *Conscious Acts and the Politics of Social Change*, eds. Robin L. Teske and Mary Ann Tétreault (Columbia: University of South Carolina Press, 2000), pp. 170–187; Tétreault, "Kuwait's Parliament Considers Women's Rights, Again."

28. Shultziner, "Struggles of Recognition."

29. Interviews of male and female Kuwaiti activists by the author, Kuwait, December 2004.

30. The 2003 election marked what was widely reported as a "defeat" for Kuwaiti liberals, whose representation dropped to three seats. Less widely noted was that the number of Salafi members rose while the number of Shi'a and Ikhwan

declined. Thus, the 2003 parliament substituted antifeminist Islamists for Islamists who had supported women's rights to varying degrees.

31. Interviews of activists in Kuwait, December 2004; Shultziner, "Struggles of Recognition."

32. Shaikh Salim had been acting prime minister for several years due to the deteriorating health of Shaikh Sa'ad al-Abdullah, who held the position of both prime minister and crown prince. He was described by contemporary feminists as a supporter despite a history that older feminists remember as anything but supportive.

33. Shultziner, "Struggles of Recognition."

34. Widely rumored at the time, confirmation came several months later, during an altercation within the ruling family over the amiri succession. See text below.

35. Tétreault, "Civil Society in Kuwait."

36. Tétreault, *Stories of Democracy*, pp. 70–72.

37. At one of Rola Dashti's *diwaniyyas*, I met two women who brought their daughters. At the first campaign *diwaniyya* that hosted female speakers (the candidate was Saleh al-Yaseen, the year 1992, and the speakers Moudhi al-Hmoud and Badriya al-Awadhi), women brought daughters just as men brought sons. See Mary Ann Tétreault, "Civil Society in Kuwait: Protected Spaces and Women's Rights," *Middle East Journal* 47, no. 2 (1993): 279–280; and Tétreault, *Stories of Democracy*, pp. 104–105.

38. Edmund Ghareeb, "New Media and the Information Revolution in the Arab World: An Assessment," *Middle East Journal* 54, no. 3 (2000): 395–418; Naomi Sakr, *Satellite Realms: Transnational Television, Globalization and the Middle East* (London: I. B. Tauris, 2002); Jon W. Anderson, "New Media, New Publics: Reconfiguring the Public Sphere of Islam," *Social Research* 70, no. 3 (2003): 887–906; Hugh Miles, *Al-Jazeera: The Inside Story of the Arab News Channel That Is Challenging the West* (New York: Grove, 2005).

39. Deborah L. Wheeler, *The Internet in the Middle East: Global Expectations and Local Imaginations in Kuwait* (Albany: SUNY Press, 2005).

40. Attorney and journalist Mohammad al-Jassem, interviewed by the author, Kuwait, July 3, 2004. The visibility of Mohammad's blog led to his arrest in November 2009 for insulting the ruling family. After months of imprisonment, which, according to a local human rights activist, included beatings by a jailer, Mohammad was released on bail in June 2010. On November 20, 2010, he was sentenced to a year in prison for his statements criticizing the prime minister.

41. Sam Dagher, "Gulf Bloggers: A New Breed of Arab Activists," Middle East Online, August 4, 2006, www.middle-east-online.com (August 9, 2007); also human rights activists Ghanim al-Najjar and Mudhaffar al-Rashid, interviewed by the author, Kuwait, March 6 and 7, 2006, respectively.

42. Mary Ann Tétreault, "Women's Rights and the Meaning of Citizenship in Kuwait," Middle East Report Online, February 10, 2005, www.merip.org (July 4, 2007).

43. A shortened form of "Nabiha khamsa min ajl al-Kuwayt," or "We want five for Kuwait." "Nabiha 5" became the ubiquitous logo of the effort, appearing on posters, buttons, hats, and, of course, orange T-shirts.

44. Interviews of movement organizers and demonstrators by the author, Kuwait, May 2006.

45. Interviews of demonstrators, including the one who was struck, by the author, Kuwait, May–June 2006. See also Nathan J. Brown, "Pushing Toward Party Politics? Kuwait's Islamic Constitutional Movement," Carnegie Endowment for

International Peace Democracy and Rule of Law Project, Carnegie Papers no. 79 (Washington, DC: January 2007).

46. Oman Hassan, "Young Kuwaitis Turn 'Orange,'" Middle East Online, May 29, 2006, www.middle-east-online.com (August 8, 2007).

47. Jamie Etheridge, "Historic First: Kuwaiti Women Vote, Run," *Christian Science Monitor*, April 5, 2006, www.csmonitor.com (June 16, 2007); Oman Hassan, "First Woman Candidate Breaks Taboo in Kuwait," Middle East Online, March 22, 2006, www.middle-east-online.com (August 8, 2007); and notes taken by author, March 3–17, 2006, of conversations and observations in Kuwait.

48. Conversations and observations of Jenan al-Boushehri and potential supporters in Kuwait, March 2006; and conversations and observations of female parliamentary candidates and supporters in Kuwait, May 2006.

49. An incumbent running in the same district as Rola Dashti was charged with bribing women voters with Chanel handbags full of dinars. A female Alliance member captured video footage on her mobile phone of Dashti's workers attempting to bribe her.

50. Parliamentary candidate Rola Dashti, interviewed by the author in Kuwait, December 29, 2006. Vote trading is revealed in the vote matrices compiled by campaign workers when the votes are counted. Ballots are read one by one so that each pair selected can be recorded. If "second votes" are floating, there will be a random distribution of second votes. In this election, a disproportionate number of pairs were identical.

51. "Government of Kuwait Steps Down," BBC News, March 4, 2007, http://news.bbc.co.uk (August 8, 2007).

52. "Kuwaiti Energy Minister Ousted to Appease Winners of Parliamentary Elections," Cera Reports Online, July 11, 2006, http://cera.ecnext.com (August 8, 2007).

53. "Opposition MPs Want Kuwait Oil Minister Sacked," Middle East Online, June 25, 2007, www.middle-east-online.com (August 8, 2007).

54. Tétreault, *Stories of Democracy*, pp. 192–193.

55. Michael Herb, personal communication with the author, June 26, 2007; and Michael Herb, personal communication with the author, June 27, 2007; also "Opposition MPs Want Kuwait Oil Minister Sacked." In his personal communication on June 27, Herb said that he had asked the head of Transparency International, during a "conference earlier in the year held by the Kuwaiti branch . . . about him, and he said that so far as he knew, Ali Jarrah was clean."

56. "Most Kuwaiti MPs Involved in Corruption," Middle East Online, June 23, 2007, www.middle-east-online.com (August 8, 2007). Elections are not enough to clean the Augean stables of Kuwait's parliament and government, however, although small improvements have been made. By 2009, Kuwait's ranking on the Transparency International index of perceived corruption had fallen to 66, the seventh year of decline. In 2010, its ranking rose to 54, but this is small cause for rejoicing as its corruption score of 4.4 shows little movement from prior years (it was 4.3 in 2007). Its improved ranking is rather a function of rising corruption worldwide. See the annual tables at http://www.transparency.org.

57. Raed Yousef, Ayed al-Enezi, Hadi al-Ajmi, and Ben Arfaj al-Mutairi, "Arrest in Death Threat to MP on Co-education," *Arab Times*, February 7, 2008, www.zawya.com (July 27, 2008).

58. "Kuwait Parliament Asked to Lift Two Shia MPs' Immunity," Agence France Presse, Gulf in the Media, March 12, 2008, www.gulfinthemedia.com (March 18,

2008); "Shia Crackdown Fuels Tensions in Kuwait," Khaleej Times Online, March 13, 2008, www.khaleejtimes.com (July 28, 2008).

59. Joanne Yao, "Kuwait: The Italy of the Gulf?" *Middle East Times*, April 14, 2008, www.metimes.com (July 27, 2008).

60. Interviews in Kuwait, December 2006, January 2007, May 2008.

61. Gavrielides, "Tribal Democracy." Blogger Kevin Anthony Stoda, who is less convinced than Gavrielides that tribal primaries are equivalent to democracy, calls them an electoral oligopoly. See Kevin Anthony Stoda, "Tribe, Tribalism and Cultural Change—Kuwait 2008," April 12, 2008, http://www.opednews.com/articles.

62. Stoda, "Tribe, Tribalism"; see also "Kuwait Police Disperse Protestors," Al-Jazeera.net, March 27, 2008, http://english.aljazeera.net (July 27, 2008); Rania El Gamal, "Kuwait Curbs Tribal Primaries Ahead of Election," Reuters, March 27, 2008, www.reuters.com (July 27, 2008); and interviews in Kuwait, May 2008.

63. Successfully running a tribal primary did not ensure success in the general election, however. In District 1, only one of the four candidates chosen in the al-Awazem tribal primary won in the general election, and he had Islamist backing. The large tribes dominated in Districts 4 and 5. In District 4, Al Mutairy took six seats and Al Rashaida took four. Veteran parliamentarians from other blocs, including three from the Ikhwan and two from the Popular Bloc, lost their seats. In District 5, Al Awazem and Al Ajman won four seats each; one of the other winners had been accused of vote-buying. B. Izzak, "Islamists Make Strong Gains," *Kuwait Times*, May 19, 2008, pp. 1, 13.

64. Candidate's representative, interviewed by the author in Kuwait, May 13, 2008.

65. Conversations and observations in Kuwait, May 2008.

66. Conversation with Aseel al-Awadi, candidate, in Kuwait, May 20, 2008.

67. One, Ma'souma Mubarak, came in first in her district; Aseel al-Awadhi took second in hers and Rola Dashti was seventh in that constituency. The fourth woman, Salwa al-Jasser, came in tenth in a small district with a highly mobilized salafi group and many wealthy merchants, including Speaker Khorafi, who long considered themselves to be proprietors of "safe seats."

68. "Kuwait's Prime Minister Survives Key Vote," Reuters, December 16, 2009, www.themalaysianinsider.com.

69. For the text of the decision, see www.law.umkc.edu.

70. The distinction I make here is between elections where only one name appears on the ballot and those where voters have choices. These choices may be circumscribed by higher authorities, as they are in Bahrain and Iran, or by financial considerations, as they are in Kuwait, but they still offer an opportunity to reject incumbents or regime-favored candidates.

71. Tétreault and al-Ghanim, "Transitions *in* Authoritarianism."

72. Significantly, statistics on turnout and voting by gender by neighborhood have not been released by the government for the past two elections, making it difficult to chart the impact of repeated trips to the ballot box. The reason given is that some candidates contested the results, but this happens in virtually every parliamentary election, while the rapid decision by the courts with regard to the three contested elections in 2009 did not result in the issuance of a complete set of election statistics.

73. Russell E. Lucas, *Institutions and the Politics of Survival in Jordan: Domestic Responses to External Challengers, 1988–2001* (Albany: SUNY Press, 2005).

74. See, for example, Angrist, "The Outlook for Authoritarianism"; and Steven Livitsky and Lucan A. Way, *Competitive Authoritarianism: Hybrid Regimes After the Cold War* (New York: Cambridge University Press, 2010).

75. Immanuel Kant, *Perpetual Peace: A Philosophical Sketch*, 1795, www.mtholyoke.edu (July 27, 2008).

76. AFP, "Kuwait's Emir Blasts Parliament," *Maktoob*, April 26, 2010, http://business.maktoob.com.

5

Oman Faces the Twenty-First Century

J. E. Peterson

OMAN IS THE often forgotten member of the Gulf Cooperation Council (GCC), perhaps because of its geographical isolation at the end of the Arabian Peninsula and its mostly outside-the-Gulf location. In terms of population and financial might, it ranks in the lower GCC tier; distance is a significant factor that insulates Oman from strife elsewhere in the Gulf. But far more important determinants of Omani insulation and its facility of quietly conducting its business as usual are the natures of Omani polity and society. A productive modus vivendi has quietly emerged during the reign of Sultan Qabus (r. 1970–). Under it, armed opposition has become a phenomenon of the past. Thousands of Omanis previously residing abroad have returned to live and work in Oman. Politics is a subdued affair left to an elite (albeit mostly self-interested) while the majority of the population simply gets on with life in a small oil-producing country with a modest standard of living.

Oman has done its best to protect itself from a threatening international environment by remaining on correct, if not always good, terms with all its neighbors. It is a founding member of the GCC, and has broadened its long-standing security relationship with Britain into a US umbrella. The costs of these measures have been relatively small measured in terms of domestic dissent, and are outweighed by the benefits of regional security protection, trade, and an absence of friction with neighbors. Thus, internally and externally, Oman continues to be a quiet corner of the Gulf. But although they are muted at present, significant problems do exist that must be resolved.

The emergence of this quietly confident Oman is due to the leadership of Sultan Qabus b. Sa'id Al Bu Sa'id. Despite occasional missteps, the sultan has done much to advance the standard of living, adding to public contentment. Oman remains socially cohesive, with a strong emphasis on traditional values, behaviors, and interactions. Economically, however, it has changed considerably. Its modest oil income has skewed an economic scene increasingly away from traditional activities to one dependent on consumer imports financed largely by oil revenues. Oman also has a high birthrate, leading to problems of resource scarcity and burgeoning unemployment. Political change also has not kept up with Oman's economic growth, remaining patriarchical and hierarchical. As a consequence, challenges for the future center on both political transformation and economic development. Oman's future is directly tied to how these challenges are met.

Key Challenges That Will Determine Oman's Future

There are multiple challenges to development and sustainability that must be urgently confronted and resolved. One of the most pressing is the scarcity of water. Simply put, Oman is a barren country whose population through the ages has subsisted on irrigated crops grown in mountain valleys and along the northern Batinah coast as well as on fishing. But the post-1970 prosperity and growth in population (which includes both indigenous Omanis and a half-million expatriates) are putting increasingly severe pressure on dwindling water supplies. Overpumping from the aquifers is common throughout the country. Oman's traditional *falaj* (underground channel) irrigation systems have also suffered, with a number of them falling out of use as groundwater levels dropped. A local survey conducted in Wadi al-Ma'awil in the mid-1990s recorded that only 40–50 liters of water were replenished for every 100 liters used. The highly cultivated and populated Batinah coast has suffered particularly severely from the introduction of large-scale commercial farming and the proliferation of weekend farms. Both have depleted the aquifer and increased salination from the incursion of seawater, making most traditional farming impossible. Palliatives such as the construction of a number of recharge dams scattered across the sultanate have had only limited success in stemming water depletion, making further development of agriculture, as well as water-intensive industry, problematic. Nearly all the capital's water comes from desalination, a fundamentally oil-era luxury that is unsuitable for widely scattered rural populations.[1]

A second challenge is controlling runaway population growth. The pre-1970 population estimates are not entirely trustworthy, but most estimates conclude that no more than 500,000 people inhabited Oman in 1970. According to the 2003 census, that figure had more than quadrupled to over 2 million, a quarter of whom were expatriates. Population growth may have been as high as 4 percent per annum during the 1980s and 1990s, although the World Bank estimated it at a lower 2.1 percent rate in 2007.[2] In common with third world countries and GCC neighbors, Oman's population is increasingly becoming younger. Apart from the need to finance the feeding, clothing, and educating of a mushrooming number of children, there is a serious problem regarding the future those children will find when they become adults.

Oman is experiencing rapidly rising rates of unemployment. The government has been reluctant to create jobs simply to disguise unemployment. Oil and natural gas are the largest economic concerns in the country, but both are capital-intensive industries that offer relatively few employment opportunities. One reason that Oman emphasizes tourism as a strategy for diversification is that it is labor-intensive. Indeed, filling jobs in hotels and restaurants with Omani workers is a striking and successful example of training Omanis to take up occupations that only a decade ago would have been considered beneath them. Unfortunately, the prospect of expanding such employment opportunities is limited. The government has placed considerable stress on *Omanization*; that is, the restriction of certain occupations to nationals only. But the private sector, whether willing or otherwise, can absorb only a small proportion of the more than 40,000 youths who leave secondary schools every year.

Despite current high prices, Omanis are worried that oil income will decline. Oman was always a relatively small oil producer. Total production peaked at 956,000 barrels per day (BPD) in 2001, declined to about 710,000 BPD in 2007, and has risen only slightly since then.[3] Output is falling in mature oil fields. But bringing new, smaller fields on line is expensive, and production from them cannot replace income from depleting reserves because the new fields yield heavier crude. The recent dramatic rise in oil prices diminished these concerns temporarily, but the subsequent collapse a few years later brought renewed problems. Even limited oil dependency distorts development and foreshadows economic problems to come.

A final challenge is whether evolution in the political system will enable the country to cope with and resolve the other challenges. The unsettled near-term question of succession is the most obvious aspect of this challenge, but political change must be more fundamental. There is increasing disquiet with regard to the domination of Oman's decisionmaking machinery by a small political-economic elite whose members often act in their personal interests as much as those of the country. Demands for expansion of the narrow scope of political participation are bound to grow as Omani society changes in a globalizing environment.

Development and Diversification

The problems outlined above point to a pressing need for economic diversification in Oman. But this is a difficult task for Oman as well as for its GCC neighbors. While the GCC countries are often referred to as oil-rich, they lack most other natural resources. Oman, like Bahrain, has smaller hydrocarbon reserves than its neighbors and, consequently, does not have an easy way to amass capital for investment.

Oman's economic history developed along three themes: subsistence agriculture, fishing, and maritime expansion. The first two are the bedrock on which the Omani economy was founded. The scarcity of natural resources limited the size of the population that could be sustained by agriculture and fishing. Maritime expansion occurred in cycles as Oman became unified internally and strong rulers turned their attention to opportunities overseas. The accumulation of wealth was made possible only by external activities, consisting partly of conquest but mostly of trade. The era of petroleum exports in the past forty years can be seen as a variation on maritime expansion that has brought unparalleled prosperity to the country. Unfortunately, a timeless lesson of Oman's history is that the bounty provided by outside expansion lasts for relatively brief periods. Meanwhile, the tripling of Oman's population since the oil era began has made a return to dependence on the traditional mainstays of agriculture and fishing virtually impossible.

At the beginning of the 1970s, the best estimate of Oman's population was 435,000 persons, with a labor force of about 100,000 workers. Some 80 percent of these workers were believed to be employed in agriculture and fisheries.[4] By mid-2007, the Omani population had ballooned to 1,923,000 nationals and 820,000 expatriates. A total of 312,000 residents were employed in 2004,[5] but the proportion employed in agriculture and fisheries had shrunk to 5 percent. The agriculture sector's contribution to gross domestic product (GDP) was only 201 million riyals (about US$518 million), a little more than 1 percent of the total GDP, and slightly more than 2 percent of nonpetroleum activities.[6]

Oman began to address the decline in oil, its most lucrative natural resource, by investing heavily in natural gas. Oman began exporting liquefied natural gas (LNG) in 2000; a second production train was brought into operation shortly afterward and a third train began operating in 2006. By 2007, LNG exports accounted for nearly 10 percent of total oil and gas income. Yet natural gas supplies are finite, expensive to develop, require reaching long-term sales contracts over several decades, and face stiff competition from other regional suppliers, especially Qatar. Furthermore, as Oman grows economically, there will be increasing domestic demand for LNG, which will reduce exports further. Finally, as a capital-intensive industry, natural gas does little to alleviate the growing burden of unemployment.

Oman must expand into new arenas of economic activity, both to compensate for future declines in hydrocarbon revenues and to expand the number of jobs available for a growing population. A critical World Bank study prepared for the Omani government in 1994—and released to the public only after news reports of its conclusions emerged—listed a number of development constraints. Among them were the impact of the oil-financed public sector on private sector development, Oman's low level of human resource development, its shortage of water, its continued reliance on expatriate labor, and the low level of private capital and entrepreneurship due in part to the country's dependence on oil revenues.[7] In particular, the World Bank recommended (1) eliminating the public sector deficit, mainly by cutting public expenditures; (2) placing part of national income in foreign investment; (3) narrowing the scope of government, strengthening the private sector by reforming the legal framework, eliminating monopolies, attracting foreign capital, and phasing out most subsidies; and (4) intensifying Omanization efforts by taxing the importation of expatriate workers, improving Omanis' education and skills, and encouraging Omanis to accept a wider range of jobs.[8]

The government has followed some of these recommendations. During the 1990s, the budget deficit steadily decreased, from 578.5 million riyals in 1992 to only 40.0 million riyals in 1997. Two years later, however, the deficit had jumped back to 472.9 million riyals. Only the rising price of oil has allowed the budget to move into the black, climbing to a surplus of 230.3 million riyals in 2004. Over the same period, government expenditures increased every year except one, rising from 1.7 billion riyals in 1992 to 2.7 billion riyals in 2004. A significant proportion of these expenditures went toward investment. Spending on development more than doubled, amounting to 26.5 percent of all state expenditures in 2004 compared to 20.8 percent in 1992. As oil prices continued to rise, so did Oman's budget surplus, reaching an estimated 1.1 to 2.0 billion riyals in 2006.[9] A temporary setback occurred in mid-2007 when Cyclone Gonu roared through the country, leaving a trail of devastation and causing more than fifty deaths. Early estimates pegged the economic damage at about $1 billion, but the government declined outside assistance and pledged that reconstruction of damaged infrastructure would be carried out within the current five-year development plan.[10] A more serious setback has been the drop in oil revenues, which fell by nearly half in the first quarter of 2009 compared to the first quarter of 2008.[11] With the subsequent partial recovery of oil prices, Oman expected to return to a budget surplus and, in early 2010, announced its largest budget ever.[12]

Government support for private sector expansion has grown. This includes the privatization of national enterprises such as the national telecommunications organization Omantel and Oman Air. Other efforts include investment in privately owned infrastructure projects, most notably power generation and distribution, with the first private power plant in the

Gulf built in the interior in the mid-1990s and three more added over the next decade.

Government initiative was behind the creation of a container port at Salalah in the south. It is operated by a private company, Salalah Port Services, a joint venture of the government, the major shipping firms Sea-Land and Maersk, and private Omani investors. The port and the adjacent free trade zone were designed to attract transshipments destined for the western Indian Ocean away from other Gulf port and manufacturing complexes, particularly Dubai. It has not been the success for which the government hoped. The construction of a new industrial port at Suhar on the northwestern coast embodied some of the same elements as Salalah and a private company was formed to operate it. The new port was expected to service anticipated exports from large-scale industrial development around Suhar, including an aluminum smelter, fertilizer plant, and the country's second oil refinery. In addition, it was seen as both relieving pressure on the country's main port at Matrah outside of Muscat and directing trade to the Batinah coast (where Suhar is located), which has the highest population in Oman. There was also some hope that the port might serve as a transit point for goods intended for elsewhere in the Gulf, particularly the United Arab Emirates (UAE), but the lack of success with similar schemes, such as the development of al-Fujayrah and Khawr Fakkan on the Gulf of Oman side of the UAE, has not been encouraging.

The government also has encouraged small import substitution industries, many located in the Rusayl industrial estate outside of Muscat. Expansion of manufacturing industries is limited by Oman's small domestic market and the overwhelming advantage enjoyed by Dubai. Oman liberalized its investment law in the mid-2000s to permit 100 percent foreign ownership (rather than the existing ceiling of 49 percent in joint ventures) and permitted non-Omanis to purchase real property in resort complexes as a way to attract foreign capital.

Over the past decade, increasing emphasis has been placed on tourism. This is an attractive sector not only because of its contribution to national income but because, as a labor-intensive industry, it offers significant opportunities for private sector employment in travel agencies, hotels, restaurants, car rental services, tour agencies, and so forth. Like other Gulf states, Oman is copying one of Dubai's strategies: plans have been announced for an ambitious $15 billion resort and residence complex called Blue City to be located on the Batinah coast not far from Muscat. It is expected to attract 200,000 inhabitants.[13] The Wave is a similar megaproject planned outside Muscat, and the capital area has experienced a small boom in resorts and luxury hotels. But Oman has suffered from economic adversity similar to Dubai's such that, by mid-2010, the Blue City project teetered on the edge of collapse. Salalah has become a popular destination during the summer monsoon for visitors from the Gulf, but the tourism industry remains small. By 2007, tourism contributed only about 1 percent to Oman's GDP.[14]

Economic diversification remains a formidable challenge, given scarce natural resources and the still uneven development of human resources. The rise in oil income in the first decade of the twenty-first century has provided more opportunities for the government to sponsor and encourage selected areas of development, but it remains an unreliable income source and does not in and of itself constitute diversification.

Social Continuity and Change

Omani society is perhaps the least changed of all the GCC states. Family life is central, and tribal identity continues to influence local lifestyles. Private residences are built to incorporate gendered living spaces, and most marriages continue to be arranged between first cousins. Long-standing patterns of stratification are based on family connections and tribal ties, relative wealth, and religious education. The influx of wealth into the country, however, particularly in the capital area, is beginning to create new distinctions.[15]

Despite this evidence of continuity, Oman also is undergoing substantial social change. Urbanization has been most evident in the expanding capital region of Muscat, where the population approaches 500,000 compared to between 25,000 and 50,000 in 1970. This not only heralds changes in occupations, lifestyles, living arrangements, the mixing of sexes, and consumerism, but also tends to dilute the importance of tribal and family ties. Urbanization is spreading throughout the country, with sustained growth in regional centers and consequent subtle transformation of many villages through migration, changing housing patterns, and new occupations. Like their Gulf neighbors, Omanis find themselves confronting alcoholism, drug use, petty crime, and diseases such as heart attacks and diabetes, all-too-familiar problems associated with prosperity.

The government recognizes that sustainable economic development requires investment in human resources. While near-universal education at least in the early years is now standard, the quality of education in state schools remains low and most Omanis seeking work after they leave school are unqualified to hold skilled labor positions. A number of government and private sector vocational training institutes are springing up to rectify this deficiency. Economic need means that Omanis are increasingly willing to accept jobs that are lower-paying and lower-status than they would have taken previously.

Oman has always been more liberal in its attitude toward women than some of its neighbors. In the post-1970 state and society, the role played by women in development, education, business, and government has expanded steadily and significantly. Prior to 1970, there were no schools for girls in Oman, but then there were hardly any for boys either. During 2007, 269,000 Omani girls comprised nearly 49 percent of total enrollment in Omani schools.[16] Women received 53 percent of the degrees at Sultan Qabus University. Women moved into higher-level positions in the government as more and more of them completed postgraduate education. By the mid-2000s, four women held ministerial positions, two were elected to the Majlis al-Shura (although both lost their seats in the 2007 election), and eight more were appointed to the Majlis al-Dawlah. Other women made their mark in the business world. In 1999, the first female member joined the board of the chamber of commerce and industry, and the first female chair of the board of directors of an Omani bank took her seat in 2002.

The path for women outside of educated and elite circles has been more difficult, however, although the number of employed women has risen. The 2003 census reported that some 17 percent of employed Omanis were women.[17] Not surprisingly, many women work in traditionally female occupations in education and health care. Of the 36 percent of women in the Omani civil service in 2004 (30,000 persons), 90 percent were employed by either the Ministry of Education or the Ministry of Health. Employed women are more visible in Muscat than elsewhere in Oman. The first target of Omanization was the banking sector and women are now a majority of Omani bank employees. In other examples, many of the first Omanis hired when shops in the capital were required to have at least one Omani on staff were women. Growing numbers of women drivers prompted a growth in the number of female driving instructors who take both men and women as students. In 2001, women were given the right to drive taxis and carry male passengers. Economic pressures send women into the workforce, where illiterate rural Omani women seek low-skill work as cleaners, kitchen help, and hospital orderlies.[18] Despite encouragement from the sultan, however, obstacles to the advancement of women remain in the form of social restraints from traditional families on the one hand, and from religious conservatism with its strict views of women's proper roles in an Islamic society on the other.

Political Rigidity and Slow Steps Toward Participation

The legitimacy of hereditary monarchies continues in the Gulf states, and whether this will persist is a question that involves them all.[19] As these countries develop, it seems almost certain that socioeconomic change will increase popular demands for government accountability and greater formal political participation. The tight circle of support on which rulers most depend—close relatives, extended families, and allies, among other national elites—will necessarily expand. Constitutional frameworks have been adopted by most of the Gulf states, but have not been in place for long enough time to take root. If one can imagine a GCC scale of constitutionalization with Kuwait at the high end and the UAE at the low end, Oman would rank somewhere in the middle.

Oman's political evolution has followed a slow and steady pace over the past thirty-five years.[20] The most significant development has been the growth in administrative capacity from a barely functional minimalist apparatus in 1970 to a fully articulated cabinet system in 2009. While Sultan Qabus has engineered a far more responsive, responsible, and complex system of government than his predecessors, he is unquestionably the ruler of the country and has devolved little responsibility for governance.

Oman's political future depends on the answers to two key questions. The first involves succession. Since 1888, the line of succession has been through the eldest suitable son. This pattern will be broken when the present sultan dies, however, because he has no direct heir. This has led to considerable concern over how to proceed. The Basic Law of 1996, Oman's first constitutional document, says that succession should be a matter of deliberation by the ruling Al Sa'id family (the inner core of the larger Al Bu Sa‘id family). If the family is unable to decide on a ruler after a period of three days, the next step is for the Defense Council to meet and read out the name of the candidate chosen by the late sultan. This unusual approach is both cumbersome and impractical. For example, there is no guarantee that the Defense Council would appoint the late sultan's candidate: it may name a candidate that it prefers or even seize power upon the death of the incumbent sultan to prevent unrest. This possibility is likely to have occurred to Sultan Qabus, who revealed several years after issuing the Basic Law that he had hidden the name of his candidate in various places around the sultanate, increasing the likelihood that his wishes would become known even if the Defense Council were to evade the letter of the law. There are at least three possible developments that could ensue following the death of Sultan Qabus: selection of a successor from the Al Sa'id family, selection of a new imam from outside the ruling family, or establishment of an alternative form of government such as a republic.

Unlike other ruling families in the Gulf, the Al Sa'id family is small. The senior members were never particularly impressive and age is diminishing their ranks. The only suitable senior member is Sayyid Fahd b. Mahmud, the deputy prime minister for council of minister's affairs. Yet he is not well liked—reportedly, even by the sultan. Further disadvantages are that mental illness is a factor in his branch of the family, and, because he is married to a French woman, his children are not full Arabs, an essential requirement.

The next generation of the Al Sa'id family also boasts few suitable candidates. Most of them are concentrated among the sons of Sayyid Tariq b. Taymur, the late uncle of Sultan Qabus and the only prime minister that Oman has ever had. Of Tariq's six sons (he also had a daughter who was briefly married to Sultan Qabus), one is deceased and two are not regarded as suitable. Thus, the likely path to succession lies with one of the remaining three sons: As'ad, the sultan's representative and formerly armor commander in the Sultan's Armed Forces; Shihab, an adviser to the sultan and formerly commander of the Royal Navy of Oman; and Haytham, minister of heritage and culture and formerly secretary-general of the Ministry of Foreign Affairs.

Should the family find itself deadlocked, another possibility would be to select a ruler from outside of the family. This poses considerable problems too, in terms of both legitimacy and practicality. Oman was governed for nearly a millennium by the Ibadi imamate.[21] The imam was elected from the adult, male, Ibadi population and chosen for his religious qualifications and his temporal skills in governance and community defense. Admittedly, the voters in this election were limited to an elite of religious notables and tribal shaikhs and the *bay'a* by the people was largely pro forma. Nevertheless, the legitimacy of the institution was unchallenged. The difficulty in the system lay in finding competent officeholders and rescuing the imamate from dynastic tendencies.

The first Al Bu Sa'id ruler, Ahmad b. Sa'id, claimed the title of imam, but did not have the necessary religious qualifications. His descendants dropped the title after a few generations. Their continued legitimacy as rulers depended essentially on British support when the family and the state in Muscat were weak, and then on the ability of individual rulers to hold the country together, provide prosperity, administer the law, and maintain order. This legitimacy has been enhanced by the present sultan whose emphasis on modernization and development has raised the standard of living for nearly all Omanis.

No other family or individual in Oman can claim the same legitimacy. A number of government ministers hail from Muscat and thus have nontribal backgrounds—for this reason alone they would not be acceptable to the majority of Omanis. While there are numerous examples of capable individuals in the government and armed forces who do come from prominent tribes and shaikhly families, their selection would automatically provoke opposition from other tribes and the opposite tribal confederation. Dhufaris are prominent in government circles and Sultan Qabus is half Dhufari (through his mother, who is from a *jabbali* tribe in the Dhufar mountains). However, a certain amount of tension still exists between northern Omanis and Dhufaris, and few northern Omanis would accept a Dhufari ruler.

The option of establishing a republic has been discussed in Muscat, but such a course of action would also be problematic. First, there is neither tradition nor machinery available to support a move toward republicanism. Such a step would require close collaboration between civilian political figures and senior members of the security forces. Not only is consensus unlikely between them, but such a deliberation would have to take place before the death of Sultan Qabus and he is unlikely to welcome any such move.

Furthermore, Oman both is a highly patriarchal polity and has a highly patriarchal society. Authority is respected not just on the merits of the authority figure, but on his background, lineage, and lines of support. It is difficult to imagine how a presidential figure could emerge naturally. Most Arab republics were established as the result of a military coup and most of their leaders have military or security backgrounds. Not only is Oman's military apolitical, but its leaders belong to the whole panoply of Omani tribes. The selection of, or seizure of power by, any one leader would provoke opposition by other tribes and confederations.

Oman's experiment with political participation so far has been limited and gradual.[22] In common with other Gulf states (and to a greater extent than some, such as Kuwait and Bahrain), rights to political participation have been conferred from the top down. Oman has been cautious in this regard, under the frequently made argument that its people are not ready for serious political change. The motivations behind the sultan's top-down moves are not clear. Desire for formal participation seems to be concentrated among educated Omanis and even they are not very assertive in this regard. External pressures from Western states, particularly the United Kingdom and the United States, may also have played a role in encouraging political opening, but it is likely that the sultan has acted on his own convictions that the country must eventually adopt such changes and gradual steps are the best way to achieve them.

Civil society institutions are weak or nonexistent with the exception of the Oman Chamber of Commerce and Industry. Formal political participation is limited to the establishment of consultative councils. The first such body to be established was the State Consultative Council (SCC) in 1981. As its Arabic name suggests (*al-majlis al-tashiri lil-dawlah*), the SCC was intended to be a forum to provide advice to the government, but only when the government sought advice. All its members were appointed and initially could serve only two terms, reflecting a perhaps laudable desire to bring in new blood but one that also prevents the accumulation of expertise and the acquisition of authority.

In 1991, the SCC was dissolved and replaced by the Majlis al-Shura (Consultative Council). This was a first step in experimenting with elections. The government chose a restricted electorate in each *wilayah* (district) to select three nominees for a seat in the Majlis, from which the government would appoint one. This policy was gradually liberalized. In the 2003 election, when all adult Omanis (men and women) were permitted to stand for office and vote for the candidate of their choice, the winner in each *wilayah* automatically became a member of the Majlis. Another adjustment over the years was to review the decision to make the populations of the *wilayahs* unequal in size. Population disparities across election districts seem to have been intentional from the beginning. Prior to the first appointments to the SCC, an additional four *wilayahs* were created in the sparsely populated central region of Oman (subsequently referred to as al-Wusta). This inflated the proportion of conservative rural members to the SCC, persons who were expected to be progovernment. In 1994, a partial correction was applied by giving two seats to those *wilayahs* whose populations were larger than 30,000. This did not eliminate population disparities, however. For example, each member from the Muscat governorate represents approximately 32,000 Omanis while each member from the Southern governorate (Dhufar) represents about half of that number. The figures for Musandam (1:5,000) and al-Wusta (1:4,250) show an even greater skew. The election of October 2007 was based on the same malapportionment of population across election districts.

In 1997, the Majlis al-Dawlah (State Council) was created. It is an appointed body that initially was made up of forty-one members. It subsequently was expanded to fifty-seven. Composed largely of former senior civil servants, former senior security officers, retired ambassadors, and prominent businessmen, the council appeared to be designed to serve as an appointed counterpoint to the elected Majlis al-Shura. The two bodies together form the Majlis Oman, whose significance seems purely ceremonial. For example, the Majlis Oman convenes when the sultan opens each session.

The creation and expansion of this formal apparatus for political participation should not be allowed to obscure basic facts about politics in the sultanate. It cannot be emphasized too strongly that Oman remains a patriarchal and hierarchical state. That is, the sultan plays a dominant, central role. All significant decisions are referred to him and all policies emerge from the Royal Office, often without advance warning, generally without explanation, and out of an almost totally opaque process. Cabinet meetings are largely pro forma photo opportunities and are not always chaired by the sultan. The appointment of ministers and other senior officials can sometimes be described as whimsical; no public review or explanation is ever given for the sultan's choice.

Once appointed, however, a minister has full control over his ministry and is answerable only to the sultan. Ministries compete for scarce resources and ascendancy on the list of national priorities. Success comes when a minister is permitted a rare audience with the sultan and gains approval for a pet project. In addition, appointment to a ministerial portfolio can be a nearly lifetime sinecure. Some ministries have remained in the hands of the same person for decades. In the late 1990s and early 2000s, a few steps were taken to retire long-serving ministers holding portfolios in information, oil, communications, and heritage and culture, but others (e.g., in the Royal Office and Ministry of Foreign Affairs) continued in office. Even when ministers are superannuated, they may return in another guise. For example, after the long-serving minister of information was replaced in 2001, he was appointed the sultan's adviser for cultural affairs and soon had offices and a staff rivaling that of his former ministry.

The drawbacks of such a system are manifold. First, a ministry becomes inextricably identified with the personality of its minister. Its policies, organization, strength, and dynamism reflect his character and personality. Ministries with long-serving ministers often acquire undersecretaries and directors-general from the same tribe or region as the minister. As time goes on, they become more secretive because public scrutiny could expose errors, incompetence, or, in some cases, corruption. Successive ministers of land affairs, responsible for allocating residential and commercial land to citizens, were abruptly removed in the 1980s because the ministers and their senior staff were found to be corrupt.

While formal political participation in Oman has enjoyed a limited expansion, informal participation remains nearly as proscribed as ever. The media—newspapers, magazines, radio, and television—do not feature debates or commentary on political issues, or publish "letters to the editor" or editorial pieces. Other likely fora for discussion of current issues, such as the Graduates' Club, are either moribund or eschew such a role. A round of mass arrests in 1994 apparently was sparked by informal gatherings of relatives and friends to complain about the course of government. A self-described Omani human rights activist who spoke to international news media regarding another round of arrests in 2005 was himself detained, as was an outspoken female former member of the Majlis al-Shura who was sentenced to one and a half years in jail. A professor at Sultan Qabus University who overstepped boundaries in his outspokenness was dismissed in November 2005, and action was taken in 2008 against bloggers and the online site Sablah on similar grounds.

One might well ask whether the restricted political climate in Oman is likely to encourage political opposition, and, if so, from what quarter or quarters. Without a doubt, Islamist orientations have swept much of the Arab world, and the more extreme expressions of this political trend have attracted global attention. While many Islamists are primarily concerned with personal religiosity and social values, political Islam is prominent in the political arena in the Gulf as elsewhere. Overall, however, perhaps because Oman remains a socially conservative country that has undergone less social change than its neighbors, Islamism seems to have less appeal.

A rare exception to the absence of political Islamism in Oman occurred in 1994, when the government questioned or detained perhaps as many as a thousand individuals, arresting some 135 who were tried and convicted of subversion in a special state security court. In his National Day speech of that year, the sultan unambiguously branded the movement as Islamist and declared that the country would not accept such behavior or beliefs. Despite the sultan's categorization, however, considerable doubt was expressed that the people detained were part of an organized Islamist group or movement. Some were clearly not Islamists and there was no evidence of clandestine organization. One reason why the sultan might have seen these persons as constituting an Islamist threat appears to have been a warning from Egyptian president Husni Mubarak, made on a visit to Oman, that there had been contact including financial transfers between some Omanis and the Egyptian Ikhwan al-Muslimin. In addition, some of those arrested had tried to organize a *khayriyah* (Islamic charitable society) in conjunction with counterparts in Dubai. Observers noting the large number of Sunnis among those detained or arrested opined that it was a reaction against Ibadi oppression. This simply is not credible. First, there is no such thing as Ibadi oppression: Ibadis and Sunnis in Oman do not have sectarian grievances. Second, so many Sunnis were involved because there was a high proportion of Dhufaris and people from Sur, where the proportion of Sunnis in the population is higher than elsewhere in Oman. Their participation is not surprising because both areas were among the last to be integrated fully into the sultanate, and their inhabitants are known for their more direct manner and words than other Omanis.

One unresolved historical precedent for the Omani state is the vacant imamate. A renascent imamate existed in interior Oman from the early twentieth century in counterpoint to and autonomous from the sultanate. The death of a respected imam in 1954 and his replacement by a weak figurehead dominated by his brother and a tribal shaikh, who solicited the controversial assistance of Saudi Arabia and Egypt, eventually resulted in the restoration of the interior to the sultan's control and the permanent exile of the imam to Saudi Arabia. Since the 1970s, the top religious figure in the country has been the mufti, a position created by and subservient to the sultan. Undoubtedly some sentiment remains in Oman, particularly in the Ibadi areas of the interior, for the restoration of the imamate. It is impossible to judge the seriousness of this sentiment. The arrest and trial in early 2005 of thirty-one Omanis on charges of seeking to disrupt the state and restore the imamate did not, in fact, throw much light on the situation. It seems reasonable to conclude that an active movement to restore the imamate is not likely to develop as long as the sultan and the sultanate government continue to satisfy the basic demands of the population. Of course, the current quiescence could evaporate if oil revenues fall, the numbers of unemployed youth rise, or the disappearance of Sultan Qabus from the scene sparks widespread uncertainty about the future.

There remains the possibility of an emergence of liberal opposition. While the term "liberal" in this context is not accurate, it seems preferable to calling such a movement secular. The heyday of secular antiestablishment ideologies in Oman occurred during the 1960s and 1970s. It is associated with the emergence in the north of a small opposition movement of students and émigrés influenced by Arab nationalist and socialist ideas and, in Dhufar in the south, the evolution of a nationalist rebellion into a Marxist-dominated front. The last remnants of the first faded away with the accession of Sultan Qabus. The second ended after a hard-fought war in the defection of all but a small number of hard-core activists from the front, the integration of Dhufar into the sultanate, and the extension of the fruits of oil income to all Dhufaris, including former rebels.

While it is possible that a liberal opposition might emerge in the near future, it is unlikely to be Marxist or Arab socialist in orientation. Rather it might be built by disaffected graduates who are liberal in the sense of supporting and advocating laissez-faire economics and participatory government. Their approach and goal probably would be oriented to reform and would open up the existing system rather than overthrow it. If such a movement should develop, it would form Oman's first loyal opposition. Yet despite continued political quiescence on the surface, murmurs of dissatisfaction with misdirected government spending, the stranglehold of a small elite over politics and commerce, a pattern of corruption among some members of that elite, and the state's external alliances are slowly spreading. This trend undoubtedly will continue with the emergence of a better-educated, more informed, and more assertive Omani citizenry.

An Objective and Inclusive Foreign Policy

Oman's foreign policy through the past few decades is noteworthy for its evenhandedness and astuteness.[23] This is all the more remarkable when the country's situation in 1970 on the eve of the present sultan's accession is considered. Oman was only a few years removed from a struggle for control of the interior in which Saudi Arabia and Egypt had backed the imamate. Elements of that conflict regrouped in Iraq, which offered its assistance to overthrow the old sultan. In the southern region of Dhufar, a major rebellion was in full swing, directed by a Marxist front supported by the Soviet Union, China, and a newly independent South Yemen. The government called on Britain, Jordan, and Iran for help, but the old sultan, Sa'id b. Taymur, had kept the country in virtual isolation. He refused to join either the Organization of Petroleum Exporting Countries (OPEC) or the

Organization of Arab Petroleum Exporting Countries (OAPEC) and effectively was barred from membership in the Arab League and United Nations. The only two countries with resident diplomatic representation in Muscat were Britain and India. An isolated Oman was clearly a vulnerable Oman.

Thirty-five years later, Oman's foreign affairs are a virtual model of pragmatism. Dissidents who had fled abroad during the 1950s and 1960s have returned, and many have assumed important positions in the government. Reconciliation also marked the government's attitude toward former foes from the uprising in the south who also were welcomed back into normal life. Step by step, relations have been repaired or started fresh with all of Oman's neighbors. Membership in major international bodies has been secured, and Oman has achieved at least correct or better relations with all regional and great powers.

Foremost among Oman's foreign policy goals is preservation of international security. For this, Oman has relied principally on Britain and the United States. Throughout the twentieth century, Omani rulers looked to Britain for support and protection. London played a fundamental role in creating Oman's first proper armed forces in 1958 and provided the necessary manpower and military assistance to bring the war in Dhufar to an end. When Britain relinquished its role in the region after its political and military withdrawal from the Gulf in 1971, Oman turned to the United States. An agreement permitting US use of Omani military installations, including as prepositioning sites for stockpiles of arms and ammunition, was signed in 1985 and has been renewed at five-year intervals. Oman opened its facilities to the United States as part of its contribution to the Kuwait War of 1990–1991 and played a similar, although less overt role, during the Iraq War that began in 2003.

On a regional level, the cornerstone of Omani policy has been to strengthen relations with its neighbors in the Arabian Peninsula. Oman was a founding member of the Gulf Cooperation Council in 1981 and generally has tried to remain above the spats that have marked relations between other members of the organization. Oman's history as a mediator in regional disputes and its preferred position in the neutral middle of contentious issues have worked in its favor in both multilateral GCC activities and bilateral relations with each of its fellow GCC members. The sultanate has supported closer coordination of GCC efforts, such as the establishment of a common tariff structure and the elimination of government subsidies to industries that export goods across the frontiers of GCC members. It has, however, opted to remain out of the adoption of a Gulf currency. At the same time, and like the four other small GCC members, it is wary of moving too quickly toward integration inasmuch as that inevitably would strengthen Saudi dominance.

Oman also established diplomatic relations with South Yemen in 1982, a country with which it had nearly gone to war a few years earlier. It expanded on those relations with the merged Republic of Yemen in 1990 and after. Although relatively sympathetic to the south during the 1993 Yemeni civil war, Oman remained aloof from the fray and quickly resumed its budding relations with Sanaa once the war ended. Oman also has signed border treaties with all neighbors.

From the 1960s to the mid-1970s, Oman and Iraq were adversaries. The Baathist regime in Baghdad played host to Omani opposition groups and gave assistance to those seeking to overthrow the government. As part of its general policy of reconciliation, Oman established diplomatic relations with Iraq in 1976 and continued to remain on a correct footing for some time. It was neutral during the Iran-Iraq War and prevented a furtive Iraqi attempt to launch an air strike on Iran from Omani territory during the tanker war phase of that conflict. Oman condemned the Iraqi invasion of Kuwait, but did not break off diplomatic relations with Iraq even though its troops had participated in the 1991 liberation of Kuwait and suffered some casualties. Diplomatic relations continued through the sanctions period, although the two countries had few substantive issues in common.

Inevitably, Oman was affected by the Iraq War, just as it had been by the Kuwait War. Directly, Oman served as a staging post for US and British forces bound for Iraq, as it had done in 1990–1991, but Omani troops were not part of the anti-Iraq coalition in 2003 as they had been in 1991. This reflects a major difference between the two wars from Oman's perspective. There was full official and widespread popular support for the Kuwait War but, even though the government of Oman cooperated fully with US requirements for the Iraq War, popular opinion in Oman as elsewhere in the Gulf coalesced against the invasion. Despite being deeply apprehensive about the George W. Bush administration's preparations to invade Iraq, Oman quietly permitted US and British use of its military facilities and muzzled domestic critics. But above all, it should be kept in mind that Muscat is about as far from Kuwait and Iraq as Milwaukee is from Washington and Madrid is from London. While concern is evident in Oman about developments in Iraq, it remains muted.

Oman has a long history of ties to Iran, dating back to Persian occupation of the country in the pre-Islamic period, but relations during the modern period date only from the early years of Sultan Qabus on the throne. The change was marked by the first meeting between the sultan and the shah at the 1971 celebrations in Persepolis, and by the shah's subsequent provision of military assistance to Oman in the Dhufar War. The last Iranian soldiers did not depart from Oman until shortly after the 1979 Iranian Revolution, but relations between the two countries remained civil, more so than those between Iran and the other GCC states. The Iran-Iraq War presented bilateral challenges on those occasions when Iran's Revolutionary Guards attacked shipping in Omani territorial waters near the Strait of Hormuz and were challenged by Omani coastal patrols. But this did not produce a break between the two neighbors, and Oman helped broker the late 1990s thaw in Saudi-Iranian relations.

The desire to remain neutral in foreign policy and open to all parties has not abated. Relations with Iraq have continued into the period after Saddam Hussein and have remained fraternal, if not enthusiastic, with the new regime. Official ties continue with Iran despite growing Western displeasure with Iran following the election of Mahmud Ahmedinezhad and in response to Iran's drive to acquire nuclear technology. There are no significant disputes with fellow GCC members and relations have steadily improved with the neighboring UAE. Oman's security relationship with the United States has strengthened. The US government has seen little need to pressure the sultanate on domestic policy given the country's gradual liberalization, the absence of any significant Islamist extremist presence, and, perhaps most of all, because of the sultanate's strategic value to Washington.

Oman After Oil

A strong advantage of the meteoric rise in oil prices in the first decade of the twenty-first century was that it both allows increases in needed government spending and, more importantly, offers an opportunity to augment the State General Reserve Fund. The reserve is intended as a cushion during the transition from oil dependency to the time when oil income will cease. Continued liberalization of the economy, membership in the World Trade Organization since 2000, the privatization of public sector entities, and competitive adjustments to ensure Oman's participation in the global economy are other well-intended and necessary steps toward economic sustainability. But much also depends on taking a broader view of sustainability through steps such as reducing water consumption, lowering the rate of population growth, and improving education.

Oman's economic future is likely to require sacrifices and, somewhere along the line, a politically difficult step toward redistribution of income. Other equally difficult political adjustments may also be necessary. The question of succession will be resolved one way or another, probably along the course of least resistance. With luck, a capable close relative of the sultan will take over the reins of government and continue his pragmatic approach. Oman's cautious political liberalization is likely to continue, pushed by rising expectations among Omanis. The desire to have some say in the decisionmaking process is increasing among widening circles of citizens, and a younger generation, poor and jobless, is growing restless.

Notes

1. World Bank, Technical Cooperation Unit, Country Department IV, Middle East and North Africa Region, *Sultanate of Oman: Sustainable Growth and Economic Diversification,* Report no. 12199-OM (Washington, DC, May 31, 1994), p. 115; Sultan Kamal Abdurredha, "Effective Water Management Plan Needed," *Oman Daily Observer*, March 11, 1995.

2. World Bank, *World Development Indicators* (Washington, DC, April 2007), http://ddp-ext.worldbank.org. See also Alasdair Drysdale, "Population Dynamics and Birth Spacing in Oman," *International Journal of Middle East Studies* 42 (2010): 123–144.

3. Sultanate of Oman, Ministry of National Economy, *Statistical Yearbook 2008*, Muscat, 2008, www.moneoman.gov.om.

4. Whitehead Consulting Group, *Economic Survey of Oman 1972* (London: Harold Whitehead, 1972).

5. Sultanate of Oman, Ministry of National Economy, *Final Results of 2003 National Census*, Muscat, 2004, www.moneoman.gov.om.

6. Sultanate of Oman, Ministry of National Economy, *Statistical Yearbook 2003*, Muscat, 2004, www.moneoman.gov.om.

7. World Bank, Technical Cooperation Unit, Country Department IV, Middle East and North Africa Region, *Sultanate of Oman: Sustainable Growth and Economic Diversification*, Report no. 12199-OM (Washington, DC, May 31, 1994), pp. 115–116.

8. Ibid., pp. ix–x.

9. Sultanate of Oman, Ministry of National Economy, *Statistical Yearbook 2005*, Muscat, 2005, www.moneoman.gov.om; Economist Intelligence Unit, Oman Country Report, March 2007.

10. *Khaleej Times*, June 14, 2007.

11. Reuters, May 25, 2009.

12. *Gulf States Newsletter*, no. 872, March 5, 2010.

13. As of 2010, the Blue City project was in serious financial trouble becuase sales were far below projections.

14. Sultanate of Oman, *Statistical Yearbook 2008*.

15. Fredrik Barth, *Sohar: Culture and Society in an Omani Town* (Baltimore: Johns Hopkins University Press, 1983); Unni Wikan, *Behind the Veil in Arabia: Women in Oman* (Baltimore: Johns Hopkins University Press, 1982); Christine Eickelman, *Women and Community in Oman* (New York: New York University Press, 1984); Jörg Janzen, *Nomads in the Sultanate of Oman: Tradition and Development in Dhofar* (Boulder: Westview, 1986); Dawn Chatty, "Women Working in Oman: Individual Choice and Cultural Constraints," *International Journal of Middle East Studies* 32, no. 2 (2000): 249–250; Corien Hoek, *Shifting Sands: Social-Economic Development in al-Sharqiyah Region, Oman* (Nijmegen: Nijmegen University Press, 1998); Dawn Chatty and J. E. Peterson, "Oman," in *Countries and Their Cultures*, vol. 3, eds. Melvin Ember and Carol R. Ember (New York: Macmillan Reference USA, 2001), pp. 1681–1689; J. E. Peterson, "Oman's Diverse Society: Northern Oman," *Middle East Journal* 58, no. 1 (2004): 32–51; J. E. Peterson, "Oman's Diverse Society: Southern Oman," *Middle East Journal* 58, no. 2 (2004): 254–269.

16. Sultanate of Oman, *Statistical Yearbook 2008.*

17. Peterson, "Oman's Diverse Society"; Sultanate of Oman, *Statistical Yearbook 2005.*

18. Chatty, "Women Working in Oman."

19. Michael Herb, *All in the Family: Absolutism, Revolution, and Democratic Prospects in the Middle Eastern Monarchies* (Albany: SUNY Press, 1999); J. E. Peterson, "Succession in the States of the Gulf Cooperation Council," *Washington Quarterly* 24, no. 4 (2001): 173–186.

20. Ian Skeet, *Oman: Politics and Development* (London: Macmillan, 1992); Calvin H. Allen and W. Lynn Rigsbee II, *Oman Under Qaboos: From Coup to Constitution, 1970–1996* (London: Frank Cass, 2000); J. E. Peterson, "Oman: Three and a Half Decades of Change and Development," *Middle East Policy* 6, no. 2 (2004): 125–137.

21. Dale F. Eickelman, "From Theocracy to Monarchy: Authority and Legitimacy in Inner Oman, 1935–1957," *International Journal of Middle East Studies* 17, no. 1 (1985): 3–24; John C. Wilkinson, *The Imamate Tradition of Oman*, Cambridge Middle East Library (Cambridge: Cambridge University Press, 1987).

22. See Abdullah Juma Alhaj, "The Political Elite and the Introduction of Political Participation in Oman," *Middle East Policy* 7, no. 3 (2000): 97–110; Abdullah Juma Alhaj, "The Politics of Participation in the Gulf Cooperation Council States: The Omani Consultative Council," *Middle East Journal* 50, no. 4 (1996): 559–571; Dale F. Eickelman, "Kings and People: Oman's State Consultative Council," *Middle East Journal* 38, no. 1 (1984): 51–84; J. E. Peterson, *The Arab Gulf States: Steps Toward Political Participation* (New York: Praeger, 1988); J. E. Peterson, "The Arab Gulf States: Further Steps Towards Political Participation," Gulf Papers (Dubai: Gulf Research Center, 2006); and Jeremy Jones and Nicholas Ridout, "Democratic Development in Oman," *Middle East Journal* 59, no. 3 (2005): 376–392.

23. Joseph A. Kechichian, *Oman and the World: The Emergence of an Independent Foreign Policy* (Santa Monica, CA: RAND, 1995).

6

Political Reform in Qatar

Jill Crystal

QATAR'S RULER, Shaikh Hamad al-Thani, came to power in 1995—undemocratically, but not unprecedentedly—by overthrowing his father in a bloodless coup. Yet once established in office, he initiated a number of prodemocratic reforms: holding elections, enfranchising women, lifting press restraints, and introducing a new constitution with an impressive array of civil and political rights. While heralded in the West as prodemocratic breakthroughs, these reforms, initiated during what we now know to have been a brief window of regional calm between two wars in the Gulf, were instead tactical responses to uncertainties surrounding the transition to power. These included a concern that portions of Qatar's large ruling family, along with its clientele base, might rally around the amir's deposed father—a concern realized in 1996 when just such a counter-coup attempt was launched. Rather than the first step in a larger reconceptualization of the state, reform initially was a strategy to head off potential unrest connected to taking power in this manner. In this chapter, I analyze the forces driving those reforms, then and now, and discuss the prospects for their consolidation.

Political Reform

Although hardly a democracy, Qatar has never been a repressive state. It has been ruled since independence by a series of relatively benign autocrats who have never tried to impose their will much beyond the palace (and, indeed, have often been unable to impose their will within the palace). Even in the 1950s and 1960s, when public protest and demonstrations were common, opponents of the regime generally were not treated harshly. Dissent in more recent times has been muted, but not muzzled. After the Gulf War, Qatar and the other Gulf states experienced some popular pressure for political liberalization. In 1992, dozens of prominent Qataris presented a petition to the amir calling for an elected council with real legislative and investigatory powers and for a constitution to guarantee democratic freedoms. Their demands were neither embraced nor rejected with force; they were simply ignored. Even before the current wave of reform, Qatar did not rank among the more repressive states of the region: reports of torture were rare, political prisoners were always few in number. Over the years, Western (and sometimes even Arab) human rights groups occasionally protested modest abuses. The police and military, while responsive to the amir, did not typically intervene in the political process. From time to time, the press did politely question specific government policies, but generally avoided the more explicitly political issues of ruling family politics.

But if Qataris have never experienced great repression, neither have they had much input in political decisionmaking until recently. With Amir Hamad's accession, however, a series of reforms raised the possibility of change. In 1995, the amir abolished the Information Ministry and, with it, press censorship. In 1996 he established Al-Jazeera, a satellite television station that soon gained international fame (and notoriety) for its critical coverage of politics around the globe (most notably for its coverage of the Iraq War and its airing of Osama bin Laden tapes; see also Chapter 10). In 1998, the amir took the first steps toward representative democracy by allowing members of the Chamber of Commerce to elect their own board, which previously had been appointed.

Two other reforms received much international attention. First, in March 1999 (and again in April 2003 and in April 2007), Qatar held relatively free and open elections for a twenty-nine-member Central Municipal Council with full suffrage for adult Qatari citizens. The amir also promised to hold future elections for thirty of the forty-five members of a new advisory council that would have some legislative responsibility. Second, in 1999, the amir established a constitutional committee that submitted a draft constitution in 2002. In April 2003, Qatar's new constitution was adopted by popular referendum, replacing the provisional constitution drawn up at independence in 1970. The new constitution called for the creation of a new partially elected legislative body; granted universal suffrage to adult Qataris; and guaranteed protections of civil, political, and social rights.

Other reforms soon followed. In October 2004, long-promised court reform occurred when Qatar's dual court system (comprised by *sharia* and secular courts) was finally unified, a move welcomed by local attorneys, who hoped it would end confusion and consequent delays regarding where to file particular cases.[1] In 2005 a new (*sharia*-based) personal status law that would apply to all residents was drafted, standardizing practice and limiting previously broad judicial discretion. The law would also expand women's rights in some areas, notably regarding child custody.[2]

In early 2004 the government announced sweeping changes in the educational system, promising to introduce and maintain more rigorous standards (with more testing), but also granting schools much more flexibility, in part with the stated goal of underpinning the new democratic process.[3] English-language instruction was increased. Religious instruction decreased. The amir also inaugurated a new Education City and attracted branches of several elite US universities, including Cornell's Medical School, Carnegie Mellon, and Texas A&M. Even earlier, in 2003, the amir established a committee on human rights. That year the government also appointed Shaikha bint Ahmad al-Mahmud as minister of education, making her the first woman to hold a ministerial post. The amir also named another woman, Shaikha Abdallah al-Misnad, to head Qatar University. Women were permitted to study in the college of engineering. The following year, another woman, Aisha al-Mannai, was named head of the law department at the university.

In May 2004, a new labor law was introduced granting Qatari workers a host of rights, including the right to form associations and to engage in collective bargaining.[4] In public speeches, the amir continued to press for political reform throughout the region. He admonished other rulers and was particularly caustic about their using the Israeli-Palestinian conflict as an excuse for inaction on reform.[5] For his efforts, the amir was hailed by many in the West as a progressive leader on the cutting edge of political reform in the region.

Despite Western encomiums, it is perhaps useful also to note what the amir's reforms did not accomplish. To begin with, they were not quite so pathbreaking as they initially appeared. Upon coming to power in a coup of his own in 1972, the current amir's father and predecessor also had consolidated his hold on the government with an initial blast of reform, including a provisional constitution and promises of democratic elections, only to revert to more autocratic ways once a measure of control over his opponents was established. Moreover, the current reforms, for all their fanfare, are still quite limited in scope. Despite promises, the amir has not yet held elections for a legislative body. Article 77 of the constitution calls for elections but, if held, they would be used to choose only thirty of the forty-eight members of a proposed council that would have limited legislative power. The elected Municipal Council's voice is advisory only. Its purview remains modest, restricted to advising the minister of municipal affairs and agriculture on those matters (not a large sector of Qatar's economy) and to overseeing implementation of decisions already made at the ministerial level. Permits are still required for public gatherings and demonstrations, and the government grants them reluctantly. Nongovernmental organizations (NGOs) require government permission to operate, and most groups, from political parties to women's organizations and human rights groups, have had requests for licenses refused. Even under the new constitution, the amir continues to rule with few restraints: he can override legislation, rule by decree, and even dissolve elected bodies. Despite the lifting of formal censorship, considerable self-censorship remains and the government continues to close newspapers for publishing critical articles. In March 2002, the government promulgated a new press law that allowed the imprisonment of journalists for their writings.[6] And while the outspoken Al-Jazeera is willing to take on the United States it all but ignores domestic Qatari politics.[7] The constitution may be a fine document, but it remains largely aspirational. It remains to be seen whether, for example, institutions guaranteeing the constitutional review of legislation that the new constitution envisions are in fact created. Until now, Qatar has stood out as an anomaly in the region, with no agency responsible for such review.[8]

The state security forces were merged into one in June 2003, and it remains under the direct control of the amir. Those who displease the ruler have little recourse; the legal system does not protect them from state abuse in any systematic way. For example, in May 2001 an appeals court affirmed a lower court's death sentence of nineteen people, eighteen of them Qatari, for their involvement in the 1996 counter-coup attempt. In 2005 the government summarily stripped some 5,000 Qatari members of a clan from the al-Murra tribe of their citizenship in connection with the involvement of some clan members in the 1996 counter-coup attempt, asserting that they possessed Saudi as well as Qatari citizenship. This decision was later reversed, but not as a result of a judicial process. Instead, it was reversed by fiat, after the rulers of Qatar and Saudi Arabia effected a reconciliation in 2008. Following the reconciliation, Saudi Arabia also allowed Al-Jazeera to return and it then became less critical in its coverage of Saudi Arabia.

Perhaps more disturbingly, the government's reforms generated little debate. Although similar reform efforts elsewhere in the region (in Kuwait and even in Saudi Arabia), whether related to women's rights, elections, or economic liberalization, have generated substantial public debate, Qatar's reforms have been introduced without discussion. While silence may suggest consent, fear is also a possibility. The few who have questioned specific policies have been quickly silenced. For example, in 1998 in an unusual display of public dissent, the Islamist Abd al Rahman bin Umar al-Nuaimi presented a petition to the amir signed by eighteen others, which objected to government policies regarding women and alcohol. The government responded not with dialogue, but with detention. In the words of one observer, the reforms are "photogenic":[9] they look good to the Western press and media but, on closer examination, are less substantive than they first appear. Why, then, have they occurred?

Internal Pressures for Reform

In Qatar, political reforms have not been instituted in response to visible public demands as they have elsewhere in the Gulf. While the Qatari public may welcome such reforms, they have neither clamored for them nor argued about them as have their counterparts in Kuwait, Bahrain, and Saudi Arabia. Dissent outside the family has been tepid. A few liberals have called for political liberalization. Some Islamists have called for greater orthopraxy, although even their numbers thus far have been few. This is either because the amir has not tolerated much dissent or because he has been supportive generally of the Islamic establishment (creating, for example, a new Ministry of Awqaf in 1992, in the turbulent period following the Gulf War, and allowing it more influence over the judicial system than before).

If reform has been a response to perceived public demands, it has been an anticipatory tactical act, embraced in the hope that reform would tame the opposition; marginalize the more radical elements by eliminating any claim that only violence can bring real change; and, should reform fail, reveal the identity of his opponents to the ruler. The reforms remind Qataris that those who can vote are privileged, different from those many expatriates who cannot enjoy the political or the economic privileges of nationals. This is particularly important today when foreigners carry a powerful transnational message of political dissent (just as in the 1950s when a transnational Arab nationalism connected successfully with local labor-based dissent). Perhaps the primary driving force behind these reforms was the amir's need to consolidate power at home and abroad after acquiring it in a coup. While he seemingly had the support of the bulk of his family, pockets of resistance nevertheless remained; the foiled counter-coup in 1996, led by some family members, apparently with support from Saudi Arabia and other Gulf states, is evidence of this.

External Pressures for Reform

Another source of pressure for reform came from outside Qatar. Qatar's ruler is keenly aware of reforms in neighboring states. Certainly, Shaikh Hamad did not begin his term in office particularly receptive to pressures from regional states, notably Saudi Arabia, that had backed domestic elements seeking to reverse his accession to power. The inauguration of Al-Jazeera that same year did little to win the affection of neighboring governments. In fact, Qatar's history of disputes with Saudi Arabia was a factor prompting Qatar to launch the station. Yet Gulf rulers have a long history of adopting (and adapting) each other's political reforms. As Michael Herb argues, the particular form of monarchical power in the Gulf pioneered in Kuwait, complete with sovereign ministries (specific powerful ministries guaranteed to members of the ruling family), was quickly adopted by all the neighbors.[10] Kuwait also pioneered the use of elected bodies on a significant scale, and these too were copied throughout the Gulf. Competition plays a role in facilitating political reform. Qatar and Bahrain compete with each other in political liberalization as they do in other arenas. The extension of suffrage to women was perhaps partly an element of that monarchical competition: Qatar was unwilling to expand contestation, but it could outdo Kuwait in expanding representation. It might not allow as much debate over its own policies as some other states, but it could, through Al-Jazeera, give the appearance of allowing substantial debate (and tweak its neighbors). Qatar's grant of women's suffrage in turn placed more pressure on the Kuwaiti government to ultimately do the same, just as Al-Jazeera paved the way for Al-Arabiyya and other stations. Elections throughout the Gulf likewise put pressure on Saudi Arabia to hold elections and, finally, on the United Arab Emirates (UAE), which had been the last holdout. Reforms in each state raise the bar for the others.

If regional pressure to expand participation was one factor pushing liberalization, another was pressure from outside the region, especially from the United States. At least at the rhetorical level, the United States has been a fervent, if recent, convert to political reform in the Middle East. The US prodemocracy initiative embraces a cluster of related issues, including elections, promotion of civil society, expansion of women's rights, educational reform, and open markets. After September 11, 2001, the George W. Bush administration set forth an ambitious plan to foster democratic transition throughout the region. It began in December 2002 with the Middle East Partnership Initiative, which led to the Greater Middle East Initiative. The latter, launched at the Group of 8 summit at Sea Island, Georgia, in June 2004, had the goal of fostering political, economic, and social reform through dialogue and a series of US-backed projects. Interestingly, Qatar was not invited to the summit owing to tensions with the United States over Al-Jazeera's reporting of the Iraq War. Reinvented in more modest form after an unenthusiastic response in the Middle East and Europe and renamed the Broader Middle East and North Africa Initiative, it was presented at the Forum for the Future in Rabat, Morocco, in December 2004. Its aim was more limited than the aim of the Greater Middle East Initiative, to bring together Arab foreign and finance ministers and Group of 8 representatives to examine areas for potential reform. At the second Forum for the Future, held in Manama, Bahrain, in 2005, the Egyptian delegation torpedoed its now considerably scaled-down goals of fostering civil society and encouraging NGOs.

While much of the region was hesitant about embracing this new presidential approach, Qatar was more responsive both to these specific initiatives and to US pressure to liberalize, largely owing to the close relationship it had built up with the United States. The relationship between the two states deepened as the United States sought, after the Gulf War and particularly after 9/11, to extricate itself from its destabilizing presence in Saudi Arabia. In December 2002, the United States and Qatar signed an agreement to upgrade Qatari military bases in the likely event of war in Iraq. In 2004 the United States moved forces stationed in Saudi Arabia to Qatar, which became the command center for the Iraq War. Qatar, for its part, had its own interests in this arrangement: the US air base at al-Udaid was located on disputed territory near the Saudi border. More broadly, the US presence (along with Al-Jazeera) simply gave Qatar a much more visible regional and international presence. But the US presence also made Qatar more susceptible to US pressure for political reform.

Qatar has certainly been vocally responsive to US pressure for democratic openings in the region, urging other Arab states to consider US proposals for democratic reform—a significant gesture in a region where leaders are, with good reason, skeptical of both prodemocratic reforms and US intentions.[11] The Doha declaration, issued in June 2004 at the end of a conference hosted by Qatar University and signed by participants from across the Arab world, called clearly for democratic change. It accused Arab governments of using the Israeli-Palestinian conflict and the Iraq War as an excuse to postpone needed domestic political reform. The declaration affirmed the goal of free and fair elections and called for a transition toward constitutionalism, the extrication of the military from politics, and greater freedom of association for all, along with the abolition of the judicial structures and laws that impede democracy. Not only has the Qatari government hosted and itself called for more democracy, it also has made reforms in apparent response to US pressure.

Some of the reforms introduced in Qatar—notably educational reform; women's suffrage; the public expansion of the political presence of high-profile women, led by the amir's wife; and holding elections—are typical of the kinds of reforms touted by the United States in its public pronouncements. While these are important reforms, one can imagine others less frequently touted by the United States, but often raised by local dissidents. Of equal or greater importance in promoting real democratic openings, they include an unfettered and critical press, reform of the police and security forces, election of a body with genuine legislative responsibilities, budgetary transparency, constitutional review of new legislation, and explicit movement toward constitutional monarchy. Reform in Qatar, however, has largely been in keeping with US government public pronouncements about what Middle East democracy should look like.

One reason for the limited nature of Qatar's efforts is that a broader reform initiative might conflict with other US goals, notably the war on terror. Where the war on terror was concerned, the United States pushed Qatar and its neighbors in a very different direction. The United States has not, for example, pressured Qatar to allow a more vocal local press. Here as elsewhere in the region, the problem lies in the fact that public opinion in Qatar, when openly expressed, is typically and increasingly anti-American. This is due both to US policy vis-à-vis Iraq and the Israeli-Palestinian conflict and to more immediate concerns about delays in getting visas and the required interviews as well as the often rude treatment received by Qataris who once traveled regularly to the United States but now do so in decreasing numbers. The government can please the United States by muting the public criticism flowing from such sentiments, but not without also muting the democratic opening. Indeed, instead of pushing for a free press, the US government has tried to restrain Al-Jazeera. A variety of US officials have complained loudly about Al-Jazeera's reporting on the US presence in Iraq. These concerns heightened dramatically with Al-Jazeera's coverage of the growing insurgency and civilian casualties in Iraq as the US occupation deepened. In April 2004, Secretary of State Colin Powell raised these and other concerns about Al-Jazeera directly with Qatar's foreign minister.[12]

The government proved somewhat responsive to the US complaints: Al-Jazeera's management was changed and, in July 2004, it adopted a new code of ethics. Even so, in August 2004, the US-led Iraqi government closed Al-Jazeera's Baghdad office for a month (extended indefinitely in September 2004), asserting that the station fomented sectarian violence, provided an outlet for terrorists, and encouraged kidnapping by showing hostage footage.[13] In 2005, US pressure led the Qatari government to begin exploring Al-Jazeera's privatization.[14]

When weighing these contradictory pressures, the regime is doubtless mindful of the US tendency to throw its weight where its interests lie, particularly those interests linked to oil and to the war on terror. Expressions of support for democratic reform by the United States have not prevented it from developing close strategic ties with both Egypt (which has been ambivalent if not openly hostile toward US pressure to open its political system) and, more importantly for Qatar, Saudi Arabia, whose democratic opening remains modest. Even though the United States has employed that democratic rhetoric for decades, its de facto policy has always been to favor stability, regardless of regime type, particularly where secure access to oil is a concern. And there is little in US policy to suggest that it is ready to jeopardize its relations with useful authoritarian states in the region. In Qatar, these contradictory signals are resolved by implementing highly visible but modest reforms.

For the amir, there is an additional problem that anti-American sentiments are also present within his unruly family. These include, most disturbingly for the United States, allegations that Shaikh Abdallah bin Khalid al-Thani (who became interior minister in January 2001), known to be sympathetic to the jihadist salafis, helped Al-Qaida members when he was minister for Islamic affairs. He is said to have used both his personal wealth and his ministry's funds to support the mujahidin in Afghanistan and to move funds to Al-Qaida.[15] He was also suspected of harboring Al-Qaida members, including the alleged mastermind of the 9/11 attacks, Khalid Shaikh Mohammad, on his own compound. After the Qatari government was notified in 1996 of the US intent to arrest Khalid Shaikh Mohammad for his connection with the 1993 World Trade Center bombings, he escaped before Federal Bureau of Investigation (FBI) agents arrived because, some suspect, he had been tipped off by al-Thani. The continuing active presence in Qatar of Egyptian Shaikh Yusif al-Qaradawi, head of the London-based International Association of Muslim Scholars and popular TV host, who has condoned attacks on US civilians in Iraq, suggests that the government is not uniformly swayed by US pressure. While al-Qaradawi's presence, like Al-Jazeera's, can in part be explained as an effort by the amir to demonstrate a degree of independence, it may also reflect his inability to control powerful members of his own family, which has been a constant problem for Qatari amirs over the years.

Just as the United States has pushed for political liberalization in the region, it has pressed with perhaps more enthusiasm for economic liberalization. This pressure comes in many forms, the most notable being the Middle East Partnership Initiative, designed to free up the private sector as well as empower civil society and foster democracy through preferential trade agreements, free trade zones, and targeted assistance to the private sector. The official reasoning behind this initiative is that free trade and market reform will lead not only to long-term growth, but also to democratic transition, regional peace, and a reduction in terrorism.

Like the other Gulf states, Qatar has been more receptive than in the past to recent US pressure for economic liberalization and has been open to the idea that economic liberalization will generate faster growth. The amir took power with an agenda of economic reform, eager to deal with the lack of transparency and accountability that had led to corruption on a massive scale and slowed economic growth in the 1980s.[16] One indication of the scope of the problem is that the previous amir left power, taking with him some \$3 billion to \$8 billion in state funds invested abroad. The dispute was eventually settled thanks to the intervention of British courts and Saudi mediators, and most of the money was returned to Qatar.

After that, the amir moved forward with economic reform. He streamlined the energy sector and introduced a significant degree of transparency there. According to Transparency International's 2008 annual survey, Qatar ranked 28 out of 175 countries surveyed, ahead of all the other Middle East states.[17] Some corruption, typically in the form of generous commissions for large government contracts that usually go to members of the ruling family, remains a problem. The amir is hampered in his reform efforts by the limits of his own authority and his inability to rein in the strongest shaikhs (notably his foreign minister, Shaikh Jasim) who have long ruled over semi-autonomous ministerial shaikhdoms. The amir has also not sent clear signals regarding transparency and accountability, having, for example, granted himself the authority in the new constitution (Article 17) to set his own salary.

One of the more important drivers of Qatar's economic liberalization program initially was its need to attract foreign direct investment (FDI) to develop the energy sector. Although Qatar has less oil than its neighbors, its natural gas reserves are the world's third largest, after Russia's and Iran's. Its North Field is the largest single reservoir of natural gas anywhere. After taking power, the amir invited international oil companies to expand oil production, locate and develop new oil fields, invest in advanced oil recovery systems to extend existing fields, and expand production of natural gas. He signed major new liquefied natural gas (LNG) deals with ExxonMobil and ConocoPhillips, and with Shell to build the largest gas to liquid (GTL) plant in the world. Qatar is also planning to build an Energy City to house a spot market for LNG sales (now sold largely through long-term contracts).

As a result of these reforms, Qatar's oil exports more than doubled in a decade, with the additional income largely reinvested in natural gas projects. Qatar, which had deficits until 1999, has experienced the highest real growth rate in the region in recent years, and now earns as much from natural gas as from oil.[18] By 2005 Qatar was, in the words of *The Economist*, a "global gas powerhouse."[19] The astronomical rise in oil and natural gas prices up to 2008 gave Qatar the ability to move forward more rapidly with economic liberalization, but in a more nuanced manner. By 2009 Qatar was, in per capita terms, perhaps the richest country in the world, with a per capita income of $119,500.[20] Unlike in previous periods of price increases, Qatar did not allow complacency to set in and has continued to move forward with many of its reforms. At the same time, the new revenues allowed Qatar, no longer dependent on foreign capital, to proceed more carefully. In 2005, Qatar decided to impose a moratorium on new natural gas projects in the North Field until 2008, which was later extended to 2010 because of concern about Qatar's ability to increase gas output without damaging the reservoir's potential. However, Qatar did open four offshore exploration rounds in 2008. In April 2008, Qatar Petroleum International (QPI, created in 2005 to develop overseas business in energy up- and downstream) began working on an agreement with Russia's Gazprom on joint projects at home and abroad. In the following years QPI bought into exploration projects in

Mauritania, and in 2008 signed an agreement with PetroChina to develop a refinery and petrochemical complex in China. The new revenues have deepened the pockets of Qatar's sovereign wealth fund, the Qatar Fund, managed by the Qatar Investment Authority. While the Qatar Fund has tried to avoid publicizing its investment strategies, according to one report the fund has assets of $60 billion. Its recent investments have included acquiring a 10 percent stake in the London Stock Exchange and a 2 percent stake in Switzerland's second largest bank, Credit Suisse.[21]

The high energy prices, however, also created new problems. Qatar experienced inflation rates far above even the high Gulf Cooperation Council (GCC) average, hitting 25 percent in 2008. That, combined with the falling dollar to which Qatar's currency is pegged, created distress, especially among Qatar's large expatriate population, which saw its real earnings and remittances fall. This led Qatar to consider dropping its dollar peg, as Kuwait had done, and even to consider cutting back on government spending. Rapid growth also led to a housing shortage and, consequently, to rising rents. In February 2008, the government placed a cap on rent increases, but the underlying pressures remained. Rising commodity prices, especially for food, have also been felt by the population. Like the other Gulf states, Qatar has been looking outside the region to establish a secure food supply. To that end, in 2008, Qatar signed an agreement with Sudan to establish a joint holding company to focus on agriculture and animal husbandry.[22]

The amir also embarked on economic liberalization outside the energy sector. In December 2002, the government announced the privatization of all water and electricity generation projects and cautiously welcomed FDI in civil aviation and health care. Qatar also opened up higher education to private, notably US, foreign investment. Where foreign investors were once required to take local partners, they now may own 100 percent of some projects. In 2005, the government partially opened its stock market to foreign investors, allowing them to own up to 25 percent of listed firms. Like the ruler of Dubai, but on a more modest scale, Amir Hamid encouraged Western investment in the tourist sector. In May 2004, he unveiled an ambitious $15 billion plan to turn Qatar into a tourist destination.[23] In 2005, the government also began construction of a new $5.5 billion airport (complete with a separate royal terminal), aiming to rival the current Dubai hub.[24]

Qatar aspires to compete with Bahrain and Dubai as a regional center for financial services. In 2005, the government hired Phillip Thorpe, the regulator fired by Dubai's International Financial Center in a cloud of controversy in 2004.[25] These moves in the direction of economic liberalization were particularly striking in Qatar because so few independent actors were pushing for it. Over the decades, Qatar's indigenous business elite has been replaced by a new economic elite that is economically dependent on and subordinate to the state. The few institutions that aggregate business interests are weak and state-dominated. The Chamber of Commerce exists, but lacks the independence of, for example, its Kuwaiti counterpart. (In 1997, when the business community was first allowed to elect a Chamber of Commerce board, it chose as chair the incumbent shaikh.)

Working with the other GCC states, Qatar has also made impressive strides in the direction of freer movement of goods and services, agreeing on a unified tariff in 2002, ahead of schedule, and going ahead with an agreement in 2004 to move toward monetary union. In October 2004, the GCC states agreed to levy a unified, if modest, value-added tax.[26] Some restrictions on capital movements have been lifted. In 2004 the Doha Securities Market announced it would open to foreign investors, and the government also issued a new labor law that allowed workers a limited right to organize and strike; established equal employment rights for women; and established regulations governing employment contracts, working hours, and maternity and health care. The new labor law also offered businesses a clearer legal framework for employment, but it excluded domestic workers (e.g., drivers and maids) entirely and barred expatriate workers from union activities.

Future Prospects

Economic and political liberalization appeared simultaneously in Qatar, but have now developed independent trajectories. Initially, economic liberalization was driven by several forces. One was the need to attract FDI in order to develop the natural gas sector. Another was the need to shore up public support following a controversial accession to power. The amir did what other autocratic rulers, including his own father, have done upon taking power: buy support for, or at least acquiescence to, reform by offering the national population a bit more money, including making a significant percentage of shares in many downstream projects available at below-market price to Qatari nationals. Yet a third force was external pressure to liberalize, although the amir appears to share the US government's belief that at least a bit more free trade and market-oriented reform will lead to long-term growth. Qatar has thus far handled the dangers of both low and high oil prices (the tendency to set aside economic reforms while high prices last) relatively well. It was better suited than most countries to weather the global financial crisis of 2008–2009. Although growth slowed, the investments in natural gas and rise in gas exports in the years leading up to the crisis gave Qatar a financial cushion. While the government of Qatar is no longer as dependent on external capital owing to high oil prices, it has continued its economic reforms especially in the energy sector, largely because of the success of previous reforms there.

Political reform is a more problematic process. Whether there is a clear link in Qatar, or indeed anywhere, between a more open economy and democratic transition (let alone regional peace and a reduction in terrorism) is far less clear. As Pete Moore and Andrew Schrank point out, the main assumption that guides US policy, that trade will lead to peace and prosperity, is not borne out by history.[27] Trade, they argue, is more likely to underpin than undermine existing political relationships and power-holders. This does appear to be the case in Qatar where ruling family members are best positioned to take advantage of any government-driven economic openings. Qatar's recent political reforms may be the first steps toward more open politics and, ultimately, democracy.

Reforms, introduced for any reason, raise expectations and thereby develop a momentum of their own. This may occur in Qatar. As Elisheva Rosman-Stollman notes, the members of the Municipal Council, once elected, took their positions seriously.[28] They fought for an expansion of their powers, and took complaints to the press. Continued democratization could generate further spillover if, for example, elected representatives and, subsequently, the Qatari population actively push for public debate. If other GCC states continue to open up politically, reforms elsewhere in the Gulf could have a cascade effect. The Kuwaiti government's decision to grant women suffrage is one example, as are the recent elections in the UAE. One scenario that would increase the likelihood of continued democratic opening in Qatar is movement toward greater participation in neighboring states. Historically, this has been a factor accelerating political reform. Qatar's amir might feel encouraged, perhaps even pressured, to expand his experiment in political liberalization if the Kuwaiti system remains lively; if Bahrain, Oman, and the UAE continue their cautious political openings; and, perhaps most importantly, if Saudi Arabia's tentative opening blossoms into real reform.

As long as domestic pressures for reform remain present but modest, gentle (and not unduly heavy-handed) pressure for political reform from the United States continues, and no international dangers emerge to threaten the amir, the next decade could see a gradual expansion of the political liberalization project. Reducing the US presence in the region also could lessen anti-American sentiment, allowing the amir to tolerate more dissent (as long as it did not also embolden radical Islamist opposition, which thus far has been modest in Qatar). Were a withdrawal of US forces from Iraq to be followed by visible diplomatic progress in resolving the Israeli-Palestinian conflict, the amir's responsiveness to US pressure for liberalization would be less objectionable regionally. Historically, the Gulf monarchs have been more open to US pressure on other matters when they felt that the United States was actively trying to resolve the Israeli-Palestinian conflict, even though this issue is not as central to the Gulf states, and certainly not to

Qatar, as it is elsewhere in the Middle East. Should a change in Israeli leadership or position on the conflict occur simultaneously with high-maintenance negotiations, these changes could also contribute to enduring political reform in the region and in Qatar.

A second, more likely, option is that the reform process will stall or even reverse. Qatar's reforms were undertaken as a top-down effort by the amir, driven primarily by a desire to consolidate his own initially shaky position and, to a lesser degree, to accommodate the United States. Having largely served this purpose, they need go no further: the amir has consolidated his rule, and US pressure to expand political participation has abated. It should be remembered that the current amir's now-deposed father had himself come to power in 1972 by deposing his cousin in a coup. He too promised elections and a constitution, but the legitimacy crisis passed with neither promise fulfilled. Moreover, the United States seems satisfied with the limited liberalization thus far and, in any event, ultimately is more concerned with terrorism than with democracy. Should oil and natural gas prices drop, contestation over the distribution of scarce resources would most likely prompt the closing of any institution where these issues could openly be debated. This is particularly likely in Qatar where the combination of a large, demanding ruling family and weak family discipline would likely leave little income from oil and gas exports for the rest of the population. When oil prices fell in the 1980s, the government initially engaged in deficit spending in an effort to defer austerity measures it feared might provoke political unrest. Ultimately, freezes and cutbacks in state expenditures, reductions in state employment, and the delay of several major development projects were introduced. But ruling family allowances were not cut and political debate was not allowed.

Yet if low prices threaten democratic openings, high oil prices do not necessarily fuel them. High oil and natural gas prices and better management of the energy sector have strengthened the current amir's financial position and allowed him to consolidate his rule. In 2003, he announced the appointment of a new heir apparent, his son Tamim (replacing another son, Shaikh Jasim). Amir Hamid settled his financial differences with his deposed father and his political differences with opponents to his rule (by jailing those involved in the 1996 counter-coup attempt), after which he felt sufficiently comfortable to allow his father to return to the country in October 2004 for a funeral. Once power was consolidated, the amir's interests in democratic opening appeared to wane. The amir can continue to hold elections for bodies with little real authority. Even elections for a partly appointed and partly elected legislative council (thus far, repeatedly delayed) could proceed as long as the council demanded no real authority and did not attempt to interpellate al-Thani ministers or raise troubling questions about the role of women, economic liberalization, Islam and politics, or other issues elsewhere debated at length. The new constitution can remain aspirational, generating no new institutions. As its irrelevance becomes obvious, public interest in political liberalization, already low, could decline further. The amir might calculate that the US government would raise few objections, particularly if he continued to pay lip service to liberalization. He could appoint a few more women, even if from his own family, to highly visible if hardly central positions, moves likely to be noted with approval by the Western press. Until the US government is willing to call for democratic elections in Saudi Arabia (perhaps when the war on terror is won), Qatar's amir need fear no genuine pressure from the United States. Existing reforms need not be rolled back completely, but the liberalization process could halt where it is and ultimately wither from lack of interest.

Should the regional situation deteriorate, the reforms might halt more precipitously. Qatar's foreign minister has already expressed his fears that Iraq is becoming a fertile ground for terrorists.[29] Were Islamist violence to appear in Qatar, it would certainly cause the amir to rethink his prodemocratic opening. Unlike Saudi Arabia and Kuwait, Qatar has thus far been largely spared such attacks, so it is not yet clear how they would reverberate in the political system. In February 2004, the government reacted swiftly to the assassination in Doha of former Chechen president Salim Khan Yandarbiyev (killed in a car bombing). As violence hits closer to home, as it did in March 2005,[30] the government might respond with still more strength. As with Saudi Arabia before 2003, there are reports that the government of Qatar is paying large sums in protection money to Al-Qaida in return for a promise to spare it from terrorist attacks.[31] Should a serious attack occur in Qatar, the government might respond differently. The jihadist salafi movement has been consistent in its hostility to the Gulf monarchies; it simply has turned its attention to more distant enemies in recent years. Were it to turn its attention back to the region, the Gulf monarchies would top its list. What makes Qatar different is that, as noted above, at least some senior al-Thanis have sympathized rather openly with the movement in the past. While it is possible that such a crisis could cause family members to largely hang together, as they have in Saudi Arabia, in Qatar the opposite is also a possibility. The Saudi (and Kuwaiti) ruling families have long demonstrated far more internal discipline in the face of regime crisis than Qatar's ruling family, which has just as often split apart. It is within the realm of distant possibility that an alliance could be made between Islamist-leaning al-Thanis and more radical, perhaps newly naturalized, Islamists. Coupled with regime crisis, such as a conflict over the succession, fundamental regime change away from liberalization might occur quite rapidly. Shaikh Hamad has consolidated power, for now, and even appointed a successor, but succession has always been contested in Qatar. Family dissent forced

Abdallah's abdication to Ali in 1949, Ali's to Ahmad in 1960, Ahmad's to Khalifa in the 1972 coup, and Khalifa's to Hamad in the 1995 coup. Not only could a succession crisis in the context of a heightened concern with terror end any nascent democratic experiment, but the United States surely would not tolerate a radically Islamist regime in Qatar and, perhaps with Saudi help, might intervene in an attempt to save or restore the monarchy.

While not likely, a regime change in any GCC state could affect all the others, given the similarity of both their regimes and their populations. If one felt threatened, all would. If a stable Shi'ite-dominated regime were to consolidate in Iraq, it might embolden Bahrain's Shi'a into more sustained open political action. While Qatar has fewer Shi'a, Bahrain's mere proximity could cause the regime to clamp down on any kind of opposition, especially if Shi'i activism in Bahrain prompted a jihadist salafi Sunni response there. Given Saudi Arabia's size, proximity, and history of meddling in Qatar's affairs, any regime change in that country would deeply worry Qatar's rulers.

Qatar's democratic opening in the past decade has been quite notable. Nonetheless, it remains precarious. It is dependent largely on the calculations of one amir, whose initial commitment to the project was probably always modest and who must maneuver through a difficult regional and international environment. Perhaps the prospects in the coming decade are not as bright as they originally seemed.

Notes

1. "Lawyers Welcome Unified Court System," *The Peninsula*, October 3, 2004.

2. "Qatar's Personal Law Aims to Strengthen Family Stability," *Gulf News*, May 14, 2005.

3. Rand-Qatar Policy Institute, "Education for a New Era: Design and Implementation of K–12 Education Reform in Qatar," 2007.

4. The (lengthy) law can be found in *The Peninsula*, "Emir Issues New Labor Law," May 20, 2004.

5. Emir Hamad Bin Khalifa al-Thani, "Out of the Fog Through Arab Reform," *Daily Star* (Lebanon), June 21, 2004, www.dailystar.com.

6. Elisheva Rosman-Stollman, "Qatar's Road to Democracy: Truth or Dare?" in *Economic and Political Liberalization in the Gulf*, ed. Josh Teitelbaum (New York: Columbia University Press, 2009).

7. Notably, for example, in April 2005 when the government revoked citizenship from some 6,000 Qatari members of the al-Ghafran clan (a subset of the al-Murra, one of Qatar's largest tribes) in connection with the involvement of some clan members in the 1996 coup attempt. Abdul Ghafour, "Qataris Stripped of Citizenship Cry Foul," *Arab News*, April 2, 2005; "Spotlight on Qatar's Human Rights Record," *Financial Times*, May 18, 2005.

8. See Nathan Brown, *The Rule of Law in the Arab World: Courts in Egypt and the Gulf* (Cambridge: Cambridge University Press, 1997), p. 183, n. 66.

9. Rosman-Stollman, "Qatar's Road to Democracy."
10. Michael Herb, *All in the Family: Absolutism, Revolution, and Democracy in the Middle Eastern Monarchies* (Albany: SUNY Press, 1999).
11. "Qatar: US Reform Plan Should Be Considered," Reuters, April 5, 2004.
12. See Christopher Marquis, "U.S. Protests Broadcasts by Arab Channels," *New York Times*, April 29, 2004, p. 15; "Al Jazeera Reports Affect US-Qatar Ties," Reuters, April 28, 2004.
13. "Iraq Tells Media to Toe the Line," Reuters, November 12, 2004.
14. Steven Weisman, "Under Pressure, Qatar May Sell Jazeera Station," *New York Times*, January 30, 2005.
15. See Josh Meyer and John Goetz, "Qatar's Security Chief Suspected of Having Ties to Al Qaeda," *Los Angeles Times*, March 28, 2003.
16. Freedom House, *Freedom in the World: Qatar*, www.freedomhouse.org.
17. Transparency International, Corruption Perceptions Index, 2008, www.transparency.org.
18. Nadim Kawach, "Qatar Records Budget Surplus for Fourth Successive Year," *Gulf News*, February 21, 2004.
19. "Qatar Is Now a Global Gas Powerhouse," *The Economist*, January 6, 2005.
20. Central Intelligence Agency, *World Factbook, Qatar,* 2010, www.cia.gov.
21. Jean-Francois Seznec, "The Gulf Sovereign Wealth Funds: Myths and Reality," *Middle East Policy* 15, no. 2 (2008): 97–110.
22. "Qatar, Sudan in Farming Tie-Up," *Gulf Times,* July 22, 2008.
23. "$15b. for Qatar Tourism."
24. "Qatar Unveils $5.5bn Airport Development," Agence France Presse, January 13, 2005.
25. "Qatar Hires Regulator Dismissed by Dubai," *Financial Times*, March 2, 2005.
26. Dalal Abu Ghazaleh, "Gulf States to Levy VAT from 2005," *Gulf News*, October 18, 2004.
27. Pete W. Moore and Andrew Schrank, "Commerce and Conflict: U.S. Effort to Counter Terrorism with Trade May Backfire," *Middle East Policy* 10, no. 3 (2003): 112–119.
28. Rosman-Stollman, "Qatar's Road to Democracy."
29. "Qatar Fears Civil War in Iraq," Reuters, April 6, 2004.
30. One man was killed and several people wounded after a suicide car bomb, the first of its kind in Qatar, went off outside a Doha theater favored by Westerners.
31. Uzi Mahnaimi, "Qatar Buys Off al-Qaeda Attacks with Oil Millions," *Sunday Times*, May 1, 2005.

7

The Saudi Shi'a and Political Reform in Saudi Arabia

Jerzy Zdanowski

FOLLOWING THE EVENTS of September 11, 2001, and the 2003 US invasion of Iraq, Saudi Arabia became a focus of international and domestic concern. In 2005, Crown Prince Abdullah succeeded King Fahd and lively discussions of the future of domestic politics and Saudi Arabia's role in the international community soon spread widely in Saudi society. The Saudis are aware of the need to reform: the question is no longer whether to change, but how fast to go about it and in which direction.

In this chapter, I consider the role of the Saudi Shi'a as important agents among the various forces urging the liberalization of the Saudi political system. There are several reasons to focus on this minority group for analyzing constraints on liberalization. The Saudi Shi'ites represent an integral part of the Saudi society and, at the same time, a religious minority. They live under a state regime that adheres to Wahhabism, a strict doctrine of Sunni Islam.[1] The Saudi Shi'a themselves are a local community well rooted in Arabia, devoted to the doctrine of Shi'ism, and strongly determined to preserve their religious practices. This religious factor can hardly be neglected in the context of social and political change in the country. In addition, the Saudi Shi'a are concentrated in the Eastern Province, the world's most important oil-producing area. Because this area generates a substantial portion of Saudi gross domestic product, the government is sensitive to local dissent and to any form of local protest. For a long time, Shi'a in Saudi Arabia simply reacted to government policies that discriminated against them. But recently they have become more assertive in seeking changes that would improve their status.

For most of Saudi Arabia's history, members of the Shi'i minority have been treated as second-class citizens. The fall of Saddam Hussein and the political ascendancy of Iraq's Shi'a population raised hopes among Saudi Shi'a for fairer treatment. The changing status and rising aspirations of Shi'a in the Gulf put political pressure on Saudi authorities to take steps to address Shi'i grievances. Thus, Shi'ism has become an important issue in Saudi politics. To understand why the Saudi Shi'a are a bellwether of broader reform efforts, one needs to understand the context and constraints of liberalization arising from Saudi history and the history of the Gulf as a region.

Demographics and History

Muslims in Saudi Arabia belong to several schools of thought (*madhahib*), some originating from the earliest development of Islam. The Hanbali School of Law is the official sect endorsed by the state, but it is dominant only in the central region of the country. The Shafi'i, Maliki, and Hanafi sects dominate in the west. In the south, there is a mix of Shi'i Ismailis, Shi'ite Zaidis, and some Hanbalis. The Ismailis, or Seveners (they recognize only seven imams), live along the border with Yemen in a region called Najran. The eastern region is inhabited by the Shi'ite Jafaris and some Shafi'is and Hanbalis. The Shi'ite Jafaris, called Twelvers because they recognize twelve imams, also have big communities in al-Madina and Wadi Fatima, and smaller communities in Jeddah and Riyadh. Most Saudi Shi'a live in strategically sensitive locations, in the economically important Eastern Province and in Najran on the long-contested border with Yemen.

The number of Ismaili Shi'a in the remote province of Najran is estimated at around 200,000, which means that they form a large majority in this region, whose population was put at 420,000 in a 2004 census.[2] Their grievances include their gross underrepresentation in all branches of government, the state-directed population transfers that settle Sunni bedouin in the region, and their ritual humiliation in courts and schools that are run entirely by Wahhabis. Children are not immune to the effects of anti-Shi'a prejudice. Some young Ismaili boys were sentenced to death for blasphemy in Najran.[3] The size of the Shi'a community in the Eastern Province is not precisely known. It is in the interest of the Saudi government to downplay the numbers to show that the Shi'ites are an insignificant minority. It seems that some Shi'i sources overestimate the numbers when claiming that the community represents as much as 25 percent of the total population. The number of Shi'ites in the entire kingdom is generally thought to be between 400,000 and 700,000, but some estimates run as high as 2.5 million. From these estimates, the Shi'ites probably made up between 2 percent at the lowest and a little under 10 percent at the highest of the total population of Saudi Arabia, a figure that includes expatriates. The proportion of Shi'a goes up to 12 percent to 15 percent when the comparison base is the native population alone.[4] Despite the wide range in estimates, however, there is no doubt that the Shi'i community constitutes a large part, perhaps even the majority, of the population in the oil-rich Eastern Province. Today, these proportions are likely to be somewhat lower than those taken from a 1913 report by anthropologist F. S. Vidal,[5] who thought that Shi'a made up about 40 percent of the population of the province as a whole.[6]

Shi'a had inhabited the eastern parts of the Arabian Peninsula for about 1,300 years before the state of Saudi Arabia was established in the 1930s. From the beginning of Shi'ism, al-Ahsa was a Shi'ite religious center, and the home of a number of *ulama* (religious scholars) of considerable repute, the most prominent of whom was Ahmad al-Ahsa'a (1753–1826), a great Muslim philosopher and mystic. The leading *ulama* families reached positions of influence and some were part of the ruling elite, especially in Qatif. In the nineteenth century, under Ottoman occupation, the religious life of Shi'a in al-Ahsa flourished. Between 1872 and 1913, many religious schools were established in Qatif. Along with numerous mosques and *husainiyyahs* (places for gathering and worship), they were supported by rich religious foundations. Local religious life then was oriented toward Najaf (in what is now Iraq), where aspiring *ulama* traveled in order to study and get their *ijazas* (diplomas) from *mujtahids* (teachers) based in Iraq's holy cities. Although some local *mujtahids* were highly qualified, and acted as *marja'as* (sources of emulation), the majority of Shi'a in al-Ahsa followed *marja-e taqlid* (the ultimate source of authority) from Najaf.[7]

Following the rise of Wahhabism in the eighteenth century, the Shi'a in al-Ahsa were exposed to one of the strictest revivalist movements in Islam. Their situation dramatically worsened when Ibn Saud's troops entered the region in 1913, at a time when it formally was part of the Ottoman Empire. A group of *mujtahids* from Qatif, led by Hasan Ali al-Badr, urged the others to oppose the conquerors and to fight them. But the majority, along with a leading cleric, Abu Abd al-Karim al-Khunayzi, opted for staying out of the conflict between the Turkish authorities and Ibn Saud. As a result, a party of Shi'a accompanied Hasan Ali al-Badr when he left Qatif for Bahrain. The Shi'a who stayed in al-Ahsa pledged allegiance to Ibn Saud and for two years enjoyed considerable religious freedom.[8]

But conditions changed as Ibn Saud, trying to consolidate his emerging state, came under strong pressure from Wahhabi *ulama* who persisted in their attempts to convert Shi'ite "heretics." This pressure increased with the rise of the Ikhwan, a puritan movement based on tribal affiliation that was defeated in 1929. Wahhabism, with its emphasis on the doctrine of *tawhid,* which stresses the singular nature of God,[9] strictly prohibits the veneration of saints, rituals held at tombs and graves, and many other aspects of theology and ritual life essential to Shi'a doctrine and practice. Among the most important are ritual processions, especially the Ashura mourning celebrations and passion play reenacting Husayn's death at Karbala.[10] To the Wahhabi *ulama*, Shi'a were polytheists (*mushrikin*), innovators (*mubdi'in*), and unbelievers (*kufar*), which justified attacking them and correcting their so-called Satanic practices.[11] As the influence of the Wahhabi *ulama* rose, the policy of the first Saudi ruler toward the Shi'a became harsher. Shi'a rapidly became socially marginalized and religiously alienated.[12]

In 1929–1930, the Shi'a population of Qatif rose up against Saudi authorities. Their leader, Mohammad bin Nasir bin Nimr, was a well-known religious scholar from al-Awamiyya village. He urged his co-religionists to fight, but the majority of Saudi Shi'ites did not accept the idea of military resistance. When the *mujtahids* and notables led by Abu Abd al-Karim al-Khunayzi appealed to the rebels to lay down their arms, the rebellion collapsed and its leaders left for Bahrain and Iraq. Some of them contacted British political agents in the Gulf to ask for protection. Ibn Saud announced a general amnesty for the rebels, but some were publicly beaten to death.[13]

Outside the Mainstream

State policy toward the Shi'a has not changed much since the death of Ibn Saud in 1953. In spite of a 1959 fatwa from al-Azhar University, which recognized Shi'ism as the fifth school of Islamic jurisprudence, Wahhabis continued to regard Shi'a and other schools of Islam as heretics and Shi'ism as incompatible with Islam.[14] Madawi al-Rashid reports that being considered heretics, the Shi'a were "regarded as a social 'anomaly' in Arabia."[15] Sunni courts do not recognize testimony from Shi'a, whom hard-liners call "infidels."[16] At the beginning of this decade, the interior ministry still controlled citizens' names through the civil record administration. Names used exclusively by Shi'a, such as Abd al-Nabi, Abd al-Rasool, and Abd al-Hussain, were banned, forcing Shi'i citizens to change their names. This policy continues in force.[17]

Censorship is another source of contention. Most Shi'ite books are forbidden to be imported or distributed. In contrast, several institutions, among them the World Assembly of Muslim Youth (WAMY), financed by the Saudi government, publish in several languages and distribute free books that claim Shi'ism to be a Jewish conspiracy against Islam. Saudi authorities recognize only two holidays, Eid al-Fitr (after Ramadan) and Eid al-Adha (after Hajj). Other Muslim holidays celebrated by Shi'a and many Sunnis, such as the Prophet Muhammad's birthday, are not allowed or acknowledged by local media. King Abdul Aziz City for Science and Technology, which regulates Internet access in the country, blocks numerous Shi'ite websites, but anti-Shi'a websites advocating the murder and expulsion of Shi'ite citizens are freely accessible. Sites such as sahab.net and muslim.net are full of terms used against Shi'a by some religious zealots. Following a fatwa of May 11, 2000, by the Grand Mufti Shaikh Abd al-Aziz Al ash-Shaikh that permitted hacking "suspicious" websites, many hackers attacked and disabled Shi'i sites. This has been referred to as "Cyber Jihad."[18]

Among the many forms of oppression experienced by Saudi Shi'a is the government's refusal to allow access to the graves of Shi'ite saints buried in Medina. Of these, the primary site of veneration is the grave of Fatima, the daughter of Prophet Muhammad, located together with the graves of four Shi'ite imams in a graveyard called "Jannat al-Baqee."[19]

Religious alienation is combined with social marginalization. Saudi officials have repeatedly denied that Shi'a are in any way discriminated against, saying that they are Muslims and citizens of Saudi Arabia. In fact, Shi'a can participate in many areas of Saudi life, including work in the oil fields, although authorities quietly restrict their numbers.[20] By 1976 a Shi'a from Tarut Island, off Qatif, was appointed to head the Jubail Industrial City project and a substantial number of Shi'ites were employed on it, most as junior employees.[21] Shi'ites can work in schools and universities teaching subjects like economics, but they cannot teach religion or proclaim their religious beliefs. After 1990, although the authorities permitted processions on the Shi'ite holiday of Ashura, they continued to forbid displaying banners or engaging in self-flagellation. Another problem is the government's unwillingness to permit the private construction of Shi'ite mosques.[22]

Shi'a also face discrimination in professional life. For example, there were no Shi'ite winners in any category of the King Faisal Prize, the nation's most prestigious annual award. The prize is given in multiple categories, including medicine, literature, and service to Islam. Since 1970, the prize has been awarded to over 110 recipients from thirty-one countries, including the United States. There was only one Shi'ite nominee, Seyyed Hossein Nasr, the famous Islamic philosopher and the head of the Imperial Iranian Academy of Philosophy. He was notified that he had won the prize in 1979 but, with the arrival of the Islamic Revolution in Iran, the decision was withdrawn with no explanation.[23] Job opportunities for Shi'a also are limited. In recent years, as Iranian-Saudi relations have improved, there has been some involvement of Shi'a in government affairs. Two respected Shi'i professionals were appointed in 2001 to the 120-member Majlis al-Shura, the kingdom's legislative council, but no Shi'a has ever served as a Saudi government minister.[24] In June 2009, the Saudi Ministry of Interior announced the names of 208 citizens who had been appointed to the thirteen regional councils around the kingdom. Even though Shi'a are the majority in the Eastern Province, the ministry appointed only one Shi'a to the local council.[25]

The Saudi government has also been fairly repressive toward any form of Shi'ite political opposition. According to Amnesty International, Saudi authorities detained many Shi'ite opposition figures without trial during the 1980s. Under the Statute of Arrest, Temporary Confinement and Preventive Detention of November 1983, issued by the minister of interior, security forces were empowered to arrest and detain any person simply on suspicion. From the moment of arrest, detainees were denied access to defense counsel and those who refused to admit to the substance of the accusations were placed in solitary confinement and subjected to repeated interrogation and torture until they recanted.[26]

Shi'ite Activism and the Iranian Revolution

The Iranian revolution (1978–1979) had a strong impact on the Shi'a of the Eastern Province, raising their awareness of their second-class religious and economic status as well as bringing about their political emancipation. The process of political maturity started even earlier. In 1968, the Movement of Vanguard Missionaries (MVM, Harakat al-Risaliyin al-Talai) was created in Karbala, Iraq, by the followers of Ayatollah Mohammad al-Shirazi, who was one of the most important *marja-e taqlid* for Shi'ite Muslims. Al-Shirazi and his students supported the idea of the rule of clerics based on *sharia* until the return of the Mahdi, but they did not believe that political power should be concentrated in the hands of only one cleric. In 1974, Saudi Shi'i activists like Hasan al-Saffar and Mohammad Taqi al-Mudarrasi joined the MVM in Kuwait, where Ayatollah al-Shirazi had moved after having been expelled from Iraq. For Hasan al-Saffar and his followers, joining the MVM was a protest against the traditional Shi'i clerics from the Eastern Province who were staying out of politics. The next year they established the Organization of the Islamic Revolution (OIR) in the Arabian Peninsula (Munazzamat al-Thawra al-Islamiyyah fi al-Jazira al-Arabiyya), which was ideologically close to the MVM, but not to the followers of Ayatollah Ruhollah Khomeini. The leaders of the OIR were influenced by Sunni Islamists like Hasan al-Banna, Sayyid Qutb, and Abul Ala Mawdudi.[27]

After the revolution in Iran, the first sign of a new consciousness among Saudi Shi'a came in the summer of 1979 when religious leaders announced in Qatif that they would celebrate the Ashura ceremonies, which had formerly been banned. In November 1979, a large-scale demonstration by Shi'a took place in the province. Shi'ite religious leaders in Qatif insisted on performing the traditional procession on Ashura, but the authorities dispatched 20,000 National Guard soldiers to disperse the mourners. As a result, riots broke out and at least seventeen people were killed. Almost simultaneously, on November 20, 1979, a group of Sunni rebels led by Juhayman al-ʻUtaybi attacked and captured the Grand Mosque in Makkah. The seizure of the Grand Mosque was unrelated to the Shiʻi uprising in the Eastern Province, however, although the combination of these two internal events with the revolution in Iran and the Soviet intervention in Afghanistan created a new situation for the Saudi government. Especially problematic was that protests in the Eastern Province continued; on February 1, 1980, Saudi Shiʻa organized a large demonstration to celebrate the first anniversary of the return of Ayatollah Khomeini to Iran. This too was suppressed by the National Guard and four demonstrators were killed. Riots broke out in Qatif, Safwa, al-Awamiyya, and on Tarut Island. These disturbances became known to Shiʻi activists as the intifada (uprising).[28]

Trying to alleviate tension, the government promised to allocate substantial funds to the development of the Shiʻite region. By 1984, the local administration was replaced by a new one headed by Prince Mohammad ibn Fahd, a son of the king. However, Saudi Shiʻa continued to be denied full religious freedom and the Ashura rituals continue to be forbidden. People who attempt to stage them are arrested.[29]

The Iranian revolution strengthened radical political tendencies among Saudi Shiʻa, deepening the mistrust of the Saudi government, which suspected that Saudi Shiʻa were secretly loyal to Iran. These suspicions were aggravated by broadcasts on Radio Teheran urging Shiʻa to topple the Saudi elite, by Shiʻite demonstrators in Saudi Arabia carrying pictures of Ayatollah Khomeini, and by Saudi Shiʻite membership in the OIR. This group published a magazine, *al-Thawra al-Islamiyya*, from 1980 to 1991, and also broadcast messages from Iranian radio stations and operated an information office in Teheran at the same time that its leaders denied that they enjoyed Iran's patronage. Hasan al-Saffar was evidently influenced by events in Iran, and declared that the Islamic Revolution was a religious duty for all Muslims, believing that the Saudi regime was illegal.[30] Finally the OIR was banned and individuals who were suspected of being members, including religious scholars, students, merchants, and employees of Aramco, were arrested and detained without trial in the Mabahith al-Amma, the general security prison in Dammam.[31] Other detentions included the arrest in March 1992 of two Shiʻite students on the Jeddah campus of King Abd al-Aziz University following a dispute they had had with a professor about a textbook they considered insulting to Shiʻi beliefs. In September of the same year, a Shiʻa from Qatif was beheaded after being convicted of blasphemy.[32]

A group of Saudi Shiʻa founded Saudi Hezbollah, a militant Islamic opposition group focused primarily on attacking the Saudi authorities for allowing US troops to stay in the country after the end of the Gulf War (1990–1991). Saudi Hezbollah appeared to draw most of its members from young men living in the Eastern Province, who were approached by members of the organization during visits to the Sayyeda Zeinab Shrine in Damascus. Those who wished to join Saudi Hezbollah were transported to Hezbollah-controlled areas in Lebanon for military training. Saudi Shi'a trained by the Hezbollah in Lebanon were implicated in the June 25, 1996, bombing of a US military housing complex near the Saudi air base at Dhahran, where the United States had a military presence, killing 19 US servicemen and injuring 373 others.[33]

The authorities' policy against the OIR encouraged vocal opposition among Shi'ite exiles. In the 1990s, however, Shi'ite opposition intellectuals such as Hamza al-Hasan, Tawfiq al-Sheikh, Abd al-Amir Musa, Abd Allah al-Hasan, and their spiritual leader Shaikh Hasan al-Saffar sought new forms of resistance. Recognizing the limitations of open confrontation with the regime, they stressed the cultural authenticity of the Shi'ite minority and their rights as Saudi citizens.[34] In 1991, the OIR changed its name to the Reform Movement (al-Harakat al-Islahiyyah) and started two monthly magazines, *al-Jazira al-Arabiyyah* in London and *Arabian Monitor* in Washington, DC, both of them moderate in tone. Calling for gradual reform in the kingdom, they also addressed issues concerning Shi'a. Some articles criticized the Wahhabi religious establishment for its rigid interpretation of Islam and its refusal to accommodate new interpretations. The authors of these articles tried to build bridges to a dissident Sunni Islamist movement, called al-Sahwa al-Islamiyyah (the Islamic Awakening), which used Wahhabi doctrine to criticize the Saudi Wahhabi establishment. The Sahwa's demands focused on rejection of both the corruption of the ruling group and the use of foreign troops to defend the "land of Islam." Although some of these demands corresponded to those of the Shi'ite opposition, serious doctrinal differences separated the two groups. The young Wahhabi clerics who sympathized with al-Sahwa al-Islamiyyah continued to regard Shi'a as infidels and innovators.[35]

In 1993, Shi'ite leaders sent a petition to the king in which they demanded an end to discrimination against Shi'a. They also supported the establishment of a consultative council, and two of their leaders were included in this new institution.[36] In October 1993 the ruling family reached an agreement with an exiled group of the Reform Movement, which promised to stop resistance activities abroad in exchange for greater civil liberties at home.[37] The dialogue was initiated by the Saudi ambassador to London, Ghazi A. al-Gossaibi.[38] In September 1994, four Shi'i opposition leaders returned from London and the United States to Saudi Arabia. This group included Tawfik al-Seif, Ja'far al-Shayib, Sadiq al-Jubran, and Isa al-Muzil.[39] In August 1996, the Reform Movement accepted an agreement with the government that provided for the release of Shi'i prisoners, a review of the ban on travel for 2,000 Shi'ites, and the issuance of passports to those Shi'i exiles who wanted to return to Saudi Arabia.

Both sides had reasons to reach the agreement. The government was facing militant Sunni Islamist opposition and needed to find new support. It also was negotiating with liberals during this time, and hoped to garner support for its "reformist" outlook. The Shi'i community wanted to end government protection of radical Sunni groups. Shortly before that, Shaikh Abdallah al-Jibrin, one of the founders of the Committee for the Defense of Legitimate Rights (Laynbat al-Difa' 'an al-Hukuk al Shar'iyya), an organization within the sahwa movement, had issued a fatwa stating that Shi'ites were infidels and, as such, could be killed without any religious consequences.[40]

This new opening, however, was derailed by the Khobar Towers bombing. In January 1997, the head of Saudi intelligence, Prince Turki bin Faysal, announced that a Saudi Shi'a, Ahmad Mughassil, was the mastermind behind the bombing and that he was thought to be in Iran. In March, another Saudi Shi'a, Hani Abd ar-Rahim al-Sayigh from the eastern city of Sayhat, was arrested in Canada on suspicion of involvement in the attack. He had entered Canada in August 1996 and applied for refugee status. The Saudi authorities argued that al-Sayigh had contacted an Iranian intelligence officer two years before the bombing and had called the Iranian embassy on the day of the attack. These allegations were attempts to confirm the Saudi government's theory that Saudi Shi'ites had carried out the attack with Iranian help and that their loyalty to the Saudi state was questionable.[41]

The Impact of the March 2003 Invasion of Iraq

Saudi authorities closely monitored the resurgence of the Shi'i majority in neighboring Iraq after the US-led invasion in March 2003. On the eve of the fighting, the Saudi government expressed concern that Iraq might fragment along ethnic and religious lines, triggering conflicts that could spread to its neighbors.[42] The Shi'a question resurfaced in Saudi Arabia itself just a few days after Baghdad fell to the US-British occupation on April 9, 2003. Shaikh Hasan al-Saffar, a leading Shi'i activist, appeared on satellite television stations to call for an end to the injustice done to Shi'a in Saudi Arabia.[43] He pointed out that Shi'i areas, such as al-Ahsa and Qatif in the eastern parts of the kingdom, were not getting enough development assistance, while Shi'a were kept out of sovereign institutions such as the army, the interior ministry, and the foreign ministry. Worse, Saudi Shi'a were forced to study religious curricula that denigrated their beliefs. These demands all came down to one: end the quiet, but long-running, discrimination against Shi'a.[44]

Undoubtedly, the resurgence of the Shi'i majority in Iraq emboldened Saudi Shi'ites, resulting in unprecedented political activity. First, on April

18, 2003, Shaikh Hasan al-Saffar and thirteen other Shi'i leaders from the eastern region issued a statement welcoming the "collapse of the Iraqi dictator." Al-Saffar said that all "citizens in the Kingdom and the Arab states feel the need for political reforms,"[45] placing Shi'i inequality within the broader problem of the need for political reform. The statement called on all Saudi political tendencies to stand together and adopt a course of forgiveness and dialogue in which the public interest would transcend personal and factional concerns.[46]

On April 30, 2003, Saudi Shi'a presented to Crown Prince Abdullah a document signed by more than 450 Shi'i men and women from across Saudi Arabia. Entitled "Partners in the Homeland," the document included two sections: "National Unity" and "Reinforcing National Unity." It called for a thorough investigation of the condition of the Shi'ite community; increased representation of Shi'a in government posts, the Shura Council, and religious institutions; equal treatment for Shi'a; the creation of an agency affiliated with the Ministry of Awqaf (endowments) and Islamic Affairs to oversee Shi'i religious affairs; and the cancellation of restrictions on Shi'i rites. The document also demanded that Shi'a be allowed to print and distribute their own publications throughout the kingdom and consult their own religious courts when necessary. The document concluded with a call for a national dialogue on these matters.[47]

An eighteen-member delegation led by Shi'i activist Ja'far al-Shayib met with Crown Prince Abdullah. The thirty-minute meeting was described as focusing on the constant trouble Shi'a face in Saudi Arabia. According to al-Shayib, the crown prince encouraged an "open and frank" discussion and "suggested a government-sponsored religious forum to be set up so the Sunnis and Shi'ites in Saudi Arabia could better understand one another."[48]

The crown prince accepted the Shi'i petition privately rather than in a public forum, but everyone in Saudi Arabia knew that the meeting had taken place. News of the petition was publicized outside of Saudi Arabia, both in the London Arabic press and in the Egyptian press. The Shi'ite initiative provoked an immediate reaction from the most conservative Sunni clerics and added to the tensions between the religious communities. During the week after the petition was presented, three Shi'i places of worship in the Tarut Island area in the Eastern Province were attacked by unknown arsonists. According to the Saudi Institute, the historic Prophet al-Khoder Mosque was the first to be torched, on May 4; on May 6, the Shaikh Alaa Mosque and al-Saif Hussainiyyah were set on fire. The Saudi Institute transmitted other reports of sectarian strife as well.[49] Such clashes continued in 2004. Among the most spectacular were an attack on the main Ismaili mosque in the southern city of Najran, the closure of several Shi'i mosques and *husainiyyahs*, the arrest of several Shi'i clerics, and the proliferation of hateful religious websites.[50]

Even if the rise of Shi'i activity was connected to events in Iraq, it would be misleading to discuss the situation of the Saudi Shi'a separately from other political developments in Saudi society as a whole. The Shi'a were not alone in organizing petitions. There was an upsurge of petitions, starting with the January 2003 letter from a group of Saudi intellectuals calling for reforms. Given that the Shi'ite community is a part of Saudi society, one decisive factor that could improve this community's status would be a general liberalization of the kingdom as a whole. Is it, however, realistic to expect such a change in a highly conservative society and state such as Saudi Arabia? And, if not, what other scenarios to improve conditions for the Saudi Shi'a might be possible?

Efforts to Liberalize the Kingdom

The debate on the necessity of political change remained muted until the Gulf War. The presence of foreign non-Muslim troops on Saudi Arabian territory in the course of the war gave discussions of the relationship between the population and the state an unprecedented dynamic. As noted earlier, liberal middle-class elements, clerics, and moderate Islamists sent petitions addressing the king and asking for general reform. These requests were often at cross-purposes. If the former sought a widening of civil and human rights, including the establishment of a consultative assembly, the latter demanded implementation of the *sharia* law in public administration, finance, the economy, the army, the information system, and foreign policy, and also an increased role for religion in the public sphere. The ferment produced, on the one hand, the women's demonstration demanding the rights of Saudi women be recognized and, on the other, a separate strand of radical Islamist opposition that ultimately became known as Al-Qaida.[51]

The beginning of the twenty-first century was marked by an upsurge of activism among some segments of Saudi society. The authorities found themselves facing grassroots pressure to implement changes and themselves appeared aware of the necessity to make them. Symptomatic of this new activism was the April 2003 Shi'ite petition to Crown Prince Abdullah, presented shortly after a group of Saudi intellectuals had given him a similar document calling for elections, freedom of speech, and other reforms in January. The January petition was signed by 104 people representing a broad spectrum of Saudi society—businessmen and professors, technocrats, and moderate religious leaders—most of them Sunni, but also some Shi'a.[52] Entitled "A Vision for the Present and the Future of the Homeland," the document expressed the idea that without reforms Saudi Arabia would be left out of history and in danger of political instability. Its authors insisted that steps be taken to build a state based on constitutionally guaranteed institutions where justice would be the basis of rule. They also advocated the formation of directly elected regional councils, so the people might run their own local affairs.[53]

The petition contained no explicit reference to Shi'a, but it appealed for reaffirmation of the proper attitudes enjoined on state and society by Islamic law (*sharia*) to spread the culture of human rights. These include tolerance, fairness, justice, respect for the right to differ, and measures to strengthen national unity without regard for divisions arising from *madhhab* (the school of Islamic law), sect, region, or social class. The reformers also called for restructuring the education system to cater to the needs of a growing job market unable to find qualified workers.[54]

The petition provoked a heated debate in Saudi Arabia. At least a dozen pro-reform articles were published in local newspapers, including a front-page story in *Okaz*, an official daily, entitled "Yes to Reforms."[55] Starting with the January petition from "the 104," the year ended with three noteworthy developments: an expansion of the powers of the appointed Shura Council; the creation of a ministerial position for consultative affairs; and the convening on June 15–18 of the National Forum for Dialogue, overseen by Crown Prince Abdullah as a means of giving voice to non-Wahhabis. The meetings brought together participants from different religious and intellectual schools, including some clerics, in addition to so-called liberals, secularists, Sufis, and Shi'ites. During the forum, the crown prince urged citizens to avoid disunity and prejudice, whether emanating from tribalism, regionalism, ideological differences, or any form of extremism. The King Abdul Aziz Center for National Dialogue (KACND) was established to run the dialogue. The second round of the forum was held in late December 2003 and religious extremism was its focus. Ten women took part through closed-circuit television. Also present was Shaikh Hasan al-Saffar from Qatif, whose participation demonstrated that the Shi'a al-Islahiyyah group stood for a strategy of gradual change by nonviolent means. The participants debated issues such as educational reform and the need to change Saudi school curricula, considered by many at home and abroad as promoting extremism and preparing the ground for inter-religious hatred.[56] In March 2004, the third forum discussed women's issues (explored in depth in Chapter 9).[57] The fourth meeting of the national dialogue was devoted to the problems and expectations of young people. It was held in Dhahran in the Eastern Province in December 2004, with 650 young people of both sexes from all over the country taking part. At Abha, scholars, intellectuals, and people of literature and culture met at the end of 2005. This forum was entitled "We and the Other: A National Vision for Dealing with World Cultures." The seventh national dialogue meeting, "Work and Employment: Dialogue Between Society and Work Related Institutions" was held in April 2008 in al-Qasim. Each forum was preceded by dozens of meetings in all regions of the kingdom.[58]

Meanwhile, in February 2003, a Saudi journalists' association was established under the government's aegis; in March, the government gave permission for women to work in factories; and, in April, work on a governmental national human rights commission was begun.[59] In July, Prince Sultan, second deputy premier and minister of defense and aviation, met with a number of reform-minded intellectuals who tendered a petition calling for urgent reforms in the educational system. All of these initiatives show that reform, state-led and promoted by the regime, was becoming a routine element in public discourse.[60]

The government itself acknowledged the necessity of reform and the legitimacy of public demands for it. Media censorship was eased and the government became more receptive to reform petitions in contrast to its hostile attitude toward such petitions a decade earlier. Crown Prince Abdullah was the first high-ranking official to use the expression "expanding political participation," stating in an address to the kingdom's Majlis al-Shura that "municipal elections will be the beginning of the Saudi citizens' participation in the political system." The foreign minister, Prince Saud al-Faisal, echoed him, saying that Saudi Arabia "has reached a stage in our development that requires expanding political participation." The necessity of reform was also acknowledged by the ailing King Fahd himself, in a speech read to the Majlis al-Shura on May 17, 2003. King Fahd had already acknowledged the importance of reform at least twice in 1982 when he first ascended to the throne, and again in 1990. By the time of his speech, such acknowledgments could be considered as routine within a mechanism of state-sponsored reform. The king did not provide specific details, but pledged that "we will tighten control on the performance of governmental agencies, broaden the scope of popular participation, and open wider horizons for the work of women within the framework of Islamic teachings." In practice, this included streamlining government institutions to improve performance in the public sector and establishing, by royal decree, a state-run human rights commission to enhance human rights in the kingdom along with new laws to modernize civil and criminal judicial procedures. The new laws and regulations will provide equal access to justice for all citizens, prevent violations, and respect basic human rights. As the king noted in the conclusion of his speech, Saudi Arabia "cannot stand still while the world changes."[61] On March 13, 2004, senior members of the Majlis al-Shura announced that the kingdom soon would hold its first-ever municipal elections, to be followed eventually by general elections. All Saudi men of voting age were proclaimed eligible to vote, although Saudi women were not granted suffrage.[62]

When Abdullah came to the throne in August 2005, many predicted that reform efforts would speed up. As crown prince, Abdullah had enjoyed a reputation as a reformer and, shortly before becoming king, he endorsed an element of choice in local elections.[63] A new law allowed universities to form student unions, a form of grassroots democracy on campuses. In 2005, limited elections were first allowed for the reinstated municipal councils, which had been suspended in the 1960s. The new ruler promoted measures to modernize the economy and create an economic elite able to counter radical clerics. Abdullah also initiated the modernization of state schools and courts.[64] His announced reforms included the creation of a supreme court as well as specialized courts for criminal, commercial, and labor cases, and the training of legal staff. These plans were especially welcomed by foreigners doing business in Saudi Arabia.[65]

The accession of Crown Prince Abdullah to the throne was widely supported in the Eastern Province and gave Shi'a hope for political reform and an end to discrimination. In mid-August, a group of Shi'a, along with Hasan al-Saffar, the leader of the Reform Movement, met with the new king in Jeddah. The Shi'a expressed loyalty and pleaded for the release of political prisoners. In September, Ismaili leaders from Najran met with the king and offered personal oaths of loyalty. They used the meeting to ask for inclusion in the political and social life of the country. Abdullah's willingness to speak with both groups can be regarded as another sign of the new ruler's attitude toward the Shi'ite minority.[66]

Domestic Changes and Tensions

Saudis today think differently from their forebears about many issues. Some are no longer content merely to satisfy basic needs for a decent living, but rather aspire to exercise an influence on the legislative process and on judicial institutions. As the Internet draws the young into the outside world, irritation at restrictions against movies, against music, and even against jingles in mobile telephones has been growing. Fawzia abu Khaled, professor of sociology at King Saud University, argues that "maybe 20 years ago we were a happy family. But society is changing and people know what's going on in the rest of the world. Different social forces have developed in the last two decades. People are not children anymore."[67]

This liberal-minded tendency is not organized, however. It consists of a few people who have to compete against opposition from extremely powerful and well-organized conservatives. The Grand Mufti of the country, Shaikh Abd al-Aziz Al ash-Shaikh, declared that Saudi liberals were just as dangerous as militant religious extremists.[68] Any attempt to make the Saudi system more liberal provokes an attack from those who want to preserve the system and appeal for its complete Islamization. In September 2008, Islamists called on Saudi leaders to act against "dangerous" liberal ideology. They presented a memorandum to Shaikh Abd al-Aziz Al ash-Shaikh in which they expressed their dissatisfaction with the steps taken to curb the phenomenon, which they claim contradicts Islamic teachings. Among their demands, the Islamists requested a halt to media campaigns that "promote vice and evil." They also asked the government to refuse to meet with visiting female delegations. Finally, they asked that Saudi leaders not yield to liberalizing pressure from influential people inside the government. When responding to this attack, the liberals had to confirm their position in Saudi society by saying that they considered themselves to be Muslims in all respects, and that Saudi liberalism was an enlightenment movement aimed at correcting wrong ideas in society.[69]

Most telling, however, was the voice the Sahwa, a Sunni movement of young clerics.[70] In 2003, responding to calls of the liberals for a more open system, Salman al-Awdah and Safar al-Hawali, the chief activists and ideologues of the movement, demanded its complete Islamization.[71] The Sahwa expected the government to prevent the Westernization of Saudi society and to maintain faithfully the place of Islam as the central framework of political life in the kingdom. This demand was taken seriously by the ruling family, which believed that the young clerics who were so critical of the Wahhabi religious establishment could not be ignored because a challenge to the position of *ulama* was, ultimately, a challenge to the entire system.[72] As Gwenn Okruhlik argues, their critique of the regime was highly dangerous because it was both symbolic and material. They accused the regime, including the official religious authorities, of having deviated from the straight path. In material terms, they criticized the mismanagement, maldistribution, and waste of national assets. They also contested the dominant historical narrative depicting the founding of the kingdom that justified the rule of Al Saud.[73]

Liberal Saudi reformers, whether in or out of government, confront strong resistance to much of what they propose. Recent changes in school textbooks, undertaken in response to external pressure to remove paragraphs hostile to Christians and Jews, show how difficult it is to implement changes opposed by clerics and conservative citizens. Attempts to reform education provoked a January 2004 statement signed by more than 150 religious scholars and university professors who asserted that Christians and Jews would never cease their efforts to lure Saudis from the path of true Islam. They described liberals as "partisans of infidelity, polytheism and delusion."[74] Later in March 2004, three Saudi dissidents, Ali al-Domeini, Abdullah al-Hamad, and Matruk al-Faleh, were arrested, accused of describing the kingdom's educational system and Wahhabi ideology as causes of extremism.[75]

On May 30, 2008, twenty-two leading Wahhabi clerics, including Abdullah bin Jibrin, Abd al-Rahman al-Barrak, and Nasir al-Umar, sent a letter to the king attacking the Shi'a as "an evil among the sects of the

Islamic nation, and the greatest enemy and deceivers of the Sunni people." The Shi'i cleric Shaikh Tawfik al-Amir who spoke out against this letter was arrested. Of the twenty-two signatories, eleven were government officials.[76] This occurred right before the Makkah conference entitled "Introducing Islam to non-Islamic Countries: Reality and Aspirations," which had been promoted by the Saudi ruler and to which he had invited the participation of more than 500 Muslim leaders and scholars from around the world. Among them was Ali Akbar Hashemi Rafsanjani, the former president of Shi'ite Iran. A crucial factor behind this push for interfaith dialogue was to dilute the influence of the more radical elements of Wahhabism, which itself provoked resistance. Many Saudi Wahhabi clerics who were not directly told to attend the conference chose to stay away.[77]

Change in Saudi Arabia has moved at a snail's pace. Fear of fracturing the society, such as along sectarian lines, has often been cited by officials as an explanation for the timidity of the reforms so far.[78] Thus, like all the other petitions, the Shi'i petition setting out a reformist vision of the Saudi future was carefully couched in the language of national unity and acknowledged the rule of the Al Saud family. "We have no alliance with anyone outside the country, and indeed want to resolve this issue so that it doesn't leave any space for outsiders to exploit," said Jaffar Al-Shayeb.[79] Other Shi'i leaders underlined the fact that they were part of the homeland and solidly loyal to it. Hasan al-Saffar said that his community was loyal to Saudi Arabia and had no ambitions for greater autonomy—even if a possible blueprint for a looser federal state were to emerge in post-Saddam Iraq. "The Saudi government knows the loyalty of the Shi'a citizens to their country," al-Saffar told Reuters in an interview on February 8, 2004, noting that Shi'i demands were modest. "There is no special Shi'ite request apart from equality with other citizens. The government knows that," he said. He admitted that he was in constant touch with Iraq's leading Shi'i cleric, Ayatollah Ali al-Sistani, but emphasized that those contacts were purely religious. "As for politics, our decisions are local and are not taken by any party outside the country."[80] Aiming to diminish suspicions that Shi'a constitute a fifth column, some Shi'i activists have opted for Saudi-based clerical training in order to establish a Saudi *marja-e taqlid*, which in their opinion would promote the national integration of Saudi Shi'a and remove any basis for blaming them for loyalty to any foreign religious or political authority.[81]

Reform also is progressing slowly because, like people in other countries, many Saudis are not eager to embrace rapid changes while the Wahhabist clergy are strongly opposed to making Saudi Arabia a more liberal and secular society. Conservatives are somewhat more in tune than liberals with the values of rural Saudis who resist the calls to change their understanding of Islam even though a more flexible interpretation is acceptable to most of their fellow citizens.[82] Symptomatically, when King Abdullah called in March 2008 for a dialogue among Muslims, Christians, and Jews after having discussed the idea with Pope Benedict XVI, the kingdom's leading official cleric, the Grand Mufti Shaikh Abd al-Aziz Al ash-Shaikh, denied issuing an invitation to Israeli rabbis to take part in a conference.[83] Few Saudis want the royal family to be replaced, considering it to be a stabilizing force, but many believe that strong government institutions could run the country more effectively.[84] One strategy of the Saudi royal family is to balance competing voices and eliminate the most radical elements on both sides.

The one step forward, one step back pattern noted in Chapter 1 can also be seen in Saudi Arabia, however. A plan to retrain 40,000 prayer leaders to disseminate a moderate interpretation of Islamic tradition as a counterweight to militant Islam was adopted and a campaign to remove the most radical imams was initiated. By 2003, 1,700 clerics had been relieved of their duties or sent for retraining.[85] Yet in 2004, a new law was adopted that put extensive limits on every form of expression. Under this law, state employees were prohibited from criticizing policies and programs of the government.[86] Similarly, in March 2004, the country's first human rights watchdog organization was established. Billed as an independent body charged with monitoring the kingdom's compliance with human rights standards, its members were carefully selected by the government, resulting in a group unlikely to provoke confrontation or openly embarrass the regime.[87]

When compared to 2005, the year that King Abdullah came to the throne promising change, both Saudi and international human rights activists say that in 2007 and 2008, repression intensified and the climate for political dissent worsened.[88] The government tried to stabilize the situation by curbing radical tendencies, an approach that affected Shi'a. In January 2007, Shi'i leaders from the Eastern Province signaled that the government had stopped short of recognizing Shi'a as a minority. They stressed that there were still no Shi'ites in positions of authority, and they were rarely promoted to managerial positions in state companies. There were also no Shi'i headmasters in public schools and the government did not react to the hard-line Sunni clerics who stepped up their preaching against Shi'ites.[89]

Relations between Shi'a and Sunnis have deteriorated since 2006 as a result of developments in Iraq and the war between Israel and Lebanon's Hezbollah. The Saudi authorities suppressed demonstrations by Shi'a and Sunnis expressing solidarity with Shi'a in Lebanon. People in the Eastern Province who carried symbols and pictures of Hezbollah and its leader, Hasan Nasrallah, were arrested.[90] In May 2008, a group of Ismaili activists from Najran handed King Abdullah a 300-page report detailing abuses by the governor of the province. The leader of the group, Ahmed Turki al-Saab, was subsequently detained by the police in Riyadh, along with five other activists. Only two years earlier the Ismailis had successfully petitioned King Abdullah to halt the settlement of up to 10,000 Yemeni tribesmen outside Najran city.[91]

Numerous resistance efforts were recorded in 2009. Saudis demonstrated their anger on the streets and at unprecedented sit-ins. On May 13, 2009, seventy-seven human rights activists and lawyers signed an open letter addressed to the king and twenty prominent politicians demanding substantial changes in the political system. The petitioners called for parliamentary elections and the election of a prime minister from outside of the royal family. Another demand was to halt the secret trials of hundreds of people alleged to be members of Al-Qaida and accused of being involved in acts of terrorism from 2003 to 2005. The beginning of these trials was announced by the minister of interior, Prince Nayef bin Abdul Aziz, in February 2009. The Saudi authorities ignored the letter and arrested some of the activists. Then, on March 23, 250 jobless graduates gathered in front of the building of the Ministry of Education and Teaching. The demonstrators brought makeshift beds showing their intention to sleep at the doors of the building. The next day, some twenty-five young unemployed primary school teachers gathered in front of the king's palace in Riyadh and demanded jobs. Finally, these young protesters handed a letter to the Saudi sovereign, asking that he listen to their grievances. The social and economic protests inside Saudi Arabia stimulated the Movement for Islamic Reform in Arabia (MIRA), the main Saudi opposition exile group in London, to act. Its head, Sa'ad al-Faqih, called on Saudis to go en masse to particular mosques throughout the country on May 29 to protest against injustice and the lack of political freedom. MIRA had tried several times to organize similar demonstrations, most notably in 2003 and 2004 when protesters clashed with riot police. The state has forbidden demonstrations in mosques.[92]

On February 14, 2009, the eighty-six-year-old king, evidently frustrated with the glacial pace of reform, decreed important changes in the government. He reshuffled top posts in education, the courts, the armed forces, the central bank, the health and information ministries, and the religious police and the state-appointed religious hierarchy as well as in the royally appointed Majlis al-Shura. The most striking change was the appointment of reformers to positions in the school and court systems. The new minister of education is the king's son-in-law, Prince Faisal bin Abdullah bin Muhammad. He was expected to implement a new curriculum emphasizing tolerance in Islam, while the firing of several senior judges, including Shaikh Saleh Luhaydan, head of the Supreme Judicial Council (al-Majlis al-'ala lil-Shu'un al-Islamiyyah), suggested a new push to modernize the courts. Similarly, the dismissal of the head of the Commission for the

Promotion of Virtue and Prohibition of Vice (Hay'at al-Amr bil-Ma'ruf wa-al-Nahy'an al-Munkar) can be seen as a response to demands to curb the morality police. The Supreme Judicial Council, a twenty-one-member board of senior clerics that issues official religious rulings, now for the first time includes representatives of all four schools of Sunni Islam, ending the monopoly of the archtraditionalist Hanbali school associated with Wahhabism.[93]

The opening of the highest religious institution in Saudi Arabia to the Maliki, Hanafi, and Shafi`i schools of Sunni Islam has had important consequences. This body still excludes Shi'a, and King Abdullah has compensated the Shi'i community in part by naming five new Shi'ites to the 150-member Shura Council. Yet some Shi'i circles, speaking from Shi'i websites, called for the establishment of religious pluralism and demanded the inclusion of Shi'i clerics on the Judiciary Council. This idea was immediately opposed by Shaikh Kalbani, one of the imams at the Grand Mosque in Makkah. The shaikh declared that Shi'i clerics were not entitled to join the Supreme Judiciary Council because they are "heretics." "I think Shi'i clerics are heretics," said Shaikh Kalbani in an interview with BBC Arabic. "Indeed, I cannot consider a Muslim anyone who knows the value of Abu Bakr (the faithful companion of the Prophet Muhammad), and still insults and curses him and warns Muslims against him."[94]

In March 2009, the king appointed Prince Nayef, the powerful interior minister and a contender for the Saudi throne, to the post of second deputy prime minister. This appointment, which placed Prince Nayef next in line to the throne after Crown Prince Sultan, reinforces the hard-liners and casts a long shadow over the future of the kingdom's still tentative steps toward reform. Prince Nayef is known for extreme conservatism on such issues as political reform and the rights of women and religious minorities.[95]

In February and March 2009, a series of demonstrations by Saudi Shi'a took place in the Eastern Province. They were provoked by confrontations between Shi'ite pilgrims and religious police in Medina, in the west of the country. The demonstrations began on February 20, when a group of female pilgrims visited the most revered Shi'ite site in Saudi Arabia, a cemetery in Islam's second-holiest city, Medina, where hundreds of the Prophet Muhammad's descendants are buried. The pilgrims screamed when they spotted a religious policeman filming them from the top of a security wall. Their male relatives, outraged by this invasion of modesty, demanded the footage. Instead, the all-Sunni police force arrested eighteen of them, sparking a riot by thousands of Shi'ite pilgrims that led to more arrests and injuries.[96] In support of the pilgrims, Shi'a in the Eastern Province took to the streets and expressed their solidarity by work stoppages. At the end of March, at least ten Shi'a in the Eastern Province were reported by Amnesty International to be held incommunicado by Saudi authorities, allegedly for taking part in a protest on February 27 in Safwa, Eastern Province. At least four others were arrested for participating in gatherings on March 19 in al-Awamiyya, also in the Eastern Province. The gatherings were held to protest an order for the arrest of Sayyed Nimr Hassan Baqir al-Nimr, a leading Shi'i cleric and mosque imam in al-Awamiyya, for criticizing the attacks on Shi'a in Medina and protesting religious discrimination against the Shi'i community.[97]

Tensions were eased by King Abdullah's decision to release all the detainees, but the situation remained volatile for several months. The hard-line policy of Saudi authorities encouraged Shi'i radicals to declare that the Saudi Shi'ite community would seek to secede from the kingdom if the hard-line approach continued. The radical tendency was revealed by al-Nimr, although his extreme position was quickly moderated and even renounced by others. The preacher avoided arrest, but several of his followers were detained.[98] On April 6, 2009, Shi'i religious leaders and Qatif intellectuals issued a statement concerning the events in al-Awamiyya, and called for ending all forms of hatred and sectarian discrimination.[99] In response, Sunni extremists accused Saudi Shi'a in Bahrain and Saudi Arabia of acting as a fifth column for Iran along with the Shi'a of Bahrain. References to Bahrain carried particular resonance because, in December 2008, Bahrain's authorities had accused thirty-five Shi'a of plotting to overthrow the state.[100]

These events signaled growing Shi'i anger against their treatment by the Saudi authorities. Their hopes for greater representation were dashed in February 2009 when King Abdullah reshaped the Saudi government and religious institutions. Although the king appointed reformers to strategic positions in government and the senior *ulama* council, Shi'ite clerics were not invited to join the Judiciary Council.[101] Some of them expressed fear that the dormant militant groups could come back as a result of the unequal treatment of Saudi Shi'a.[102]

Conclusion

Saudi Shi'a could serve on the front line of reform if their loyalty to the Saudi state were not in question. Most come from Arab tribes but, religiously, they have much more in common with fellow Shi'a in Iraq, Iran, Lebanon, and Bahrain than with fellow Saudis who follow the puritan Wahhabi school of Islam. At a time when many Arab officials point to predominantly Shi'i Iran as the most serious security threat they face, there is a general attitude in the Arabic media suggesting that Saudi Shi'a are somehow led by or follow an Iranian agenda. Saudi Shi'a have repeatedly denied this and attempted to demonstrate allegiance to their homeland, even as they protested discrimination against themselves. These accusations have been supported by human rights organizations and Western governments, led by the United States, which has repeatedly expressed concerns about religious freedom in Saudi Arabia.[103]

Most Saudi Shi'a ignored Iran's call to rebel during the Iran-Iraq War in the 1980s, remaining loyal to their country. In January 2007, Shaikh Hasan al-Saffar, a leading Shi'i cleric from the Eastern Province, declared once again that Saudi "Shi'ite citizens are proud of their nationalism and don't see themselves as an element in regional political struggles in Iran, Iraq and Lebanon."[104] But the question is how long they will be willing to wait, especially as the regional and international situation changes. Before 2003, the strong position of Saddam's anti-Shi'a regime in Iraq and Iraq's US-supported alliance with the Al Saud did not leave much space for Saudi Shi'i emancipation. Since the overthrow of Saddam, however, Saudi Shi'ite consciousness has changed radically.[105] On the eve of the US-led invasion of Iraq in March 2003, people in the Eastern Province believed that the invasion would liberate Iraq's majority Shi'ite population and that any move toward democracy there would give Iraq's Shi'ites unprecedented power that they could use to end the persecution of the Saudi Shi'ites.[106]

There is a direct linkage between political reform in Saudi Arabia generally and the situation of the Shi'a in particular. Serious reform in the kingdom means instituting government accountability to society through procedures such as elections and rules governing representation. It also could lead to a measure of self-rule in the provinces, including the Eastern Province. In itself, that would constitute a breakup of the Wahhabi monopoly. Saudi Shi'i claims of entitlement to a role in the Sunni-ruled system test the ability of Saudi authorities to implement political reform of a broadly liberal type. Reform may threaten internal stability in the short term, but fairer treatment of religious minorities could be a better strategy than repression for maintaining national unity as well as stability over the long run.

For the ruling family it is essential to look at the strategic political relationships between the state and domestic groups. The closest allies and the most adamant adversaries of the Saudi rulers are the *ulama*, and relationships with them are of particular importance for the family. The Wahhabi religious establishment remains powerful and pervades all aspects of life in the kingdom. It has shaped Saudi society for generations and, as a result, its sectarian principles are commonly perceived as universal truths. Holding elections, issuing identification cards to women, and reforming the judiciary are cast by this establishment in doctrinal terms that frame resistance to them and to dialogue with the Shi'a as religious duties.[107] There is little support for liberal ideas or their exponents who seek an alternative concept of social development, ideas that place them outside the official religious framework.[108] Thus, the status of the Saudi Shi'a still depends on Wahhabism and its ability to revise its orientations. Madawi Al-Rasheed is correct when arguing that "refuting Wahhabi religious discourse that denounces them [Shi'a] as *rafidha* (rejectionists) and polytheists is the beginning of a process of regaining recognition on the religio-political map of Saudi Arabia."[109]

Yet there are glimmerings of hope. There is no clear position on the Sunni-Shi'ite dialogue among the leaders of the Sahwa, but the absence of a dogmatic position offers an opportunity for reconciliation. There are many contacts and meetings between liberal Sunni intellectuals and moderate Shi'i clerics. Wahhabi clerics and independent preachers are being invited to attend meetings and conferences in the Eastern Province. Shi'i activists are also continuing a practice of dialogue with Sunni reformists in the western part of the country. In 2007, Hasan al-Saffar visited the Wahhabi strongholds of al-Unayzah and al-Buraydah. He was invited by the governor of al-Qasim Province to attend Unayzah's first Cultural and Heritage Festival. In 2007 another Shi'i activist, Mohammad Mahfouz, edited a book entitled *Sectarian Dialogue in the Kingdom of Saudi Arabia* (*al-Hiwar al-Madhhabi fi al-Mamlaka al-Arabiyyah al-Sa'udiyyah*).[110] It was written in response to a call for a dialogue among the adherents of the different Islamic schools in Saudi Arabia that Shaikh Abdullah bin Mani had made in March 2006. The call was promptly supported by Shaikh Salih al-Sadlan of Imam Muhammad bin Saud Islamic University. The book included contributions from leading scholars from Sunni and Shi'i schools of thought. All of them expressed their wish for peaceful coexistence.[111]

The slow process of reform has begun to improve the status of Saudi Shi'a. They can construct mosques and observe Ashura and other religious festivals publicly, if quietly. At the 2006 Riyadh book fair, volumes on Shi'ite subjects were available for the first time. Qatif and other towns in the Eastern Province have their own local councils with Shi'ite majorities. According to Shaikh Hasan al-Saffar, the Saudi Ministry of Religious Affairs has started to limit anti-Shi'a rhetoric in mosques.[112] In consequence, tensions between the region's Sunni and Shi'i Muslims tend to stay belowground. But when pressures build and a ready channel is cleared, they can bubble to the surface with alarming force, as witnessed in the spring of 2009. With Iran sounding more aggressive under President Mahmud Ahmedinezhad, small incidents once again are triggering bigger eruptions. Shi'i Arabs tend to look to their own spiritual leaders for guidance instead of Iran but, with Iran inclined to confront the Gulf Arabs' US ally and with Shi'i Arabs still experiencing political exclusion and social stigma, unrest is always possible.

The Saudi Shi'a want an end to discrimination and are committed to negotiating a settlement of Shi'i grievances. Liberals and left-wing intellectuals cooperate with Sufis and their Islamist co-religionists to call for more respect for human rights, yet symptoms of impatience are evident. A September 2005 report from the International Crisis Group entitled "The Shi'a Question in Saudi Arabia" notes that King Abdullah, widely believed to have been at the forefront of efforts to engage Shi'a and promote their integration, may now be in a position to effect greater change.[113] But the leaders of a newly established Shi'ite opposition movement, Khalas (Salvation), note that during the past fifteen years there have been plenty of opportunities for the government to reform its policy toward the Shi'a that were not taken.[114]

The best-case scenario for national development would be to grant Saudi Shi'ites full citizenship rights and increase their involvement in national affairs as soon as possible. When discussing the possibility of the emergence of a Shi'i transnational radical movement in the Gulf, Laurence Louër stresses that it is not impossible and that such "development could be the result of the failure of the current strategy of integration."[115] The results of the second round of local polls, held in Saudi Arabia on March 3, 2005, when Shi'a turned out in large numbers and swept the board in Qatif to win five out of six seats, show that the Saudi Shi'a are eager to be involved in national affairs. Commenting on the events in the Eastern Province in February and March 2009, al-Nimr noted that "it is the right of the majority to take [control of] the government, but they should take care of the minority. The solution is to open the country, give freedom for political action, and accept others as they are. . . . There has to be a minimum of democracy."[116]

Notes

1. Wahhabis are Muslims who subscribe to a particularly strict version of the Hanbali school, influenced by the teachings of Mohammad ibn Abd al-Wahhab, an eighteenth-century scholar.

2. "Saudi Shi'ite Held After Meeting King," *Kuwait Times*, May 19, 2008.

3. Such sentences were commuted to prison and administered public lashes. See "Glacier in the Desert," *The Economist*, January 5, 2006; Human Rights Watch has documented Saudi government discrimination against Ismaili Shi'a in religious practice, employment, and education. For a list of documents see http://www.hrw.org/en/search/apachesolr_search/Saudi+Arabia_Shia?Array. School textbooks continue to teach Saudi students that adhering to the Ismaili faith constitutes the sin of "major polytheism," effectively declaring its adherents infidels.

4. Leading experts on Saudi Arabia stress the rapid growth of Saudi Arabia's population—at least 300 percent between 1973 and 2000; see Anthony H. Cordesman, *Saudi Arabia Enters the Twenty-First Century: The Political, Foreign Policy, Economic, and Energy Dimensions* (Westport, CT: Praeger, 2003), p. 6. But estimates for the total and native Saudi population vary; for example, *MENA: 2008 Economic Developments and Prospects* (Washington, DC: International Bank for

Reconstruction and Development/World Bank, 2009), p. 104, www.worldbank.org. According to the CIA *World Factbook* the population of Saudi Arabia in 2009 was 28,686,633, including 5,576,076 non-nationals; Central Intelligence Agency, *World Factbook, 2010* (New York: CIA, 2009), www.cia.gov. But the Saudi Labor Ministry reported a much higher number of expatriates—almost 8.8 million. See, for example, Madawi Al-Rasheed, "The Shi'a of Saudi Arabia: A Minority in Search of Cultural Authenticity," *British Journal of Middle Eastern Studies* 25, no. 25 (1998): 132. Heba Saleh estimated that Shi'a numbered about 1.5 million out of a total population of 23 million and this seems to be a good compromise figure; Heba Saleh, "Iraq Conflict Leaves Saudi Shi'a Anxious of Backlash," *Financial Times*, May 4, 2006, p. 3.

5. F. S. Vidal estimated that, at the beginning of the 1950s, Shi'ites made up about 50 to 60 percent of the total population of the Eastern Province; F. S. Vidal, *The Oasis of Al-Hasa* (Dammam: Aramco Arabian Research Division, 1955), p. 34. According to Laurence Louër, the author of the most recent comprehensive study of Shi'a in the Gulf, the Shi'a constituted one-third of the population of the province; Laurence Louër, *Transnational Shia Politics: Religious and Political Networks in the Gulf* (New York: Columbia University Press, 2008), p. 7.

6. Cordesman, *Saudi Arabia Enters the Twenty-First Century*, p. 206.

7. Guido Steinberg, "The Shi'ites in the Eastern Province of Saudi Arabia (al-Ahsa'), 1913–1953," in *The Twelver Shi'a in Modern Time: Religious Culture and Political History*, eds. Reiner Brunner and Werber Ende (Leiden: Brill, 2001), pp. 239–240. On the theological Shi'i school of Najaf, see Jawdat al-Qazwini, "The School of Najaf," in *Ayatollahs, Sufis and Ideologues: State, Religion and Social Movements in Iraq*, ed. Faleh Abdul-Jabar (London: Saqi, 2002), pp. 245–264.

8. The description of the events of 1913 in al-Ahsa can be found in the British documents kept in the India Office Records, R/15/5/27, "British Relations with Ibn Sa'ud 18 March 1911–1 Oct 1920."

9. In a word, *monotheism* is the act of believing and affirming that God is one and only. Certain movements in Islam, and among them the Wahhabis, have claimed to represent strict monotheist orthodoxy better than others whom they consider to be polytheists.

10. These ritual processions remained banned until the beginning of the 1990s; see Helen Chapin Metz, ed., *Saudi Arabia: A Country Study* (Washington, DC: Government Printing Office for the Library of Congress, 1992), http://country studies.us.

11. Madawi Al-Rasheed admits that, although the practice of labeling Sh'ia as polytheists continued in the twentieth century, the acts of excommunicating individuals were rare and under control; Madawi Al-Rasheed, *Contesting the Saudi State: Islamic Voices from a New Generation* (Cambridge: Cambridge University Press, 2007), p. 40.

12. See India Office Records, R/15/5/27. For more recent events, see Madawi Al-Rasheed and Loulouwa Al-Rasheed, "The Politics of Encapsulation: Saudi Policy Towards Tribal and Religious Opposition," *Middle Eastern Studies* 32, no. 1 (1996): 96–119; Hasan al-Hamza, *Shi'a fi al-Mamlaka al-Arabiyya al-Sa'udiyya*, part II (Beirut: Mu'assasa Baqi li-Ahya al-Turath, 1993), pp. 241–259.

13. See the British documents on these events: India Office Records, R/5/2/1859, "Political Agency, Bahrain; Miscellaneous Correspondence with Amir and Notables of Najd, Hasa and Qatif"; India Office Records, R/15/7/706, "Bin Saud's Relations with Trucial Chiefs 18/3/1923-5/10/1939"; India Office Records, R/15/1/334, "Ibn Saud's Relations with Shaikhs: Najdis Agent's Activities 15 Apr

1923–31 Jul 1931"; Agency, Bahrain, 14 March 1930"; and, especially, India Office Records, R/15/2/95, "Ibn Saud's Relations with Bahrain and Qatif, 19 Dec 1929–23 May 1930."

14. Al-Rasheed and Al-Rasheed, "The Politics of Encapsulation," p. 110.

15. Al-Rasheed, *A History of Saudi Arabia*, p. 146.

16. John R. Bradley, "Emboldened Shi'ites," *Al-Ahram Weekly*, May 15–21, 2003, http://weekly.ahram.org.eg.

17. "Religious Freedom in Saudi Arabia: Incitement for Hatred Is Still Ongoing," *Saudi Shi'a: The Affairs of the Shi'ites in Saudi Arabia*, May 16, 2009, www.saudiShi'a.com (Saudi Shi'a is a civil, nonprofit informational project established in 2005).

18. Shi'a News Agency, "Religious Freedom in the Kingdom of Saudi Arabia—Focus on Citizens," Shi'a News Agency, October 15, 2001, www.Shi'anews.com.

19. Human Rights Watch, *World Report 1997: Events 1996* (New York: Human Rights Watch, 1996), p. 298; Irfan al-Alawi, "Saudi Interference with Muslims During the Hajj," Hudson New York, January 22, 2010, www.hudson-ny.org.

20. Helen A. Lackner, *House Built on Sand: A Political Economy of Saudi Arabia* (London: Ithaca, 1978), p. 88.

21. See James Buchan, "Secular and Religious Opposition in Saudi Arabia," in *State, Society and Economy in Saudi Arabia*, ed. Tim Niblock (London: Croom Helm, 1982), p. 125.

22. Cordesman, *Saudi Arabia Enters the Twenty-First Century*, p. 209.

23. "Religious Freedom in the Kingdom of Saudi Arabia—Focus on Citizens." The 2003 US State Department report on human rights said that Saudi Arabia's Shi'a were subject to "officially sanctioned political and economic discrimination." Sayyed Hossein Nasr himself emigrated to the United States after the revolution and took the position of professor of Islamic studies at George Washington University.

24. Nora Boustany, "Shi'ite Muslims in Saudi Arabia Emboldened by Hussein's Fall," *Washington Post*, April 23, 2003, p. A32.

25. The appointed member was Ghassan al-Nimr, a distinguished businessman from Al-Ahsa; see "Religious Freedom in Saudi Arabia: Incitement for Hatred Is Still Ongoing."

26. Human Rights Watch, *Empty Reforms: Saudi Arabia's New Basic Laws* (New York: Human Rights Watch, May 1992).

27. Leo Kwarten, "Why the Saudi Shiites Won't Rise up Easily," *Khitat Loubnaniya: A Lebanese Window on Shia Affairs*, January 6, 2009, www.khitat.info.

28. Gwenn Okruhlik, "Rentier Wealth, Unruly Law, and the Rise of Opposition: The Political Economy of Oil States," *Comparative Politics* 31, no. 3 (1999): 300. Toby Craig Jones, "Rebellion on the Saudi Periphery: Modernity, Marginalization, and the Shi'a Uprising of 1979," *International Journal of Middle East Studies* 38, no. 2 (2006): 213–233. Thomas Hegghammer and Stephane Lacroix, "Rejectionist Islamism in Saudi Arabia: The Story of Juhayman al-'Utaybi Revisited," *International Journal of Middle East Studies* 39, no. 1 (2007): 103–122.

29. Amnesty International, "Saudi Arabia: Detention Without Trial"; Joshua Teitelbaum, *Holier Than Thou: Saudi Arabia's Islamic Opposition* (Washington, DC: Washington Institute for Near East Policy, 2000), p. 83.

30. Kwarten, "Why Saudi Shiites Won't Rise up Easily."

31. In July 1989 Amnesty International issued urgent appeals on behalf of eight of the detainees, expressing concern at reports that they were being subjected to torture and ill treatment. Among them were two religious scholars: Sayyid Tahrir al-Shimimy and Shaikh 'Ali 'Abd al-Karim al-'Awa.

32. Amnesty International, "Saudi Arabia: Detention Without Trial."

33. Cordesman, *Saudi Arabia Enters the Twenty-First Century*, pp. 197–198.

34. Al-Rasheed, "The Shi'a of Saudi Arabia," pp. 125, 129.

35. Teitelbaum, *Holier Than Thou*, p. 84. This movement first emerged in the 1960s, rose to prominence in the 1980s, and gained widespread popularity during the Gulf War after the Saudi authorities decided to rely on US forces to defend the peninsula against potential Iraqi aggression. See also Joe Stork, "Violence and Political Change in Saudi Arabia," *ISIM Review* 19, no. 19 (2007): 54–55.

36. Mamoun Fandy, *Saudi Arabia and the Politics of Dissent* (New York: Palgrave Macmillan, 2001), pp. 197–198; Kwarten, "Why Saudi Shiites Won't Rise up Easily."

37. "Chronology," *Middle East Journal* 48, no. 2 (1994): 351.

38. Al-Rasheed and Al-Rasheed, "The Politics of Encapsulation," p. 113.

39. Fandy, *Saudi Arabia and the Politics of Dissent*, p. 200.

40. Tim Niblock, *Saudi Arabia: Power, Legitimacy and Survival* (London: Routledge, 2006), p. 102; Fandy, *Saudi Arabia and the Politics of Dissent*, p. 206.

41. Teitelbaum, *Holier Than Thou*, p. 89.

42. "Kingdom Warns of Turmoil in Region After Iraq," *Arab News*, February 6, 2003. Al-Sayegh denied all allegations, but confirmed that he had studied in Iran; see www.search.com/refernce/Hani_Abdul_Rahim_al_sayegh; Anthony DePalma, "Saudi Case Casting a Light on How Militants Infiltrate and Exploit Canada," *New York Times*, May 4, 1997.

43. On Shaikh al-Saffar, see Fandy, *Saudi Arabia and the Politics of Dissent*, pp. 195–226.

44. Hasan Abu Taleb, "The Shi'ite Question in Saudi Arabia," *Egypt Commentary,* no. 9, March 11, 2004, www.ahram.org.eg; "Saudi Shi'ite Call for Fairness," *Arab News*, April 24, 2003.

45. The statement was widely distributed inside Saudi Arabia and from Washington, DC, by the Saudi Institute, a privately funded Shi'i organization critical of the Saudi government; see www.saudiinstitute.org.

46. "Saudi Shi'ite Call for Fairness"; Boustany, "Shi'ite Muslims Emboldened."

47. Abu Taleb, "The Shi'ite Question in Saudi Arabia"; Toby Jones, "Seeking a 'Social Contract for Saudi Arabia,'" *Middle East Report,* no. 228 (2003): 42–48.

48. Bradley, "Emboldened Shi'ites"; Teitelbaum, *Holier Than Thou*, pp. 84–88.

49. Bradley, "Emboldened Shi'ites." Some Shi'i students were expelled from Jubail Industrial College in the Eastern Province after a fight with Sunni students who spoke against their religious practices. A Shi'i cemetery in Anaak was desecrated two months earlier.

50. Paul Cochrane, "Saudi Arabia's Energy Infrastructure Faces Terror Threat," *Daily Star* (Lebanon), December 2, 2004, www.dailystar.com.lb.

51. Gwenn Okruhlik, "Making Conversation Permissible: Islamism and Reform in Saudi Arabia," in *Islamic Activism: A Social Movement Theory Approach*, ed. Quintan Wiktorowicz (Bloomington: Indiana University Press, 2004), pp. 250–269.

52. Catherine Taylor, "Saudi Arabia's Quiet Voices of Reform Start to Speak Up," *Christian Science Monitor*, January 15, 2003. One of them was Abdel Khaleq Abdallah al Abdel Hai, a political scientist at King Saud University in Riyadh and himself a Shi'a, originally from the Eastern Province.

53. "Reformists in Free, Frank Talks with Abdullah," *Arab News*, February 2, 2003.

54. Ibid.

55. "Reform Debate Rages in Saudi Arabia," *Gulf News*, March 4, 2003.

56. Raid Qusti, "Scholars Urge Moderation and Dialogue," *Arab News*, June 21, 2003; "Thousands of Saudi Shi'ites Observe Ashura," *Gulf News*, March 3, 2004.
57. "Adapt or Die," *The Economist*, March 4, 2004.
58. King Abdulaziz Center for National Dialogue, www.kacnd.org/eng/all_national_meeting.asp.
59. Roula Khalaf, "There Is a Dangerous Period Coming: Between Reform and Repression, the House of Saud Faces Its Greatest Peril," *Financial Times*, November 18, 2003, p. 13.
60. Raid Qusti, "Reforms in Kingdom Are Under Study, Sultan Says," *Arab News*, July 21, 2003.
61. John R. Bradley, "Can Saudi Arabia Reform Itself?" *The Daily Star* (Lebanon), September 5, 2003, www.dailystar.com.lb.
62. "Chronology," *Middle East Journal* 57, no. 4 (2003): 656; "Chronology," *Middle East Journal* 58, no. 3 (2004): 490.
63. "No Time to Lose," *The Economist*, February 19, 2009.
64. Anne Penketh, "Succession at House of Saud: The Men Who Would Be King," *The Independent*, June 17, 2008, www.independent.co.uk.
65. "Saudi Arabia's Promised Reforms: King Abdullah of Saudi Arabia," *New York Times*, January 4, 2008.
66. See Toby Jones, "The Iraq Effect in Saudi Arabia," *Middle East Report*, no. 237 (2005): 22; AFP, "Saudi Ismailis Want Greater Say in Kingdom," *Daily Star* (Lebanon), September 22, 2005, www.dailystar.com.lb.
67. Cited in Khalaf, "There Is a Dangerous Period Coming."
68. "The Limits of the Reform," *The Economist*, March 25, 2004.
69. Mariam Al Hakeem, "Islamists Call on Saudi Leaders to Act Against 'Dangerous' Liberal Ideology," *Gulf News*, September 8, 2008.
70. According to the International Crisis Group, "The young *Sahwa* Islamists espoused a blend of the traditional Wahhabi outlook (mainly on social issues) and the more contemporary Muslim Brotherhood approach (especially on political issues)." In "Saudi Arabia Backgrounder: Who Are the Islamists?" *Middle East Report,* no. 31 (2004): 2.
71. Teitelbaum, *Holier Than Thou*, pp. 101–107. On the Sahwa Islamists, see also Al-Rasheed, *Contesting the Saudi State*, pp. 137–140, 153–174, 178–185.
72. Al-Rasheed, *Contesting the Saudi State.*
73. Gwenn Okruhlik, "Networks of Dissent: Islamism and Reform in Saudi Arabia," *Current History*, January 2002, p. 25.
74. See David B. Ottoway, "Pressure Builds on Key Pillar Supporting Saudi Royal House," *Wall Street Journal Europe*, June 9, 2004, p. 6.
75. "The Suffocating Limits of Reforms," *The Economist*, May 19, 2005.
76. Human Rights Watch, *Denied Dignity: Systematic Discrimination and Hostility Toward Saudi Shi'a Citizens*, New York, September 3, 2009, www.hrw.org.
77. Andrew England, "King Abdullah Seeks Stability by Reaching Out on Religion," *Financial Times*, June 24, 2008.
78. The fear was shared by a US intelligence report of November 2003; see Guy Dinmore and Roula Khalaf, "The US National Interest Is Caught Up with the Saudis in a Very Complex Way: They Are More Than a Gas Pump," *Financial Times*, November 19, 2003, p. 13.
79. Bradley, "Emboldened Shi'ites."
80. Kwarten, "Why Saudi Shiites Won't."
81. Fred Wehrey, "Shi'a Pessimistic About Reform, but Seek Reconciliation," *Arab Reform Bulletin*, June 19, 2007.

82. "Saudi Reforms: No Time to Lose, " *The Economist,* February 19, 2009.

83. Ian Black, "Intellectuals Condemn Fatwa Against Writers," *The Guardian*, April 3, 2008.

84. Neil MacFarquhar, "Saudi Uneasy Balance Between Desires for Change and Stability," *New York Times*, May 4, 2004.

85. Magdi Abdelhadi, "Hundreds of Saudi Clerics 'Dismissed,'" BBC News, May 30, 2003, http://news.bbc.co.uk.

86. Khalid al-Dakhil, "Quiet Time," *New York Times*, November 27, 2004.

87. Heba Saleh, "Saudi Arabian King Approves Selected Human Rights Group," *Financial Times*, March 11, 2004, p. 7; Carlyle Murphy, "Saudis Slowly Opening Dialogue About Rights," *Christian Science Monitor*, March 28, 2008.

88. Roger Hardy, "Whatever Happened to Saudi Reform?" BBC News, February 6, 2008, http://news.bbc.co.uk.

89. Hassan M. Fattah and Rasheed Abou al-Samh, "Saudi Shiites Fear Gains Could Be Lost," *New York Times*, February 5, 2007.

90. Human Rights Watch, *Denied Dignity.*

91. "Saudi Shi'ite Held After Meeting King."

92. There is no information about any response to this appeal; see Habib Trabelsi, "Saudis Learn to Protest," *Saudi Wave*, May 26, 2009, www.saudiwave.com.

93. "Tiptoeing Towards Reform," *The Economist*, February 19, 2009; Jeffrey Fleishman, "Saudi Arabia's King Abdullah Appoints Moderates to Key Posts," *Los Angeles Times*, February 15, 2009; Carlyle Murphy, "With Shi'ites Rising Across the Region, Saudi Arabia's Grow Impatient," *Christian Science Monitor*, April 27, 2009.

94. Habib Trabelsi, "Sheikh Kalbani: All Shi'ite Clerics Are Heretics," *Saudi Wave*, May 6, 2009, www.saudiwave.com.

95. "Saudi Arabia's Prince Nayef: A Rising but Enigmatic Prince," *The Economist*, April 2, 2009.

96. Abeer Allam, "Riyadh Confronts Growing Shia Anger," *Financial Times*, March 25, 2009.

97. Trabelsi, "Saudi Learn to Protest"; Amnesty International, "Shi'a Men and Teenagers Held Incommunicado by Saudi Arabian Authorities," London, March 23, 2009. In al-Awamiyya, the radical tendency was expressed in the following graffiti: "Death to Wahhabi," "Down with the government," and "We will not forget our prisoners"; see Carlyle Murphy, "With Shi'ites Rising Across the Region"; Human Rights Watch, *Denied Dignity.*

98. Allam, "Riyadh Confronts Growing Shia Anger."

99. "Statement of Shiite Leaders and Qatif's Intellections over Alawammia Events," *Saudi Shia: The Affairs of the Shiites in Saudia Arabia,* June 4, 2009, www.saudiShi'a.com.

100. "Shi'a Unhappiness Is Rattling Regimes in Saudi Arabia."

101. Allam, "Riyadh Confronts Growing Shia Anger."

102. Fattah and al-Samh, "Shiites Fear Gains Could Be Lost."

103. Anees al-Qudaihi, "Saudi Arabia's Shi'a Press for Rights," BBC Arabic Service, March 24, 2009, http://news.bbc.co.uk.

104. Andrew Hammond, "Saudi Cleric Says Shi'ites Loyal to Kingdom, Not Iran," Reuters, 29 January 2007, www.alertnet.or.

105. Yaroslav Trofimov, "Saudi Shiites See Hope in an Invasion of Iraq: Marginalized Muslims Transfer Hopes Away from Iran, to U.S.," *Wall Street Journal*, February 3, 2003, www.sullivan-county.com/x/saudi_shiite.htm.

106. Yaroslav Trofimov interviewed leading Shi'i intellectuals at Qatif, and among them Sayyed Hassan al-Awami, an Islamic lawyer who runs a Shi'ite community center in this city; see Trofimov, "Saudi Shiites See Hope."

107. Cochrane, "Saudi Arabia's Energy Infrastructure."

108. On the Saudi liberals, see Richard Dekmejian, "The Liberal Impulse in Saudi Arabia," *Middle East Journal* 57, no. 3 (2003): 400–413.

109. Al-Rasheed, *Contesting the Saudi State*, p. 212.

110. Mohammad Mahfouz, ed., *Sectarian Dialogue in the Kingdom of Saudi Arabia* (Qatif, Saudi Arabia: Aafaz Center, 2007).

111. Wehrey, "Shi'a Pessimistic About Reform"; Kwarten, "Why Saudi Shiites Won't"; Huda al-Saleh, "Saudi Clerics Seek Dialogue Among Various Sects," *Asharq Alawsat*, January 5, 2007, www.aawsat.com.

112. Saleh, "Iraq Conflict Leaves Saudi Shi'a Anxious of Backlash."

113. "The Shi'a Question in Saudi Arabia," *Middle East Report,* no. 45, September 19, 2005, p. 13.

114. Al-Qudaihi, "Shi'a Press for Rights."

115. Louër, *Transnational Shi'a Politics*, p. 300.

116. Murphy, "With Shi'ites Rising Across the Region."

8

Economics Trumps Politics in the United Arab Emirates

Christian Koch

WITH THE PASSING of Shaikh Zayid Bin Sultan Al-Nahyan, the "Father of the Nation," in November 2004, the United Arab Emirates (UAE) entered a new era. For almost sixty years, Shaikh Zayid had embodied the development of first the Trucial Coast and then the UAE. He served as the Ruler's Representative in Al-Ain beginning in 1946 while his brother Shakhbut was still ruler of Abu Dhabi, and assumed the leadership mantle in Abu Dhabi himself twenty years later. Shaikh Zayid was the driving force behind the economic and social development made possible by the discovery of oil in the late 1950s, and he led the disparate emirates to form a federation after Britain announced in 1968 that it would soon withdraw from the region "east of Suez." He presided over the establishment of the UAE in 1971 when most observers were convinced that such a federation would not last. Shaikh Zayid's firm belief in unity drew the seven distinct and highly individual emirates together and his vision and determination ensured that this arrangement would persist.[1]

Even before Shaikh Zayid's passing, the UAE had emerged as the model of an economically prosperous and politically stable society. Since its establishment, the UAE has displayed an economic openness that actively sought close contact with the rest of the world. Led by the emirates of Abu Dhabi and Dubai, the UAE demonstrates a strong determination to forge a well-diversified economy based on cutting-edge projects, a willingness to challenge conventional wisdom, and a political culture that has proven adaptable while avoiding large-scale discrimination both among Emiratis of the different emirates and with respect to the large expatriate community that outnumbers nationals by a ratio of 5:1. Without a doubt, the country has been fortunate in its leadership, which has laid the groundwork for further progress. Due to an effective blending of tradition and modernity, it has made an apparently seamless transition from a backwater tribal conglomeration to a modern and increasingly institutionalized state. The UAE's domestic tranquility and economic prosperity stand out in the turbulent region of the Gulf, where conflict and instability are closer to the norm. The degree to which the UAE had evolved and matured over the years became clear when the transition to the new leadership of Crown Prince Shaikh Khalifa Bin Zayid Al-Nahyan was carried out in an orderly manner and in accordance with constitutional provisions. A similarly smooth process took place in early 2006 in Dubai with the passing of Shaikh Maktoum Bin Rashid and the assumption of the leadership mantle there by Shaikh Mohammad Bin Rashid Al-Maktoum.

The UAE's unique political structure is the key to its past development and current success. Although the country has acquired an increasingly unified national character since its founding, the individual identity of the emirates has been maintained such that politically, socially, and even economically, each is distinct.[2] The development of the country has been driven by political realism and sensitivity to local traditions rather than grand visions of Arab unity.[3] The astuteness and pragmatism of its leaders on the ground have been the cornerstones of the UAE's success.

This strategy also explains why the UAE by and large remains a loose federation rather than a centralized state. The federation's relative openness is countered by interdependencies generated by the uneven distribution of wealth across the set of emirates: Abu Dhabi and Dubai are the wealthiest; Sharjah and Ras al-Khaimah occupy the middle ground; and Ajman, Umm al-Quwain, and Fujairah are geographically small and have limited resources. In spite of disparities in wealth, even the most ardent proponents of the federation agree that a successful union cannot be forced on its participants, but rather must come about through individual commitments identifying the levels of engagement. Thus, Ras al-Khaimah was not pressed to join the union in December 1971, but agreed on its own accord to join a couple of months later, while the provisional constitution remained in effect for over twenty-five years before a permanent agreement was devised. Similarly, Dubai's ruler, Shaikh Rashid, was ultimately given the post of prime minister of the UAE in 1979 as a means to channel Dubai's influence through an emerging federal structure. The leitmotif has been one of flexible arrangements and this has served the UAE well.

In more recent times, globalization and interdependence have encouraged convergence, a trend that was made particularly clear in the wake of the global financial crisis of 2008–2009 when Dubai found itself severely affected and having to seek financial support through the federal framework to avoid more serious consequences to its economic well-being. In the end, the support from Abu Dhabi was never in doubt and the economic crisis resulted simply in some hard lessons being learned, especially as far as international finance was concerned. Overall, the model character that Dubai[4] and the UAE as a whole had begun to assume in terms of its economic development and diversification efforts survived largely intact despite the fact that this impression was not conveyed by the mainstream media.[5] That is not to say that the episode did not also highlight many of the shortcomings of the institutional setup within the UAE, such as those with regard to transparency, accountability, and the rule of law. These shortcomings are especially apparent when it comes to business transactions, the mixture and overlap that exist between the public and private sectors, and the overall framework for attracting foreign investment. None, however, have ever threatened the concept of the UAE as a viable federation and effective governing system.

As the UAE's political leadership has emerged from its first significant political transition and solidified its position within the country, it seems an opportune moment to take stock of its internal development and make some assessments about the status of its integration and consolidation. The Gulf region as a whole has undergone some significant transformations in the last decade of the twentieth century and the first decade of the twenty-first century brought about by a mixture of domestic factors, regional developments, and external intervention. The death of Shaikh Zayid occurred during a crucial period in the political development of all the Gulf Cooperation Council (GCC) states (Bahrain, Kuwait, Oman, Qatar, Saudi Arabia, and the United Arab Emirates). First, in the wake of the September 11, 2001, attacks on the United States, the George W. Bush administration concluded that the political status quo in the entire Middle East region was contributing to Islamic extremism, and its response was to make a determined push for political liberalization and democratization.[6] Out of this developed the infamous Middle East Partnership Initiative (MEPI) and the Greater Middle East Initiative agreed upon at the Group of 8 summit in June 2004. While these approaches were almost unanimously rejected by the regional states as blatant external interference in their domestic affairs,[7] other leaders say that the president's announcements acted as an impetus for the Gulf states to undertake political reform measures themselves.[8] Second, the US-led invasion of Iraq in 2003 removed one of the harshest dictatorships in the Middle East, paving the way for a different political leadership to emerge in Baghdad. As a Gulf state itself, Iraq's events have repercussions throughout the region. The fall of Saddam Hussein's regime, in particular the violence and instability that characterized Iraq in the invasion's aftermath, increased pressures on the other Arab Gulf states to concentrate on domestic stability in conjunction with political reform.

While these events focused debate on the political status of the region, the invasion of Iraq and its consequences confirmed the status quo as much as it precipitated a domino effect supporting democratic political change in the Gulf. Far from being able to inaugurate a new era of democratic politics inside Iraq, the United States lost both credibility and legitimacy as a result of its mismanaged postinvasion policies. Instead of putting pressure on neighboring states to reform their political systems, Iraq became the example of what to avoid and therefore actually strengthened the determination of Gulf leaders to eschew taking radical steps that could result in the same chaos and anarchy evident in Iraq. Moreover, given the deteriorating security situation elsewhere in the Middle East—such as in Lebanon and the Palestinian territories, and concerns over renewed conflict with regard to Iran and its pursuit of a nuclear program—within a short time the United States itself effectively abandoned its liberalization agenda and returned to a policy that placed a premium on regional stability rather than bringing about democratic transitions. In this context, it is more than arguable that the transformation taking place at the political, social, and economic levels in the UAE should be viewed less as the result of external events imposing themselves on internal processes than as domestic patterns in train for more than a decade that are increasingly coming to the forefront. The response from UAE authorities to implement reforms reflects this clearly. With the primacy placed on regime security, the ruling families in the UAE have historically responded pragmatically regarding changes to internal ruling arrangements, including challenges from within the families themselves, and implemented changes that have in turn been greeted positively by the population at large and have further enhanced the legitimacy of the rulers themselves. The period since 2003 has been no exception. At the same time, the rulers have returned to their cocoon when external or internal developments required no response. The result is that, while the impetus toward reform continues to follow a step-by-step and evolutionary approach, the UAE, similar to the other Arab Gulf states, has in fact been undergoing broader and deeper societal changes that will necessarily lead to a further opening of its political system. Thus, transition must be seen not as a linear and straightforward process, but as a path with many curves that nevertheless moves forward.

Forces Promoting Reform in the United Arab Emirates

Since the time of its establishment as a federation in 1971, the UAE has undoubtedly undergone a "subtle evolution" of its tribally based structures. Modernization and globalization both are increasing pressure on the system to respond. Previously, the enormous rentier wealth available to most Gulf societies shielded these states from some political demands. But oil wealth gradually generated a new set of expectations in citizens who have grown accustomed to high living standards. In addition, younger generations have been shaped by a political socialization different from that of their forebears, one driven by access to higher education and the global information revolution. As a result, Gulf governments find themselves in a constant spiral, implanting various reforms only to be confronted by demands for further changes. These ever-rising demands come from regional and global forces as well as domestic populations and external actors. In this context too, the UAE is no exception to the rest of the region; thus, the transformative processes visible in other GCC member states are also visible in the UAE.

At the same time, at least on the surface the UAE is regarded as having pursued a path of development that diverges from the norm. Economically, the country has experienced explosive growth in its national gross domestic product (GDP), which rose by nearly 500 percent from 1994 to 2007. The global financial crisis also affected the UAE, but not to such a pronounced degree as elsewhere. By the beginning of 2010, the prospect of positive growth had returned, albeit at a more moderate rate than prior to the downturn. More importantly, the UAE remains a state with modern infrastructure and services comparable to those available in the developed world. This is largely a consequence of deliberate policy choices designed to keep the UAE competitive internationally while making it a positive example for the region.[9] Furthermore, as the UAE strives to take an active part in the overall process of globalization, it also persists in its commitment to invest its oil wealth to sustain further development and assist various diversification efforts.[10] For 2007, non-oil sectors accounted for 65 percent of the GDP, according to the Ministry of Economy.[11]

The UAE's remarkable economic advancement has not been matched by a similar rate of political development, however. Following the municipal elections in Saudi Arabia held between February and April 2005, the UAE remained the only state on the Arabian Peninsula that continued to rely exclusively on appointed instead of elected or semi-elected consultative and policymaking institutions. Only in December 2006 did the country introduce elections for its legislative body, the Federal National Council (FNC), but even then the right to vote was limited to selected members of an electoral college. In the end, this included only 6,689 citizens, or 0.88 percent of the total Emirati population.[12] Moreover, little information has been released about the next stage of elections, originally scheduled to be held in the latter half of 2010. As one member of the FNC has expressed it, "nothing is happening. Nobody knows."[13]

In addition, other shortcomings have been exposed in the race for economic opportunism. On the one hand, both federal- and emirate-level institutions have seen only minimal movement toward a system of accountability and transparency, something that became quite apparent in the wake of the announced status of Dubai's debt issues and the subsequent uncertainty about the actual size of Dubai's outstanding commitments.[14] On the other hand, due in part to the continued generation of economic opportunities, civil society in the UAE harbors no substantial political reform movement. An independent UAE Society for Human Rights was established, but approval came only after a lengthy delay by the Ministry of Social Affairs. Moreover, the society's powers are limited and its activities are closely watched by authorities. Similarly, promises by the government to enact a legal framework for the establishment of nongovernmental organizations have not been followed through and the overall process by which organizations are allowed to operate and what activities they can pursue continues to be arbitrary and nontransparent.

The lack of visible political change has several causes. First, it is quite apparent that in the current climate there is little sense of urgency within the leadership to undertake adjustments to existing political structures. Second, as far as the UAE leadership is concerned, managing change while maintaining economic and social stability within existing religious and social frameworks continues to be an imperative. Buoyed by high per capita income and supported by a high degree of internal legitimacy, the ruling families of the UAE have so far felt little need to expand political participation or raise substantially the capacity of governmental institutions. A third factor comes from the UAE's position as a reliable ally of the United States and a moderate voice in regional affairs. Its conformity to US expectations has kept the UAE out of the spotlight shone on states expected to enact political reforms. Thus, during the initial push by the George W. Bush administration for political reforms in Bahrain, Qatar, and Saudi Arabia, a similar level of debate did not emerge within the UAE or between the UAE and the United States.

In the UAE and elsewhere in the Gulf, political evolution toward greater responsiveness has thus lagged behind development in the economic and, to some degree, the social field. Here, it should be noted that, in general, economic policy decisions tend to be less contentious than political changes. The route to consensus on change in the political realm tends not only to be more difficult, but also to take longer. While the UAE is now home to over 120 different nationalities that are more or less able to pursue lifestyle choices without interference from federation authorities, the same kind of openness and tolerance is not visible in the policies of the government toward its own national populations or with regard to broadening their access to the political system. Clearly, the traditional Gulf social contract based on the exchange of wealth for power remains in effect in the UAE. And despite globalization trends encroaching on existing political arrangements, the UAE retains its tradition as a patriarchal society whose political loyalties are substantially defined by tribal elements. Its political system remains fundamentally pyramidal, hierarchical, and patriarchal.[15] Power is centralized and flows from the ruling families that govern the seven emirates. As Christopher Davidson argues, "essentially the family itself has become an institution and has formed a layer of structural legitimacy in its own right."[16] In this system, moves to broaden access to the political process are slow to materialize.

The argument that I make here, however, is that this situation is unlikely to remain static. While there is a social consensus that gradual change is the best mechanism to reform society, the pace of change in the UAE has been involuntarily accelerated by pressures from globalization and political fallout from events such as 9/11 and the Iraq War. Given their own determination to portray the UAE as a progressive country, the ruling families themselves see no other way but to accommodate certain international norms (e.g., abiding by World Trade Organization rules as a member in good standing) if they want to continue on the path of economic openness as well as to be taken seriously as a member of the international community. As such, the emphasis as far as the UAE leadership is concerned is on a broad commitment to modernizing the state at all levels, including solidifying the fundamentals of a market economy, improving and expanding the efficiency of institutions, and increasing the overall administrative capacity of the state. A related development comes from new demands for reform from within the UAE. These demands have indigenous roots grounded in the growing political awareness produced by a better education system and a freer media environment, and also from local observation of reform measures implemented elsewhere in the region.[17] It is in this context that questions are being raised by citizens themselves as to why political development continues to lag behind in the UAE when other GCC states have progressed further and more rapidly.

Despite outward appearances of stasis, the UAE is thus experiencing the beginnings of movement toward political change. Inside ruling family circles, there is an increased recognition that subtle adjustments to current political arrangements are necessary if only to maintain the families' own legitimacy. The decision to hold limited elections to the FNC was one such example. As a step seen as being taken in the right direction, this move has brought forth new ideas and encouraged a broader debate about how the UAE can continue on its economic growth path while, at the same time, being able to accommodate rising citizen demands on the government. The appointment of Shaikha Lubna al-Qassimi as the first female minister of the country in November 2004 was another prominent example of change, not only because she is a woman but also because she came from a private sector business background where she had earned a reputation for being able to get things done. A cabinet reshuffle in February 2008 increased the representation of women in the UAE cabinet to four persons.[18] Other examples include the introduction of best business practices in several ministries, the establishment of an electronic wage protection system to curb the practice of delayed salary payments to sections of the labor force, and numerous investigations and court cases in conjunction with corruption as a result of Dubai's debt crisis. In fact, the public prosecutor in Dubai has listed fighting corruption as the top priority, stating that "any employee exploiting his position to make illegal profits will not have immunity."[19]

Dubai's crown prince Shaikh Mohammad Bin Rashid al-Maktoum is a vocal and highly visible proponent of such change. At the 2004 Arab Strategy Forum, he stated:

> We are at our best when we are talking about change, but our will to change is shaky, or perhaps weak. For decades, we have been talking about unity and cooperation, but the talk in some parts of our Arab world is not about the unity of the nation, but about preventing the collapse of some states. . . . I say to my fellow Arabs in charge: If you do not change, you will be changed. If you do not initiate radical changes, responsibly discharge your duties and uphold the principles of truth, justice and responsibility, your peoples will resent you. More than this, the verdict of history on you will be severe.[20]

Shaikh Mohammad has acknowledged the fact that, in addition to introducing changes from the top, demand for reform is pushing up from below as a new, politically conscious generation seeks greater input into the decisionmaking process. For the UAE, the issues that will have a particular impact on the political environment are economic dynamism; institutional capacities; and the role played by education, the media, and labor markets.

Among GCC members, the UAE has the second largest economy after Saudi Arabia. Its GDP has soared from $33.3 billion in 1990 to $253.4 billion at the end of 2008.[21] More importantly, some of the expanded national income has been transformed into human capital, with the UAE positioned in the "well advanced" category and holding a ranking of 35 in the UN 2009 Human Development Report. In 2008, the UAE's per capita income stood at $53,188, bested only by Qatar among the GCC states.[22] The UAE also is noteworthy for its successful efforts at diversification and privatization, with a large proportion of GNP now coming from non-oil sectors. Despite having the sixth largest oil reserves in the world, the oil sector accounts for less than one-third of the UAE's GDP. In 2006, the non-oil sector's contribution to GDP actually increased by a whopping 77.3 percent to $102.4 billion, contributing 64.3 percent of the total.[23] In Dubai, where oil reserves are shrinking, income from oil has dropped below 5 percent of gross national income.

To maintain economic growth momentum, governments at both the federal and the local emirate level have initiated reforms that include a phased implementation of performance-based budgeting within a newly introduced, three-year, medium-term budget framework, and the privatization of manufacturing and public utilities such as water and power. Having successfully adopted a range of diversification strategies, the pressing economic policy challenges for the UAE are no longer to maintain economic stability, but rather to continue policy reform and ensure implementation and compliance. Concrete initiatives in this regard included the September 2004 establishment of a Financial Supervisory Bureau and the establishment of the Dubai Ethics Resource Center in October 2003 to promote transparency and combat practices such as insider trading. As a result, the UAE improved its ranking on Transparency International's Corruption Perception Index to 6.5 in 2009 from 5.2 in 2003, the first year the UAE was included in the survey, locating it at thirtieth place worldwide.[24] Overall, it can be said that there is a broad and strong commitment among all of the constituent elements of the federation to improve the services and the efficiency of state institutions. The Abu Dhabi government issued a law in December 2008 to set up an independent accountability authority to ensure that government departments are managed efficiently.[25] This followed the release in April 2007 of the first UAE national strategy to improve public administration by setting targets for the federation's sixteen ministries, including improving cooperation between federal and local authorities, looking into the policymaking role of the ministries, increasing the efficiency of government bodies, and updating laws and regulations.[26]

Even more important were the strategic visions and policy agendas put forth both at the federal and the emirate level. Dubai's Strategic Vision 2015 document, released in February 2007, established the areas of economic and social life, infrastructure and environment, security and justice, and government excellence as the pillars around which to achieve prosperity and sustainable growth.[27] Particular emphasis was placed on public sector excellence that included items such as transparency, sound financial performance, accountability in a result-based culture, and the development and promotion of human resources.[28] This was followed by a three-year UAE development plan that called for adopting international best practices in all areas of governance, with specific objectives to be met in social and economic development, modernizing the civil service, promoting rural development, and strengthening coordination between federal and local authorities.[29] In August 2007, Abu Dhabi released its policy agenda 2007–2008, which "signifies a beginning of a new era for our Government and public sector, in terms of accountability and transparency."[30] The idea of a secure society and a vibrant economy was based on the pillars of premium education, empowerment of the private sector, creation of a sustainable knowledge-based economy, a transparent regulatory environment, and national manpower resource optimization.[31]

In addition, laws were enacted to protect and expand foreign direct investment and relax sponsorship rules, especially through the creation of so-called economic free zones. As a result, Dubai hosts such zones as Dubai Internet City, Dubai Media City, Dubai Health Care City, and Dubai Academic City. Overall, as demands on the system have expanded over recent years, the government has undertaken a number of initiatives to improve the institutional framework within which economic activity takes place. The result is that the system's responsiveness also has improved. Furthermore, a number of regulations, especially with regard to financial institutions, have come into effect, including a regulatory framework for the establishment of the Dubai International Financial Center. All of this is not to suggest that the UAE has managed to overcome the issues and problems accompanying its emergence as a modern nation-state, but it does point to the fact that reforms are moving in the right direction and that there exists a level of responsiveness within the system. The global financial crisis did not change this level of responsiveness; in fact, it accelerated the demand for more accountability because confidence in various business sectors had to be restored quickly, especially in the Dubai real estate sector, which was particularly affected by the global tightening of credit markets and project financing.

The Emerging Role of Institutions

Moving from the economic to the political arena, UAE federal institutions and the accompanying political system have reached a certain level of maturity, as reflected in the conflict-free political transitions following the deaths of Shaikh Zayid and Shaikh Maktoum mentioned earlier. Immediately upon the announcement of the death of the UAE president, the mantle of the presidency was passed to Vice-President Shaikh Maktoum Bin Rashid Al-Maktoum, the ruler of Dubai. This was followed on November 4, 2004, by the announcement of Shaikh Khalifa Bin Zayid Al-Nahayan, the crown prince of Abu Dhabi, as the new president. Shaikh Khalifa was selected by consensus in the Supreme Council under Article 51 of the constitution.

Another key moment saw the issuing of Federal Decree No. 51 in November 2004, just prior to the passing of Shaikh Zayid.[32] The decree announced the formation of a new cabinet, the seventh in the country's history, along with changes in the structure of the cabinet itself. On the one hand, the decree showed an intention to introduce greater efficiency into the political system. It consolidated related agencies into new units: Education and Youth and Higher Education were merged into one Ministry of Education; Economy and Commerce and Planning became one Ministry of

Economy and Planning; Petroleum and Mineral Resources and Electricity and Water were merged into one Ministry of Energy; and GCC Affairs and the Minister of State for Supreme Council Affairs became one Ministry of Supreme Council Affairs and the GCC. A new Ministry of Presidential Affairs was created to provide a better institutional framework for the Office of the President. Most significant was the appointment of Shaikha Lubna Al-Qassimi to be the new minister for economy and planning.[33] A further reshuffle in February 2008 in which a new Ministry for Foreign Trade was created and the number of women members was increased to four is another example of the government's attempts to respond to both domestic and global developments and ensure a level of transparency through its actions.[34]

The attention placed on highlighting and expanding the role of women reflects the fact that women outnumber men in higher education enrollment by almost three to one. Yet their high level of education has not been translated into a widespread integration of women into the workforce. Unemployment rates remain high. Women are reported as being 70 percent of job seekers; they comprise 60 percent of the public sector workforce, which is the employer of last resort.[35] Even so, the employment of women in business has been rising. Women's participation in the private sector labor force tripled between 1980 and 2000, rising from 5.1 percent to 14.8 percent.[36] The Board of Businesswomen had approximately 12,000 members as of May 2003, managing investments worth 25 billion UAE dirhams.[37] The initial appointment of Shaikha Lubna as well as the gradual expansion of women in government positions should be viewed in this context. As listed in the *UAE Yearbook 2008*, the "pursuit of gender equality is not just a social policy initiative, it is generally recognized that full female participation is also pivotal for sustainable economic development."[38]

After the federal law to govern the elections scheduled for December 2006 was passed, membership in the FNC also was expanded to women. Several women ran for council posts and one succeeded in winning a seat on the Dubai council. Additional women were appointed such that women occupied 22 percent of the seats in the FNC during the 2006–2010 term. Women are also taking seats on governing bodies at the individual emirate level. In 2004, Sharjah counted five women members on its consultative council while the Dubai Chamber of Commerce and Industry saw three women assigned to its board of directors following a 2003 amiri decree allowing women to be chosen.[39]

In the social sphere, Federal Decree No. 38 of 2004 marked the accession of the UAE to the Convention on the Elimination of All Forms of Discrimination Against Women, although the government added reservations to some of the clauses in the text of the convention, including parts of Article 2; Article 9, clause 1; Article 15, clause 2; and Article 29, clause 1.[40]

Meanwhile, discussions on changing personal status laws have continued. The General Women's Union has asked the Ministry of Justice, Islamic Affairs and Awqaf to amend a draft law dealing with issues like dowries, polygamy, and financial support for divorced women.[41] The UAE ranked thirty-eighth in the 2009 United Nations Development Report in the Gender-Related Development Index and thirty-fifth in the Gender Empowerment Measure.[42]

With the release of the UAE Federal Government Strategy, there has also been an emphasis on improving the performance and function of the executive branch of the government, although on this front progress has remained limited. For example, the FNC has not experienced any structural transformation since its establishment in 1971 despite regional trends toward expanding legislative capacity. The election of council members was introduced in December 2006, but there has been no effort to expand the institution's functional capacity such as in areas related to the initiation of legislation. The council's role remains purely consultative, restricted to providing commentary and advice on proposed bills.[43] Unlike the past, however, when such a situation would have been accepted quietly, a number of academics have voiced criticism about the slowness of the government's response to calls for reforming the council. Even prior to the introduction of elections, Abdulkhaleq Abdullah, a professor at the UAE University, stated:

> It is high time for us to have a fully elected house . . . enough of an appointed council that is without legislative powers, lagging behind us in development and failing to express people's concerns. It has become embarrassing for the UAE to lag behind others politically in the region. This does not fit the country and its stature. At a time when more than 10 million Arabs in Palestine, Iraq and Saudi Arabia exercised their right to vote and be elected, it is completely unacceptable that the UAE still has an appointed house.[44]

Abdullah's criticism did produce an initial response, and his call brought FNC members together to demand that the council focus its debates on specific topics and introduce measures to ensure that the government be held accountable for its performance. In May 2004, for example, several members publicly criticized the government for ignoring the needs of rural areas.[45] The FNC also began to elect its speaker by secret ballot in March 2003. But since then, no further progress has been achieved. But there has been increased criticism within the country about the failure of the government to announce either the next phase of elections scheduled for the end of 2010 or plans to extend greater legislative authority to the FNC. On these fronts, the impetus to enact change and move forward as far as the government is concerned has certainly waned.

The same can be argued for various local councils in Abu Dhabi,

Sharjah, and Ras al-Khaimah where capacity also has expanded slowly. After assuming power, President Shaikh Khalifa quickly put his stamp on the new government by ordering the Abu Dhabi Executive Council to be restructured.[46] But no further steps have been taken. Similarly, the formation of the Dubai Executive Council in February 2003 and the decision in April 2003 to form district councils were designed to enhance public participation in decisionmaking and promote the development of the respective districts.[47] But this has been as far as it goes. According to the country's federal arrangement, each emirate retains the prerogative to decide whether reforms will be instituted and how local consultative councils will be composed and selected. As in other federations, local governments can experiment with innovations before they are applied at the federal level. As a result, in addition to the UAE Federal Government Strategy released in April 2007, there is the Abu Dhabi Policy Agenda of August 2007 and the Dubai Strategic Plan released in February 2007. All are meant to streamline government operations, increase transparency, and clearly outline and focus government strategies whether at the individual emirate level or for the UAE as a whole. In essence, however, they are economically and not politically driven, and these plans simply strive to display an active government that provides the framework for stable development and growth rather than promote structural and substantive changes in the way the government is run.

Of equal concern has been the slow development of civil society within the emirates.[48] In July 2004, a number of prominent UAE nationals petitioned for the establishment of an Emirates Association for Human Rights, the first ever in the country. Their application to the Ministry of Labor and Social Affairs was a significant grassroots initiative, but the organization was not granted a license to operate until February 2006.[49] What the episode revealed once again was that individual proposals for the expansion of civil society through the establishment of voluntary organizations depend on higher-level decisions to become reality. After the application was submitted, the ministry did not even comment on it for three months.[50] When an official announcement was made in late November 2004 stating that the organization would be given the go-ahead, authorization allowing the group to begin operations did not follow for eighteen months. Similar foot-dragging can be seen when it comes to a formal law on the establishment of nongovernmental organizations. The government has indicated numerous times that it would be forthcoming, but not even a draft version has actually appeared.

The above example shows that freedom to form political organizations or the opportunity for those organizations to play an effective role in decisionmaking in the UAE does not yet exist. The UAE constitution makes no provision for the establishment of political groupings, either formalized parties or nongovernmental organizations, although the right to assembly is explicitly recognized in Article 33 of the constitution. Similar to other Arab Gulf states, in the UAE, voluntary associations can form but they are subject to licensing and control by the relevant ministries, which in turn means that any financial support by the government subjects that organization to the decisions of the ministry. Other voluntary groups do operate, but this is done on a purely private basis. Political decisionmaking thus clearly remains the prerogative of the ruling families. While individual citizens can take their grievances and voice them in a ruler's *majlis*, they have little formal influence on the decisionmaking process and even successful protests do not lead to systemic reform. As a result, civic engagement in the UAE, along with the required social trust that is essential for a functioning system of institutional governance, continues instead to be invested in personal relations. Recent improvements in this situation stem from rising levels of education and greater access to information technologies, but they are small and remain relatively slow moving. Overall, the entire process of forming and regulating independent organizations remains highly arbitrary. In addition, authorities are hesitant to proceed with the creation of institutional frameworks for political participation, instead preferring that much of this development take place via informal mechanisms.

Education, Communication, and the Labor Market

Outside of direct government control, social forces are, however, beginning to change the political landscape of the UAE. To be sure, in the area of education, the country has witnessed rapid expansion in the number and quality of institutions of higher education. The greatest need is for improvement in the quality of K-through-12 instruction and learning. Shaikh Nahyan Mubarak al-Nahyan, the minister of education, has himself admitted that the state of primary and secondary education is "very poor," with teaching continuing to emphasize rote learning and many graduates unable to meet admission standards for higher education.[51] In announcing the UAE Federal Government Strategy, even the prime minister, Shaikh Mohammad Bin Rashid al-Maktoum, criticized the lack of progress in education despite rising levels of state support: "The budget for education has increased annually for the past 20 years. . . . Yet, the outcome has constantly been weakening."[52] This has led some to warn that the country risks creating a "lost generation."[53]

While education reform was a prominent part of the George W. Bush agenda to promote democracy and liberalization in the Middle East, reforms in the UAE began well before US policy had shifted in this direction. In 1995, government authorities issued Reform Plan 2020 with the aim of revising curricula to raise standards. In 2002, the Ministry of Education created small committees to oversee the reform process. They were charged with removing material considered offensive and ensuring that curriculum content meet requirements for the modern job market. Furthermore, all policy plans and strategies issuing from the government include attention to education, thereby underlining that such changes have support at the highest level. Public statements from everyone in the UAE leadership make it clear that education reform will continue until the school system can prepare students adequately to meet present-day higher education and job market requirements.[54] As part of the 2009 budget, the UAE allocated 9.7 billion dirhams, or 23 percent of the total budget for education. In addition, Abu Dhabi and Dubai have established well-endowed foundations to support broad-based societal reform. Announcing the US$10 billion Mohammad Bin Rashid Foundation, Dubai's ruler Shaikh Mohammad stated:

> The Foundation's mission is to invest in knowledge and human development, focusing specifically on research, education and promoting equal opportunities for the personal growth and success of our youth. The Foundation's programs are also aimed at enhancing the standing of scholars and intellectuals in the Arab world.[55]

These steps have led to concrete results. The Abu Dhabi Education Council, for example, has launched a public-private partnership program for public school management, introduced English-language instruction even at the elementary level, installed computer labs, and utilized online educational resources throughout the educational system.[56] At the higher education level, the UAE has one of the highest application participation rates in the world, with 95 percent of girls and 80 percent of boys who enroll in the last year of secondary school applying for higher education both in the country and abroad.[57] At the beginning of 2010, there were three national institutions of higher education (UAE University, the Higher Colleges of Technology, and Zayid University); numerous private universities such as the American Universities of Sharjah and Dubai, Abu Dhabi University, Sharjah University, and the Ajman University of Science and Technology; and branches of several foreign institutions, including the Sorbonne and New York University. There has also been a widespread growth of vocational institutions covering areas such as banking and finance, the oil industry, and aviation services.[58]

Despite its shortcomings, education in the UAE has thus begun to make a noticeable impact on the younger generation. More literate and knowledgeable about regional and international events, young people in the emirates are increasingly conscious of their standing in society and their corresponding role within it. The effects of mass education are enhanced by modern communications, especially independent media. Satellite television channels such as Al-Jazeera and Al-Arabiyya have drawn large audiences throughout the Middle East, and stimulated popular interest in and knowledge of politics and current affairs.

The UAE constitution guarantees all citizens "freedom to hold opinions and expression of the same" as well as "freedom of communication." These rights have been slow to be translated into practice but, thanks to the globalization of the communications regime, recent years have seen relaxation of government controls on the media. The establishment of Dubai Media City drew numerous broadcast and print media to Dubai, including the satellite channels Al-Arabiyya and Middle East Broadcasting Center (MBC), and Western news services like CNN and Reuters. Media coverage of local affairs focuses on domestic issues such as job discrimination, labor disputes, the cost of living, and environmental matters. News from elsewhere in the Gulf offers a broader perspective on current affairs. UAE residents can follow in real time such events as constitutional developments and parliamentary elections in Kuwait and the opposition protests in Iran following the disputed presidential elections in June 2009.

The decision by the UAE to hold elections can only be understood in this context. The UAE is one of the most networked and wired countries in the Gulf. It has an Internet penetration rate of 67 percent, over 2.3 million Internet users (49.8 percent of the population), and 69.61 mobile phones per 100 inhabitants.[59] In what has become a relatively open media environment, remaining constraints on reporting are mainly the result of self-censorship, shaped by the government's prohibition on criticism of the ruling families and statements it considers threatening to social stability. Interestingly, the government's attempt to pass a new media law in 2009 was hampered by growing public opposition. Although in the new version of the law the government scrapped jail terms for offending journalists, the draft law retained a provision stating that it is "prohibited to publish news that causes harm to the national currency or causes damage to the national economy."[60] Numerous UAE intellectuals and citizens subsequently objected and argued that this did not advance the process of reform in the country. As a result, the status of the law remains in limbo as of April 2010. The fact that editorial matters fall under the realm of criminal law and that 90 percent of journalists are noncitizens means that self-censorship is seen as the chief means of avoiding any sort of trouble. At the same time, however, the UAE did advance twelve places in the 2007 World Press Freedom Index on the basis that "authorities have displayed a tendency to be more open-minded."[61]

Finally, the modernization process has led to the emergence of a middle class made up of civil servants, small-business owners, and skilled workers. While these groups have established a degree of independence for themselves, they continue to be dependent on the largesse of the upper elite for their livelihood and advancement. Reflecting increased differentiation in the labor market, the UAE has announced that it will permit the establishment of labor unions, thus bringing its practice into line with other GCC states that have either already established such associations or are considering the idea. Under the proposed draft labor law, UAE citizens and expatriates who have resided in the UAE for at least three years will have the right to freely join labor unions and engage in union activities.[62] Yet this step had not been taken by the beginning of 2010.

The proposed labor law is a response to the often scandalous treatment of expatriate labor, especially low-skilled workers from South and Southeast Asia. Their abuse has attracted media attention and does not conform to the country's new emphasis on accountability and transparency or protect its image. Here, the UAE has indicated that it intends to introduce further labor market reforms, including cracking down on illegal recruitment, fining companies that fail to pay salaries on time, and improving conditions in the much-criticized labor camps. Numerous fines already have been imposed on local companies for such items as nonpayment of wages and violating the midday break rule. These laws have been enforced with employers publicly named and shamed for some practices. In this context, it can be said that outside pressure has served as an element forcing the UAE government to react. This was also the case with regard to use of underage boys as camel jockeys, a practice officially outlawed in 2005. Yet external pressure also has its limits. One indication of the limited US impact on labor issues can be found with regard to the proposed UAE-US Free Trade Agreement, which has largely stalled due to the US negotiators' insistence that labor issues be a central point of discussion. In response, UAE authorities postponed further discussion on this subject indefinitely.

Labor issues are linked to the larger population dilemma faced by UAE policymakers. Since the country was founded, there have not been enough UAE citizens to satisfy labor market demands. This made the importation of foreign labor a necessity, but it has produced a number of problematic consequences. UAE citizens are a small minority in their own country. According to a February 2008 report by the Agency for National Human Resource Development and Employment Authority (TANMIA), the number of UAE nationals had fallen to 15.4 percent of the population by the end of 2006, when there were only 866,779 UAE citizens in a total population of 5.6 million.[63] Leaders and government officials fear that the large number of foreigners will dilute the traditional character of UAE society. Abdul Rahman Al Awar, director of TANMIA, stated in an interview in September 2004 that "expatriates will remain in the private sector for generations to come . . . but we cannot allow them to continue to deprive nationals of job opportunities."[64] He noted further that 99 percent of private sector vacancies go to expatriates. While so-called emiratization programs are in place, they have not been able to meet their proposed targets. Even the banking sector, long touted as the leader in recruiting nationals into the labor force, experienced an overall percentage drop in citizen employees between 2002 and 2004.[65] Neither amnesties for illegal workers and those who have overstayed their visas nor pronatalist policies directed toward nationals have been able to resolve these underlying structural parameters.

Conclusion

Using Western standards of democratization or political liberalization—including instituting elections for public officials and establishing the rule of law—the United Arab Emirates would be classified as an underdeveloped country with limited prospects that the pace of change will increase significantly in the near future. To be sure, there is a grain of truth in such characterizations. With economic resources available to support the dominant patron-client relationships actively fostered by the various ruling families in the individual emirates, there is no sense of urgency toward altering political arrangements that so far have proven to work quite well. From this perspective, the current situation in which modernization has not so far interfered with political stability or stimulated any serious domestic opposition justifies maintaining the current path and avoiding risky experiments.[66]

But beneath this placid surface, the UAE is in fact experiencing the same pressures that are also pushing other Gulf states toward greater degrees of liberalization. Among UAE citizens, there is general agreement about the desirability of broadening political participation and political reforms.[67] While the term "democracy" has acquired negative connotations resulting from the belief that it is primarily a US mechanism for imposing an external system of rule on the country, most people do hold positive views toward democracy as a form of government. A poll conducted by Zogby International in 2004 revealed that 44 percent of the UAE population has a favorable attitude toward the US democratic system. This continued to be the case in 2008 even as US policy came in for severe criticism from UAE nationals. The advances in education and communications discussed above are, in the meantime, contributing to growing pressure from within for change.

Governing elites realize that adjustments to the system will be required both to keep pace with regional developments and to support their own legitimacy. Steps to broaden political participation have been announced and more are expected, especially with regard to civil society organizations and the role of women. The UAE ruling elite appears increasingly concerned with long-term strategic policies and there is a sense that reform policies are being devised with the long-term picture in mind. Questions remain, however, on priorities. High-prestige projects continue to trump more fundamental institutional reforms.

One critical caveat is the domination of the economy over other popular concerns. Indeed, the impetus for political reform is still largely confined to the elite. The record levels of oil prices until the summer of 2008 that caused the UAE's national income to skyrocket moved political reform to the back burner. But the impact of the global financial crisis on the UAE and the rest of the Gulf region in late 2008 and into 2009, especially the more than 60 percent drop in oil prices, underlined the fact that a strategy based solely on continued economic development and growth would not be sufficient to ensure overall sustainability. Ultimately, what is required is the emergence of a new social contract under which ruling arrangements are no longer based on the handouts that the state passes on to its citizens to cement its own legitimacy, but where citizens are provided the opportunities to become productive members of society who share responsibility for the proper functioning of their country. In more practical terms, it means continued political reform that moves from the prevailing top-down decision-making system toward one that is based on the concepts of accountability, transparency, and the rule of law.

The UAE's success up to now can be attributed to the flexibility of its internal institutions. With globalization, sustainability, and political reform playing an increasingly central role in the minds of citizens as well as planners, the next decade could bring about a reevaluation in the relationship between policymaking and decisionmaking at the emirate and the federal levels. From that perspective, the UAE very much remains a work in progress.

Notes

1. Shaikh Zayid's philosophy and core beliefs about the importance of unity are laid out in Shaikh Zayid Bin Sultan Al-Nahyan, *The Leader and the Nation* (Abu Dhabi: Emirates Center for Strategic Studies and Research, 2004), especially the introduction and chapter 10.

2. Frauke Heard-Bey argues that the high percentage of foreign workers in the UAE has caused nationals to increasingly identify themselves as "UAE citizens" as a means to deal with their minority status. See "The United Arab Emirates: Statehood and Nation-Building in a Traditional Society," *Middle East Journal* 59, no. 3 (July 2005): 357–375. In his book on the UAE, Christopher Davidson characterizes the UAE as a "confederation" rather than a federation and argues that to date, little policy coordination between the individual emirates occurs. See Christopher Davidson, *The United Arab Emirates: A Study in Survival* (Boulder: Lynne Rienner, 2005), especially pp. 82–85 and 189–207. Fatma al-Sayegh, cited in Davidson, *The United Arab Emirates*, p. 206, n. 27, meanwhile describes the UAE as having gone through three distinct phases, with the period from 1971 to 1979 being the "creation of the federation"; 1980 to 1986, the "accepting of the federation"; and 1987 to present, the "maturity of the federation."

3. See Frauke Heard-Bey, "The United Arab Emirates: A Quarter Century of Federation," in Michael Hudson, ed., *Middle East Dilemma: The Politics of Economics and Arab Integration* (New York: Columbia University Press, 1999), p. 134.

4. Much has been written on the role of Dubai as an economic model for the rest of the region. A solid academic analysis of the concept is provided by Martin Hvidt, "The Dubai Model: An Outline of Key Development-Process Elements in Dubai," *International Journal of Middle Eastern Studies* 41, no. 3 (2009): 397–418.

5. Once the news broke that certain Dubai-backed companies were seeking a moratorium on their debt payments, much of the press coverage saw a 180-degree turn from praising Dubai as the next Hong Kong to suggesting that the emirate would now fail and predicting its demise. See, for example, "The Dark Side of Dubai," *The Independent*, April 7, 2009; and "Confidence Will Never Return to Dubai," *The Times* (London), December 5, 2009.

6. The development of the US democracy agenda for the Middle East is discussed in Chapter 11.

7. In an interview with the Italian daily *La Repubblica*, Egyptian president Hosni Mubarak warned that the imposition of US reform plans on the Arab world would result in "a vortex of violence and anarchy" and that the lessons of violence-ridden Algeria should serve as a clear warning in this regard ("Riforme e Pacificazione in Medio Oriente [Intervista Conil Presidente H. Mubarak]," *La Repubblica,* March 5, 2004). In a joint statement following their meeting in Egypt in February 2004 ("Riyadh and Cairo Reject Imposed Reforms," *Arab News*, February 25, 2004), President Mubarak and Saudi Arabia's crown prince Abdullah "affirmed that Arab states proceed on the path of development, modernization and reform in keeping with their people's interests and values" and that Arab states "do not accept that a particular pattern of reform be imposed on Arab and Islamic countries from outside." Such statements have been continuously repeated by various leaders since the end of 2003.

8. This line of argument was voiced by several participants at the workshop "Political Reform in the GCC States: Current Situation and Future Prospects," Dubai, September 2004, which was organized by the Gulf Research Center and the Carnegie Endowment for International Peace. See www.grc.ae.

9. Some of the arguments presented here are based on articles I wrote for the *Bertelsmann Transformation Index 2006*, a cross-country analysis based on fifty-five criteria to see "to what extent developing and transition countries steer societal change toward constitutional democracy and a socially responsible market economy." See Bertelsmann Stiftung, ed., *Bertelsmann Transformation Index 2006: Toward Democracy and a Market Economy* (Bielefeld: Verlag Bertelsmann Stiftung, 2006). Updated versions of the article are available in the UAE country chapter that appears in both the 2008 and 2010 *Bertelsmann Transformation Index*. See Bertelsmann Stiftung, ed., *Bertelsmann Transformation Index 2008: Political Management in International Comparison* (Bielefeld: Verlag Bertelsmann Stiftung, 2008); and Bertelsmann Stiftung, ed., *Bertelsmann Transformation Index 2010* (Bielefeld: Verlag Bertelsmann Stiftung, forthcoming).

10. The UAE is currently listed as having the sixth largest proven oil reserves in the world at 97.8 billion barrels, behind Saudi Arabia at 264.1 billion barrels, Iran at 137.6 billion barrels, Iraq at 115.0 billion barrels, Kuwait at 101.5 billion barrels, and Venezuela at 99.4 billion barrels. For the UAE, this represents 7.8 percent of the total world reserves. In addition, the UAE has significant gas reserves that rank as the seventh largest in the world (*British Petroleum Statistical Review of World Energy*, June 2009, www.bp.com).

11. "UAE Economy Soars 7.4 pc in 2007," *Khaleej Times*, March 10, 2008, www.grc.ae (March 11, 2008). See also "Investments in Non-oil Sectors Accelerate UAE Growth Rate," www.uaeinteract.com.

12. "Poll Opens for First UAE Elections," Al-Jazeera English website, December 16, 2006, http://english.aljazeera.net (October 23, 2007).

13. Mahmoud Habboush, "FNC Members Ask for New Elections," *The National*, March 10, 2010.

14. Suggestions have ranged from anywhere between US$60 billion and US$150 billion. See Eckart Woertz, "Implications of Dubai's Debt Troubles," Gulf Research Center Report (December 2009).

15. Al-Sayegh, cited in Davidson, *United Arab Emirates,* pp. 110, 115–116.

16. Davidson, *The United Arab Emirates*, p. 104.

17. For a broader view on how these developments are promoting change throughout the Middle East, see Christian Koch, "The Societal Sources of Change in the Middle East," *International Politics and Society,* no. 4 (2004): 54–69.

18. "Number of Women in UAE Cabinet Doubled," Agence France Presse, February 18, 2008, www.grc.ae (March 11, 2008).

19. "Dubai Government Pledges War Against Corruption," Emirates News Agency (WAM), August 18, 2008.

20. The speech by Shaikh Mohammad Bin Rashid was reprinted in "Need of the Hour Is the Will to Change," address of Shaikh Mohammad Bin Rashid. Reprinted in *Gulf News*, December 14, 2004.

21. GDP is calculated using a 3.685 conversion rate (the UAE dirham is permanently pegged to the US dollar at the rate of $1:3.685 UAE dirham). The data are from the International Monetary Fund, *Regional Outlook Middle East and Central Asia*, Washington, DC, October 2009. See also *Emirates Business 24/7*, July 28, 2009.

22. *Emirates Business 24/7*, July 28, 2009. See also IMF, *World Economic Outlook: Crisis and Recovery* (Washington, DC: IMF, April 2009).

23. AME Info, April 24, 2007, www.ameinfo.com. See also www.menafn.com (June 29, 2009).

24. Of the GCC states, only Qatar stood above the UAE with an index of 7.0 in position 22. Oman came in thirty-ninth place with an index of 5.5, Bahrain ranked in forty-sixth place with an index of 5.1, followed by Saudi Arabia at sixty-third place and a 4.3 index and Kuwait at sixty-sixth place and a 4.1 index rating. The full corruption perceptions index is available from Transparency International, "Corruption Perception Index 2009," www.transparency.org (April 12, 2010).

25. "Accountability Authority Set Up to Improve Government Efficiency in UAE," *Khaleej Times*, December 21, 2008.

26. "HH Sheikh Mohammad Bin Rashid Unveils the UAE Federal Government Strategy," AME Info, Dubai, April 17, 2007, www.ameinfo.com (June 29, 2009).

27. "Highlights: Dubai Strategic Plan 2015: Dubai . . . Where the Future Begins" (Dubai: Government of Dubai, n.d.), http://egov.dubai.ae (October 24, 2007).

28. "Highlights: Dubai Strategic Plan 2015," p. 13.

29. *Gulf News*, April 18, 2007; see also "Highlights of the UAE Government Strategy: Leadership . . . Integration . . . Excellence," www.wam.ae (October 24, 2007). It can also be downloaded at www.dubai.ae. No date or place of publication is provided.

30. "The Executive Council, Policy Agenda 2007–2008: The Emirate of Abu Dhabi," www.gulfnews.com (October 24, 2007).

31. "Abu Dhabi Policy Agenda 2007–2008, Executive Summary," Abu Dhabi, General Secretariat of the Executive Council, 2007, www.abudhabi.ac.

32. "New Ministers Vow to Strengthen Nation," *Gulf News*, November 3, 2004; "Ministry a Big Boost for Presidential Affairs," *Gulf News,* November 22, 2004; and "Restructuring of Sixth Cabinet Sees First Women Minister," *Gulf News,* November 2, 2004.

33. "Zayed Reshuffles Cabinet," *Gulf News,* November 2, 2004. There was also an interesting case in Ras al-Khaimah where it was suggested that the dethroning of the crown prince in June 2003 was due in part to the activities of his wife, who was regarded by some as a strong advocate of women's rights. See "Emirate Prince Ousted in Women's Rights Row," *Daily Telegraph*, June 15, 2003, www.telegraph.co.uk (March 11, 2008). Also, "The Ras al-Khaima Succession Crisis," *The Estimate*, July 4, 2003, www.theestimate.com (March 11, 2008).

34. See "Seven New Faces as Cabinet Reshuffled," *Khaleej Times*, February 18, 2008, www.grc.ae (March 11, 2008).

35. "Women Form 70pc of National Job Seekers," *Gulf News*, September 22, 2004.

36. Similar trends were witnessed throughout the GCC member states, with the participation of women in the labor force doubling in Bahrain, Kuwait, Qatar, and Saudi Arabia and almost tripling in Oman; ILO, *Yearbok of Labour Statistics 2002* (Geneva: ILO, 2002).

37. *Khaleej Times*, August 27, 2004; Ebtisam Al-Kitbi, "Women's Issues in the GCC Countries in 2004," *Gulf Yearbook 2004* (Dubai: Gulf Research Center, 2005), p. 135; Meena Janardhan, "UAE: Women's Participation Is the Norm," IPS News, February 25, 2009, http://ipsnews.net (June 29, 2009).

38. UAE Ministry of Information, *UAE Yearbook 2008*, www.uaeinteract.com.

39. "Three Women in New DCCI Board of Directors," *Gulf News*, November 17, 2003.

40. Al-Kitbi, "Women's Issues in the GCC Countries in 2004," pp. 127–129, especially n. 14; also "Political Future of Women in UAE Promising," *Khaleej Times*, August 27, 2004.

41. "Ensuring Women's Rights," *Gulf News*, January 15, 2004.

42. UNDP, *Human Development Report 2009, Overcoming Barriers: Human Mobility and Development* (New York: UNDP, 2009), http://hdr.undp.org.

43. There are still only forty members divided along the same representation as originally suggested (eight each for Abu Dhabi and Dubai, six for Sharjah and Ras al-Khaimah, and four each for the smaller three emirates).

44. Quoted in "Nationals Push for Polls to Elect FNC Members," *Gulf News*, February 23, 2005.

45. "Government Slammed for Ignoring Rural Areas," *Gulf News*, May 19, 2004.

46. "President Issues Three Decrees Restructuring Abu Dhabi Executive Council," *Emirates News Agency,* December 9, 2004.

47. "Dubai Plans District Councils," *Gulf News*, April 2, 2003; and "Dubai Sets Up Executive Council," *Gulf News,* February 26, 2003.

48. Francis Matthew, "UAE's Civil Society Is Weak," *Gulf News*, February 18, 2010.

49. *Gulf News*, September 4, 2006.

50. "Deadline Over, Rights Panel Waits for Official Approval," *Gulf News*, October 5, 2004.

51. "Public School Education Poor, Must Be Reformed—Minister," *Gulf News*, October 5, 2004.

52. "Mohammad Calls for Cautious Emiritization," *Gulf News*, April 18, 2007.

53. "Nation in Danger of 'Losing a Generation,'" *The National*, February 10, 2010.

54. In this capacity as Abu Dhabi crown prince, Shaikh Mohammad Bin Zayid has equally argued for greater attention to the quality of education in both public and private schools at all grade levels. See "Nahyan: Education Will Become High Priority for UAE's Future," *Gulf News*, August 25, 2004.

55. Press Release of the World Economic Forum from May 19, 2007, www.weforum.org (October 25, 2007).

56. UAE Ministry of Information, *United Arab Emirates Yearbook 2007* (Abu Dhabi, 2007), especially the chapter on social development, pp. 213–264.

57. Ibid, p. 230.

58. Ibid, p. 237.

59. "Internet Penetration in the UAE Increasing," *Emirates Business 24/7*, August 6, 2008; "Just the Good News Please: New UAE Media Law Continues to Stifle Press," April 2009, http://hrw.org (April 13, 2009). See also Internet World Stats, "Usage and Population Statistics" (Miniwatts Marketing Group, 2010), www.internetworldstats.com (June 29, 2008).

60. See Human Rights Watch, "Just the Good News Please: New UAE Media Law Continues to Stifle Press," April 13, 2009, www.hrw.org.

61. "UAE Fares Well in World Press Freedom Index," *Khaleej Times*, October 17, 2007.

62. "Trade Unions Will Help Cut Worker Woes," *Gulf News*, July 30, 2004.

63. "75 pc of Labour Force in UAE Belongs to Asian Countries," *Khaleej Times*, February 25, 2008, www.khaleejtimes.com (March 11, 2008).

64. "Women Form 70pc of National Job Seekers."

65. "Worker Groups Law Nears," *Gulf News*, June 12, 2004.

66. William A. Rugh, "The United Arab Emirates: What Are the Sources of Its Stability?" *Middle East Journal* 5, no. 3 (1997): 14–24.

67. This is reflected in a number of unpublished surveys conducted by the Emirates Center for Strategic Studies and Research (ECSSR), a UAE government think-tank based in Abu Dhabi.

PART 2
The Regional Context

9

Women in Civic and Political Life: Reform Under Authoritarian Regimes

Eleanor Abdella Doumato

GENDER EQUALITY—whether in terms of economic opportunity, employment, education, or participation in politics and civil society—is a crucial component of Western-style democracy. The paradox of the Gulf experience with democratizing initiatives, however, is that reform efforts bring women into the political arena only when nondemocratic, authoritarian regimes open the door for them. At the same time, wherever reform initiatives on behalf of women are implemented, these reforms are exposed to critical opposition from a conservative public given new political voice by the same democratic processes through which women seek inclusion and empowerment.

Without exception, the Gulf's authoritarian regimes have facilitated women's emergence into commerce, the professions, civic organizations, and public affairs more generally. In all the Gulf states, women are underrepresented in the workforce and their participation is constrained by paternalistic labor laws, sex segregation rules, and prohibitions against their working in specific areas. At the same time, however, Gulf rulers have instituted policies to encourage their participation, such as providing generous maternity benefits, providing access to unemployment insurance and training, and increasing the number of positions for women by featherbedding in the public sector. Women are being appointed to high-level positions in government and civil society organizations, including the once-forbidden terrain of the Islamic judiciary.

The most notable successes of Gulf regimes have been in the field of education for women and girls. Between 1990 and 2000, the historical gap between boys' and girls' access to education closed: as in the rest of the Middle East, gender differences in enrollment at every level of education are now almost negligible.[1] These advances are most dramatic at the college and university level, where the number of female students is equal to or greater than the number of male students.[2] Furthermore, in every Gulf state, coeducational and women-only English-language colleges and universities designed to follow a US curricular model have been founded by heads of state and by private initiative following approval by heads of state. In Kuwait, the state university and the private American University of Kuwait began as coeducational institutions, although both have been segregated by sex as a result of a law passed by Kuwait's National Assembly. Even in Saudi Arabia, where gender segregation is the cornerstone of official morality, the King Abdullah University of Science and Technology opened in 2009 as a coeducational institution for graduate education.

In this chapter I look principally at Saudi Arabia, but also include the other Gulf Cooperation Council (GCC) states—Bahrain, Kuwait, Oman, Qatar, and the United Arab Emirates—to address women's empowerment by exploring the following questions: In what ways are women engaging in civic and political affairs, and have the Gulf's authoritarian regimes helped or hindered their participation? Are there common barriers that women face across the region, and where are the "red lines" that Gulf regimes will not cross? Do democratizing initiatives expand women's opportunities or rein them in?

State Feminism in Saudi Arabia

Following the attacks of September 11, 2001, in which fifteen of the nineteen airplane hijackers turned out to be Saudi citizens, the kingdom came under intense international scrutiny. Held up as contributory factors motivating the 9/11 hijackers were Saudi Arabia's political repression, lack of personal liberties, low standards for educational achievement, and high rates of unemployment, along with a government-sponsored form of Islam that encourages hostility toward non-Muslims and rejection of Western culture. As a result, the Saudi regime faced pressure for social and political reform not only from the United States, but also from liberal thinkers and radical opposition groups within the kingdom.

A brief springtime of optimism for Saudi liberals followed. Media censorship was loosened and subjects that had been off limits, including issues related to women, were openly debated. Saudi women became more visible physically. Female newsreaders reappeared on television, and women's photos, which once were forbidden, became a daily staple in the press. Crown Prince Abdullah, who became king in 2005, appeared to take the lead by calling for more work opportunities for women. He routinely met with feminist delegations and female journalists, professors, and business leaders at home and on his trips overseas.[3] Abdullah brought women into government-controlled organizations and appointed women to high positions in the civil service. In 2000 his government ratified the Convention on Elimination of All Forms of Discrimination Against Women, albeit with a potentially self-negating reservation, exempting the kingdom from observing obligations under the convention that contradict Islamic law."[4]

Having expanded women's access to education, entrepreneurship, the civil service, and the professions, the Saudi regime opened new public spaces to women: museums; research libraries; public festivals; civic organizations; and new media, including and especially satellite television and Internet access.[5] Recent appointments of women to ministerial posts, university deanships, and directorships in quasi-governmental civic organizations continue embedding systemic changes in society, with women emerging in spaces previously considered the exclusive domain of men.

Human Rights Activism

One of the most dynamic areas of civic engagement for women is human rights activism. The National Society for Human Rights (NSHR) is an independent organization licensed by the Saudi government (Royal Decree No. 2412, 2004). It is the brainchild of Saudi professionals and academics, a number of whom were educated in the United States. Three of the nine members of the NSHR's Executive Council are women, including Al-Johara Mohammad Al-Anqari, who is vice president for family affairs.[6] Al-Anqari deals with complaints about sexual abuse, failure to pay alimony and child support, domestic violence, and other issues of concern to women. In 2009, the society issued a series of recommendations aimed at curbing abuses on the part of the *mutawwa'in,* Saudi Arabia's religious police force. Overseen by the government-funded Commission for the Preservation of Virtue and Prevention of Vice, the religious police direct much of their activity toward controlling women's dress and behavior in public.[7]

Another organization, the Committee of Social Protection, came into being in 2008. Nawaf Al-Herthy, who is chairman of the committee's Jeddah branch and director of the Jeddah Psychiatric Hospital, coordinates efforts among health care facilities, the police, and the Ministries of Health, Social Affairs, Justice, and Education to address reported cases of domestic violence and child abuse.

The Human Rights Commission, established by royal decree in 2005, is a government agency that has yet to reconcile its human rights mission with its civil service status under royal patronage.[8] A hopeful indicator for the future, however, lies in the 2008 opening of a women's section of the commission in Riyadh under the directorship of Wafiqah Al-Dakhil, "to create awareness about the laws relating to women and children through campaigns and define rights as established by Islam" and "handle complaints relating to violence, sexual harassment, arbitrary divorce, rape and personal cases."[9]

Other Saudi organizations concerned with women's rights function tenuously online, with the apparent goal of creating international awareness of human rights problems as opposed to taking action within the kingdom to solve them. These include the Arabic website Voice of Saudi Women (www.sawomenvoice.com) and the Human Rights First Society (http://hrfssaudiarabia.org), which tried to work openly in the kingdom but was unsuccessful at obtaining a license.

In the civil service, there has been a series of "firsts" when it comes to high-level appointments. Female physicians were appointed deputy director of health affairs for the Mecca region and head of the General Directorate of Nursing in the Ministry of Health.[10] Moreover, in 2009 Nourah Al-Fayez was appointed deputy minister of education for women's education, the first woman to be appointed to the Council of Ministers, and a member of the royal family, Princess Al-Jawhara Fahad bin Mohammed bin Abdel Rahman Al-Saud, was appointed director of the new university city for women in Riyadh. While women are not yet eligible for judgeships, they are now permitted to enroll in a new women's department in the Law Faculty at King Saud University in Riyadh, raising the possibility of judicial appointments for women in the future. One positive indicator for women in the legal professions is the endorsement of appointments of female legal scholars to the Council of Senior Scholars, and their entitlement to issue fatwas,[11] which was issued by Abdullah ibn Suleiman Al-Manea, a member of the all-male council.

Women are gaining visibility through professional associations. However, the trajectory of their participation is not as promising as might have been expected in 2004, when the government first allowed women to cast their own votes for board membership on municipal chambers of commerce and industry. Previously, men had voted on behalf of female chamber members, who are now allowed not only to vote but also to run as candidates. In Jeddah, women candidates experienced some successes initially: in 2005, Nadia Bakhurji, 1 of only 20 women among a membership of 5,000 in the Saudi Engineers Council, was elected to the council's board;[12] in the same year, also in Jeddah, where there are 3,000 women among 40,000 members of the Chamber of Commerce and Industry,[13] 17 Saudi businesswomen filed as candidates and 2, Lama Al-Sulaiman and Nashwa Taher, won seats on the chamber's board.[14]

These successes are not representative of elections in other parts of the country. In 2004, no women were elected to the Riyadh Chamber of Commerce and Industry; even though the chamber had about 2,750 female members, only 46 women cast votes in the board election.[15] Time has shown a pattern of low female participation and lack of male support for female candidates. For example, in 2009, 7 women ran as candidates for the Jeddah Chamber board. Of these 7, only 1, an incumbent, was successful; the other incumbent was defeated; and only 160 out of more than 3,000 women members voted—a small fraction of the 6,400 ballots cast.[16] The pattern was repeated in the Eastern Province's Chamber elections. In January 2010, Commerce Minister Abdullah Zainal Alireza appointed 2 women to the board, but these were women who had not been among the 3 female candidates in the elections, all of whom lost after having failed to garner even 100 votes among them. The election outcome illustrates the obstacles women across the kingdom face when seeking positions of public influence. First, there are cultural values in play: the candidates were tainted when men from the local community lodged a complaint with the Eastern Chamber for allowing women to run for office. Although the complaint was denied by the Chamber, the accuation that women's participation is a violation of *sharia* served as a reminder that, in local schools of thought, it is. Moreover, everywhere in the region, women fail to support other women: in the Eastern Province, only 60 of the nearly 900 women eligible to vote participated in the election.[17]

Beginning in 2006, obtaining a state-issued identity card with a photograph became compulsory for women. The requirement may signal a shift in the relationship between women and the state: previously, with the exception of passport holders, all female Saudi citizens were registered with the state only as a name included on the identity cards of their male guardians. The lack of an individual identity document made it difficult for women to obtain government benefits or services in their own names, open bank accounts, or conduct any sort of business independent of male guardians. The government's main concern could be security: photo IDs give law enforcement personnel a way to determine who people are. Yet the card can also be seen as a breach by the state of the barrier represented by the male guardian, who stands between a woman and everything outside her home. Under the new law, if a woman already holds a passport (obtained with her guardian's permission), she does not need a guardian's permission to obtain the ID. For a woman without a passport, a male guardian must agree to her obtaining an ID card since only he can verify her identity when she makes her application.[18] (The paradox of an ID being compulsory, yet also requiring permission of a woman's male guardian to obtain it, must be put aside.) Over time, however, as female citizens are issued IDs at birth, the issue of the guardian's permission will become moot.

Antecedents to the new ID policy include a May 2003 decree by the Council of Ministers allowing women to obtain commercial licenses in their own names without a male guardian's permission. Yet the interjection of the state between male relatives and the women in their families is far from universally accepted. In January 2008, for example, the College of Education at the University of Riyadh required female students to register using their state ID cards: some students complained that the state was breaking the rules of religion, accusing the Ministry of Education of intending to allow male employees to view their photographs.[19]

These gestures of liberalism toward women have been greeted with some skepticism. In January 2004, the Saudi and international press reported, as if it were a groundbreaking event, the presence of Saudi businesswoman Lubna Al-'Olayan at the Jeddah Economic Forum to speak on economic growth in the kingdom. It was not the speech that was newsworthy, but the fact that both men and women in the audience were sitting in the same room. To some observers, the event was a momentous step forward for women; to others, like the Grand Mufti Shaikh Abd al-Aziz Al ash-Shaikh, the mixed-sex event was a moral outrage. Some observers felt that the excitement generated over the presence of women and men together simply highlighted how limited women's options really are. Abd al-Rahman al-Rashed, former editor of the Arabic language daily *As-Sharq al-Awsat*, wrote in the January 26, 2004, edition of the paper: "What is the worth of 10 businesswomen at a conference, when their real activities end the moment the participants depart and the cleaners come in." Al-Rashed notes that, during the conference, the government decided against establishing a women's faculty for technology studies to match the faculty available to men, thereby denying women equal access to education in these fields. The Jeddah forum cannot even be credited with normalizing the mixing of the sexes in professional settings: more than a year later, in February 2005 King Abd al-Aziz University hosted a conference on higher education at which the female participants were assigned seats in a segregated area away from the main hall, which was reserved for men.

Saudi Arabia's Experiment with Democratic Elections

Every Gulf state has some form of democratic elections. In almost every case voter eligibility is circumscribed, and most elections are for councils with limited or no legislative functions. Saudi Arabia began holding elections for seats on municipal councils in February 2005. This first such experiment in over forty years was hardly a paragon of democracy at work. Not only were women excluded from voting, but also men in military service and municipal employees. Political campaigning by liberals was not allowed, although conservative candidates had campaign tents set up all over the country. Only half the seats on the councils were filled by election; the other half was appointed. The municipal councils, furthermore, are merely advisory, without executive or legislative authority. Yet the inclusion of women as voters, if not as candidates, would have marked a milestone of sorts. Women were hopeful because, when the Saudi Consultative Council (Majlis al-Shura) announced the plan for elections in October 2003, no criteria for voting or running for office had been included, but an endorsement of women's participation had come from then–crown prince Abdullah's personally appointed Advisory Working Group. That was the body that had proposed municipal elections, and also explicitly called for full voting rights for women. Support came from the Justice Ministry as well. As reported in the Saudi newspaper *Okaz*, a ministry spokesman said that "there is no reason to stop them from participating in the elections. . . . Trends coming from the West which are beneficial and do not contradict our laws and religion should not be banned."[20]

For the better part of a year the government vacillated over whether or not to allow women to vote, holding a collective finger to the wind to gauge the reaction of the Saudi public while the establishment *ulama*, among others, made their objections known.[21] Meanwhile, women put themselves forward as candidates: Nadia Bakhurji, a Riyadh interior designer, and Fatin Bundaqji, director of women's empowerment and research at the Jeddah Chamber of Commerce and Industry, continued to lobby for their right to run for office[22] even after interior minister Prince Naif bin Abd al-Aziz announced that women would not be allowed to vote. He did not close the door on the possibility of women voting in future elections, citing logistical reasons such as that polling places would have to be sex segregated and so would the city council sessions in which women hoped to participate.[23]

Perhaps in compensation, three women were appointed to serve on an advisory council to the all-male Shura Council, which had 150 members as of May 2009. Some at first had thought these women would serve as members of the council but, as it turned out, they were not even invited to sit in and listen during council deliberations. In fact, their duties as advisers were never made clear.[24] In July 2006, with considerable media publicity, six more women were appointed as part-time advisers to the council, but their portfolio remains equally nebulous. They may be asked to represent Saudi Arabia at conferences outside the kingdom, or to give advice to the Shura Council on "women's issues" such as high dowries—if they should be asked.[25]

Hatoon Al-Fassi, an associate professor at King Saud University and one of the women appointed, commented that, "if the committee is to be as described, there is no need for it and I object to being included. This is not a first step; it is very much the same as what we have now. Women are asked as consultants with no right to make decisions, no authority and their opinions are not taken."[26] What women want, she said, is an independent women's council supervising all issues relating to women, with the right to make suggestions to the Shura Council and report directly to the king.[27] On the other end of the spectrum are members of the Shura Council who are not prepared to admit women in any capacity. Saleh bin Humaid, the speaker, stated that in his view any discussions about women members of the Consultative Council were "premature."[28]

In 2009, the approach of scheduled elections for municipal councils prompted renewed discussion about women's participation. A conference of municipal council members in the Eastern Province agreed that women should have the right to vote, but not to put themselves forward as candidates. No decision on women's participation in elections was issued from Riyadh, however, and the following month the whole question was rendered moot, for the time being at least, when the Saudi cabinet extended the term of the municipal councils from four years to six, effectively postponing the elections for two years. The decision came in the wake of a petition sent to the king asking for swifter democratization, including an elected parliament and a prime minister who is not a member of the royal family.[29]

Women in Grassroots Reform Initiatives

Even though women were ultimately shut out of municipal elections, they were politically assertive during Saudi Arabia's post-9/11 springtime for liberal thinkers, writers, and activists.[30] Democratizing initiatives followed one after another in the form of petitions to the government, every one submitted by both men and women who pledged allegiance to the monarchy but also asked for changes in the system of governance. In January 2003, a letter signed by 104 citizens entitled "A Vision for the Nation and Its Future" was sent to the crown prince. It called for social justice; public election of the Shura Council; an end to corruption; an independent judiciary; and freedom of speech, assembly, and association. In April, a second petition entitled "Partners in One Nation" was signed by 450 Shi'ite men and women expressing sympathy with the signatories of the January letter, and asking for relief from discrimination and more Shi'ite representation in government positions, education reform, and religious freedom.[31]

On September 24, 2003, 306 Sunni and Shi'ite men and women sent another petition, "In Defense of the Nation," repeating the same calls for political reform and separation of powers, freedom of speech, right of assembly, and religious tolerance. The signers openly blamed existing political restrictions for terrorist activity in the kingdom, and its development.[32] The petition cited the second-class status of women among issues that need addressing, and advocated elections for the 120-member Consultative Council. Then–crown prince Abdullah, who among all the senior princes has been most responsive to citizens' concerns, met personally with the petitioners. On October 14, the government opened a conference on human rights sponsored by the Saudi Red Crescent Society, but this conference marked the limit of the regime's toleration of dissent. When protestors turned up at conference headquarters to advocate political reform and the release of political prisoners, Saudi police used live ammunition to break up the demonstration, and arrested 271 people.[33]

Two months later, on December 16, more arrests followed a public demonstration in Jeddah instigated by Saad al-Faqih, the Saudi dissident who heads the London-based Movement for Islamic Reform in Arabia, which is not friendly toward women's rights. Fifteen demonstrators demanding an elected government, an independent judiciary, and a new Islamic constitution were sentenced in January 2004 by a religious court to 100 to 250 lashes and from two to six months of imprisonment for having demonstrated against the government.

In March 2004, thirteen petition signers met personally with the crown prince, after which they too were arrested for "promoting a constitutional monarchy and using Western terminology in demanding political reforms." Ten were released after agreeing in writing to never petition the government again. The remaining three, Matrouq al-Faleh, Abdullah al-Hamid, and Ali al-Demaini, refused to accept such a trade-off. The good news, since having access to legal representation has been one of the key demands of liberal reformers, is that after three months in prison all three men were assigned a lawyer. The bad news is that when the three were finally brought to court, nine persons attempting to attend the trial were arrested, including journalists from the newspapers *Saudi Gazette* and *Al-Madina.* In August 2005, the three petitioners were finally released, not because they had been acquitted but because they had received a royal pardon.[34]

The political fallout from the arrest of these three petition signers is significant for charting the route of future feminist activism. In September 2004, the Council of Ministers reaffirmed the regime's position on political activity, forbidding public employees to challenge government policies by "participating, directly or indirectly, in the preparation of any document, speech or petition, engaging in dialogue with local and foreign media, or participating in any meetings intended to oppose the state's policies."[35] The ruling family also made it clear that even well-intentioned intervention from the outside is unwelcome. After sentences ranging from six to nine years for the three imprisoned petition signers were announced in June 2005, US secretary of state Condoleezza Rice expressed disapproval. In response, Prince Naif in essence replied that she ought to mind her own business.[36]

National Dialogues: Controlling the Conversation

The regime responded to the initial round of petitions by organizing public debates, the so-called National Dialogue sessions, to co-opt opposition movements and influence their agendas.[37] In the second debate, which took place in Mecca in December 2003, ten women, seated in a separate room from the men, were allowed to participate. Various political, social, and educational problems were openly discussed. The meeting ended with the formulation of eighteen recommendations that were later formally presented to then–crown prince Abdullah. They echoed some of the demands put forth in the petitions, including holding elections for the Consultative Council and local consultative councils; encouraging establishment of trade unions, voluntary associations, and other civil society institutions; separating the legislative, executive, and judicial powers; and broadening freedom of expression.[38]

The third National Dialogue session, held in Medina in June 2004, was totally devoted to "Rights and Duties of Women." Half of the seventy participants were women, but the meeting was dominated by conservative men, and controversial topics such as lifting the ban on women drivers or allowing them to travel without a male guardian were avoided. The agenda of the session was so sanitized that a delegation of women went separately to see the crown prince with specific recommendations, which Abdullah politely promised to consider.[39] It was clear that a public meeting on the subject of women had nowhere to go because, a few days before the session had begun, a group of nearly 130 religious scholars issued a joint statement protesting the planned discussion about women and women's rights as yet another "vicious campaign from the [Muslim community's] enemy, led by the American government, to divert it from its faith."[40] The statement also criticized several Saudi newspapers for being "proponents of Westernization" with regard to women, and asserted that total equality between men and women would contravene Islam.

Red Lines and Waffle Lines: The Power of Values

The brass ring for women's empowerment, the right to drive a car, is still beyond the grasp of Saudi feminists. Driving is important for women because they may not travel without permission from their male guardians and are not supposed to ride as passengers in a car operated by an unrelated male driver. Furthermore, Saudi Arabia does not have adequate public transportation. It is considered shameful and also dangerous for a woman to walk in public, veiled or otherwise, so access to a car and driver is critical to her mobility. For many, having a car and driver may determine whether and where a person will work, whether and when she will socialize or even visit her family, and whether she can get a child to a doctor or a hospital in an emergency. Indeed, the right to drive may determine whether a person can act as an independent and responsible adult. Yet women's driving is resisted; it is a red line that cannot be crossed. Female mobility would signal a sea change in hegemonic attitudes about men's right to control women, the value of gender segregation, the meaning of modesty, and the all-consuming prospect of illicit sex that pervades—and threatens—Saudi society. One might say that sex segregation and the invisibility of women in Saudi Arabia's conservative society are fused with the very definition of what it means to be Muslim.

One could argue, therefore, that there is little reason to expect that women will be offered the opportunity to apply for driver's licenses anytime soon, and past attempts to promote women's driving have not produced hopeful outcomes. For example, in June 2005, Mohammad al-Zulfa, a member of the Shura Council, attempted to place on the council's agenda a discussion about doing a study to look into the feasibility of women driving. He was not asking to allow women to drive. All he asked was to discuss it and to consider the economic implications of hiring hundreds of thousands of foreign drivers at heavy cost to do for women what they could do for themselves. In response, there were calls for him to be expelled from the council and even stripped of his citizenship. One of his most virulent critics was a member of the Council of Senior Scholars, Shaikh Saleh Ibn Fawzan Ibn Abdullah al-Fawzan, who argued that "the financial cost of importing foreign drivers is nothing compared to the loss of honor from letting women drive."[41]

In society at large, however, opinion is mixed. In June 2005, 102 Saudi men and women filed a petition with the Saudi Human Rights Commission in support of women's driving,[42] and polls suggest that a majority of Saudis agree that women should be able to drive. In one poll conducted in 2004, 63 percent of those interviewed thought women should be allowed to drive.[43] Another survey conducted a year later found a similar percentage in support.[44] On the other hand, there is active opposition to women driving by conservative women as well as men, some of whom view driving as a symbol of encroaching Westernization that threatens the privileged status they believe women hold in Islam. In July 2005, some 500 women, including university professors, doctors, journalists, and teachers, sent a petition to King Abdullah saying they wanted things to stay the way they were.[45] Lubna al-Tahlawi argues that "women in Saudi Arabia are safer, and better taken care of, and have more status and privilege than women in the West." Western women are viewed as sex objects, suffer from a high rate of prostitution, and do not even make the same salary as men for the same job as women here do, she continued. "Driving has not improved their lives."[46]

The position of the Saudi leadership fluctuates, reflecting the different perspectives of members of the royal family and changing political contexts. In the summer of 1990, in the wake of the infamous women's driving demonstration that took place as US forces deployed on Saudi soil, Saudi rulers joined in the chorus of outrage led by the religious police and the head of the Council of Senior Ulama, Shaikh Abd al-Aziz bin Baz (of blessed memory), who condemned the demonstration as an assault on Islamic standards of decency. Reasoning in the tradition of the logically fallacious "slippery slope" argument, he bases his opinion on the premise that "whatever leads to forbidden things should be forbidden," and since women's driving leads to evil consequences, women's driving must be forbidden.[47] The royal leadership's approach in the post-9/11 era has been to make no promises, to mollify feminist activists with kind words, and to displease no one in the hope that the controversy will go away. As Prince Naif remarked, "these matters are decided according to the general good and what is dictated by women's honor, but I urge everybody to put a stop to this and not make an issue out of it that pits one group against another."[48]

King Abdullah claims that he supports women's driving, but he avoids making commitments, saying that he "would not impose women's driving against the will of [his] people."[49] In December 2005, Crown Prince Sultan took the same noncommittal stance, saying that the government had no objection to allowing women drivers as long as their fathers, husbands, and brothers approved.[50] Accordingly, petitions for the right to drive continue to evoke polite evasions instead of outright rejection. A January 2008 petition presented to King Abdullah expressed the hope that "2008 will be the year in which Saudi women obtain their natural right to drive a car."[51] After that, the government put out a lethargic feeler to test the political winds, announcing through the Information Ministry that a royal decree allowing women to drive would be issued "at the end of the year."[52] In March 2008, the Shura Council, the very same body that three years earlier refused to discuss the question of women's driving, recommended that women be allowed to drive. The council also issued a list of restrictions as if to anticipate criticism in advance: the driver should be under a certain age; she should have permission of a *mahram* and undergo driver training; she should dress modestly, carry a cell phone, and drive only on weekdays during daylight hours. Out of further concern for women's safety the council included punishment of a prison sentence and a fine to be imposed on anyone talking with a woman driver from another car or sexually harassing her.[53] As of April 2010, after another round of rumors and denials regarding Shura Council support for women's driving, the right of women to drive is yet to be made into law.

Selling Underwear

In the spring of 2006, the government ordered shop owners who sell women's underwear to hire all-female sales staff by July 2006 to help solve a growing unemployment problem among Saudi women. But there was another reason: the obvious mortification that women experience in buying intimate clothing from men.[54] By 2007, the policy was to have been extended to stores selling dresses and abayas (the black cloak worn over street clothes). The Labor Ministry organized training courses to prepare women for these jobs, and also produced a raft of conditions under which saleswomen would be allowed to work.[55]

The policy also became a victim of emotional reactions. Since shop windows would have to be papered over and doors kept locked, women shoppers complained that they would feel as though they were committing an illicit act when they went to buy underwear. Grand Mufti Shaikh Abd al-Aziz Al ash-Shaikh denounced the presence of saleswomen in retail shops as a "step towards immorality and hellfire."[56] The labor minister who had suggested the change became a hated figure among conservative Saudi clerics. In a May 2006 audio message, even Osama bin Laden called him a "heretic" who should be killed. At that point, the government, ever ready to withdraw under fire, postponed the replacement of male sales clerks by women in lingerie shops. In the fall of 2007, a year later and with passions cooled, women lingerie salespersons savored triumph in Jeddah, and so did their customers who were no longer compelled to ask men for assistance in purchasing nightgowns, padded bras, and thongs.[57] The catch is that the only place where women are allowed the privilege of buying and selling underwear without male intervention is in women-only shopping areas.

Privacy as Peril

A defining moment for locating the regime's red lines when it comes to women and values occurred in the aftermath of a fire in a public school for girls in Mecca on March 11, 2002. Eight hundred girls had been crammed into a building designed for 250 people. There were no emergency exits, no fire alarms, no fire extinguishers, and no way out in an emergency. Like most public buildings that house girls and women, the outside doors were locked and guarded by men, and so was the main gate of the school. Windows are usually barred and, like all schools, the buildings were surrounded by high walls.[58] The immediate culprits in the tragedy according to witnesses were the *mutawwa'in*, who beat girls trying to get out through the gate because they were not wearing abayas, and intervened when male passersby tried to help the girls escape.[59]

The fire resulted in the deaths of fifteen students and injury to fifty-two others. Afterward parents, journalists, and others demanded prosecution of those responsible, including officials at the General Presidency for Girls' Education, the *ulama*-controlled agency in charge of girls' schools. No one, however, was prosecuted, and there was no public reprimand of the religious police. Instead, the General Presidency was folded into the Ministry of Education, and dissolved the following year.[60] The Ministry of Education now administers the girls' schools and colleges and supervises kindergartens and nursery schools as well as literacy programs for women within a new department that functions under an undersecretary of the Ministry of Education for girls' education affairs. The change was accompanied by new education policies that equalized course offerings for boys and girls, but not safer building codes for girls' schools. Seven years later, in 2009, a woman was put in charge of girls' education when Nora bint Abdullah Al-Fayaz was appointed deputy minister for girls' education, the first woman to be given ministerial rank in Saudi Arabia.

Why the Regime Will Not Cross Its Red Lines

A woman from the town of Qatif on the Gulf coast was gang-raped by seven men in 2007. She subsequently was sentenced to 200 lashes and six months in jail upon the recommendation of Saudi Arabia's Supreme Judiciary Council, which heard the case on appeal. Originally, she had been sentenced to ninety lashes and no jail time by the Qatif General Court, but a statement from the Justice Ministry said that the sentence did not reflect the seriousness of the crime. The woman had, by her own admission, met privately in a car with an acquaintance where they were seen together and assaulted. The Ministry of Justice stood behind the Qatif judiciary. A statement issued on November 21, 2007, noted that the Qatif court's sentence of ninety lashes was correct, if too lenient, according to *sharia*, because the woman had gone out without her *mahram* (her legal guardian) and engaged in illegal *khalwa* (being alone with a man who is not a close relative).[61] According to the ministry she and the man accompanying her, not the rapists, were the primary culprits. "The main reason for the occurrence of the crime was the woman and her accompanying person exposing themselves to this heinous crime (the rape) and causing its occurrence because they violated the provisions of Islamic Law."[62]

In the face of embarrassing international criticism, King Abdullah issued a pardon for the "Qatif Girl," which relieves her of punishment, but does not clear her of guilt.[63] Justice Minister Abdullah Al ash-Shaikh defended the Supreme Judiciary Council's verdict, noting that the king's pardon was an act of kindness to alleviate suffering, "although he (the king) trusts that the verdicts are just and fair."[64] The verdicts were just and fair given Saudi Arabia's moral universe in which women as individuals are responsible for the behavior of men in general. It is this moral responsibility of women that burdens their access to justice, employment, and empowerment, and underscores a red line that the regime is loath to cross.

Why is the issue of women's empowerment a red line for the regime? The well-worn explanation lies in the historical symbiosis between Saudi rulers and their Wahhabi clerical supporters: the rulers provide their hand-picked *ulama* with jobs and religious authority, and the *ulama* provide a cloak of legitimacy for the rulers under the pretense that under the Al Saud, religion and state are partners. The establishment *ulama* on the Supreme Council of Senior Scholars endorse regime policies,[65] whether debunking Juhaiman Al Utayba's justification for laying siege to the Grand Mosque in 1979 or producing quranic legitimacy for US military assistance after Iraq invaded Kuwait. Since 9/11, council members have helped to shield the regime from international criticism by condemning "excessiveness" in religion and calling for a rejection of bin Ladenist interpretations of jihad. Grand Mufti Shaikh Abd al-Aziz Al ash-Shaikh stands by the regime against salafi jihadists and liberal reformers alike. After the bombings of housing compounds in May and November of 2003, he reminded Saudi citizens to obey their ruler even if he is oppressive since "he who rebels against the Emir rebels against God." Following the arrest of reform advocates in March 2004, the grand mufti issued a rationalizing fatwa, arguing that "those who cause the 'umma to doubt its leadership and its religion are truly enemies, even if they claim to call for reform."[66]

Indeed, reform advocates who would be the natural allies of liberal feminists are vulnerable to being incarcerated, admonished, or fired from jobs for authoring petitions or engaging in public demonstrations in the cause of democratic reforms, including reforms relating to women's issues.[67] For example, the law license of the Qatif Girl's lawyer, Abd al-Rahman al-Lahim, was revoked for him having taken the case on appeal and bringing it to the attention of the media. The absence of legitimate channels for dissent and the absence of freedom to organize for political purposes have the effect of magnifying conservative, religious, and institutionalized voices because there is no viable liberal political constituency to compete with them. Reform advocacy on behalf of women is further minimized in that some democratizing reformers, in their search for political partners, have turned to liberal Islamists who share their desire for popular participation in government decisionmaking, but see this participation as taking place within the context of Islamic law. The result is that any alliance between the two ultimately compromises liberal reformers' commitment to a feminist agenda.[68]

Since schools for girls began to open in 1961, there has been widespread support for women's education, including and especially at the university level, and today the demand for jobs for women is high at all income and skill levels. The Saudi leadership is not immune to these demands, which are being addressed in the expansion of course options for women, in the Eighth Development Plan's analysis of women's potential role in the workforce,[69] and in the establishment of quotas for female employees in the public sector, even though the quotas are unrealistic.[70]

Work and education for women are not issues of contention for the Saudi public. What is at issue is anything that compromises the two building blocks of Saudi Arabia's value structure: men's legal control over female relatives and sex segregation. Hence, there is widespread resistance when it comes to women as equal actors in society; as individuals entitled to equal access to medical care, divorce, child custody, and nationality rights; and the rights to hold public office, drive a car, or travel without a guardian's permission.

For a great many Saudis, whatever their political or religious stripes, the public invisibility of women is a source of pride, and the segregation of women from men, with its implicit hierarchy of power between the sexes, remains at the heart of personal identity. The 2004 Obaid poll of Saudi social values showed that 59 percent of the Saudi population support the official clergy, implying support for its conservative social agenda.[71] An earlier poll based on a much smaller sampling of the Saudi population showed a large majority (81 percent) responding that women are always obligated to obey their husbands; 45 percent approving of polygamy without reservation; and 67 percent agreeing that religious authorities adequately respond to "people's spiritual needs, moral problems, family needs, and social problems."[72] Indeed, one explanation for the Saudi regime's catering to its conservative *ulama* is the presumption that the Saudi public in general subscribes to the values they represent and agrees with the conservative social policies they endorse.

This is an erroneous assumption. Social values in the abstract are not the same as the laws and regulatory systems that claim to reflect those values: the prerogative of men to control and protect their wives, for example, is a commonly accepted social value, but not commonly accepted is its logical extension ad absurdum: a hospital regulation denying medical care to a wife whose husband is unavailable to consent to her treatment. The lack of free speech and a free press that are fundamental to democracy helps to perpetuate the illusion of widespread satisfaction with such harmful regulations: pockets of individuals grumble, sign petitions, and even meet with the king, but they cannot sway the public without a public airing of views.

Yet there is a Saudi public ready to listen: even if 59 percent of the population supports the official *ulama*, 41 percent does not. Unfortunately, a dialogue on women that would raise the consciousness of society as a whole cannot be fully opened up without also opening up the Saudi public to a dialogue on democratization, which the Saudi rulers are not prepared to tolerate. Consequently, what we see when it comes to women's rights are piecemeal offerings calculated to appease activists willing to work within the system while not offending the regime's conservative supporters.

Women in the Gulf Cooperation Council States

Saudi Arabia's exclusion of women from voting and candidacy for political office is unique in the Gulf region, as is women's exclusion from driving and working with men, and the use of religious police to compel women to cover their faces in public. The social conservatism that gives rise to women's exclusion and separation, however, is not unique, and neither is the initiative of authoritarian regimes in placing women in high-profile positions. A look at the electoral experience and rising visibility of women in neighboring GCC states tells us two things: first, that when it comes to women and values, conservatism remains an obstacle, with women just as reluctant as men to elect women to political office; and, second, that women's ability to participate in politics and attain high positions has been effected not by pressure from below, but by fiat from above, from authoritarian regimes that are attentive to the deployment of human resources and are experimenting with democratizing initiatives.

Kuwait

The ruling family of Kuwait has been placing women in high-profile positions since 1979, when women were appointed as assistant deputy ministers at the Ministries of Social Affairs and Labor, Finance, and Education. In 1995, a woman from the ruling family was appointed president of Kuwait University. In 2004, Nabila Abdullah al-Mulla served as Kuwait's ambassador to the United Nations; she previously was ambassador to South Africa, Zimbabwe, Namibia, Mauritius, and Botswana, in addition to holding other high-level posts in the United Nations, including chair of the Board of Governors of the International Atomic Energy Agency. In June 2005, two women were appointed to the municipal council, which has six seats reserved for appointed members. In April 2009, Kuwait's first female police officers graduated from the country's police academy, despite some conservative opposition, and were placed as trainers at the academy and in the airport and women's prison.

In May 2005, Kuwait's National Assembly granted women the right to vote and stand for political office at both the municipal and national levels (see Chapter 4). The assembly's decision came fourteen years after the end of the Gulf War, which brought about the reopening of the National Assembly with voting rights for men only and the resumption of an aggressive lobbying campaign on behalf of women's suffrage. The National Assembly, with an Islamist majority, voted down a 1999 decree issued by Amir Shaikh Jaber al-Sabah granting women full political rights, and in 2003 rejected a decree authored by the deputy prime minister that would have allowed women to participate in city council elections.[73] The National

Assembly had also displayed its conservative colors by voting in 1996 to segregate the University of Kuwait's then-coeducational classrooms.

Does the 2005 enfranchisement of women signal a shift in conservative values when it comes to women in political life? To the contrary, some would argue. Supporting women's voting rights could benefit conservative agendas because the lesson to be drawn from women voters elsewhere in the region and from the Islamist women's movement in Kuwait is that women who vote are likely to support conservative candidates, not their liberal opponents.[74] Furthermore, the bill to amend the electoral law incorporated a last-minute amendment that had broad appeal to conservatives of all stripes: women voters and candidates would be required to abide by Islamic law. Given the elasticity of Islamic meanings when it comes to women, assembly members would be free to make assumptions about what the amendment intended, opening the door for resurrecting religious limitations on women's participation in the future. The most benign restriction, for example, might require women to cast their votes at sex-segregated locations, a procedure followed in elections subsequent to this change.

Wielding Islamic law as a cudgel to discourage women's political participation has continued unabated on the part of some members of parliament (MPs), but has not succeeded in excluding them. Following the passage of the women's voting rights law, then–prime minister Shaikh Sabah al-Ahmad Al-Sabah appointed Ma'souma al-Mubarak minister of planning and minister of state for administrative development affairs, a position entitling her to ex officio membership in the parliament. Tribal and Islamist parliamentarians protested the appointment as unconstitutional, but could not get her removed. As a liberal Shi'i academic with a degree from the University of Denver, this headscarf-wearing veteran women's rights activist had her own supporters. Her appointment reflected the aspirations of progressive Kuwaiti women as well as Kuwaiti Shi'ites, dissatisfied with their lack of representation in the cabinet. Similarly, the 2007 swearing-in ceremony of Nouria al-Subeih, Kuwait's second female cabinet member to become minister of education, was marred by shouting MPs, angered that al-Subeih was "breaking the law" by not wearing a head covering.[75] Yet these conservative MPs failed to unseat al-Subeih or force her to cover her head in the National Assembly. On January 22, 2008, she won a vote of confidence in the parliament after defending herself, first from charges of mismanagement brought by Islamist MP Saad al-Shurai, and then from a legal challenge to her position on the grounds that *sharia* forbids women to assume high government positions (see Chapter 4).

The enfranchisement of Kuwaiti women more than doubled the number of eligible voters, with women comprising 57 percent of the electorate.[76] However, the outcome of the first postenfranchisement parliamentary election in June 2006 suggested that, as male Islamist assembly members had calculated, women voters are socially conservative and cannot be presumed to support other women. The government had automatically registered all eligible women as voters to encourage voter turnout,[77] but even with 194,614 registered female voters and twenty-eight women running against 252 men for 50 seats, not a single woman was elected.[78] The outcome was the same in municipal elections that had taken place the previous month: two women competed among eleven candidates for a single vacant seat on the district of Salmiyya's municipal council. Even though women were the majority of voters, the female candidates lost by wide margins. The conservatism of women voters was reaffirmed in the May 2008 election, when only 3 percent of women voters cast ballots for women candidates, and none of the twenty-seven female candidates for seats in the National Assembly was successful.[79]

Despite these initial setbacks, the tenacity of women cabinet members and electoral candidates ultimately led to success in National Assembly elections in May 2009, when four of sixteen women candidates won seats: US-educated professors Salwa al-Jassar and Aseel al-Awadhi, former professor Ma'souma al-Mubarak, and economist Rula Dashti. After the swearing-in ceremonies, fourteen of the newly elected MPs staged a walkout, but not because of the presence of women parliamentarians. A few were miffed that some of the women were not wearing *hijab*, but their real concerns stemmed from unresolved tensions between the National Assembly and the amir, who had dissolved the parliament two months earlier in a dispute involving control over government priorities. Although voter turnout was low and the political landscape unsteady, the successful women candidates won their seats without the help of organized political parties or a quota system, making Kuwait a beacon for women political aspirants throughout the Gulf.[80]

Bahrain

Women's engagement in politics in Bahrain began in 2000, when the king, Shaikh Hamad bin 'Īssà Āl Khalīfah, appointed four women to join Bahrain's all-male, membership-by-appointment Shura Council. In the same year, Bahrain became a constitutional monarchy through an amendment to the National Action Charter, which decreed that all citizens are equal in the eyes of the law regardless of religion, sect, or social class and called for a bicameral parliament, with a Shura Council composed of forty appointed seats and a Chamber of Deputies with forty elected members (see Chapter 2).

The first election in which women were allowed to participate took place at the municipal level. Over 300 candidates, including 31 women, were registered to run for five ten-seat councils. The majority of the winners were religiously affiliated candidates. Even though half of the 51 percent of the Bahraini electorate who actually voted were women, not a single female candidate won. Female candidates face structural disadvantages such as a lack of access to mosques and religious community centers to campaign; male candidates use these locations to attack their female opponents.[81]

In the October 2002 parliamentary election, 8 women competed among 190 candidates. A survey conducted ahead of the election revealed that 60 percent of Bahraini women were opposed to the participation of women, and no woman was elected. Yet women continued to serve in parliament. The king appointed 6 women to the Shura Council, among them Alice Sama'an, a Christian. Something of the depth of social conservatism among Bahrain's parliamentary members can be judged, however, by a proposal put forth during the 2004 legislative session to segregate the sexes at University of Bahrain.[82]

Despite domestic opposition, the king continues to encourage women's participation in political life. In August 2006, he appointed six additional women to parliament, two female cabinet ministers, and the first woman judge in the Gulf.[83] In 2005, the Supreme Council for Women, a state body headed by the king's wife, Shaikha Sabeeka bint Ibrahim Āl Khalīfah, launched a national campaign for the political empowerment of women. It called for better mental, physical, and financial preparation of female candidates running for national office, and urged voters to support women on a merit basis. The king also appointed a few women, some his relatives, to highly visible positions: Shaikha Haya Bint Rashid Āl Khalīfah, appointed royal court legal adviser, served as ambassador to France and the UN Educational, Scientific and Cultural Organization from 2000 to 2005, and was elected president of the UN General Assembly in July 2006. That year, one woman who ran for office unopposed was successful in winning a seat in the Council of Representatives.

The Bahrain Chamber of Deputies weighed in on the question of women in diplomatic missions. In August 2005, Deputy Ahmad Bahzad proposed to allow female diplomats, a number of whom work in the Ministry of Foreign Affairs, to work abroad.[84] In April 2006, his proposal was rejected in the chamber, however, and dismissed by Islamist MPs as "impractical and against family values."[85] Deputies from Al Asalah, the main salafi party, and the Minbar Islamist Bloc, the political wing of the Muslim Brotherhood in Bahrain, voted against the proposal, arguing that diplomatic work is very demanding and unsuitable for women, and would conflict with their duties to home and family, particularly in traveling for long periods of time. Preventing women from taking jobs abroad was presented as an assertion of male protection over women who would otherwise be subjected to the company of unrelated men: diplomats, they argued, also have to attend functions in non-Muslim countries and be among men. "We should make sure that our women are not forced into such settings."[86]

Conflicting notions of women's rights also have surfaced regarding nationality laws. In March 2007, Bahraini political groups, the Democratic Progressive Minbar Society and the Democratic National Action Society, called for enactment of legislation that would allow Bahraini mothers married to non-Bahraini men to pass their nationality on to their children. Opposition came from conservative religious leaders, especially Shi'ites, who claimed that family law must only be adjudicated by religious scholars in religious courts.[87]

Qatar

In Qatar women were granted the right to vote and run for the Central Municipal Council elections in 2000 by a decree of the emir, Shaikh Hamad bin Khalifa al-Thani. None of the six women who ran in a field of 248 won office. In 2003, however, a woman candidate was successful when her male opponent withdrew from the race.[88] In 2007, of three female candidates for municipal elections, one woman, Shaikha Al Jufairi, was elected by a wide margin. According to the new constitution adopted in 2005, all Qataris over eighteen years of age, men and women, are eligible to vote and run for office in the newly established parliament, the Majlis al-Shura.

In addition to opening the door to elective office, the emir and his wife, Shaikha Mozah bint Nasser al-Misned, have placed women, mostly their own US-educated relatives, in highly visible positions (see Chapter 6). The newly appointed president of the University of Qatar, for example, is Shaikha Abdullah al-Misned, and the vice president and chief academic officer is Noura Khalifa Abdulla Turky al-Subaai. The dean of the College of Arts and Sciences is Shaikha Jabor al-Thani, and the emir's sister was appointed vice president of the Supreme Council of Family Affairs. Qatar's emir has also appointed women to the positions of minister of education, public prosecutor, and dean of the University of Qatar's Faculty of Islamic Law and Islamic Studies. The emir's wife, Shaikha Mozah, in her capacity as head of the Qatar Foundation for Education, Science and Community Development, spearheaded the establishment of Education City, housing coeducational branch campuses of major US universities.

Oman

Sultan Qaboos bin Said al-Said opened the door for women to enter Omani politics in 1994. He appointed two women to his newly instituted Shura Council, then a fully appointed body, in the first instance of women's participation in the political process in any of the GCC states (see Chapter 5).[89] In 2000, when the council was opened up to elections, the sultan allowed women to both stand for election and vote for candidates. Among several hundred candidates were twenty women, two of whom were successful. They were reelected in 2003, when suffrage was made universal. However, in the 2007 elections for Shura Council, which has 84 seats, 20 of the 632 candidates were women, but none was elected. On the other hand, the fifty-eight-seat State Council (Majlis al-Dawlah), whose members are appointed, has seven, eight, or nine female members (sources differ on the actual number).[90]

Sultan Qaboos, like other Gulf rulers, has appointed women to high-profile positions. In 1998–1999, he named Oman's first female ambassador and appointed three women to serve as deputy ministers. He also appointed the first woman to the board of directors of the Omani Chamber of Commerce. In March 2003, he named a woman president of the Public Authority for Craft Industries with the rank of minister; in 2004, three other women joined the cabinet as ministers of higher education (Rawiya bint Saud bin Ahmad al Busaidi), tourism (Rajiha bint Abd al-amir bin Ali), and social development (Sharifa bint Khalfan bin Nasser al Yahya'i). The sultan also appointed five female lawyers as attorneys general, the only case of women holding high-level legal positions in a GCC state. In 2008, the person occupying Oman's most visible position on the international stage was Hunaina bint Sultan bin Ahmad al-Mughairi, ambassador to the United States. Another woman, Khadijah bint Hassan bin Salman al-Lawatiyah, is ambassador to the Netherlands. Coeducational higher education is expanding in Oman: at the new University of Nizwa, for the year 2007–2008, 90 percent of accepted students were women. In his mission to empower women, the sultan has had the backing of the mufti of Muscat, who, uniquely among religious leaders in GCC countries, gave his blessing to the inclusion of women in the political process.[91]

United Arab Emirates

There were no women among the appointments to the UAE's forty-seat Federal National Council (*Majlis al-Ittihad al-Watani*) until December 2006. That year, half of the council seats were opened for election by an appointed electoral college of 6,689 Emiratis that included 1,189 women. Sixty-five of the 456 candidates were women, but only 1, an architect from Abu Dhabi, succeeded in winning a seat (see Chapter 8).[92] Women then held nine seats on the council, eight having been appointed to office by the UAE president, Khalifa bin Zayid al-Nuhayyan, ruler of Abu Dhabi.

In the UAE, each ruler is sovereign in his domain, and conditions for women vary from one emirate to another. The progressive ruler of Sharjah, Shaikh Sultan bin Mohammed al Qasimi, appointed several women to his local consultative council in 2000. In November 2004, Lubna al-Qassemi was appointed the federal minister of planning and economy, and a year later, Mariam al-Rumi became social affairs minister. In the UAE armed forces, women serve in a special women's corps that came into being after the Gulf War and, as in Kuwait and Bahrain, Emirati women also serve in the police force.[93] In 2007, the UAE president announced his support for efforts to expand women's opportunities, including allowing women to become judges, which would require a change in the current law stating that only a Muslim man may be a judge. In 2008 the Judicial Department of Abu Dhabi named two women, Aleya Saeed Al Qaabi and Atiqqah Awad Al Qatheeri, as public prosecutors, a first for the UAE.[94]

Because, in this chapter, I focus on women in democratizing initiatives and high-profile political positions, the sparse information given for the position of women in small GCC states, the emirates in particular, is misleading. Like women in all the Gulf countries, Emirati women are prominent educators and entrepreneurs as well as independent political actors campaigning for social justice and equity in family law. One such issue has surfaced in all the Gulf countries: the inability of women to pass their nationality on to their husbands or children if they are married to non-nationals. In Dubai, twenty-three Emirati women protested outside the Labor Ministry building on January 24, 2006, to demand the reinstatement of their social security payments, which had been cut off because they were married to working expatriates. In this first public protest by UAE female nationals demanding equal rights under the nationality laws, protesters argued that their children are not allowed free university education or health care, and they cannot get passports. If the children renounce their father's nationality in order to take a five-year UAE passport, it could become nonrenewable, leaving the children stateless and unable to get any kind of passport.[95]

What Works for Women?

Initial experiments with democratic elections in the GCC countries suggest that a positive correlation between democracy and women's empowerment ought not to be presumed. The obstacles women encountered in obtaining the vote, combined with their minuscule successes as candidates and overt opposition to their political participation from members of elected assemblies in Kuwait and Bahrain, should alert us to the possibility that, for the time being, women who seek empowerment may be better off under authoritarian rulers willing to promote a feminist agenda. The lessons of the past are that women have experienced success as quota beneficiaries for jobs and political offices, appointees to high-profile positions, recipients of state-guaranteed benefits, manipulators of family networks, and, most importantly, as a result of their own efforts in business, in academic and professional achievement, and in civic activism.

The pivotal role of values in determining the parameters of women's public life is not to be underestimated, and when it comes to democratic elections, people do, in fact, tend to vote their values, even when their values are incompatible with their interests: what better example than the 2004 presidential election in the United States. The George W. Bush campaign won voters' hearts by calling for a constitutional amendment against gay marriage and promising to appoint justices to the Supreme Court who would oppose abortion. He won the election even though he also promised to take away the guaranteed social security benefits on which the middle class relies for retirement income and shift the tax burden further from the wealthiest Americans onto the middle class. As Thomas Franks argues in his book *What's the Matter with Kansas*, electoral successes such as the 2004 Bush victory demonstrate that values identification can motivate people to make political choices that feel good while, at the same time, they are harmful to the voters' interests.[96] We need look no further than the US example to recognize that democracy gives as much voice to human emotion as to reason and informed judgment.

When we look at women and the values question as it plays out politically in the Gulf, it is clear that the same issues are contested in every country, whether through the mediation of authoritarian regimes or the forum of democratic elections. In either case, women's emergence into public life has been facilitated more through the "state feminism" of Gulf rulers than through the efforts of representative institutions. The case of Kuwait is a clear paradigm: the Kuwaiti National Assembly's resistance to the emir's edict in support of women's voting rights was resisted by the National Assembly, and later accepted with the proviso that women's participation be restricted to "what Islamic Law allows." Absent the emir's initiative, in this country where women have achieved the greatest success in elections in the GCC, women's suffrage would not have come to the floor of the National Assembly in the first place.

Given the ubiquitous resistance to women's political participation, it is fair to ask why some hereditary rulers of Gulf states have encouraged it. The answer is, first, that women's empowerment is in every country's national interest economically as well as in terms of human development. Another reason is that pressure from women and liberal feminist supporters for political engagement has been building up from below and also from within ruling families, occurring hand in hand with women's soaring educational successes. Because the exclusion of women retains an emotional appeal among Gulf populations at large, the judicious course for Gulf rulers has been to give women limited access to the democratizing institutions they have created while also limiting the authority of these institutions to influence policy. At the same time, in all the Gulf countries civil liberties are restrained; pressure from either side has nowhere to be channeled except in directions chosen by the rulers and in a manner that suits their interests.

When we look at the Gulf, we see that whether or not there are democratic institutions, and whether or not women are elected or appointed to seats in these institutions, the trajectory of women's empowerment remains set in one direction. A case in point is an incident in Saudi Arabia illustrating women's ability to influence government policy even in the absence of official policymaking channels for women (or men). In August 2006, the General Directorate of the Affairs of the Grand Mosque and the Prophet's Mosque announced that a decision had been made to prevent women on pilgrimage from praying in the open courtyard in front of the Kaaba. Instead, "to avoid over-crowding,"[97] women were to have a designated, exclusive place of their own, to be located some distance away. Reaction to the prayer ban was swift. Hatoon Ajwad al-Fassi, professor of history at King Saud University in Riyadh, responded in the press, pointing out that the decision was contrary to the Muslim ideal that men and women are equal on hajj, and raising questions as to how such a ban would be viewed by pilgrims who come from all over the world to pray at the Kaaba.[98] Her critique swept through Arabic blogs and the webpages of Muslim organizations in the West, where readers responded with threats to organize protests. The globalization of the issue, put in motion by the voice of a feminist historian, created a vocal opposition that provided a counterweight to Saudi conservatives who had initiated the prayer ban in the first place. A month after the ban was first announced, Mohammad Bin Nasser Al Khozayem, deputy head of Grand Mosque Affairs, issued a statement to the press saying that the space in front of the Kaaba would instead be expanded for women's prayer, giving women even more of the total area than the space allocated for men.[99]

Values remain a persistent challenge. However, with women's success in education, attainment of professional qualifications, and achievement of income parity within the family, along with the high-profiling of women by Gulf rulers, the social structure within which these values are contested is changing. Discussion in the media, and in newly constituted consultative councils and parliaments, is making debate over issues of public concern possible. The outcome is that the kinds of definitive social control policies that were once the prerogative of Gulf rulers are now untenable, and parliamentary majorities, if far less liberal than their hereditary heads of state, are at least subject to persuasion.

Notes

1. World Bank, "MENA Flagship Report on Education: The Road Not Traveled—Education Reform in the MENA" (preliminary findings as presented at

Georgetown University, March 24, 2005), table, "Taking Stock: Access and Equity, Gross Enrollment Rate in MENA," and "Gender Difference in Gross Enrollment in MENA (1970–2000)."

2. In Kuwait, for example, women comprise two-thirds of university students; in Saudi Arabia, 58 percent; in the United Arab Emirates, 75 percent of the student body at the National University in Al-'Ain are women; in Qatar, there are two-and-a-half times the number of women as men in higher education; and in Bahrain there are twice as many women as men. UNDP, *Human Development Report 2005* (New York: UNDP, 2005), table 27, "Gender Inequality in Education," p. 307. These figures do not account for study abroad, which is more easily accessible to men than to women, and hence they exaggerate gender disparity at the university level.

3. For example, Halima Mazfar, "A King's Vision: Expanding the Role of the Saudi Women,"*Asharq Al Awsat*, August 1, 2006.

4. UNDP Programme on Governance in the Arab Region, "The Gender and Citizenship Initiative; Country Profiles: Saudi Arabia," 2007, http://gender.pogar.org.

5. For more on women in new public spaces, see Valentine Moghadam and Fatima Sadiqi, eds., "Women's Activism and the Public Sphere" [special issue], *Journal of Middle East Women's Studies* 2, no. 2 (2006).

6. Copies of the National Society's incorporation papers, bylaws, signatories, and license can be viewed in its application for membership as a nongovernmental organization in the Asian Pacific Forum of National Human Rights Institutions at www.asiapacificforum.net.

7. "Saudi Ministry of Interior Considers Special Police Unit for Domestic Violence," *Asharq Al Awsat*, January 26, 2009.

8. Khalid Al-Dakhil, "2003: Saudi Arabia's Year of Reform," *Arab Reform Bulletin* 2, no. 3 (2004); Abdul Ghafour, "First Independent Human Rights Organization Established," *Arab News*, March 3, 2004.

9. Embassy of the Kingdom of Saudi Arabia, "Human Rights Commission to Open Women's Section in Riyadh," September 4, 2008, www.saudiembassy.net; Mohammed Rasooldeen, "HRC Opens Women's Wing in Riyadh," *Arab News,* Spetember 4, 2008, http://archive.arabnews.com.

10. Maha Akeel, "Woman Appointed to Top Health Post in Jeddah," *Arab News*, July 12, 2004.

11. "Women Can Issue Fatwas, Be Muftis: Shaikh Abdullah Al-Manea," *Saudi Gazette*, August 2, 2008.

12. Somaya Jabarti, "Engineers Council Poll: One More Step for Saudi Women," *Arab News*, December 28, 2005.

13. Maha Akeel, "Women in JCCI Poll Fray," *Arab News*, October 3, 2005.

14. Maha Akeel, "Women Create History in JCCI Poll," *Arab News*, December 1, 2005.

15. *Arab News*, December 1, 2004.

16. Sabria S. Jawahar, "Women Let Down by Female Voters in Chamber Elections," *Saudi Gazette,* January 13, 2010, www.saudigazette.com.sa.

17. Ibid.

18. Raid Qusti and Somayya Jabarti, "New Identity Cards: Saudi Women Find Their Feet—and Face Too," *Arab News*, March 13, 2005.

19. Haya Al Manie, "Paranoia in Society," *Al Riyadh*, reprinted in *Arab News*, January 9, 2008.

20. www.aljazeera.com, December 4, 2004.

21. Nawaf Obaid, "Clerical Hurdles to Saudi Reform," *Washington Post*, March 9, 2004.

22. "Saudi Election Delayed; Government Employees Silenced," *Reform Bulletin* 2, no. 9 (October 20, 2004).

23. BBC News, November 10, 2004; "Women Shut Out of Upcoming Saudi Vote," Associated Press, October 12, 2004.

24. In 2004 the Carnegie Endowment published a chart on "Women in Parliament in the Arab World," which included "two or three" women in the Saudi Majlis, with the caveat that for Saudi Arabia reports differed and no confirmation was available.

25. Maha Akeel, "More Women 'Consultants' Join Shura," *Arab News*, June 29, 2006.

26. Ibid.

27. Maha Akeel, "New Panel Disappoints Women," *Arab News*, January 1, 2006; Maha Akeel, "More Women 'Consultants' Join Shura."

28. Roshan Muhammed Salih, "No Role for Women in Saudi Council," Al-Jazeera, October 27, 2003.

29. "Saudi Arabia Mulls Allowing Women to Vote," *Khaleej Times*, April 26, 2009; "Saudi Municipal Polls Put Off Two Years," Agence France-Presse, May 19, 2009.

30. Andrzej Kapiszewski, "Elections and Parliamentary Activity in the GCC States: Broadening Political Participation in the Gulf Monarchies," in *Constitutional Reform and Political Participation in the Gulf*, eds. Abdulhada Khalaf and Giacomo Luciani (Dubai: Gulf Research Center, 2006), pp. 88–131.

31. Toby Jones, "Seeking a 'Social Contract for Saudi Arabia,'" *Middle East Report*, no. 228 (2003): 42–48. See Chapter 7 in this volume.

32. "In Defense of the Nation," Gwenn Okruhlik and Sara Youssef, trans., 2004, www.ccc.nps.navy.mil.

33. Toby Jones, "Violence and the Illusion of Reform in Saudi Arabia," Middle East Report Online, November 13, 2003, www.merip.org (September 24, 2006).

34. "PEN American Center Hails Release of Saudi Reformers" (International Freedom of Expression Exchange, n.d.), www.ifex.org.

35. Quoted from "Saudi Arabia: Elections Delayed; Government Employees Silenced."

36. Agence France Presse, July 1, 2005.

37. Kapiszewski, "Elections and Parliamentary Activity in the GCC States."

38. *Asharq Al Awsat*, January 4, 2004.

39. *Al Hayat*, June 15 and 18, 2004.

40. Iris Glosemeyer, "Checks, Balances and Transformation in the Saudi Political System," in *Saudi Arabia in the Balance: Political Economy, Society, Foreign Affairs*, eds. Paul Aarts and Gerd Nonneman (London: Hurst, 2005), p. 227.

41. Raid Qusti, "Saudi Men and Women Petition Rights Body on Women Driving," *Arab News*, June 28, 2005. Arguments by Saudi religious scholars in support of banning women from driving have been published in many sources, over many years, as early as 1979 in my experience. A collection of these arguments can be seen in English in *Islamic Fatawa Regarding Women*, comp. Muhammad bin Abd al-Aziz Al-Musnad (Riyadh: Darussalam, 1996).

42. Raid Qusti, "Saudi Men and Women Petition Rights Body."

43. Nawaf Obaid, "What the Saudi Public Really Thinks," *Daily Star* (Lebanon), June 24, 2004. The survey was conducted under the auspices of the Saudi National Security Assessment Project, a private, nongovernmental research body that includes seventy-five researchers, and covered all of the kingdom's thirteen provinces between July and November of 2003. The results (with a margin of error

of 3 percentage points) were based on a total of 15,452 respondents (62 percent men and 38 percent women). The objective was to survey Saudi perspectives on political reform, the religious establishment, women's empowerment, and terrorism.

44. "Poll Claims Support for Allowing Women to Drive," *The Guardian*, December 28, 2005.

45. Faiza Saleh Ambah, "Saudi Women Recall a Day of Driving: Women Who Protested in 1990 Reunite as Debate over Women Drivers Returns," *Christian Science Monitor*, December 7, 2005.

46. Ibid. A similar argument is made by liberal feminist Fatma Mernissi in *Scheherazade Goes West: Different Cultures, Different Harems* (New York: Washington Square, 2001), which reminds readers that Westernization is not a panacea for women in the Middle East.

47. On the "slippery slope" concept in Islamic jurisprudence (*sadd al-dhari'ah*), see Khaled Abou El Fadl, *Speaking in God's Name: Islamic Law, Authority and Women* (Oxford: One World, 2001), pp. 190–192. A further discussion may be found in Gwenn Okruhlik, "Religious Revivalism and Its Challenge to the Saudi Regime," in *Religion and Politics in Saudi Arabia*, eds. Mohammed Ayoob and Hasan Kosebalaban (Boulder: Lynne Rienner, 2009), pp. 109–123. On the discussion among Saudi *ulama* regarding women's driving, see Saad al-Matrafi, "Scholars Frustrate Extremists on Women Driving Issue," *Arab News*, May 31, 2005. For a fatwa on women's driving by Shaikh bin Baz, see Muhammad bin Abd al-Aziz Al-Musnad, *Islamic Fatwa Regarding Women* (Riyadh: Darussalam, 1996).

48. "Driving Ban Stays for Women," BBC, June 13, 2005.

49. Maha Akeel and Hassan Adawi, "Abdullah Wins Applause for Assurance on Women Driving," *Arab News*, October 15, 2005.

50. "Poll Claims Support for Allowing Women to Drive," *The Guardian*, December 28, 2005.

51. "Saudi Women Petition for Right to Drive," Agence France Presse, January 3, 2008.

52. Damien McElroy, "Saudi Arabia to Lift Ban on Women Drivers," *The Telegraph*, January 21, 2008.

53. alarabiya.net, March 19, 2008.

54. Arifa Akbar describes an incident in a lingerie shop in the hypermodern Al Faisaliah shopping mall in downtown Riyadh where a male sales assistant advised a veiled woman on the benefits of buying a pink, lacy underwear set. The woman listened with her head bowed, mortified; Arifa Akbar, "Hello Boys: Lingerie Leads the Fight for Saudi Women's Rights," *Independent News*, April 27, 2006.

55. "Hiring of Foreign Women in Lingerie Shops Ruled Out," *Gulf News*, April 11, 2006.

56. Anton La Guardia, "Muslim Clerics' Anger Delays Saudi Plan to Let Women Sell Lingerie," *The Telegraph*, May 16, 2006.

57. Rym Ghazal, "New Saudi Law Ends Glaring Contradiction," *Daily Star* (Lebanon), September 19, 2007.

58. For more on the fire and the condition of public buildings for women, see Eleanor Doumato, "Separate and Unequal: Sex Segregation Is a Saudi National Obsession," op-ed, Brown University News Service, March 2002.

59. Saudi Gazette, March 14, 2002, al-Eqtisadiah.

60. Kingdom of Saudi Arabia, Ministry of Education, "General Education," 2003, http://www.moe.gov.sa/openshare/EnglishCon/About-Saud/Education1.htm_cvt.htm.

61. Saudi Arabia, Ministry of Justice, "Explanatory Statement by the Ministry of Justice About Qatif Girl," November 21, 2007, www.mofa.gov.sa.

62. "New Explanatory Statement by the Ministry of Justice on Qatif Girl," Saudi Press Agency, November 24, 2007, www.spa.gov.sa.

63. In addition to the focus of the international press on the case of the Qatif Girl, the UN Committee on the Elimination of Discrimination Against Women criticized Saudi Arabia for restricting "virtually every aspect of a woman's life"; "UN Questions Saudi Rules for Women," *Los Angeles Times,* January 18, 2008; "Saudi Restrictions on Women Questioned," *Los Angeles Times*, January 18, 2008.

64. Ebtihal Mubarak, "Abdullah Pardons 'Qatif Girl,'" *Arab News*, December 18, 2007.

65. One exception was the council's refusal to endorse Saudi Arabia's participation in the 1995 UN Population and Development Conference in Cairo because of disagreement over the birth control issue.

66. *Al-Hayat*, March 21, 2004, pp. 1, 6; F. Gregory Gause III, "Saudi Islamists: Challenge or Support for Saudi Stability and Security?" paper presented at the National Defense University conference, Washington, DC, April 14, 2004.

67. See, for example, Human Rights Watch, "Teachers Silenced on Blasphemy Charges," November 17, 2005, http://hrw.org; Human Rights Watch, "Saudi Arabia: Lift Travel Ban on Government Critics," February 14, 2007, http://hrw.org.

68. For more on the relationship between reformers and Islamists, see International Crisis Group, "Saudi Arabia Backgrounder: Who Are the Islamists?" *Middle East Report*, no. 31 (2004): 8–11.

69. The kingdom's eighth Five-Year Development Plan (2005–2009) aims at increasing the percentage of women in the Saudi workforce from 5.4 percent to 14.2 percent. The eighth plan signifies government recognition of women's advancement in all fields as necessary for the advancement of society as a whole. According to Saudi analyst Noura Al-Turki, the plan links a woman's education with her employment, and her economic advancement with the social well-being of herself and her family, and calls for greater opportunities for women "to occupy decision-making positions" and for "solutions that would lead to enabling women in terms of education, health, and employment"; Noura Al-Turki, "Gender Analysis of the Eighth National Development Plan (2005–2009)," unpublished manuscript, Khadijah Bint Khuwailid Businesswomen Center, Jeddah, August 27, 2007. To meet these challenges, the plan notes the absence of women from productive activities such as information technology, trade, banking, and communications, and recognizes that the reason for this absence, in part, is women's lack of educational opportunities in the sciences and technology. As Al Turki notes, the plan fails to set specific goals or policies to ensure women's advancement or to designate agencies to carry them out, but it does call for a restructuring of the national education system from the elementary through the university level, which has begun to be fulfilled in the two new coeducational universities for science and technology.

70. In 2007, Prince Sultan announced plans to allocate one-third of government jobs to Saudi women, but similar quotas for women in the workforce have been announced with some regularity, with no possible means of creating sufficient job opportunities to bring such a quota to reality; P. K. Abd al-Ghafour, "One-Third of Government Jobs for Women: Sultan," *Arab News*, May 27, 2007.

71. Nawaf Obaid, "What the Saudi Public Really Thinks," special to the *Daily Star* (Lebanon), June 24, 2004, www.dailystar.com.

72. Pippa Norris and Ronald Inglehart, "Islamic Culture and Democracy: Testing

the 'Clash of Civilizations' Thesis," in *Human Values and Social Change: Findings from the Values Surveys*, ed. Ronald Inglehart (Leiden: Brill, 2002).

73. For more on women and politics in Kuwait, see Mary Ann Tétreault, "Women's Rights and the Meaning of Citizenship in Kuwait, Middle East Report Online, February 10, 2005, www.merip.org (July 4, 2007); Abdullah Alshayeji, "Beyond Women's Suffrage in Kuwait," *Arab Reform Bulletin* 3, no. 6 (2005); Haya al-Mughni and Mary Ann Tétreault, "Political Actors Without the Franchise: Women and Politics in Kuwait," in *Monarchies and Nations: Globalization and Identity in the Arab States of the Gulf*, eds. Paul Dresch and James Piscatori (London: I. B. Tauris, 2005), pp. 203–221; UNDP, www.pogar.org. UNIFEM maintains a website dedicated to women's development issues in the Middle East. For more information, see www.arabwomenconnect.org.

74. Abdullah Alshayeji, "Women's Suffrage Means Deep Change in Kuwaiti Politics," *Daily Star* (Lebanon), July 27, 2005.

75. "Veil Protest Dogs Kuwait Minister," BBC, April 2, 2007.

76. Ali Taqi, "Kuwaiti Women Voters Have the Upper Hand," *Gulf News*, May 22, 2005. This result is a product of different registration rules for women and men. The difference in registration rates is likely to narrow in future elections, with or without a change in registration procedures.

77. Brian Whitaker, "More Women Win Vote in Kuwait," *The Guardian*, January 6, 2006.

78. "No Women Win Office in Kuwait," Associated Press, July 1, 2006.

79. For an analysis of Kuwaiti elections, see Nathan Brown, "Kuwait's 2008 Parliamentary Elections: A Setback for Democratic Islamism?" Carnegie Endowment for International Peace, Web Commentary, May 2008, www.carnegie endowment.org; see also Nathan Brown, What's at Stake in Kuwait's Parliamentary Elections?" Carnegie Endowment for International Peace, Web Commentary, May 7, 2008, www.carnegieendowment.org. On the 2008 election results, see "Kuwait, a Moment of Great Promise: Four Elected Women Sworn in for First Time in Kuwaiti Parliamentary History," UNDP press release, May 31, 2009.

80. For an analysis of the significance of the May 2009 elections, see F. Gregory Gause III, "Question Time," *National Newspaper* (UAE), June 18, 2009, www.the national.ae.

81. *Gulf News*, May 20, 2002.

82. N. Janardhan, "In the Gulf, Women Are Not Women's Best Friends," *Daily Star* (Lebanon), June 20, 2005.

83. Habib Toumi, "Six Women to Be Named in Bahrain's Council," *Gulf News*, August 6, 2006.

84. Habib Toumi, "Bahrain Allows Female Diplomats to Work Abroad," *Gulf News*, August 16, 2005.

85. Habib Toumi, "Bahraini MPs Reject Motion to Boost Number of Female Diplomats," *Gulf News*, April 13, 2006.

86. Ibid.

87. Habib Toumi, "Liberals Seek Law to Grant Citizenship to Children of Non-Bahraini Fathers," *Gulf News*, March 9, 2007.

88. US Department of State, Bureau of Democracy, Human Rights, and Labor, *Qatar: Country Reports on Human Rights Practices, 2003*, Washington, DC, February 25, 2004; "Apathy Reflects Women's Mindset," *Gulf News*, June 28, 2006.

89. Abdullah Juma Alhaj, "The Politics of Participation in the Gulf Cooperation Council States: The Omani Consultative Council," *Middle East Journal* 50, no. 4 (1996): 560–571.

90. Ibitisam al-Kitbi, "Women's Political Status in the GCC States," *Arab*

Reform Bulletin 2, no. 7 (2004); US Department of State, Bureau of Democracy, Human Rights, and Labor, "Oman," *Country Reports on Human Rights Practices*, March 6, 2007, www.state.gov.

91. C. J. Riphenburg, *Oman: Political Development in a Changing World* (Westport: Praeger, 1998), p. 152.

92. Samir Salama, "More Than 1,000 Women Eligible to Vote," *Gulf News,* September 13, 2006, http://archive.gulfnews.com; "UAE Head Announces First Election," BBC News, December 1, 2005; US Central Intelligence Agency, "UAE," *The World Factbook*, December 13, 2007.

93. Shaikh Mohammed bin Rashid Al Maktoum, "Women in the UAE," www.sheikhmohammed.co.ae.

94. "UAE to Have Women Judges Soon," *Arab News*, January 7, 2008; Eman Mohammed, "UAE's First Female Judge Says Not Afraid of New Role," *Gulf News,* April 1, 2008.

95. Diaa Hadid, "National Women Demand Equal Rights as Men," *Gulf News*, January 25, 2006.

96. Thomas Franks, *What's the Matter with Kansas* (New York: Holt, 2005).

97. Ibid.

98. Hatun Ajwad al-Fassi, "Haqq al-Nisa' fi al-Salaat fi al-Haram al-Mecca," *al Iqtisadiah*, August 4, 2006.

99. "Saudi Clerics Backtrack on Female Prayer Ban Near Kaaba," Reuters, September 12, 2006.

10

New Media: In Search of Equilibrium

N. Janardhan

WHEN IRAQ INVADED Kuwait in August 1990, it took days for Saudi newspapers to report the "tension." But when the United States and its allies invaded Iraq in 2003, the media's new freedom in Gulf Cooperation Council (GCC) countries was showcased. Often accused of toeing the official line at the cost of objectivity, the media, much of it local, used the Iraq War to overcome government restrictions and its own history of self-censorship. The "new media"—television, Internet weblogs, mobile text-messaging, and radio—have traveled a nearly full circle in less than a decade, both evoking and satisfying popular thirst for news and, in the process, making a noticeable impact on the political foundations of the GCC states.

This dynamic is fueled by improvements in technology and a tectonic shift in relations between media and the Gulf governments. It appears that the governments are caught in their own trap—they do not wish to allow the media free rein, yet they are unable to check the flow of information absolutely. Technology has made not only news, but also views, increasingly difficult to restrain. As a result, the governments in the region have lost their control over the aspirations of liberals, reformers, and innovative political activists and groups.

On the ground, regional media—both print and electronic—have evolved a style that suits nondemocratic governments that do not appreciate evaluation or criticism of their policies and performance. While the media largely adhere to government diktats in the domestic context, there is a perceptible difference in the way they approach international issues and events pertaining to local interests in the international arena.

That does not mean, however, that the media in the region are either bland or monolithic. The vastly expanded range of news, views, and images the media made available to the average Arab is shaped by a quest to appear comprehensive and balanced. Media outlets attempt to reflect multiple views and trends by providing a variety of features and programs. At the same time, the media reflect changing Arab attitudes by criticizing US policies and gently, but surely, evaluating the performance of local regimes.

Evaluations of the impact of new media on the politics of the region vary. According to Jon Alterman, conventional media in the Gulf "rail against the unfairness of purported US and Israeli control of international institutions, they are blind to domestic news, and they cover neither intellectual developments nor human interest stories." In contrast, Alterman believes that the new media have made the Arab countries resemble the West because now governments have a "voice but not a veto" about how and whether the public is informed about their activities.[1]

Deborah Wheeler argues that the Internet is an important tool for breaking social and gender barriers. Her study of Internet use in Kuwait suggests that youth use the Web primarily for communicating and entertainment, although she also emphasizes that the Internet gives young people "new autonomy on how they run their lives," and has the potential to "stimulate processes of change over time."[2] At the least the new media, in their own humble way, have become a channel of expression that acts as a safety valve, allowing pent-up frustration to ease without adverse political consequences for regimes while opening a space for political participation among the people. Even so, and despite growing evidence of the proliferation of new media tools in the politics of the region, Naomi Sakr feels that any final verdict on the impact of new media on people and politics in the Arab world is premature.[3]

In this chapter, I focus on developments related to the new media in the GCC countries in the context of media coverage of events in the Gulf, particularly in Iraq. These developments vary by country. Some, like Kuwait, Saudi Arabia, and Bahrain, are actively engaged while others, like Qatar and the United Arab Emirates (UAE), have shown more caution in media experiments.

The deployment of new media for information dissemination has produced both opportunities and challenges. The scope of freedom in the realm of information has expanded vastly, but abusing that freedom when the desire to be popular overcomes social responsibilities has exacted costs. Consequently, although political consciousness has risen in response to the greater flow of information, its impact on political development remains at an early stage.

Weblogs Win

Most analyses of the new media question whether they are a catalyst for modernity and democratization in a region bound by tradition, and then answer that question by crediting them with promoting debates and alternate opinions.[4] There are reasons to believe that media have liberalized Arab political culture and boosted fledgling reform movements. Their most unambiguous success is to have broken the monopoly of state-owned, government-controlled broadcast organizations that formerly had dominated the region. Now there is more news than "regime propaganda" available, both on television and from Internet sources.[5] Wide coverage of the Palestinian and Iraqi elections, pro- and anti-Syria rallies in Lebanon after the assassination of former prime minister Rafiq Hariri, and the Kifaya (Enough) movement in Egypt during the first half of 2005 were not viewed simply as discrete Arab political events. They also reinforced the efforts of activists elsewhere, such as Kuwaiti women, whose long campaign for political rights finally achieved success in May 2005.

Television was the first medium to inspire political change, but blogs have taken it further to serve as a key activist tool in GCC countries. Citizens use blogs to demand political rights and civil liberties. From 2004 to 2006, the number of Arab bloggers in the GCC countries is estimated to have grown fivefold.[6] Bloggers post their views in Arabic, English, and some in a combination of both. The opinions expressed in citizen blogs are often quite different from the views of established newspaper and Web columnists.

Blogs, according to Marc Lynch, "allow ordinary Arabs to re-engage with politics, and escape the red lines that limit even the most independent of Arab media. National blogospheres create a space in which citizens are able to engage in sustained, focused political argument, and perhaps even hold national leaders to account." Lynch reports Arabs as engaging in three kinds of political blogging: "activism" (politically engaged), "bridge-blogging" (bridging the gap with Western audiences), and "public sphere engagement" (arguments about politics, culture, and society).[7]

The impact of blogs in the Gulf is most evident in Kuwait. Blogs were used to great effect to coordinate rallies in April 2006 in support of election law reform. Bloggers ran a virtual campaign that spilled into the streets in the form of an Orange Revolution, in recognition of the orange T-shirts and other insignia worn by demonstrators. A handful of university bloggers translated a call by proreform members of parliament to fight corruption by reducing the number of electoral districts into a "5 for Kuwait" campaign logo. The message was spread online, attracting hundreds of youth to demonstrate in front of the National Assembly building, waving orange banners.[8] The effect of these campaigns and protests led to a bitter standoff between parliament and the government, forcing Emir Shaikh Sabah Al-Ahmed Al-Sabah to dissolve the parliament in May and call for new elections in June.

The Orange Movement leadership itself maintained a blog—KuwaitJunior (www.kuwaitjunior.blogspot.com)—that originated in the

United States. The blog provided complete coverage and analysis of the emiri succession drama in January of 2006, posting information gleaned from *diwaniyyas* (see Chapter 4). During the 2006 election campaign, the blog highlighted electoral corruption, and participants investigated one allegation by mounting a sting operation.

Another innovation in Kuwait was television broadcasts of candidates' debates by private satellite stations. The programs telecast by the Alliance, an opposition group formed in 2004, featured speakers critical of the government. When officials sought to curtail the programs, the group shifted stations. Blogs were important here as well, offering video streaming to viewers who did not receive the less popular channel that the Alliance was forced to employ.[9]

Bahrain's smaller blogging community includes many former political prisoners. One led an online campaign calling for a boycott of the country's government-owned telecommunications company, Batelco, for levying excessive tariffs. Blogs posted controversial statements and also challenged the government over human rights violations. By 2005, about sixty Bahraini blogs were actively engaged in political debates. Among them were protests organized in late 2004 following the arrest of Abdulhadi Al-Khawaja of the Bahrain Centre for Human Rights, and the alleged government-orchestrated "Bandar-gate," a vote-fixing scandal in 2006.

Bahraini blogs are complemented by Internet sites like BahrainOnline, which is frequented by members of virtually every group interested and engaged in politics, including the royal family, members of parliament, and other politicians. The opposition Shi'ite group is the most prolific user and beneficiary of the site. In 2002, it used the Internet in its successful campaign to boycott the national election (see also Chapter 2).[10] The nature, intensity, popularity, and impact of the debates on the site led the government to arrest the moderator, Ali Abdel Iman, on charges of "defamation . . . inciting hatred against the regime and spreading rumors and lies that could cause disorder," in 2005.[11] He subsequently was released. Three years earlier, the Information Ministry had censored Internet sites on the grounds that they were "inciting sectarianism or propagating lies, sparking protests by Bahraini activists."[12]

Saudi Arabia may have the most active bloggers. "Are we destined to just listen to the news of all the big changes around the world as we await a good deed from our king?" is an example of the prevailing blog trend.[13] The freedom conferred by anonymity has encouraged Saudi women to embrace the Internet. More than half of Saudi blogs are written by women and, as a result, women's issues are regularly addressed on blogs. While political issues as such are not a priority for women, the social issues that do occupy them have acquired political overtones. Blogs are seen as a safe platform from which women can call for change and empowerment. Popular Saudi blogs that are managed by women include "Farah's Sowaleef," "A Thought in the Kingdom of Lunacy," and "Saudi Eve." Such blogs are usually critical of male domination in Saudi society and record the experiences of those who dare to challenge established norms.

While most Saudi female bloggers write journals, some use blogs to further a cause. Saudi-yat.blogspot.com calls for Saudi women's Islamic rights. Activists, male and female, used blogs to start a movement for women's rights called "Ween Al Bagi" (Where Is the Change?).[14] In their quest to gain permission to drive, a group of Saudi women submitted a petition to the government. The petition remained posted on different Saudi websites and circulated via e-mail for several weeks so that Saudis, as well as people around the world, could sign.[15] According to one activist,

> although the latest petition is unlikely to put women behind the wheel and on their country's multi-lane highways anytime soon, the use of the internet—emails, blogs, and social networking websites—to circulate it showed how adept Saudi women have become at navigating the information highway, which has become one of the most exciting tools for change in the Arab world.[16] [See also Chapter 9.]

In the UAE, which has the region's second-largest weblog community, a citizen was censored for attacking religious leaders one week after launching "The Land of Sands" in 2004. But after finding a way to circumvent the Internet servers of Etisalat (the state telecommunications monopoly) so that he could continue his postings, he found himself blocked again.

Because bloggers are testing government control of information flow by writing about everything from human rights to the region's rulers and even Islam, Internet activists have become the fifth estate, one that is tracked and penalized by the authorities. Human rights groups have accused several governments in the Gulf and elsewhere in the Middle East of suppressing the Internet by blocking websites and detaining bloggers. Five Middle East countries—Egypt, Iran, Saudi Arabia, Tunisia, and Syria—are on a list of the thirteen worst Internet freedom enemies.[17] The jury is still out on whether online opposition will graduate from "venting to acting" and whether it can be transformed into social and democratic reform in the region. Authorities have not hesitated to appreciate its potential, however, and they have been quick to censor content, particularly content posted in Arabic.

Text-Messaging

Another instrument of the new media—cell phone text-messaging—has also become a powerful channel of political expression. In a region where independent political parties are banned, text-messaging helps organizers to assemble lists of participants in loose political groupings, rapidly spread news about detained activists, aid in scheduling meetings and demonstrations, encourage voting, and give prominence to emerging issues.

In Kuwait, as noted above, protesters used text-messages to mobilize supporters for demonstrations under the radar of government authorities, particularly youth. Lessons learned from the women's rights movement and the Orange Movement were applied both by candidates contesting National Assembly elections who used text-messaging as a campaign tool and by their political rivals who used the same tool to disseminate negative publicity. By 2008, electioneering by text-message was so ubiquitous it was regarded as spam.

The movement for women's political rights was an early example of activist use of text-messaging. One of the most effective campaigns occurred in 2005 after text-messaging became an integral part of the suffrage campaign. "People who use those messages are denouncing, insulting opposition figures, members of parliament and the government . . . new technology encourages unrestrained personal invective as new democratic cultures are formed." A message targeted at the speaker of the Kuwaiti parliament, Jassem al-Khorafi, who did not support political rights for women, accused him of being more interested in making money from business contracts than women's rights: "If you want Khorafi to vote for women's political rights just issue the right as a tender contract."[18]

In Bahrain, opposition groups were warned against using text-messages to organize demonstrations. Yet when an economic reform report was released in 2005, the Al-Wefaq National Islamic Society, a Shi'ite movement that is the kingdom's largest opposition group, paid a commercial service to publicize the following text-message: "Economic reform without political reform is like a bird with only one wing. How can it fly?"[19]

Using communication technologies for political propaganda in the Gulf was originally the forte of Saudi exiles and Islamic activists who engaged in a war conducted by faxed pamphlets in the early and mid-1990s. Before text-messaging went commercial, black marketeers sold CDs containing lists of cell phone numbers. (This task has now been taken over by mobile phone companies who carry it out for a fee.) Taking television channels off the air and blocking websites have been effective means to counter political opposition, but blocking text-messages on mobile phones is a more difficult proposition.[20]

Other Internet Innovations

Exiles, by necessity, rely heavily on new media to further their political agenda. The first to produce and disseminate texts from abroad was the

Saudi opposition in London, led by Mohammed Al-Masari and Saad al-Faqih, who disseminated information against the royal family through faxes. Saad al-Faqih now runs the London-based Islamist opposition Movement for Islamic Reform in Arabia, and uses a website to call for political reform in the kingdom and the removal of the Saudi monarchy. One such attempt to organize a protest in the kingdom in December 2004 fizzled out under a heavy security blanket.

In a video posted on the Internet, the chief of the Al-Ajman tribe in Saudi Arabia requested support for the exiled Movement for Islamic Reform in Arabia. Ali Al-Dumaini, who was jailed in 2005 along with two other activists for demanding political reforms, said his "Dialogue and Creativity" forum was blocked because it had discussed issues related to human rights, tolerance, and democracy.[21]

Like the women's rights activists noted earlier, other proreform groups in the kingdom also post petitions to solicit signatures before presenting them to the government. Some of them have been arrested and released, but the posting of the text of petitions on various websites accessible within the kingdom has kept the political reform agenda prominent in the public consciousness.[22]

The growing use of new media to advance political reform is a natural corollary of the rapidly rising number of Internet users in the Arab world—an estimated 42 million in 2008. This represents an impressive Internet usage growth rate of 1,177 percent between 2000 and 2008, although it began from a small base, and Arab Internet user penetration remains well below the world average.[23]

Government initiatives, mostly supported by information technology (IT) companies and private organizations, to increase the PC-installed base at educational institutions and homes also contribute to growth in Internet use. The UAE is ahead in terms of Internet penetration in the Arab world at 49.8 percent, followed by 37.8 percent in Qatar, 34.7 percent in Bahrain, and 34.7 percent in Kuwait. In terms of numbers, Egypt ranks first with 8.6 million Internet users; Saudi Arabia, 6.2 million; and the UAE, 2.3 million.[24] The growth in Internet subscriptions is expected to rise across the region in response to plummeting charges, improved services, and expanding competition among service providers.

New media expansion has given birth to some "daring free-zone" enterprises such as Dubai Media City and Dubai Internet City in the UAE, which promise potential customers that they will not "censor broadcasts or meddle with programming."[25] A study by the Arabic Network for Human Rights Information, however, finds that many Middle East Internet users face shutdowns of websites and Internet cafes, and prosecution for Internet-related crimes. In 2004, the study reported that some 400,000 webpages were banned and filtered in Saudi Arabia to "protect Islamic values and culture."

The Saudi government also blocked several Shi'ite and other Islamic websites that offer interpretations different from the official Wahhabi line (see also Chapter 7).[26] This practice is also common in the UAE, although the service provider may be able to reverse the ban based on a satisfactory justification by the Internet subscriber.[27] The study also found that Qatar is among the least repressive states in the Arab cyberworld. By contrast, in March 2005, Bahraini authorities detained three Bahrainis for links to a banned Arabic Internet forum, which was accused of inciting hatred against the government and spreading false information that could jeopardize state security.[28]

Web of Rage, Terror, and Counterterror

Extremist organizations are enthusiastic users of the Internet for planning, spreading, and executing their goals.[29] Al-Jazeera interviews with terror suspects Khalid Shaikh Mohammad and Ramzi bin Al-Shibh in 2002 suggest that the September 11, 2001, attackers communicated openly using prearranged code words such as the "faculty of urban planning" for the World Trade Center and the "faculty of fine arts" for the Pentagon.[30] Since 9/11, numerous software programs have been developed to disguise or hide messages in other ways.[31]

Youth are a primary target audience of Internet activists. One example is www.alsaha.com (The Forum). Originating from the UAE, it is considered to be one of the first and most successful Arabic weblogs, with forums on religion, politics, and sports, among others.[32] Since most forums are not moderated, bloggers use them not only to share ideas, but also to express their fury. Saudi intellectuals, often using false identities, are especially prominent in The Forum, making up a majority of the participants, and an estimated 80 percent of the discussions revolve around Saudi Arabia. On most political debates, opinions are usually evenly distributed; some estimate that about 30 percent of the participants are Al-Qaida sympathizers and supporters.[33]

In June 2004, the UAE shut down an Internet forum (www.qal3ati.net/vb) that carried statements by militants and Saudi dissidents. In May, an Al-Qaida-linked site (www.al-ansar.biz) was shut down after it posted the video of American Nicholas Berg's beheading in Iraq.[34] Kuwait also blocked at least three Islamic websites accused of inciting violence following clashes between extremists and security forces in January 2005.[35]

Other incendiary websites include the now interrupted Al-Daawa (The Call) website at www.D3wa.net, an Arabic-language website based in Kuwait and believed to be associated with Al-Qaida. Once known as jahara.org, it even offered manuals on how to make bombs. In 2003 www.alneda.com, a website believed to be Al-Qaida's primary medium of communication with its sleeper cells, was very active. Since then the website has been checked and blocked on several occasions, but keeps finding its way back in another form. Al-Muhajiroun (The Migrants)—an active English-language website—and Al-Qalaa (The Fortress) at www.qal3ah.org, which carried a statement by Saudi Al-Qaida operative Abdul Aziz Al-Muqrin prior to the attack in Khobar in June 2004, are other popular sites.

Opposition to the US occupation of Iraq encouraged the proliferation of websites. Extremists used two Arabic websites, Kuwaiti.com and Symphoniyat Loli Nagham Al-Mawaqi Al-Arabiya (names as published) to disseminate images of the abduction and murder of US citizens.[36] Others, such as www.qal3ah.net and www.al-ansar.biz, were flooded with reports on the abuse of Iraqi prisoners by US guards. Internet sites reproduced graphic pictures of prisoners abused at Abu Ghraib and called for retribution.[37]

Al-Qaida members defied a crackdown and the loss of senior leaders in Saudi Arabia, including a leading Web magazine editor, Issa Saad bin Oshan, by using the Internet to win new recruits. The group continued to publish its two widely distributed e-magazines. Oshan was in charge of "Sawt Al-Jihad" (Voice of Holy War)—the most important propaganda tool, which detailed how Saudis could contribute to the armed struggle. It reappeared in Saudi Arabia in April 2005 after several months of unexplained absence with a question: "Why Muslims on the Arabian peninsula have not heeded a call to hunt down Americans? [*sic*]."[38] Another publication is the "Muaskar Al-Battar" (Battar Barracks), a guerrilla manual advocating the killing of officials and instructing readers on the use of arms, including one post explaining how to use a mobile phone in a bomb attack like the one in Madrid in March 2004.

There are also progovernment activists on the Internet. For example, Mohsen Al-Awaji, a Saudi dissident who was briefly imprisoned for blaming terrorism in the region on despotic regimes, hosts a political website with the knowledge of the authorities concerned.[39] And, in response to hate messages from the United States that followed the killing of an American in Riyadh, "thoughtful" e-mail replies helped set the record straight. Articles written by Saudis condemning the killing also were posted on the Internet, which helped the hate mail subside. The power of the Internet was touted as being "stronger than any PR campaign."[40]

Saudi Arabia openly acknowledged the positive impact of online media by claiming to have changed the ideological thinking of more than 250 Al-Qaida sympathizers through the Islamic Affairs Ministry's Counterterrorism Program conducted over the Internet. The program includes direct counseling as well as a hotline for families worried that their sons may be drawn toward Al-Qaida. According to the Saudi Islamic affairs minister Saleh Al-Asheikh, following a ministry dialogue with 800 people, "more than a quarter were convinced. . . . The Internet is a fertile field. We have used many Islamic and cultural sites to increase awareness of the dangers of terrorism."[41]

Online *Diwaniyyas*

In view of the adoption of Web-based media tools to monitor postelection developments in Iran in June 2009, it would be useful to track briefly the emergence and impact of Facebook and Twitter, which are primarily social networking tools, in the GCC countries. As part of the 2009 Kuwait election campaign process, a Facebook page displayed the following slogan: "The vote that matters most! Make a difference—Say no to tribalism! Say no to fanaticism! Say no to corruption!"[42] Facebook, also known as online *diwaniyyas,* had about 10,000 members in Kuwait in mid-2007.[43]

The August 2008 case of a Saudi father killing his daughter for chatting on Facebook reveals the domestic strife that new media are causing. The young woman was reportedly beaten and shot after her father found her in the middle of an online conversation with a man. The case led some religious exponents to criticize Facebook for corrupting youth. "Facebook is a door to lust and young women and men are spending more on their mobile phones and the Internet than they are spending on food." Critics also allege that the social networking site serves as a tool to encourage homosexual relations in the conservative kingdom.[44]

That has not deterred an estimated 30,000 young Saudis from interacting on Facebook. More than 6,500 people signed an online petition in a bid to stop Riyadh from banning Facebook from local Internet servers. The site is also used by women. Many employ nicknames and post comic images or drawings on their pages instead of photographs, leading some Saudi bloggers to dub the network "Faceless."[45] The impact of online interaction in the region is extensive. Even the vice president and prime minister of the UAE and ruler of Dubai Shaikh Mohammed bin Rashid al-Maktoum has a Facebook page (www.facebook.com/SheikhMohammed). Shaikh Mohammed has used the Internet on several occasions to reach the public, including to answer questions about the economic crisis that affected Dubai following the global financial meltdown in late 2008.[46]

Since the Telecommunications Regulatory Authority unblocked Twitter in August 2008, the UAE has had the most Tweeters in the GCC region, about 1,000 users. Saudi Arabia has 360, and Qatar 120 Tweeters.[47] The extensive use of Twitter in Iran's postelection protests may influence Gulf Arabs, but is unlikely to have any dramatic impact.

BlackBerry Ban

The impact of BlackBerry, however, has been rather different. Al Wefaq, the largest political and religious society in Bahrain, with seventeen seats in the forty-member lower house of parliament, has been using the BlackBerry chat function to share its views. Newspapers also use the service to break news. In April 2010, Bahrain suspended "Breaking News," started by a Bahraini journalist and sent to more than 13,000 BlackBerry subscribers, because it created "confusion and chaos." The free service provided a summary of front-page news in Bahrain's six newspapers. Journalist Muhannad Sulaiman informed subscribers:

> I am sorry about the inconvenience, but as you do know, it is well beyond my capabilities. . . . I will suspend the service in compliance with the law, but it will be only for a few days until I complete the procedures to get the license. I will not give up this right to freedom of providing information, and I thank all those who have expressed their support, including the many ministers and senior officials who I discovered were members of the group.[48]

First Change

The first new medium to generate an alternative discourse was television. As satellite access expanded, the rising information flow charted a growing freedom of expression. One example is Al-Jazeera's twenty-four-hour Arab equivalent of C-SPAN—Al-Jazeera Live—which was launched in April 2005 and covers everything political in the region and the West. The fact that Al-Jazeera's correspondents were unwelcome in Saudi Arabia, Kuwait, Algeria, Tunisia, Iraq, and even Iran, after it had aired reports of unrest among Iran's Arab minority, is testimony to the popularity of the programs and perhaps a reflection of their antiestablishment tilt.

Talk shows have proven to be the ideal forum for the political- and reform-minded to air their views. A promotion for Al-Jazeera's "The Opposite Direction" program poses some blunt questions: "Why is it that when an Arab leader dies, people moan and wail as if the nation can't live without him? What have these leaders ever achieved for us? Aren't they symbols of corruption and backwardness and tyranny?"[49] These interactive programs tend to be sensational and appeal to the emotions of the audience. Talk shows feature guests who criticize Arab regimes for their repression and, as a result, "Arab governments have denounced satellite stations as enemies, as divisive, even as terrorists. They have filed lawsuits against them, closed bureaus, attempted to jam transmissions, or even launched their own state-run satellite stations."[50]

According to a report by the US Institute of Peace:

> It is the satellite channels that show the greatest potential for ushering in political change in the region. . . . Inadvertently or not, they offer a locus for the Arab street to vent, formulate and discuss public affairs. They bring Arabs closer together, breaking taboos and generally competing with each other and their respective governments for the news agenda.[51]

Supporting that view is another question posed on Al-Jazeera: "Have the existing Arab regimes become worse than colonialism?" to which 76 percent of the callers responded affirmatively.[52] The desire for change was also reflected in Al-Jazeera's 2005 focus on voting in Iraq, rather than on the violence there. Al-Arabiyya capitalized on the mood by engaging eight satellite broadcasting vehicles across Iraq to maximize the impact of its coverage.[53]

Following the May 12, 2003, terror attack in Saudi Arabia—which many referred to as the kingdom's 9/11—and other attacks by Al-Qaida and its affiliates, the Saudi government published and broadcast the names and pictures of some of the most wanted terrorists. This was a far cry from the days when even the existence of Saudi terrorists was denied. A six-part talk show on terrorism was broadcast on Saudi television as part of a national campaign to discourage recruitment to terrorist groups. About two dozen intellectuals—academics, journalists, authors, family counselors, and religious leaders—took part, many emphasizing the role of the family in rearing tolerant youth, the role of police in providing security, and the necessity of cooperation by citizens and foreign residents with security forces.[54] In addition, the Saudi government launched Al-Fajr (The Dawn), a religious and educational channel intended to combat extremism, both acknowledging and reinforcing the influence of the new medium.

Tash Ma Tash (No Big Deal), a popular Saudi satirical comedy, has been televised since 1993. The program pokes fun at the flaws of Saudi society and was one of the pioneers of self-criticism on sensitive topics such as culture, terrorism, marital relations, and religion—issues that many agree need to be brought to public attention. The program's success could be measured by its popularity and public anticipation of its telecasts not only in Saudi Arabia, but also in other GCC countries, where the program has been replicated to reflect specific problems in those societies.[55]

The brief survey above indicates that one of the several deficits associated with the Middle East as a region—information—has been partly rectified by the burgeoning television channels and the advent of the Internet. Despite attempts to limit the spread of the new media, "it appears technology has won against repression."[56]

The Other Side of Al-Jazeera

The debate about the rise and impact of satellite television has centered on the credibility of the news-gathering and -reporting methods of satellite channels. While the initial goal was to provide an alternative to Western media, satellite television has consolidated its position by expanding its audience base, aided by popular interest in the wars in Afghanistan and Iraq, and mistrust of news originating from the West.[57] In addition to providing an alternative source of news to local audiences, regional channels appeal to a large segment of Muslim and Arabic audiences outside of the region. Critics depict television channels based in the Middle East as the mouthpieces of extremists and accuse them of fomenting hatred toward the West. Proponents assert that they reflect reality, which explains their popularity among the people. This perspective is reinforced when Western media borrow extensive footage of events in crisis areas from Middle East media. During the Iraq War, while the Western media relied heavily on "superficial sound bytes, interviews with current or former government officials, and expertise from a narrow ideological range," regional channels included reactions of local and international figures and officials, thereby representing multiple realities, including the human toll and material destruction.[58]

Much of the credit for liberating the media in the Middle East is attributed to the "CNN of the Arab World"—the Al-Jazeera network. The Qatar-based television station broadcasts world news, but focuses on regional issues and crises. By mid-2009, it was estimated to have 53 million viewers.[59] Qatar claims that Al-Jazeera, founded in 1996, is an independent, private sector channel, but many Arabs believe that it is a government mouthpiece available as needed. Qatar compares its relationship with Al-Jazeera to the one the BBC enjoys with the British government. Even so, it is well-known that Qatar's prime minister and foreign minister Shaikh Hamad bin Jassim bin Jabr al-Thani, a cousin of the emir, owns 35 percent of the channel. Sustained by a $137 million grant from the emir, it also charged up to $20,000 per minute of footage for high-demand tapes such as those with Al-Qaida messages.[60]

Al-Jazeera has undoubtedly changed the rules of the media game, but it also is a chronic headache to Middle East governments and sows discord among them. By 2004, the Qatari government had received more than 400 official complaints from Arab states about Al-Jazeera's broadcasts.[61] Qatar's five GCC partners threatened a boycott in 2002, charging that it had slandered them, thereby violating a GCC code of conduct that bans cross-border media attacks.[62]

The United States also has accused Al-Jazeera of airing "false" and "inflammatory" reports about the US-led military operations in Iraq, and it too has demanded that action be taken against the station.[63] During his service as US secretary of state, Colin Powell said that Al-Jazeera's coverage was harming otherwise strong ties between the United States and Qatar while former US defense secretary Donald Rumsfeld described its reporting as "vicious, inaccurate and inexcusable."[64] The George W. Bush administration even refused to invite Qatar as an observer to the Group of 8 summit meeting in 2004 because it had failed to curb the "excesses" of Al-Jazeera.[65] In response to Al-Jazeera's popularity and reach, however, the United States was prompted to broadcast US views in Arabic. One way, ironically, was via advertising purchased by the US State Department on Al-Jazeera to promote the US position in the Middle East.[66]

The government of Qatar acknowledges that Al-Jazeera is a headache, but refuses to shut it down. Al-Jazeera not only is a potent propaganda weapon, but also a major advertisement for the ruling family's liberal outlook in a region dominated by conservative thinking. Al-Jazeera itself reaffirmed that it would not bow to pressure from the United States and would stick to its founding policies.[67] Qatar did, however, pledge to act on sternly worded US complaints. A spokesman promised that the government would "review it because we need Al-Jazeera to be professional and we don't want anybody to send lies or to send wrong information."[68]

Although Qatar declines to defend everything that Al-Jazeera reports, it says that, on balance, "it is good to see or hear what happens in the Arab world and what reflects the mood of Arabic or Islamic public opinion." Doha also explains that all organizations go through several stages, beginning with "incipience, then growth and then maturity, before declining or leveling off," putting Al-Jazeera at the "pre-maturity" stage. As a step toward limiting the damage, Al-Jazeera's board of directors established a "re-evaluation commission."[69] US criticism prompted the commission to recommend that Al-Jazeera adopt a "code of ethics" derived from a study of charters from various networks around the world.[70]

While adverse reactions are symptomatic of the limited tolerance that governments have for criticism, credit is due to Al-Jazeera for airing a broad range of opinions running from US neoconservatives to the Israeli prime minister Benjamin Netanyahu to Osama bin Laden and his sympathizers. It is more diverse and more consistently so than any mainstream Western television channel.[71] Al-Jazeera's enterprising approach resulted in its being the first to report on the Abu Ghraib prison atrocities in Iraq. Of course, there are many issues on which coverage could be improved, such as unemployment and labor. It is also important to note that, even though Al-Jazeera has adopted good journalistic standards in its foreign coverage, it is like most other media when examining its own country's affairs—evasive.

Al-Jazeera Spin-Offs

Al-Jazeera's success sparked emulation in the region, the most prominent being the Al-Arabiyya channel. It was launched weeks before the US-led invasion of Iraq, in February 2003, with capital of $300 million drawn from the Saudi-controlled MBC, Lebanon's Hariri Group, and other investors from Saudi Arabia and Kuwait. Al-Arabiyya promised more news—sixteen hours of daily programs as compared to Al-Jazeera's eleven and a half, with no report lasting beyond two and a half minutes.

Headquartered in Dubai, Al-Arabiyya markets itself as a "balanced" alternative to Al-Jazeera, covering "news far from any deliberate provocation." Owned by Shaikh Walid Al-Ibrahim, a brother-in-law of King Fahd of Saudi Arabia, the channel did not copy Al-Jazeera's programs *Islamic Law and Life* and *The Opposite Direction.* It rather sought to distinguish itself, even in its choice of terms. It referred to US troops in Iraq not as "occupying forces" but rather as "multinational forces." One of its controversial programs, *From Iraq,* constructed a balance sheet comparing Saddam Hussein's reign with the US-British occupation. In the context of the Palestinian-Israeli conflict, it used "dead" instead of "martyr" when speaking of casualties. In consequence, well before it had become established and found an audience, Al-Arabiyya was viewed unfavorably by both the George W. Bush administration and the insurgents. US troops killed three Al-Arabiyya employees in Iraq, and at least five were killed in one car bomb blast in October 2004. Moreover, unlike Al-Jazeera, Al-Arabiyya also received threats from Islamist groups that accused it of being a "terrorist channel" and giving the Iraqi government favorable coverage.[72]

The US-installed Interim Governing Council banned Al-Arabiyya for two months, charging it with "incitement to murder" after it broadcast an audiotape purportedly made by Saddam. Former US defense secretary Rumsfeld called the channel "violently anti-coalition."[73] Al-Arabiyya, however, insisted that its coverage was "objective and precise" and, in the face of US criticism, it proved popular among Iraqis. A poll by the US State Department in seven Iraqi cities in October 2003 found that 37 percent named Al-Arabiyya as their preferred news source, followed by Al-Jazeera at 26 percent, and Iraqi Media Network (renamed Al-Iraqiyyah TV) at 12 percent.[74]

According to a 2004 poll conducted by Zogby International, although Al-Jazeera was the first choice for news among 44 percent of viewers in Saudi Arabia, within a year of Al-Arabiyya's launch, 39 percent of the viewers in all the countries polled said they watched its news coverage almost daily.[75] Over time, the United States also took more kindly to Al-Arabiyya than it did to other local channels. During the offensive by US troops in Fallujah in November 2004, Al-Jazeera focused on civilian deaths and resistance while Al-Arabiyya showed images of a terrorist haven being stormed. US officials refused to associate with Al-Jazeera, but Al-Arabiyya broadcast a four-part exclusive interview with Iraq's interim prime minister Iyad Allawi just before the elections, and US president George W. Bush gave it two exclusive interviews.[76]

A 2007 poll showed Al-Jazeera's 21.26 rating was higher than Al-Arabiyya's 5.1, but Al-Arabiyya was rated 22.23 in Saudi Arabia over Al-Jazeera's 17.33.[77] In Iraq Al-Arabiyya managed a whopping 41.29 rating, almost even with Al-Iraqiyyah, the Iraqi government channel, and well ahead of Al-Jazeera's 18.39 rating. The United States actually commended Al-Arabiyya: "They're trying. The station is more moderate, but sometimes reporters on the scene get carried away."[78]

The United States's preference for Al-Arabiyya was evident when the White House arranged President Barack Obama's first media interview after taking office with the Saudi-owned, Dubai-based channel. Reports suggest that, following an internal debate about the timing of a presidential interview to the Arab media, several advisers recommended that it be granted to Al-Arabiyya because "the channel is seen as a prominent voice of moderation in the Middle East, preferring calm analysis to what many see as rival Al-Jazeera's more sensational coverage."[79]

To counter the Arab channels and contrary to the recommendations of the US Advisory Commission on Public Diplomacy, the United States launched Al-Hurra TV in 2004. Even with $60 million in seed money, plus an additional $40 million appropriated by Congress to increase its potential coverage to 80 percent of Iraqis, Al-Hurra faded following its inability to cover the Fallujah siege from inside the city as its competitors did. A survey by the Arab Advisors Group revealed that Al-Jazeera topped the ranks in brand recognition with 82 percent, followed by Al-Arabiyya with 75 percent. Saudi Al-Ekhbaria was recognized by 33 percent, but Al-Hurra was recognized by a mere 16 percent of those polled. While 70 percent of respondents said that Al-Arabiyya was very trustworthy and 69 percent said the same of Al-Jazeera, only 17 percent felt Al-Hurra was trustworthy.[80]

The success of satellite television in the Gulf reflects the increasing space for expression and political debate in the region. When Al-Arabiyya and Abu Dhabi TV joined Al-Jazeera to offer unprecedented, locally responsive coverage of events and developments across the world, the tone of global discourse on Arab media also changed as their professionalism and technical advancement attracted notice.[81] The growing maturity and sophistication of audiences with respect to the information flow can also be judged by their refusal to accept uncritically whatever is relayed by media outlets. Thus, following the ouster of Saddam, the Arab media came under scrutiny for "misleading" people in the region into thinking that Iraq was "winning" the war when, in reality, the Republican Guard had melted into the crowd after offering little resistance.[82]

Conclusion

The new media have been more boon than bane in their role as developers of political consciousness among Gulf populations, and even as communicators of the voice of the opposition to ruling regimes and citizens. Regionally, the new media are shining light on issues that, until a decade ago, were taboo in the public domain. Governments were forced to respond when the regional intelligentsia began to question why they were denied their own channels, websites, and radio stations while international broadcasters had preferred access. Moreover, the new media, and especially their most accessible elements, cannot be perfectly monitored and controlled by the governments. Thus, the information revolution, initially the preserve of elites, quickly broadened out and transformed political discourse in the region on multiple levels.

Several challenges continue to plague the Gulf media, however. In general, traditional—shallow—presentation still predominates, along with excessive praise of leaders and celebrities. Loss of identity is a factor, with most GCC radio and television stations imitating more professional Arab counterparts. Overall, these challenges can be summed up as three not entirely convergent pressures. The first is the scope of freedom that the citizens of the GCC countries demand in order to better express their concerns. The second is the limited autonomy of the ownership and management of the main media outlets, which remain linked to government interests. The third is the impact of and reaction to punitive measures imposed on some media outlets, organizations, and staff.

Because media freedom is closely linked to democratization, ruling regimes that do not derive their political legitimacy from the masses view media development as a dangerous, even frightening, prospect. To give free rein to the media, share responsibility for governance with society, and turn decisionmaking into a process conducted collectively and not unilaterally would make governments accountable in ways that they now are still able to avoid. This is reason enough to put roadblocks in the way of media development.

There is no doubt that free and responsible mass media can be effective tools for shaping public opinion, gauging the impact of public policies, and disseminating information. The new media in the Gulf took this process one step further by giving citizens at every level a chance to disseminate information in the political realm while limiting the scope for government intervention. At the same time, the popularity and accessibility of the new media have led to abuses. While political consciousness has certainly increased, it remains undetermined how societies whose political development is at a nascent stage will use their new awareness. Even so, looking back over the past decade of rapid development offers grounds to hope for continued progress.

Notes

1. Jon B. Alterman, *New Media, New Politics? From Satellite Television to the Internet in the Arab World* (Washington, DC: Washington Institute for Near East Policy, 1998).

2. Deborah L. Wheeler, "The Internet and Youth Subculture in Kuwait," *Journal of Computer-Mediated Communication* 8, no. 2 (2003); see also Jon W. Anderson, *Arabizing the Internet* (Abu Dhabi: Emirates Center for Strategic Studies and Research, 1998).

3. Naomi Sakr, *Arab Media and Political Renewal: Community, Legitimacy and Public Life* (London: I. B. Tauris, 2007).

4. Rami G. Khouri suggests that the impact would be better if there were specialized coverage of business, environment, government spending, military, and culture; Rami G. Khouri, "Arab Satellite Marriage: Osama bin Laden and Madonna," *Daily Star* (Lebanon), November 28, 2002. See also Mohamed Zayani, *Arab Satellite Television and Politics in the Middle East* (Abu Dhabi: Emirates Center for Strategic Studies and Research, 2004).

5. Thalif Deen, "Is Al-Jazeera the New Symbol of Arab Nationalism?" Inter Press Service, October 12, 2004.

6. Haitam Sabbah, "Weblogs Soar in Gulf States," Agence France Presse, June 14, 2006.

7. Marc Lynch, "Blogging the New Arab Public: Arab Blogs' Political Influence Will Grow," April 10, 2007, www.worldpoliticsreview.com.

8. Sabbah, "Weblogs Soar in Gulf States."

9. Mary Ann Tétreault, "Kuwait's Annus Mirabilis," Middle East Report Online, September 7, 2006, www.merip.org (September 11, 2007).

10. More details available at Neil MacFarquhar, "In Tiny Arab State, Web Takes on Ruling Elite," *New York Times,* January 15, 2006.

11. Agence France Press, "Bahrain Detains Moderator of Online Forum," March 5, 2001.

12. "Online Forum Moderator Held in Bahrain," Agence France Presse, March 2, 2005.

13. Sabbah, "Weblogs Soar in Gulf States."

14. Habib Shaikh, "Blogs Fast Becoming Place of Refuge for Women," *Khaleej Times,* February 23, 2007; Rasheed Abou-Alsamh, "Saudi Women Unveil Opinions Online," *Christian Science Monitor,* June 19, 2006.

15. *Arab News,* September 16, 2007.

16. Mona Eltahawy, "Happy Birthday, Saudi Arabia," Middle East Online, September 25, 2007; see also Naomi Sakr, ed., *Women and Media in the Middle East: Power Through Self-Expression* (London: I. B.Tauris, 2004).

17. "Bloggers in Mideast Transforming Dialogue but Face Clampdowns by Authorities," Associated Press, February 9, 2007.

18. Steve Coll, "Text Messaging Is New Tool of Political Underground," *Washington Post*, March 29, 2005.

19. Ibid.

20. Ibid.

21. Agence France Presse, "Saudi Tribal Chief Urges Opposition in Security Forces," August 24, 2007; "Saudis Block Liberal Internet Forum, Says Activist," Reuters, August 9, 2007.

22. "Profile: Saudi Political Opposition," BBC, February 10, 2005.

23. "Internet Usage and Population Statistics," www.internetworldstats.com.

24. Ibid.

25. Dana El-Baltaji, "Dubai: An Emerging Arab Media Hub," *Arab Media and Society,* no. 3 (Fall 2007), www.arabmediasociety.org.

26. William Fisher quotes from the HRINFO report, *The Internet in the Arab World: A New Space of Repression?* in William Fisher, "Arab Internet Users Are Caught in a Terrible Web," *Daily Star* (Lebanon), December 7, 2004.

27. See also "Internet Filtering in the United Arab Emirates in 2004–2005: A Country Study," OpenNet Initiative, www.opennetinitiative.net.

28. The site under scrutiny was www.bahrainonline.org, and another popular site is www.montadayat.org; *Arab Times*, Kuwait, March 16, 2005.

29. According to French political scientist Gilles Kepel, the development of the Internet and its use by Arab television stations have changed the face of the terrorist threat. At the Madrid antiterrorism summit on March 10, 2005, he said: "Without Al-Jazeera, there would be no Al-Qaeda."

30. Tom Zeller Jr., "On the Open Internet, a Web of Dark Alleys," *New York Times,* December 20, 2004.

31. Ibid.

32. Al-Saha is reported to have carried a warning message prior to the September 11 attacks. In 2003, it reported a clash in Mecca between militants and Saudi security forces nearly half a day before any news agency was able to confirm and report the incident. The site's political forum is no longer accessible in Saudi Arabia, but hackers have managed to keep the site busy and inform each other about changes in addresses.

33. Mohammed Alkhereiji, "The Pros and Cons of Extremist Websites," *Daily Star* (Lebanon), June 4, 2004.

34. "UAE Temporarily Shuts Down Saudi Dissident Website," Associated Press, June 22, 2004.

35. Diana Elias, "Kuwait Blocks Sites That Incite Violence," *USA Today*, February 8, 2005.

36. BBC Monitoring Service, June 22, 2004, quoting from Muwaffaq Al-Nuwaysir, "Terrorists Exploit Easy Access to Arabic Websites to Post Images of US Victim," *Al-Sharq Al-Awsat* (London), www.aawsat.com.

37. "Islamic Websites Call for Revenge After Iraqi Prisoner Abuse," Agence France Presse, May 5, 2004. A video on www.al-ansar.biz, operated by a group named Muntada Al-Ansar, was titled "[Jordanian Militant] Sheikh Abu Musab Zarqawi Slaughters an American Infidel with His Hands and Promises Bush More." The video was available at www.thememoryhole.org. The murder of Robert Jacob, an American, was also posted as a video in June 2004. See also Daniel Benjamin and Gabriel Weimann, "What the Terrorists Have in Mind," *New York Times*, October 27, 2004.

38. "Al-Qaeda Online Journal Resumes Publication," Associated Press, April 28, 2005.

39. Yaroslav Trofimov, "Saudi Arabia Switches Its Policies, Letting Some Dissidents Speak Out," *Wall Street Journal*, May 9, 2002.

40. Khaled Al-Maeena, "Saudis Should Use the Power of the Internet to Stop Hate," *Gulf News*, July 5, 2004.

41. "Saudi Clerics Reform Extremists Through Online Dialogue," *Arab News*, February 7, 2005.

42. www.facebook.com/pages/Kuwait-Kuwait-Elections-of-2009-We-The-People/75210593274?ref=mf.

43. *Friday Times*, Kuwait, June 22, 2007.

44. "Saudi Woman Killed for Chatting on Facebook," *The Telegraph*, March 31, 2008.

45. Ibid.

46. "Sheikh Mohammed Joins Facebook," *The National*, June 26, 2009.

47. "UAE Leads Gulf Region with Most Twitter Users," *The National*, March 9, 2009.

48. "Local News on BlackBerry Banned in Bahrain," *Gulf News*, April 9, 2010.

49. Jarius Bondoc, "Veronica Pedrosa Joins 'Hated' Al-Jazeera TV," *Philippine Star,* December 7, 2005.

50. Marc Lynch, "Not the Enemy: The Arab Media and American Reform Efforts," *Arab Reform Bulletin* 2, no. 4 (2004).

51. Robin Wright, "Al-Jazeera Puts Focus on Reform," *Washington Post*, May 8, 2005.

52. "The Al Jazeera Effect," *Weekly Standard*, April 21, 2004. Also see Abdel Karim Samara, "The Arab Media and the Iraq War," *Open Democracy,* August 12, 2003, www.opendemocracy.net.

53. Hassan M. Fattah, "Arab Media Focus on Voting, Not Violence," *New York Times*, January 31, 2005.

54. "Terrorism Has Saudi Television Talking," United Press International, February 7, 2005.

55. See Raid Qusti, "Tash Ma Tash: A Barometer of Self-Criticism," *Arab News*, November 3, 2004.

56. Amir Taheri, "Doesn't the Gulf Suffer from Hope Deficit?" *Gulf News*, May 21, 2004.

57. Edmond Ghareeb, "New Media and the Information Revolution in the Arab World: An Assessment," *Middle East Journal* 54, no. 3 (2000): 395–418.

58. Al-Jazeera became the only network in Afghanistan after the Taliban expelled all other journalists during the war. See "Arab Satellite Television: From the Periphery to Center," Emirates Center for Strategic Studies and Research, August 11, 2004, www.ecssr.ac.ae; and Mohammed El-Nawawy and Adel Iskandar, *Al-Jazeera: How the Free Arab News Network Scooped the World and Changed the Middle East* (Boulder: Westview, 2002).

59. Christopher Helman, "Will Americans Tune to Al-Jazeera?" *Forbes*, July 13, 2009. The Arabic network's three-year-old sister channel, Al Jazeera English, is available over cable and satellite to 140 million households in 100 countries.

60. N. Janardhan, "Al Jazeera TV Rubs Arab Governments the Wrong Way," Inter Press Service, August 13, 2002.

61. Asad Abdul Rahman, "The Sky Is the Limit," *Gulf News*, May 28, 2004.

62. "Five Gulf States Threaten to Punish Al-Jazeera TV," Reuters, October 11, 2002.

63. "Al-Jazeera Iraq Coverage Clouds US-Qatar Ties," Agence France Presse, April 28, 2004.

64. Mansour O. El-Kikha, "Al-Jazeera—Filling the Void," *New York Times*, May 12, 2004.

65. "Al-Jazeera Iraq Coverage Clouds US-Qatar Ties," Agence France Presse, April 28, 2004.

66. For more analysis of the US administration's attitude toward Al-Jazeera during the Iraq War, see Steve Tatham, *Losing Arab Hearts and Minds: The Coalition, Al-Jazeera and Muslim Public Opinion* (London: Hurst, 2006).

67. "Al Jazeera Will Not Bow to US Pressure," *The Peninsula*, April 29, 2004.

68. "Qatar to Probe Al-Jazeera After US Complaints," *Arab News*, April 30, 2004.

69. Nora Boustany, "Al-Jazeera's Learning Curve," *Washington Post*, April 30, 2004.

70. "Al-Jazeera Unveils Ethics Code," *The Peninsula,* July 14, 2004.

71. "Al-Jazeera Targeted for Unbiased Reporting," *The Peninsula*, April 22, 2004, quoting *The Guardian.* Even Israel's *Haaretz* backed Al-Jazeera against the United States; Arnaud de Borchgrave, "Tutwiler's Mission Impossible," *Washington Times*, May 7, 2004. On the flip side, there were many reports about Al-Jazeera's alleged link with terrorists, especially in Iraq. See "The Al-Jazeera Effect," editorial, *Weekly Standard*, April 21, 2004.

72. Samantha M. Shapiro, "The War Inside the Arab Newsroom," *New York Times*, January 2, 2005.

73. Ibid.

74. Peter Feuilherade, "Al-Arabiya TV—Profile," BBC News, November 25, 2003. A 2004 Gallup poll revealed that 39 percent of the Iraqi audience views Al-Arabiyya while 35 percent favors Al-Jazeera; Lee Smith, "The Road to Tech Mecca," *Wired* 12, no. 7 (July 2004). See also excerpts from the findings of media surveys in Egypt, Jordan, and the UAE in "Media Consumption in the Middle East—Examining the Data," InterMedia Surveys, September 2, 2003, www.zunia.org.

75. Shapiro, "TheWar Inside the Arab Newsroom."

76. "Arab Satellite Television—The World Through Their Eyes," *The Economist*, February 24, 2005.

77. Alvin Snyder, "Al-Jazeera and Al-Hurra Contend with TV Ratings Problems," March 27, 2007, www. uscpublicdiplomacy.org.

78. Smith, "The Road to Tech Mecca."

79. Scott MacLeod, "How Al-Arabiya Got the Obama Interview," *Time*, January 28, 2009.

80. "Al-Jazeera's Viewers' Base in Saudi Arabia Is 5 Times Larger Than United States Sponsored Al-Hurra's Audience," www.arabadvisors.com. More statistics are available in "Al-Jazeera Most Popular in Saudi Arabia," *Arab News*, September 10, 2004.

81. For more on television broadcasting in the region, see Naomi Sakr, *Satellite Realms: Transnational Television, Globalization and the Middle East* (London: I. B. Tauris, 2002).

82. N. Janardhan, "Arabs Debate 'Misinformation' During War on Iraq," Inter Press Service, June 12, 2003.

11

Permanent Interests, Variable Policies: The United States in the Gulf

Mary Ann Tétreault

THE INTERNATIONAL REPUTATION of the United States sank during the last years of the George W. Bush administration. The almost universal sympathy evoked by terrorist attacks in New York and Washington, DC, quickly evaporated, and confidence in the United States dropped to levels most US citizens found shocking. Yet this decline should not have been surprising. Thanks to its coalition's brutal invasion and occupation of Iraq, its open partisanship favoring the policies of the Israeli hard right, and its thoughtless—sometimes reckless—treatment of traditional allies and potential enemies, the United States during the Bush administration came to be seen as a source of instability in the Middle East and globally.[1] Nothing made the status of the United States clearer than the many spontaneous demonstrations by citizens in Arab countries against the perceived US role as éminence grise in the 2006 Lebanon war. They occurred even in Kuwait where citizens remain grateful that the United States delivered them and their country from Iraqi occupation in 1991.[2] Although the reputation of the United States in the Middle East and other Muslim countries rose in the months following the election of Barack Obama to the presidency, in Arab states the rise was minuscule.[3]

It is by now common to conclude that US foreign policy since 2001 is aberrant, an expression of the radical ideology of President George W. Bush and his neoconservative advisers,[4] or an overwrought reaction to the shock of the September 11, 2001, terrorist attacks—and sometimes both. I argue here that there is more continuity than change in the primary aim of US foreign policy, although how it is pursued depends on individual leaders and the means that they have at their disposal. Even so, from George Washington's realist caution to avoid entangling alliances to George W.

Bush's insistence that the United States is prepared to "go it alone," and despite President Obama's bows in the direction of consultation and multilateralism, autonomy has been a consistent goal of US presidents and their foreign policies.[5] It characterized the 1823 Monroe Doctrine as much as the 2002 Bush National Security Strategy: although the policies intended to achieve the aims that each document outlines differ (along with the tone in which they are expressed), their position is consistent. What made the Bush era so different from the recent past is that US global military predominance converged with the occupation of the heart of the executive branch by leaders determined to assert US primacy abroad and dismantle checks on presidential authority and power at home.[6] Ideological opponents of domestic power sharing and liberal internationalism, especially civil and human rights, they were determined to translate their preferences into policy and law.[7]

Throughout the Cold War, the United States and its strategic mirror image, the Soviet Union, invested heavily in military technology to increase the destructive power of their weapons and the scope of military command and control. Both superpowers field-tested these systems in client and proxy wars to achieve immediate aims, demonstrate their power, and maintain their global prestige.[8] When the collapse of the Soviet Union ended the Cold War, US hard-liners continued to press for expanded US military capability.[9] Taking refuge during the time between the fall of Richard Nixon and the rise of George W. Bush in supportive nonstate organizations, they prepared for their return to power by colonizing state institutions. With the election of George W. Bush and Dick Cheney, hard-liners achieved control of the foreign policy establishment under a president with messianic ambitions.[10]

The Bush White House gloried in the role of leader of the sole remaining superpower. US military expenditures soared; in 2005, they were higher than those of all other countries combined.[11] Massive unchecked military force allowed the party in control of the White House and Congress to project a new vision of US power. After 9/11, it was applied enthusiastically in the Middle East.[12] Despite setbacks in Afghanistan and Iraq, the United States proceeded with plans to preserve global dominance for the foreseeable future, expanding military bases worldwide and moving to weaponize space.[13]

This aggressive posture has been explained as a unique outgrowth of the worldview of the George W. Bush administration. Journalist Ron Suskind reports a conversation with an administration insider that ended this way:

> The aide said that guys like me were "in what we call the reality-based community," which he defined as people who "believe that solutions

> emerge from your judicious study of discernible reality." I nodded and murmured something about enlightenment principles and empiricism. He cut me off. "That's not the way the world really works anymore," he continued. "We're an empire now, and when we act, we create our own reality. And while you're studying that reality—judiciously, as you will—we'll act again, creating other new realities, which you can study too, and that's how things will sort out. We're history's actors . . . and you, all of you, will be left to just study what we do."[14]

Why this spirited rejection of reality was not rejected with equal spirit by citizens called on to pay the price for such hubris in blood and treasure is the product of another historical strand in US policy. Called "the paranoid style" by historian Richard Hofstadter,[15] it describes the fear and resentment with which many Americans approach those they see as alien and threatening: Others, especially when those Others transgress boundaries or take what Americans see as rightfully theirs. When US leaders evoke these emotions, aggression is often the result.

American Exceptionalism and the Paranoid Style

Even before it was a "hyperpower," the self-image of the United States was hyperexceptional—as Michael Barone remarks in *U.S. News and World Report*, "Every nation is unique, but America is the most unique."[16] Jonathan Monten examines the democratization policy of George W. Bush in terms of this "liberal exceptionalism," and locates it in the pattern of alternating interventionism and isolationism that many historians and analysts find characteristic of US foreign policy.[17] Monten believes that these alternations are influenced by what sociologists call opportunity structures. For example, liberal exceptionalism is most prominent when the United States finds itself in a favorable situation for intervention. Thus, like me, Monten argues that current US policy is a product of post–Cold War unipolarity. He finds its roots in "vindicationism," a desire to spread the "good news" of US democracy around the world. Monten identifies vindicationism as an evangelical ideology that demands active US intervention, one that "contains an underlying claim about the efficacy of US power to produce democratic change."[18]

Evangelical Protestant religious imagery is part of this definition and, indeed, is prominent in George W. Bush's public pronouncements on foreign policy, yet I disagree with Monten (and others)[19] who see American exceptionalism primarily in religious or idealistic terms. As noted above, I believe it is not a value, but rather a *mode* of politics: Hofstadter's "paranoid style" or what Michael Rogin called "American political demonology."[20] Hofstadter captures its essence well: "American politics has often been an arena for angry minds. . . . Style has more to do with the way in which ideas are believed than with the truth or falsity of their content. . . . The paranoid style is an old and recurrent phenomenon in our public life which has been frequently linked with movements of suspicious discontent."[21] Paranoid politics is not confined to one religious group or one type of demon. Whether there is an explicit foreign policy component or not, manifestations of the paranoid style always include a fear of violation by subversive, "dark" forces.[22]

The paranoid style actually predates the founding of the republic. It is detectable in accounts of the earliest days of the settler colonies, an indication of how deeply it is embedded in American domestic political life. Linda Colley explains the belligerence of the ancestors of Americans and other human instruments of British imperialism as the result of fear. Subjects of a small, relatively poor island nation, they knew that their country would not intervene to save them if they got into trouble: should things go wrong, it would be every man for himself and his own.[23] Looking at English settlers in North America, Karen Kupperman finds many concrete examples of colonial paranoia. Colonists' fears of exotic local populations led them to commit acts of savage violence that mystified and frightened native peoples, virtually ensuring that contact between them would converge toward mutual hostility.[24]

David Hackett Fischer argues that the "Englishness" of British emigrants to North America was highly varied. Their communities embodied diverse patterns of life and thought with regard to their expression of hostility to foreigners and diligence in ferreting out internal subversives. Had he been thinking of foreign policy, Fischer might have predicted that a leadership obsessed by manliness, the security of its prerogatives, and rank-centered honor, joined to millenarian constituencies who believe that honor is preserved through violence, rules are made to be broken, and outsiders are probably up to no good, would prove to be as belligerent in foreign policy as in domestic politics.[25] These social forces shaped the combination of messianic democratization and punitive human rights violations that marked US foreign policy in the Gulf for a quarter-century.

Another characteristic of the paranoid style is its resurgence following wars. Neoclassical realists see a causal arrow running from an upsurge in state power and capacity to what Gideon Rose calls "the magnitude and ambition" of foreign policy.[26] I believe that this relationship is interactive rather than simply linear. Wars increase state power and capacity;[27] alter opportunity structures; and, under the conditions described by Monten, spark power grabs accompanied by fears of judgment and punishment.[28] The complex relationship between the desire to take and resentment of both those who are despoiled and any who question the right to take is strongly evident throughout US history from the early colonial encounters recounted by Kupperman, through the behavior of slave owners in the pre–Civil War South[29] and the lynching rituals Orlando Patterson describes that constituted an integral part of how the paranoid style was expressed domestically during the Jim Crow period.[30] Such behavior is masked by assertions of proprietorship, cloaking military intervention as protection of what is "ours."

Body Boundaries

"Body boundary" denotes the subjective sense of the boundary of the self; that is, the nature and extent of the spaces around the corporeal limits of the physical body an individual needs to control to feel secure.[31] Applying that concept to the post-Westphalian sovereign state,[32] identity boundaries of countries should coincide with formal borders drawn on a map, extended to include other elements internationally recognized as legitimate properties of the sovereign state, such as airspace and territorial waters. Sometimes, leaders and citizens regard regions not formally incorporated into their nation-state as though they are also part of this body. Examples include colonies and dependencies, revanchist images of "lost" territories or of places that should be part of the state (its "manifest destiny"), and spheres of influence. During the Cold War, the architecture of the Soviet and Western blocs established superpower body boundaries. Soviet spheres of influence and control incorporated the Baltic states, the Caucasus, and central Asia, all targets of continuing post-Soviet attempts to restore Russian authority in these areas. Similarly, "domino theory" fears expressed by US policymakers during the Cold War reflected their belief that the national security boundaries of the United States included all of its allies and dependencies—what Americans then called "the free world."[33] A challenge anywhere—South Korea, Cuba, Vietnam, even Algeria[34]—evoked strong, often belligerent, responses.[35]

The United States evinced extended body boundaries early in its history, and attempted to secure them by applying military power to acquire contiguous territory on the North American continent and dependencies in Latin America.[36] Buoyed by Andrew Jackson's unexpected—if technically postwar—rout of British forces at New Orleans in 1815, they felt able to set the terms of their relationship to Europe, and to a Latin America breaking free of imperial relations with Spain. Thomas Jefferson still coveted Cuba when he recommended that the United States support Cuban independence as the best way to maintain good relations with Britain:

> I candidly confess, that I have ever looked on Cuba as the most interesting addition which could ever be made to our system of States. The control which, with Florida Point, this island would give us over the Gulf of Mexico, and the countries and isthmus bordering on it, as well as all those

whose waters flow into it, would fill up the measure of our political well-being.[37]

Jefferson sought a declaration of war from Congress to support Britain against the rest of the Holy Alliance, but was defeated by Secretary of State John Quincy Adams's insistence on US autonomy. Coupled with measures to formalize US-Russian and US-British relations in the Western Hemisphere, the cabinet announced that the United States would oppose interference by any European power other than Spain, including Britain, in the affairs of the "new governments" that had declared themselves independent of Spanish rule.

> The late events in Spain and Portugal show that Europe is still unsettled. . . . Our policy in regard to Europe, which was adopted at an early stage of the wars . . . nevertheless remains the same, which is, not to interfere in the internal concerns of any of its powers; to consider the government de facto as the legitimate government for us; to cultivate friendly relations with it, and to preserve those relations by a frank, firm, and manly policy, meeting in all instances the just claims of every power, submitting to injuries from none. . . .
>
> It is impossible that the allied powers should extend their political system to any portion of either continent without endangering our peace and happiness. . . . It is equally impossible, therefore, that we should behold such interposition in any form with indifference.[38]

The later Monroe Doctrine is a vigorous assertion of hemispheric independence from European intervention and an expression of concern to appear "manly" among other nations. The 1904 "Roosevelt Corollary" actually asserted a US obligation to intervene in the domestic politics of countries the United States had declared off limits to intervention by Europeans.

> It is our duty to remember that a nation has no more right to do injustice to another nation, strong or weak, than an individual has to do injustice to another individual; that the same moral law applies in one case as in the other. But we must also remember that it is as much the duty of the Nation to guard its own rights and its own interests as it is the duty of the individual so to do. . . . Either it is necessary supinely to acquiesce in the wrong, and thus put a premium upon brutality and aggression, or else it is necessary for the aggrieved nation valiantly to stand up for its rights. . . . Therefore it follows that a self-respecting, just, and far-seeing nation should . . . keep prepared, while scrupulously avoiding wrongdoing itself, to repel any wrong, and in exceptional cases to take action which in a more advanced stage of international relations would come under the head of the exercise of the international police. A great free people owes it to itself and to all mankind not to sink into helplessness before the powers of evil.[39]

The arrogation of authority to "take action" rather than "sink into helplessness before the powers of evil"[40] is reminiscent of Henry Kissinger's remark about how the United States should respond to the likely election of Salvador Allende de Gossens as president of Chile.[41] These moralistic pronouncements from so long ago were strongly echoed in US assertions of rectitude in promoting regime change in the Gulf.

Our Oil

In the late nineteenth century, US body boundaries expanded to embrace investments by US-based corporations in strategic industries abroad,[42] including in the Middle East, where hydrocarbon exploration and development were conducted during the first three-quarters of the twentieth century primarily by US, British, and Dutch corporations.[43] The international hydrocarbon industry has always been an agent of globalization. Underpinned by a web of contracts that allowed international oil companies (IOCs) to control the configuration, growth, and conduct of this multinational industry, the IOCs generated enormous wealth for their owners at the same time that they underwrote the strategic and economic security of their home countries.

The energy regime that the IOCs created often led to conflict among developed states. The French, for example, were convinced that an Anglo-American cabal controlled oil for the benefit of Anglo-Saxons.[44] What looked from the outside like a dual conspiracy, however, was actually another arena where US and British interests both cooperated and competed for dominance. Despite British efforts to block them, Americans succeeded in getting half of the concession leased by Kuwait in 1934, even though Kuwait was still a British dependency at the time.[45] US oil companies, helped by their government, shut British companies completely out of the largest Middle East oil bonanza, Saudi Arabia, during World War II.[46] After the war, the US government decreed that sterling could not be used for oil transactions, a grave disadvantage for a war-impoverished Britain. Dollars became the exclusive financial medium of the oil trade in Europe, cementing both the interdependence of oil and financial markets and the determination of Americans to control both.[47]

Britain and the United States did work together to protect their oil interests. The United States used the Central Intelligence Agency to overthrow the nationalist government of Iran in 1953 after its prime minister, Mohammad Mossadegh, had the temerity to nationalize British oil holdings.[48] Yet rivalry also marked the US-British struggle with Iran. The restoration of Mohammad Reza Shah brought US oil companies into Iran, reducing the former British monopoly to a minority stake in this lucrative concession. In addition, the change simplified company management of the global oil regime, called "the international oil cartel" in a report presented to the US Federal Trade Commission that same year.[49] It also marked the undisputed primacy of the United States over Britain in the global oil market.

The Cold War was the dominant paradigm guiding US foreign policy elites from 1946 to the 1990s and, for the first thirty-five years, hydrocarbon security was deeply embedded in Cold War politics. The Baghdad Pact, signed in 1955, was another US-British/senior-junior partnership, with Britain taking the public role in assembling a regional alliance including Iraq, Turkey, Iran, and Pakistan that was intended to preserve preferential Western access to oil by keeping the Soviet Union out of the Middle East. Britain's reputation was damaged by the politics of the Baghdad Pact and sank further the following year when Egypt's president, Gamal Abdel Nasser, nationalized the Suez Canal. Britain joined France and Israel in an invasion of Egypt to take back the canal, but the United States forced their withdrawal, despite its own dislike of Nasser. Throughout this period, the United States had difficulty juggling the often incompatible demands made by its leadership of the Western alliance and the need to manage conflicts in the Middle East to guarantee the continued flow of cheap oil to its major power allies and, increasingly, to itself. It sacrificed NATO integrity to Arab opinion by siding with Algerian insurgents in their war against France[50] while it opposed most other anticolonial and revolutionary movements in the Middle East, including modest efforts made by legitimate governments such as Iran's, and dissenting populations such as in Saudi Arabia, to improve their political and economic situations.[51]

During the 1956 Suez war and the 1967 Six Day War, the United States mobilized all of its global oil resources, including the services of oil multinationals, to defeat Arab embargoes against supporters of Israel.[52] But US problems intensified after the 1967 war when its policy shifted from a pro-Arab stance toward greater support for Israel.[53] Consequently, when the oil weapon was applied again in 1973 during the October war, the United States itself was an embargo target, encouraging US policymakers to devise plans to take over Middle East oil fields in the event of future attempts at "strangulation."[54] But it was not the embargo per se that most disturbed the United States. Rather, it was the effect of embargo-related production cuts that reduced total supplies of oil reaching the market. The tight market allowed producers to quadruple prices and enabled some of them to nationalize their industries. "Our oil" suddenly became theirs as ownership of these huge industrial operations and the products—and profits—they generated were transferred from mostly US-based IOCs to national governments and national oil companies.

Analysts differ on their assessment of this change. Some attribute agency to the new owners; others deny that there was an oil "revolution" at all, arguing that the United States and its oil companies still controlled global energy resources.[55] Either way, the post–October 1973 energy regime required a different approach to Middle East politics and to managing the world oil market, tasks to which the US government proved unequal.[56] The most ominous sign of ebbing US control of Middle East oil was the 1978–1979 Iranian revolution. Its antecedents were undetected by US and US-client intelligence services while among its consequences were a hostage crisis that brought down a president and an energy crisis that pushed oil prices to new highs.

Cold War politics collided with oil politics when the Soviet Union invaded Afghanistan in 1979. President Jimmy Carter asserted that the Gulf and its oil were vital national interests, making an explicit claim that the region's oil lay within the body boundaries of the United States:

> The region which is now threatened by Soviet troops in Afghanistan is of great strategic importance: It contains more than two-thirds of the world's exportable oil. The Soviet effort to dominate Afghanistan has brought Soviet military forces to within 300 miles of the Indian Ocean and close to the Straits of Hormuz, a waterway through which most of the world's oil must flow. The Soviet Union is now attempting to consolidate a strategic position, therefore, that poses a grave threat to the free movement of Middle East oil. . . . Let our position be absolutely clear: An attempt by any outside force to gain control of the Persian Gulf region will be regarded as an assault on the vital interests of the United States of America, and such an assault will be repelled by any means necessary, including military force.[57]

President Ronald Reagan took a vastly different tack with respect to energy policy, although his foreign policy remained firmly anti-Soviet. Oil from the Gulf declined in importance as market forces unleashed by Reagan's energy policy innovations made the whole world an open source of hydrocarbons. Reagan moved immediately upon taking office to end a broad range of programs that had effectively conferred price supports for crude and products produced in the United States by reintegrating the US and world energy markets, which had been insulated from one another since the 1930s.[58] Together with policies designed to raise the value of the dollar compared to Japanese and European currencies, and a general weakness in oil markets caused by declining demand following the sky-high price increases imposed during the Iranian revolution, the new US energy policy produced a bonanza for Americans.[59] Oil prices declined and then collapsed, unleashing a flood of cheap oil that persisted for about two decades. This helped the United States more than other oil-importing countries that had to pay for their oil in dollars that had become more expensive compared to their local currencies.[60] Negative effects on the United States included ever higher levels of US oil consumption and dependence on oil imports, discounted as security issues in Washington and by Americans delighted to be able to buy more gasoline for less money.

Middle East oil and US strategic security policy converged once more on the Gulf when Saddam Hussein's invasion and occupation of Kuwait threatened the advantageous energy market position of the United States and its allies. President George H. W. Bush's greatest foreign policy triumph was the 1991 liberation of Kuwait from Iraqi occupation. UN Security Council resolutions to sanction and then invade Iraq were the result of skillful US diplomacy that brought the Soviet Union into the coalition against Saddam, marking the end of Cold War politics in the United Nations.[61] Even so, Bush's actions left unfortunate legacies. Whether due to miscalculation or bad faith, his invitation to Iraqi Shi'a to rise up against Saddam was not followed by military or even diplomatic assistance to the insurgents. Postliberation pressure on Kuwait and the other Gulf states to purchase US arms and acquiesce in the maintenance and enlargement of US bases for their future defense undermined regional security strategies (see Chapter 12). It also left these states vulnerable to domestic repercussions, including terrorist attacks, motivated in part by their acquiescence to those US demands.

President William J. Clinton's intervention in the Gulf was part of his policy of "dual containment," a package of strategic and economic sanctions intended to neutralize both Iraq and Iran as dangers to US interests. Against Iraq, this included both massive bombing raids in retaliation for violations of the modus vivendi between Saddam and the victorious coalition that took shape after the second Gulf war, and highly intrusive participation in the UN-managed inspection system set up to interdict development of chemical, biological, and nuclear weapons.[62] But it was Clinton's infatuation with a theory much in fashion in academic circles that foreshadowed the rationale for the radical departure in US policy toward the Middle East inaugurated by President George W. Bush.

Democratization: President George W. Bush and the Incarnate Word

In the late 1980s, social scientists suddenly discovered that democracies do not make war on other democracies.[63] This attractive notion held out the promise that, after the long insecurity of the Cold War, world peace might be within our grasp. Politicians were as attracted to this thesis as academics. In his 1994 State of the Union message, President Clinton said:

> Ultimately, the best strategy to ensure our security and to build a durable peace is to support the advance of democracy elsewhere. Democracies

> don't attack each other, they make better trading partners and partners in diplomacy. That is why we have supported, you and I, the democratic reformers in Russia and in the other states of the former Soviet bloc. I applaud the bipartisan support this Congress provided last year for our initiatives to help Russia, Ukraine, and the other states through their epic transformations.[64]

For Americans—who made up by far the largest portion of its proponents—the "democratic peace thesis" was especially appealing because it defined the United States as the very model of a democratic nation.[65] This proposition is deeply flawed, however. It "not only disguise[s] elastic values as fixed coding rules; [it also] risk[s] mistaking the cause of these values for their effect."[66] In other words, the democratic peace thesis asserts (but fails) to examine the relationship between democratic norms and foreign policy. It also confuses democracy with conformity to a US-defined set of criteria whose content varies with changes in US strategic objectives.[67]

During the Clinton administration, domestic constraints limited US intervention to change regimes in countries termed "rogue" or "failed" states. This is not to say that Clinton's Republican predecessors were opposed to military intervention. During the presidencies of Ronald Reagan and George H. W. Bush, US forces were sent to support US clients and replace distasteful regimes with US-defined democracies in Lebanon, Libya, Grenada, Panama, and elsewhere, in addition to Kuwait.[68] But Republicans opposed intervention by Democrats where significant US economic or political interests were not at stake. Clinton's intervention in Haiti, scorned as "nation-building," was cut short by a critical Congress that, together with US military leaders, also blocked intervention in Bosnia and Rwanda. Military intervention in Kosovo was nominally a NATO policy although one indirectly blessed by the United Nations.[69] Its multilateral character may explain why peacekeeping forces continue to mediate political transition there. Republicans applauded Clinton's periodic bombing of Iraq until 1998, when they derided the withdrawal of US arms inspectors and subsequent bombing of Iraq as attempts to divert popular attention from the Monica Lewinsky scandal.[70] They mocked the 1998 bombing of mujahidin training camps in Afghanistan and a pharmaceutical factory in Sudan following terrorist attacks on US embassies in Kenya and Tanzania for the same reason. When George W. Bush began his first term as president, calls by Clinton holdovers to intervene against the Afghan bases of Al-Qaida were dismissed as overblown.[71]

Key George W. Bush administration figures had their own strategy for intervention, and regime change in Iraq was an integral part of it. Its intellectual underpinnings included a revival of Cold War concepts like the domino theory, but in a new guise. Sheltered beneath the legitimacy conferred by enthusiastic academic endorsement of the democratic peace thesis and the broad interpretation of the transitology paradigm discussed in Chapter 1, these neo-domino theorists argued that overturning Iraq would trigger a cascade of falling autocrats, leaving in its wake a stream of new democracies able to satisfy both demands for freedom by their peoples and demands for peace by other nations.[72] The power of the domino image was undiminished in the minds of such policymakers, explaining their expectation that democracy would be an automatic outcome of regime change. It also was consistent with Bush's campaign promise that he would not engage in nation-building, the pejorative neoconservative term for Clinton-era participation in postconflict reconstruction in Haiti and the Balkans.

In his book on the foreign policy inner circle of the George W. Bush administration, James Mann traces the game plan for the Gulf policy that unfolded after 9/11. Developed under the aegis of presidential commissions and conservative think-tanks, it bloomed in the writings and activities of Republicans in government and in exile during the George H. W. Bush and Clinton years. It was sustained in the persons of key actors as they entered and left public office, some as far back as the administration of Richard Nixon.[73] The very first meeting of Bush's top foreign policy officials on January 30, 2001, included a discussion of a future Iraq war, and Vice President Dick Cheney identified Iraq as one of the main US security problems in interviews with Nicholas Lemann for a May 2001 *New Yorker* profile.[74] After the 9/11 bombings, Cheney, US secretary of defense Donald Rumsfeld, and his assistant, Paul Wolfowitz, claimed that "Iraq posed nearly as serious a problem for the president and his team as Afghanistan."[75] Indeed, military resources were withheld from US forces fighting Al-Qaida and the Taliban in Afghanistan in anticipation of an attack on Iraq while intelligence was "fixed," in the words of a British official, to set the stage for the March 2003 invasion.[76]

The official casus belli, that Iraq possessed weapons of mass destruction, was discredited when no such weapons were found. But the focus of the invasion on regime change was evident from the start in a military strategy that put capturing Baghdad ahead of securing territory and military supply lines.[77] Wishful thinking contributed to poor planning and both allowed what had been advertised as a quick war to drift into an extended occupation.[78] As the United States and Britain battled resistance and insurgency, domestic and international criticism mounted. Official rationales for the invasion of Iraq returned openly to the theme of regime change when it became clear that there were no weapons of mass destruction to be found. Deposing Saddam was touted as only the beginning of democratization in the region as a whole.

It was in this context that, thanks to a document leaked to the Saudi-owned London newspaper *Al-Hayat*, the Greater Middle East Initiative burst onto the foreign policy scene in 2004.[79] Its basic premise was that US foreign policy throughout the Cold War had itself contributed to the myth of "Middle Eastern exceptionalism," which held that religion and culture made the region uniquely resistant to democratization. George W. Bush insisted that Middle East countries did have the capacity to democratize, and repeated his assertions in many public speeches and comments.[80] This change in US attitude was welcomed even by critics of Bush's war policy, especially those already committed to democratization in the region. But the critics were not satisfied with assertions alone, noting that even the original plan, watered down in response to protests from Arab governments after the release of the working paper,[81] fell short of what would be necessary for practical success.

Middle East specialist Alan Richards began his June 2004 testimony before the Senate Foreign Relations Committee by accepting some of the George W. Bush administration's assumptions. He noted several problems elided by the policy's advocates, however. One was that the Arab-Israeli conflict, an important contributor to violence in the region, could be resolved through the good offices of the United States, at that point widely regarded as both a partisan in that conflict and a power illegitimately occupying Iraq. Another was the administration's belief that the most important obstacles to democratization were technical rather than political. This was reflected in deep inconsistencies in US policy, which supported some authoritarian governments, such as Egypt's, Jordan's, and Pakistan's, while it urged the Gulf autocracies to liberalize their political and economic systems. Richards also expressed doubt that the Bush policy could be successful as long as the United States government refused to distinguish among Islamist trends and work with moderate Islamist reformers rather than lumping all aspects of Islamism together as terrorist and seeking to eliminate them.[82]

In a commentary prepared for the Carnegie Endowment for International Peace, Marina Ottaway and Thomas Carothers criticize the lack of courage in the administration's plans to implement the initiative. Having taken a strong position on the shortcomings of Middle East governments as outlined in the *2002 Arab Human Development Report*, the administration had proposed little that was new in the context of ongoing US policy while ignoring the long effort to promote greater openness by the European Union through the so-called Barcelona process.[83] Like Richards, Ottaway and Carothers lament that "the administration is unwilling to push the envelope and adopt a much more assertive policy toward nondemocratic and largely nonreforming but friendly Middle Eastern States."[84] Less persuaded than Richards that Islamists are potential democrats, their arguments about failing to distinguish technical and political obstacles to reform focused explicitly on Islamist and other regional opposition movements. They conceded that the commitment of these groups to reform might be genuine, but cautioned that what was understood by the term varied from group to group, and all diverged from the US position. Most tellingly, they identified a crucial silence in the proposal's refusal to acknowledge that one of the primary supports for Middle East authoritarianism and resistance to opening was the lack of security felt by all the states and peoples in the region. They charged that, as a result of the George W. Bush administration's support for hard-line Israeli policies, the explicit omission of security issues from the initiative made it "hollow at the core" and unlikely to have an impact even remotely close to Bush's claims for it.[85]

These conceptual and practical flaws in the most ambitious proposal by George W. Bush for peaceful democratization of the Middle East mirrored the flaws in his military approach. Epitomized by the controversial resurrection of the domino theory to guide a warfighting strategy that discounted the need to secure postconflict Iraq, they proceeded to an almost accidental occupation that proved to be too inadequately provisioned in human, material, and economic resources to rebuild the country.[86] The conduct of the occupation, particularly the failure to ensure security and restore basic services, the abuse and killing of civilians, and the systematic torture of prisoners, made the idea of US-led democracy in Iraq ring hollow to residents in the region.[87] Meanwhile, rising violence in Iraq and Afghanistan, the deterioration of conditions in Israel and Palestine, and the aftereffects of the Israeli war on Lebanon made it ring hollow even in Washington. Yet rather than pulling back, failure seemed to strengthen the resolve of hard-liners in the administration to push for extending US intervention further, to Iran in retaliation for alleged assistance to Iraqi insurgents or to halt its uranium enrichment program, or to Syria, also charged with supporting terrorist enemies of the United States in Iraq and in Lebanon.[88] Yet even in Iraq, the US commitment to liberalization was asserted most strongly in support of a law to open ownership of Iraqi petroleum to foreign oil companies.[89]

Prospects for Democracy

The failure of the domino theory to produce democracy anywhere in the Middle East is not the only tragedy of George W. Bush's foreign policy in the Gulf, but it is an important one. One unfortunate effect is that it has undermined US domestic support for democratization in the region. Critics point to the electoral victories of Hamas in Palestine, a reaction to the corruption and ineptitude of Fatah; the success of Hezbollah in gaining seats in Lebanon's post–Cedar Revolution parliament; surprise victories by members of the banned Muslim Brotherhood in Egypt's 2005 parliamentary elections; and an Iraqi government led by Da'wa Party veteran Nuri al-Maliki as evidence that the Middle East is not ready for democracy: give them elections and they will choose terrorists. As I noted earlier, Bush himself was inconsistent in his commitment to democracy. He supported Egypt's president Husni Mubarak, whose 2005 "reelection" was marked by street demonstrations featuring signs proclaiming Kifaya (Enough), the arrest of his strongest opponent during the campaign, and a voter turnout under 25 percent.[90] Suggestions that the election be open to international observers were ignored by the Mubarak government while its many post-election crackdowns on dissent, against judges, participants in antigovernment street demonstrations, and even bloggers,[91] elicited little more than platitudes from Washington.

The larger tragedy, however, is that George W. Bush's botched attempt to democratize the Middle East through military action in Iraq overshadowed progress toward political opening in other Gulf states and missed opportunities to praise and foster positive expectations about institutional development in regimes that later regressed in the darkness of nonrecognition.[92] Even more unfortunate was the inconsistent US approach to Lebanon, where the results of the Cedar Revolution and the ejection of Syrian troops in 2005 were undermined by acquiescence to Israeli military attacks in 2006. In other instances, however, encouragement of progress in instituting and strengthening elections and the expansion of women's rights built constructively on policies toward the Gulf Cooperation Council that go back to the second Gulf war.[93] This inconsistency may have encouraged what Steve Heydemann calls authoritarian "upgrading," strategic moves by leaders of autocratic regimes to check the boxes for elections, women's rights, and civil society while evading policies that could effect durable democratization.[94] Indeed, the lack of intelligent engagement with its own policies might be the most lasting generator of the many unfortunate foreign policy legacies of the Bush administration. The political openings in the Arab Gulf described in Chapters 2–8 show that Bush's assertion that people in the Middle East want democracy as much as anyone else in the world has great merit. They were let down by the first administration since the discovery of oil in the region that could have pressed those desires on reluctant rulers had its leaders acted more wisely.

George W. Bush's approach to the Gulf, like most US policy toward Cuba—not to mention Haiti—is a product of triumphalist vindicationism and the paranoid style. The president's welcome verbal commitment to democracy was undermined by an overreliance on incompetent administrators, defective theories, and military means, the just deserts of those who reject diplomacy, multilateralism, and power sharing. What happened in consequence was far from justice with regard to the Gulf states, which are less secure than they were before the invasion of Iraq, more vulnerable to terrorism and perhaps to war when US forces are withdrawn from Iraq or if US military intervention is extended to neighboring states. The casualties of this policy are the very goals it was intended to achieve: a democratic Middle East, orderly energy markets, and greater security for the United States, however its body boundaries are defined.

Notes

1. Examples include Jim Lobe, "Gap Grows Between U.S., World Public Opinion," Inter Press Service, March 16, 2004, www.globalissues.org (August 5, 2006); Pew Global Attitudes Project, "Global Unease with Major World Powers," Pew Research Center, Washington, DC, June 27, 2007, http://pewglobal.org (July 17, 2007); Tom Regan, "US in Iraq Greatest Threat to World Peace?" *Christian Science Monitor*, June 15, 2006, www.csmonitor.com (November 5, 2006). Ironically, when he was criticized for Russia's invasion of Georgia, Russian prime minister Vladimir Putin had this to say: "Of course, Saddam Hussein ought to have been hanged for destroying several Shiite villages. . . . And the incumbent Georgian leaders who razed 10 Ossetian villages at once, who ran over elderly people and children with tanks, who burned civilians alive in their sheds—these leaders must be taken under protection." See "Echoes of Iraq Haunt U.S. Effort to Calm Russia-Georgia Fight," *Detroit Free Press*, August 12, 2008, www.freep.com (August 15, 2008); and see the commentary of Juan Cole, "Putin's War Enablers: Bush and Cheney," Salon.com, August 14, 2008, www.salon.com (August 14, 2008).

2. For example, Ahmad al-Khaled, "Kuwaiti Shiite Cleric Calls for Jihad," *Kuwait Times*, July 19, 2006, p. 1; Rania El Gamal, "God Save Nasrallah," *Kuwait Times*, August 3, 2006, p. 1. Following the bombing of Qana, a Starbucks in Rumathiya was stormed by local residents demanding that it be closed down.

3. Andrew Kohut, Richard Wike, Erin Carriere-Kretschmer, Kathleen Wolzwart, and Jacob Poushter, "Confidence in Obama Lifts U.S. Image Around the World: Most Muslim Publics Not So Easily Moved," 25-Nation Pew Global Attitudes Survey, Washington, DC: Pew Research Center, July 23, 2009.

4. The radical neoconservatives in and outside of the George W. Bush administration are the subject of James Mann, *Rise of the Vulcans: The History of Bush's War Cabinet* (New York: Free Press, 2004). Among recent examples of the position that the Bush-Cheney foreign policy is sui generis are Glenn Greenwald, *A Tragic Legacy: How a Good vs. Evil Mentality Destroyed the Bush Presidency* (New York: Crown Books, 2007); and the four-part series on Cheney by Barton Gellman and Jo Becker that appeared in the *Washington Post* from June 24 to 27, 2007. All four articles were accessed July 17, 2007, at http://www.truthout.org/docs_2006/062707B.shtml.

5. An apparent exception to this generalization is the post–World War II multilateralism spearheaded by the United States. Yet during this era of "liberal internationalism," the United States's determination to have its own way even at the expense of close allies was not uncommon. See, for example, Richard N. Gardner, *Sterling-Dollar Diplomacy in Current Perspective: The Origins and the Prospects of Our International Economic Order* (New York: Columbia University Press, 1980); and Linda Melvern, *The Ultimate Crime: Who Betrayed the UN and Why* (London: Allison & Busby, 1995). The latter was the basis of Melvern's noted British Channel 4 series *UN Blues*, broadcast in January 1995.

6. In addition to the references in the previous note, see Seymour Hersh, *Chain*

*of Command: The Road from 9/11 to Abu Ghraib (*New York: HarperCollins, 2004); Jane Mayer, "The Hidden Power," *New Yorker*, July 3, 2006: 44–55; Ali A. Allawi, *The Occupation of Iraq: Winning the War, Losing the Peace* (New Haven: Yale University Press, 2007); and Charlie Savage, *Takeover: The Return of the Imperial Presidency and the Subversion of American Democracy* (New York: Little, Brown, 2007).

7. George Packer, "Fighting Faiths," *New Yorker*, July 10 and 17, 2006, pp. 93–97; Jack Goldsmith, *The Terror Presidency: Law and Judgment Inside the Bush Administration* (New York: Norton, 2007); Jane Mayer, *The Dark Side: The Inside Story of How the War on Terror Turned into a War on American Ideals* (New York: Doubleday, 2008); Barton Gellman, *Angler: The Cheney Vice Presidency* (New York: Penguin, 2008).

8. Robert Gilpin, *War and Change in World Politics* (New York: Cambridge University Press, 1981).

9. Patrick E. Tyler, "U.S. Strategy Plan Calls for Insuring No Rivals, Develop a One-Superpower World: Pentagon's Document Outlines Ways to Thwart Challenges to Primacy of America," *New York Times*, March 8, 1992.

10. Mann, *Rise of the Vulcans*; also Barry Werth, *31 Days: The Crisis That Gave Us the Government We Have Today* (New York: Nan A. Talese, 2006); and Greenwald, *A Tragic Legacy*.

11. James Surowiecki, "Unsafe at Any Price," *New Yorker*, August 7 and 14, 2006, p. 32; SIPRI (Stockholm International Peace Research Institute), *SIPRI Yearbook 2006*, "World Military Expenditures, 1988–2005," table 8A,1m, www.sipri.org (November 5, 2006).

12. But applied ineptly. Failing to capture Osama bin Laden and Mullah Omar in favor of concentrating on the planned invasion of Iraq was the first major strategic error. The second was a cascade of blunders: invading Iraq with an inadequate force, eschewing postconflict plans offered by analysts inside and outside the government, and opting for a prolonged occupation directed and implemented by poorly prepared civilian personnel. See, among many others, Hersh, *Chain of Command*; Conrad C. Crane and W. Andrew Terrill, "Reconstructing Iraq: Insights, Challenges, and Missions for Military Forces in a Post-Conflict Scenario" (Carlisle, PA: U.S. Army War College Strategic Studies Institute, February 2003); George Packer, *The Assassins' Gate: America in Iraq* (New York: Farrar, Straus & Giroux, 2005); Rajiv Chandrasekaran, *Imperial Life in the Emerald City: Inside Iraq's Green Zone* (New York: Knopf, 2006); Allawi, *The Occupation of Iraq*.

13. Tom Englehart, "Permanent Bases the World Over: Behold the American Empire," Alternet, www.alternet.org (June 14, 2007); Helen Caldicott and Craig Eisendrath, *War in Heaven: Stopping the Arms Race in Outer Space Before It's Too Late* (New York: New Press, 2007). Russian president Vladimir Putin pushed back when the United States initiated arrangements to install missile defense systems in Eastern Europe. See US House of Representatives, Committee on Foreign Affairs, Subcommittee on Europe and Subcommittee on Terrorism, Nonproliferation, and Trade, "Do the United States and Europe Need a Missile Defense System?" Joint Hearing, May 3, 2007, http://foreignaffairs.house.gov (July 17, 2007); also Michael Scollon, "Russia: A New MIRV Emerges," Radio Free Europe/Radio Liberty, May 31, 2007, www.rferl.org (July 17, 2007); and Michael Scollon,"Putin Says Missile Test Is Response to U.S.," Radio Free Europe/Radio Liberty, www.rferl.org (July 17, 2007).

14. Ron Suskind, "Without a Doubt," *New York Times Magazine*, October 17, 2004, pp. 50–51.

15. Richard Hofstadter, "The Paranoid Style in American Politics," *Harper's Magazine,* November 1964, pp. 77–86.

16. Michael Barone, quoted in Jonathan Monten, "The Roots of the Bush Doctrine: Power, Nationalism, and Democracy Promotion in U.S. Strategy," *International Security* 29, no. 4 (2005): 119.

17. For example, Arthur M. Schlesinger Jr., *The Cycles of American History* (New York: Mariner, 1999); Walter Russell Mead, *Special Providence: American Foreign Policy and How It Changed the World* (New York: Routledge, 2002). A recent popular analysis that takes this same tack is Peter Beinart, "The Rehabilitation of the Cold-War Liberal," *New York Times Magazine*, April 30, 2006, pp. 41–45.

18. Monten, "Roots," p. 125. Vindicationism is the energetic expression of what Monten and others see as a consistent US orientation toward spreading democracy around the world. The alternating passive approach is called "exemplarism."

19. Examples include Michelle Goldberg, *Kingdom Coming: The Rise of Christian Nationalism* (New York: Norton, 2006); and Kevin Phillips, *American Theocracy: The Peril and Politics of Radical Religion, Oil, and Borrowed Money in the 21st Century* (New York: Viking, 2006).

20. Hofstadter, "The Paranoid Style"; Michael Rogin, *Ronald Reagan, the Movie, and Other Episodes in Political Demonology* (Berkeley: University of California Press, 1987).

21. Hofstadter, "The Paranoid Style," p. 77.

22. The paranoid style is not unique to the United States. The Middle East also is noted for the prevalence of conspiracy theories in political and social life, a characteristic that makes US–Middle East conflicts especially nasty because each side mirrors the other's ugliest face. Another contributor to the poisoning of relations between the United States and its fancied enemies in the Middle East is the tendency of each side to demonize the other, perhaps another legacy of excessive religionism. See, for example, William O. Beeman, *The "Great Satan" vs. the "Mad Mullahs": How the United States and Iran Demonize Each Other* (Westport: Praeger, 2005).

23. Linda Colley, *Captives: The Story of Britain's Pursuit of Empire and How Its Soldiers and Civilians Were Held Captive by the Dream of Global Supremacy, 1600–1850* (New York: Pantheon, 2002).

24. Karen Ordahl Kupperman, *Indians and English: Facing Off in Early America* (Ithaca: Cornell University Press, 1998). A similar reciprocal or feedback mechanism has been postulated by Tarik Ali as one of the roots of the clash of fundamentalisms operating between Islam and the US-led West today. See Tariq Ali, *The Clash of Fundamentalisms: Crusades, Jihads and Modernity* (London: Verso, 2002); also Beeman, *The "Great Satan" vs. the "Mad Mullahs."* How these action-reaction clashes operate across multiple religions and cultures is the subject of Mary Ann Tétreault and Robert A. Denemark, eds., *Gods, Guns, and Globalization: Religious Resurgence and International Political Economy* (Boulder: Lynne Rienner, 2004).

25. David Hackett Fischer, *Albion's Seed: Four British Folkways in America* (New York: Oxford University Press, 1989), esp. pp. 207–418 and 605–782. Also, Rogin, *Ronald Reagan, the Movie*; and Peter Ehrenhaus and A. Susan Owen, "Race Lynching and Christian Evangelicalism: Performances of Faith," *Text and Performance Quarterly* 24, nos. 3–4 (2005): 276–301.

26. Gideon Rose, "Neoclassical Realism and Theories of Foreign Policy," *World Politics* 51, no. 1 (1998): 152. Rose distinguishes between realists and those he calls neoclassical realists with respect to their degree of subjection to the logic of anar-

chy. The neoclassicals do not assume that this logic always is effectively transmitted (i.e., policymakers make mistakes).

27. This relationship also holds for revolutions. See Theda Skocpol, *States and Social Revolutions* (New York: Cambridge University Press, 1979).

28. A positive interpretation of this pattern can be found in an interview with John Lewis Gaddis on the new Bush National Security Strategy; John Lewis Gaddis, *Frontline*, January 16, 2003, www.pbs.org (July 14, 2006).

29. See, for example, Garry Wills, *"Negro President": Jefferson and the Slave Power* (Boston: Houghton Mifflin, 2003).

30. Kupperman, *Indians and English*; Orlando Patterson, *Rituals of Blood: Consequences of Slavery in Two American Centuries* (New York: Basic Books, 1998); Ehrenhaus and Owen, "Race Lynching."

31. This term comes from the health professions and is used extensively by persons working in reproductive technology. For example, see Irma van der Ploeg, "Biometrics and the Body as Information: Normative Issues of the Socio-Technical Coding of the Body," in *Surveillance as Social Sorting: Privacy, Risk and Digital Discrimination*, ed. David Lyon (New York: Routledge, 2003), pp. 57–73; and Irma van der Ploeg, "'Only Angels Can Do Without Skin': On Reproductive Technology's Hybrids and the Politics of Body Boundaries," *Body and Society* 10, nos. 2–3 (2004): 153–181.

32. The relationship between Western conceptions of sovereignty and individuality is discussed in John Ruggie, "Continuity and Transformation in the World Polity: Toward a Neorealist Synthesis," in *Neorealism and Its Critics*, ed. Robert O. Keohane (New York: Columbia University Press, 1986), pp. 131–157.

33. See, for example, Theodore Draper, "Falling Dominoes," *New York Review*, October 27, 1983, www.nybooks.com (February 13, 2006).

34. Matthew Connolly, "Rethinking the Cold War and Decolonization: The Grand Strategy of the Algerian War for Independence," *International Journal of Middle East Studies* 33, no. 2 (2001): 221–245.

35. In contrast to threats to states within US body boundaries, even spontaneous uprisings against authoritarian regimes in states outside of those boundaries—such as Hungary—did not merit direct intervention regardless of the degree of rhetorical support they might have attracted. See István Deák, "Did the Revolution Have to Fail?" *New York Review of Books*, March 1, 2007, accessed www.nybooks.com (July 8, 2007).

36. This is discussed at some length in Stephen Kinzer, *Overthrow: America's Century of Regime Change from Hawaii to Iraq* (New York: Times Books, 2006).

37. Thomas Jefferson, letter to James Monroe dated October 24, 1823, www.mtholyoke.edu (February 1, 2010).

38. "Message of President James Monroe to the US Congress," December 2, 1823, www.yale.edu (June 4, 2008).

39. "Message of President Theodore Roosevelt to the US Congress," December 6, 1904, www.uiowa.edu (June 5, 2005).

40. Ibid.

41. "I don't see why we need to stand by and watch a country go Communist due to the irresponsibility of its own people"; "National Security Council's 40 Committee," June 27, 1970, cited in William Blum, *Killing Hope: US and CIA Military Interventions Since World War II* (London: Zed Books, 2003), p. 209.

42. Kinzer, *Overthrow*.

43. The classical comprehensive accounts of this fabled era are Anthony Sampson, *The Seven Sisters: The Great Oil Companies and the World They Shaped*

(New York: Viking, 1975); and Daniel Yergin, *The Prize: The Epic Quest for Oil, Money and Power* (New York: Simon & Schuster, 1991).

44. Harvey B. Feigenbaum, *Politics of Public Enterprise: Oil and the French State* (Princeton: Princeton University Press, 1985).

45. Archibald H. T. Chisholm, *The First Kuwait Oil Concession Agreement: A Record of the Negotiations, 1911–1934* (London: Frank Cass, 1975).

46. Irvine H. Anderson, *Aramco, the United States, and Saudi Arabia: A Study of the Dynamics of Foreign Oil Policy, 1933–1950* (Princeton: Princeton University Press, 1981).

47. Gardner, *Sterling-Dollar Diplomacy.*

48. Mark J. Gasiorowski, "The 1953 Coup d'État in Iran," *International Journal of Middle East Studies* 19, no. 3 (1987): 261–286.

49. US Federal Trade Commission, *The International Petroleum Cartel*, US Senate Select Committee on Small Business, Staff Report to the Federal Trade Commission, 82nd Cong., Committee Print no. 6 (Washington, DC: US Government Printing Office, 1952).

50. Connolly, "Rethinking the Cold War and Decolonization"; Gil Merom, *How Democracies Lose Small Wars: State, Society, and the Failures of France in Algeria, Israel in Lebanon, and the United States in Vietnam* (New York: Cambridge University Press, 2003).

51. On Iran, see Gasiorowski, "The 1953 Coup," and, on Saudi Arabia, see Robert Vitalis, *America's Kingdom: Mythmaking on the Saudi Oil Frontier* (Palo Alto, CA: Stanford University Press, 2006).

52. Farouk Sankari, "The Character and Impact of Arab Oil Embargoes," in *Arab Oil: Impact on the Arab Countries and Global Implications*, eds. Naiem A. Sherbiny and Mark A. Tessler (New York: Praeger, 1976), pp. 265–278. Mary Ann Tétreault, *Revolution in the World Petroleum Market* (Westport: Quorum, 1985).

53. Richard C. Weisberg, *The Politics of Crude Oil Pricing in the Middle East, 1970–1975*, Research Series no. 31 (Berkeley: University of California Press, 1977).

54. See, for example, US Congress, House of Representatives, Committee on International Relations, Special Subcommittee on Investigations, "Oil Fields as Military Objectives: A Feasibility Study," report prepared by the Congressional Research Service, 94th Cong., 1st sess., August 21, 1975 (Washington, DC: US Government Printing Office, 1975), parts I and II, pp. 1–39, www.mtholyoke.edu (July 19, 2007).

55. Compare Tétreault, *Revolution in the World Petroleum Market*; and Hans Jacob Bull-Berg, *American International Oil Policy: Causal Factors and Effects* (New York: Palgrave Macmillan, 1987).

56. G. John Ikenberry, *Reasons of State: Oil Politics and the Capacities of American Government* (Ithaca: Cornell University Press, 1988).

57. Jimmy Carter, "State of the Union Address," January 23, 1980, www.jimmycarterlibrary.org (August 3, 2006).

58. David F. Prindle, *Petroleum Politics and the Texas Railroad Commission* (Austin: University of Texas Press, 1981); Tétreault, *Revolution*; Mary Ann Tétreault, "Economics and Security: Ronald Reagan's Energy Policy," *Forum* 3, no. 4 (1988): 70–79.

59. Other contributors to glutted oil markets in the 1980s were inventory depletions and aggressive foreign oil sales by the Soviet Union, both contributing to the competition for markets by oil exporters. In response, Saudi Arabia increased production, triggering a price collapse in 1986, when crude dipped beneath $10 a barrel. Saudi Arabia also sold oil to Aramco at a special price, the "Aramco advantage,"

which allowed its four IOC owners to undercut the marketing positions of other oil companies. See Tétreault, *Revolution*.

60. Tétreault, "Economics and Security."

61. Yelena Melkumyan, "Soviet Policy and the Gulf Crisis," in *The Gulf Crisis: Background and Consequences*, ed. Ibrahim Ibrahim (Washington, DC: Georgetown University Center for Contemporary Arab Studies, 1992), pp. 76–91; also Jean Edward Smith, *George Bush's War* (New York: Holt, 1992).

62. Brian Urquhart, "How Not to Fight a Dictator," *New York Review of Books*, May 6, 1999, www.nybooks.com (August 3, 2006). Also, Scott Ritter, *Iraq Confidential: The Untold Story of America's Intelligence Conspiracy* (London: I. B. Tauris, 2005). Ritter believes that regime change was also a Clinton goal, pursued through weapons inspection.

63. For example, Michael Doyle, "Liberalism and World Politics," *American Political Science Review* 80, no. 4 (1986): 1151–1169; Bruce Russett, *Grasping the Democratic Peace: Principles for a Post–Cold War World* (Princeton: Princeton University Press, 1993).

64. William Jefferson Clinton, "State of the Union, 1994," delivered version, January 25, 1994, www.let.rug.nl (February 22, 2006).

65. Ido Oren, "The Subjectivity of the 'Democratic' Peace: Changing U.S. Perceptions of Imperial Germany," *International Security* 20, no. 2 (1995): 150.

66. Ibid.

67. Ido Oren, *Our Enemies and US: America's Rivalries and the Making of Political Science* (Ithaca: Cornell University Press, 2003).

68. Mann, *Rise of the Vulcans*; also Kinzer, *Overthrow.*

69. Václav Havel, "Kosovo and the End of the Nation-State," Paul Wilson, trans., *New York Review of Books,* June 10, 1999, pp. 4, 6.

70. CNN, "Cohen Criticizes 'Wag the Dog' Characterization: Former Defense Secretary Testifies Before 9/11 Panel," CNN, www.cnn.com (February 22, 2006); also Conservative Caucus, "Wag the Dog? U.S. Policy on Iraq," excerpted from *Howard Phillips Issues and Strategy Bulletin*, December 31, 1998, www.conservativeusa.org (February 22, 2006).

71. Richard A. Clarke, *Against All Enemies: Inside America's War on Terror* (New York: Free Press, 2004).

72. "Bush's Domino Theory," editorial, *Christian Science Monitor*, January 28, 2003, www.csmonitor.com (August 3, 2006); Paul Reynolds, "The 'Democratic Domino' Theory," BBC News Online, April 10, 2003, http://news.bbc.co.uk (August 5, 2006); Jack Beatty, "Fatal Vision," *Atlantic Unbound*, May 1, 2003, www.theatlantic.com (August 4, 2006).

73. Mann, *Rise of the Vulcans*; also Werth, *31 Days*; and "Rumsfeld's War," *Frontline*, October 26, 2004, www.pbs.org (August 4, 2006).

74. Ron Suskind, *The Price of Loyalty: George W. Bush, the White House, and the Education of Paul O'Neill* (New York: Simon & Schuster, 2004), pp. 72–75; Nicholas Lemann, "The Quiet Man," *New Yorker*, May 7, 2001, http://newyorker.com.

75. Bob Woodward, *Bush at War* (New York: Simon & Schuster, 2002), p. 60.

76. Mark Danner, "The Secret Way to War," *New York Review of Books*, June 9, 2005, pp. 70–74. The Dearlove memo reporting the results of meetings between US and British intelligence officials in July 2002 is on p. 71. Also James Risen, *State of War: The Secret History of the CIA and the Bush Administration* (New York: Free Press, 2006); and Seymour Hersh, *Chain of Command: The Road from 9/11 to Abu Ghraib* (New York: HarperCollins, 2004).

77. Michael R. Gordon and Bernard E. Trainor, *Cobra II: The Inside Story of the Invasion and Occupation of Iraq* (New York: Pantheon, 2006); Thomas E. Ricks, *Fiasco: The American Military Adventure in Iraq* (New York: Penguin, 2006).

78. The ad hoc nature of US actions in Iraq is noted in many sources. For example, see Packer, *The Assassins' Gate*; Rajiv Chandrasekaran, *Imperial Life in the Emerald City: Inside Iraq's Green Zone* (New York: Knopf, 2006); Ali A. Allawi, *The Occupation of Iraq: Winning the War, Losing the Peace* (New Haven: Yale University Press, 2007).

79. "G-8 Greater Middle East Partnership Working Paper," *Middle East Intelligence Bulletin*, February 13, 2004, www.meib.org (July 14, 2006).

80. Daniel Neep, "Dilemmas of Democratization in the Middle East: The 'Forward Strategy of Freedom,'" *Middle East Policy* 11, no. 3 (2004): 73–84.

81. See, for example, Charles Recknagel, "U.S.: Washington's 'Greater Middle East Initiative' Stumbles amid Charges It Imposes Change," Radio Free Europe, March 23, 2004, www.rferl.org (July 14, 2006).

82. Alan Richards, "Testimony Before the U.S. Senate Foreign Relations Committee," June 2, 2004, www.senate.gov (July 14, 2006).

83. Marina Ottaway and Thomas Carothers, "The Greater Middle East Initiative: Off to a False Start," Policy Brief no. 29, Carnegie Endowment for International Peace, March 2004, www.carnegieendowment.org (July 14, 2006).

84. Ibid., p. 1.

85. Ibid., p. 3.

86. On the accidental qualities of the occupation, see Chandrasekaran, *Imperial Life*; and Allawi, *Occupation*. This transpired despite warnings from military leaders, starting with then-chair of the Joint Chiefs of Staff, General Edward Shinseki, and military and civilian analysts whose prewar writings detailed the likely outcome of a US invasion and what would be needed to make it succeed. See, for example, Conrad C. Crane and W. Andrew Terrill, "Reconstructing Iraq: Insights, Challenges, and Missions for Military Forces in a Post-conflict Scenario" (Carlisle, PA: US Army War College Strategic Studies Institute, February 2003); James Fallows, "The Fifty-First State?" *Atlantic Monthly*, November 2002, www.theatlantic.com (March 4, 2003).

87. Gilbert Burnham, Riyadh Lafta, Shannon Doocy, and Les Roberts, "Mortality After the 2003 Invasion of Iraq: A Cross-Sectional Cluster Sample Survey," The Lancet Online, October 11, 2006, www.thelancet.com; and see the surveys cited in note 1.

88. Greenwald, *A Tragic Legacy*; Seymour M. Hersh, "The Redirection," *New Yorker*, March 5, 2007, pp. 54–60, 62–65; Seymour M. Hersh, "Preparing the Battlefield," *New Yorker*, July 9 and 16, 2007, pp. 60–67.

89. Ben Lando, "Iraq Gov't Oil Law in Limbo," UPI, July 19, 2007, www.upi.com (July 20, 2007); James A. Paul, "Oil Companies in Iraq: A Century of Rivalry and War," paper presented at the "Global Policy Forum Conference on Corporate Accountability," Berlin, November 2003, www.globalpolicy.org (July 19, 2007).

90. David Remnick, "Letter from Cairo: Going Nowhere," *New Yorker*, July 12 and 19, 2004, pp. 74–83; Human Rights Watch, "From Plebiscite to Contest: Egypt's Presidential Election," 2005, http://hrw.org (July 19, 2007).

91. Human Rights Watch, "From Plebiscite to Contest"; Michael Slackman and Mona el-Naggar, "Police Beat Crowds Backing Egypt's Judges," *New York Times*, May 12, 2006, p. A3; Negar Azimi, "Bloggers Against Torture," *The Nation*, February 19, 2007, pp. 11, 13–14, and 16; Borzou Daragahi and Noha El

Hennawym, "Egypt's Dissidents Held Down by Law," *Los Angeles Times*, June 12, 2007, www.latimes.com (June 19, 2007).

92. Mary Ann Tétreault, "Kuwait's *Annus Mirabilis*," Middle East Report Online, September 7, 2006, www.merip.org (September 11, 2007).

93. The importance of such external pressure is emphasized in Mary Ann Tétreault, *Stories of Democracy: Politics and Society in Contemporary Kuwait* (New York: Columbia University Press, 2000), esp. chaps. 6 and 8.

94. Steven Heydemann, "Upgrading Authoritarianism in the Arab World," Analysis Paper no. 13 (Washington, DC: Sabin Center for Middle East Policy, October 2007).

12

Defense Cooperation: Beyond Symbolism?

Matteo Legrenzi

> We in the Gulf have no liking for foreign troops to defend our own future and to defend our own sovereignty. We believe that we can, by approaching this issue collectively, ensure the survival of our sovereignty and the continuous security of the Gulf.
>
> —*First GCC secretary-general Abdullah Bishara, September 1986*

> Many of the Gulf States were very reluctant to have us around before Iraq invaded Kuwait . . . in many ways the war clearly changed attitudes in the Gulf . . . we notice a significantly enhanced willingness to cooperate on security arrangements and joint ventures with the United States and US forces. —*US secretary of defense Dick Cheney, May 1991*

The conventional wisdom is that, despite the lack of any explicit reference in the charter of the organization, the Gulf Cooperation Council (GCC) was founded to guarantee the security of its member states or, more accurately, of their dynastic monarchies vis-à-vis internal and external challenges.[1] Therefore, it would be useful to consider whether the establishment of the GCC actually enhanced the security of its member states in either the internal or external realm. After a careful review of initiatives in these areas, it is my contention that the GCC's impact on security has been meager. It would be unfair to blame the organization itself, however, because the challenges stem from structural determinants. The support of external allies, chiefly the United States, appears to be a necessary component of any strategy intended by the six members to achieve a modicum of external security. Whether this support is present or absent has more to do with Gulf security than the actions of the GCC or any individual member.

I begin this chapter with a brief analysis of the balance of power in the Gulf. To elucidate why self-reliance is inherently difficult for the GCC states, I review their attempts to institutionalize a common security policy, externally and internally. Next, I identify what I think are the main systemic constraints faced by GCC states, individually and collectively. This will help to clarify why the institutional role of the GCC is necessarily limited. I then briefly review the main challenges that the ruling families face from both within and without in trying to prevent violent change. Finally, I assess the Gulf Cooperation Council through the use of criteria developed by William Tow to measure the performance of what he dubs "Subregional Security Organizations."[2] I conclude the chapter with an assessment of the contributions of the GCC to public diplomacy in light of its actual achievements in the internal and external security fields.

The Realities of Power in the Gulf

For most of the past 200 years, neither local actors nor regional powers had much say in the management of security in the Gulf. During that time, Britain played a hegemonic role, turning this body of water into what Avi Shlaim, among others, calls a "British lake."[3] Britain's influence was visible even before the defining moment in 1793 that inaugurated British penetration of the Gulf: the opening of an East India Company agency in Basra. The first in a series of treaties with the shaikhdoms that culminated in 1892 with exclusive agreements to manage their foreign relations was actually signed in 1820, the same year that rival colonial powers withdrew from the Gulf, thereby marking the beginning of British dominance. Britain negotiated directly with the two large regional powers (the Ottoman Empire and Imperial Iran) and from the 1920s with the Saudis, but its regional hegemony was uncontested until the eve of its departure. During the turmoil of the 1950s and 1960s, marked by the rise of Arab nationalism whose Nasserite propaganda washed all the way to the shores of the Gulf, the British succeeded in providing an illusion of security even though both Arab nationalism and Gamal Abdel Nasser were seen as direct threats to the Gulf monarchies and experienced as such by several of them, notably Saudi Arabia. Indeed, the British could not have prevented a major Soviet push into the area or even a well-organized domestic insurgency. Yet their mere presence was reassuring to local rulers, including the Saudi royal family with whom Britain had clashed in the middle of the nineteenth century.[4] Consequently, the British departure left a power vacuum, which was more apparent than real, but sufficient to engender a number of experiments in regional cooperation and collective security.

If we consider contemporary realities of power in the Gulf, however, the situation is best conceptualized as a triangle whose sides are of variable and unequal lengths. The two regional powers, Iran and Iraq, are the longer sides.[5] The GCC states, in spite of their geoeconomic importance, make up the shortest side. They are always in danger of being squeezed by the two stronger powers and therefore must rely on appeals to external powers, chiefly the United States, to preserve their military security.[6]

Iran has always been the most important power among the Gulf littoral states. Its population of 70 million makes it one of the three largest states in the Middle East and North Africa.[7] It controls the entire northern coast of the Gulf from the Shatt al-Arab to the Strait of Hormuz, through which all the hydrocarbon exports from the Gulf must travel before reaching the open sea. Iran has a long military tradition dating back to the ancient world when the Persian Empire was the main antagonist of Attic Greece, continuing through the Islamic conquest, and into its modern history as a nation-state. Despite a brief period of occupation by Afghan rulers, losses of territory to Russia, and partial occupation by the Soviet Union and Britain, Iran was never a subject of direct colonial control. Like other ancient land empires, Iran benefits from considerable strategic depth because its capital and other important cities are situated in the interior of the country. Iran has harbor facilities on the mainland coast as well as on numerous islands, but its strategic vulnerability lies in its seaports, as the frequent closure of the oil terminal of Bandar al-Abbas during the Iran-Iraq War demonstrated.[8]

Iran has long claimed a hegemonic role in determining the parameters of Gulf security. It is important to note that its hegemonic claims have been advanced irrespective of regime type. Well before the establishment of the Islamic Republic, the Shah was seen by Iran's Arab neighbors as an arrogant and overbearing ruler who considered himself the natural leader of the area, a "toff" to use the expression of a British-educated leading GCC diplomat, reflecting his love of fine clothing and an implied desire to lord it over his neighbors. The seizure of Abu Musa and the two Tunbs islands on the eve of the British withdrawal is still protested by the United Arab Emirates (UAE) and remains a sore point in the international relations of the Gulf.[9] Although at that time Gulf Arabs had no reason to expect domestic tampering on the Shah's part because of his aversion to possible Nasserist and Soviet infiltration in the region, their fears became palpable in the aftermath of the Islamic Revolution. Since then, the creation of a stable security system in the Gulf appears even more distant with the coming to power of a second generation of Iranian revolutionaries.[10] This new generation, sometimes called Iran's neoconservatives, is ideologically motivated and most of its members have a well-deserved reputation for eschewing corruption if not patronage. Yet their ideological rigidity makes it difficult to reach any compromise on a security architecture for the region as a whole while their fiery rhetoric does not inspire confidence in Arab Gulf rulers.

Military maneuvers by the Iranian army near the shores of the Gulf conducted in 2008 make it clear how the lessons of the recent Iraqi and Lebanese conflicts have been internalized. The Iranian army is preparing for a "fourth-generation" network campaign. In case of armed conflict with the United States, it will avoid concentrating its forces and mounting direct resistance to US firepower. Instead, it will try to disrupt shipping in the Strait of Hormuz and mount a guerrilla campaign in the case of a US land invasion. It is far from clear that Iran could be contained as successfully as it was during the 1984–1987 tanker war. Its military technology has improved and the Iranian armed forces seem to have drawn correct lessons from their experiences in the Iran-Iraq War (1980–1988).

The second-ranking Gulf power is Iraq. Its population in 2009 was estimated at about 31 million persons. Geographically, it can barely be defined as a Gulf state because its shoreline is limited to the Fao Peninsula and access to the interior from the Gulf is limited by the capacity of the Shatt al-Arab, which is both shallow and very narrow. The Shatt is a highly vulnerable waterway that was reopened by the British in the aftermath of the Iraq War of 2003. Previously, it had been closed for more than twenty years having been blocked early in the war with Iran, and it needs to be dredged constantly to be kept operational.[11]

In political and military terms, Iraq has played a crucial role in the international relations of the Gulf ever since the British departure. From a purely military point of view, Iraq's major urban centers, communication lines, and industrial complexes are very exposed and the capital's location relatively close to the Iranian border leaves it vulnerable to air attacks. Its relative lack of strategic depth has not deterred Iraq from being a protagonist in all three Gulf conflicts. It initiated the Iran-Iraq War (1980–1988) and the Kuwait War (1990–1991), and was the object of the US-led military intervention in 2003. These three wars in the Gulf constitute a set of events of major influence on the security situation in the region. Indeed, the first helped precipitate the founding of the GCC.

The GCC states, representing the third and shortest side of my triangle model, are mostly characterized by small native populations and the extreme vulnerability of their oil installations, particularly refineries, pipelines, and shipping points. This puts them at a perpetual disadvantage from a military point of view. The capitals of the five smallest states are coastal cities dependent on water desalinization plants that also are located on the Gulf coast. Their vulnerability to enemy attack from occasionally belligerent near neighbors helps to explain why the GCC states relied on an external power to redress their deficiencies. Yet despite having had to ask for the reflagging of Kuwaiti ships during the Iran-Iraq War, the myth of GCC self-reliance was not abandoned, even at the rhetorical level, until after the Iraqi invasion of Kuwait. GCC rulers now consider self-reliance a chimera, and believe that the possibility of building a collective security system that excludes the United States is out of the question. This is the major stumbling block in devising confidence-building measures that could lead to discussions between the GCC states and Iran aimed at establishing a collective security system.[12]

It is important to keep these geostrategic realities in mind when discussing GCC attempts to institutionalize a common security policy in the internal and external fields. For example, from a military point of view, it is not realistic for Kuwait to implement a "blocking action" for more than forty-eight hours should there be a military confrontation with either Iran or Iraq. Rhetorical statements abound but analysts and, to a greater extent, the military agree with this hard-nosed assessment.[13] While there has been a steady improvement in the training and readiness of the armed forces of the GCC states, they are unlikely to reach a point where they could hold out against hostile actions from their larger neighbors. Therefore, the decisions of the GCC states to rely on US support are logical. They also are efficient because the dominance of one supplier encourages standardization of weapons and interoperability. Although a contrary argument could be made in support of a policy of relying on many suppliers so as to maximize diplomatic cover when a crisis erupts, limiting the sources of arms procurement complements and integrates a strategy of carefully balanced foreign investments aimed at forging interdependence with external powers.

External Defense

For some of the reasons outlined above it is not surprising that, after more than twenty-five years of lip service to the idea of more integrated defense policies, the security situation of the GCC states today is not much different from the one prevailing in the 1980s. They are equipped with weapon systems acquired from the United States, Brazil, South Africa, France, Italy, Britain, Russia, and France, among others. In the past twenty years, China also has played a prominent role in supplying weapons to Gulf states. Silkworm missiles purchased by both Saudi Arabia and Iran are expected to raise the cost of military hostilities to high levels. An Iranian missile attack on the UAE would wreck the investment climate there and deal a blow to the goal of establishing Dubai as a global city. This is just one example of targeted arms procurement to secure an effective deterrent. Even though the arms procurement policies of the GCC states appear haphazard to the point of driving military analysts to despair at the resulting operational hodgepodge, it is reasonable for the GCC governments to take out an "insurance policy" underwritten by as many insurers as possible. The wisdom of such an approach was demonstrated by the ability of the member states to muster extensive diplomatic support following the Iraqi invasion of Kuwait in 1990 as well as by the prominent role that defense contractors play in shoring up relations among the United States, Europe, and the GCC.

These huge outlays are often resented by local populations, however, and the amounts are indeed staggering. Two relatively recent examples are the GCC-wide US package announced in July 2007 that is expected to cost US$31 billion, and the renewal of the al-Yamamah arms deal in August 2006 between Saudi Arabia and Britain for the purchase of seventy-two Eurofighter Typhoons for an estimated $80 billion over twenty years. However, the ruling families realize that they are part of an implicit, unspoken understanding between the Arab Gulf states and the Western powers, chief among them the United States, which guarantees their external security.[14]

Locally, after more than twenty-five years of cooperative ventures, the GCC can point to the first phase of a joint air defense command-and-control system aptly named Hizam Al-Taawun (Belt of Cooperation), which became operational in 2001. This system provides secure communications between the national air defense command and control centers of the member states, but it is not a fully integrated air defense system.[15] This reflects a preference for autonomy that many military analysts omit to highlight: there is a problem of trust within the GCC that prevents a rigorously integrated defense policy from emerging. Throughout the life of the GCC, one or more of the smaller states has balked at going further, fearful of the Saudi hegemony that would result from implementing an effectively integrated defense policy.[16] Manifested in a number of ways, the genesis of this fear lies in the period leading up to the independence of what were then British-protected states. Boundary disputes, a preference for unilateral security arrangements with the United States over multilateral GCC-wide pacts, and initial resistance to formal internal security agreements are all signs of a well-rooted diffidence. Throughout the 1980s, the most reluctant small state was Kuwait; now this role seems to have shifted to Qatar. The point is that political considerations prevent further GCC defense integration. The policy of purchasing arms from a host of disparate suppliers and carefully cultivating a range of diplomatic contacts is seen as a better way to achieve external security than by establishing a vertically integrated, centralized command similar to NATO's or the US–South Korean one. Members recognize that self-sufficiency in external defense matters is simply beyond the grasp of the GCC because Saudi hegemony would be too high a price to pay for a truly integrated defense policy.

In spite of structural constraints and the political choices of the smaller GCC states, symbolic attempts at defense cooperation have persisted for more than twenty-five years. I argue that the reason behind them is the desire to present a united front to the international community. The fact that armed forces of the GCC states were projected as united vis-à-vis Iran and Iraq was seen by ruling elites as carrying positive value in international policy circles as measured by the coverage received during joint military maneuvers. These mainly cosmetic exercises, as Anthony Cordesman describes them, most conducted at the battalion level, are hyped up beyond all proportion in the local press, especially state media outlets. The joint exercises are meant to convey notions of unity, steadfastness, and independence, but the only serious military maneuvers conducted by the armed forces of the GCC states are carried out under US leadership. At the naval level, individual GCC states have increased their capacity to fulfill important missions in the Gulf, such as mine warfare and patrolling.[17] However, joint maneuvers are confined to individual navies working alongside the British, the Americans, and the French, or those conducted bilaterally.

The symbolism of GCC defense cooperation is best exemplified by the Peninsula Shield joint defense force. It was established in 1986 after a meeting in Riyadh of the GCC chiefs of staff following a three-year series of joint military exercises. Peninsula Shield is based at King Khaled Military City in Hafr Al-Batin, a strategic location in northeast Saudi Arabia about 65 kilometers from the border with Kuwait. Its nominal strength is about 5,000 soldiers, but its real warfighting capabilities are concentrated in a Saudi Army brigade that was deployed in the area long before the joint force existed. A second brigade with manpower and equipment from several GCC states is reputedly understrength and has no real warfighting capabilities.[18] The only time the Peninsula Shield force was deployed was during the successful Iranian Fao Peninsula offensive on March 3, 1986, when it was dispatched to Kuwait as a gesture of solidarity.

The symbolic nature of the Peninsula Shield force has been recognized publicly even by Abdullah Bishara, the first secretary-general of the GCC.[19] Even its alleged function as a trip-wire contingent is called into question by its immobility during the Iraqi invasion of Kuwait. Indeed, for two days, Saudi television did not even report news about the invasion. General Khaled Bin Sultan, the Saudi commander of the coalition joint forces, actually decided to disband the unit for the duration of Operations Desert Shield and Desert Storm. He judged that the single units comprising the force would be much more useful if they were attached to the contingents coming from their mother countries.[20]

In light of its modest proportions and even more modest capabilities, it is noteworthy that the establishment of the Peninsula Field force was quite controversial. A Saudi proposal to split it into two nuclei for deployment on the southwest and northeast borders was rejected by Oman on the grounds that this would constitute a "provocation" vis-à-vis Iran. Since then, in the aftermath of the GCC leaders' summit in Abu Dhabi on December 18–19, 2005, Saudi crown prince and defense minister Sultan bin Abdul Aziz announced in Riyadh that the Peninsula Shield force as we know it today would cease to exist. What will happen to it remains unclear, however, as the Saudi proposal has not yet been spelled out. It is possible to envisage the retention of an administrative structure, possibly under the aegis of the GCC Secretariat in Riyadh, to retain some element of centralized command and control able to call on individual military units in case of an emergency. Yet the fact that the force could be dissolved or at least radically reconfigured with the stroke of a pen further underlines its mostly symbolic role.

The saga of the Peninsula Shield force illustrates how differently the GCC states perceive security threats: there is no strategic consensus on what the GCC should guard against. Kuwait, Oman, and the UAE insisted on a proviso that should the force enter another member's territory, command would revert from Saudi Arabia to the host country.[21] This highlights both the preoccupation of small member states with possible Saudi meddling in their internal affairs and the mostly symbolic nature of GCC joint military enterprises. The most that can be said about the Peninsula Shield force is that it exists. That, I would argue, is precisely the reason why it was constituted: to fulfill a symbolic rather than an operational role. Secretary-General Bishara reinforces this point when he asserts that Peninsula Shield was created to prove that "the Gulf to all intents and purposes is one and that the people of the Gulf would consider any threat to one of them to be a threat to all."[22] This statement may be inaccurate in practice, but it was not made naively. Like countless other GCC declarations and communiqués, it is meant to convey the idea that the GCC stands united.[23] Even though the GCC does not constitute a "pluralistic security community," defined in Deutsch's formal terms, it strives with some success to project that image.[24]

In sum, collaboration in the realm of external defense has not moved beyond symbolism, but the symbolic impact of that collaboration is significant. The GCC has managed to project the image of a single bloc in international security discourse. From this point of view the showpiece joint military maneuvers, the token Peninsula Shield force, and the countless communiqués have achieved their purpose. In the mainstream media the GCC states are often lumped together when defense matters are discussed,[25] even if military analysts are unanimous in recognizing that what underpins Gulf security is a solid US military presence.

Internal Security

The GCC states have collaborated closely in the realm of internal security. This is an arena in which the member states can act with relative independence from external actors and they have done so since the inception of the organization. Such collaboration predates the GCC's founding and is conducted mostly informally, at the bilateral level. The Secretariat is largely excluded from dealing with internal security matters even if the Security Department of the Political Affairs section, usually chaired by an Omani official, from time to time plays a liaison role.

The main reasons why the GCC Secretariat plays only a minor role in internal security matters are twofold. First, no one in the security apparatuses of the member states wants to expose the technocrats of the Secretariat to sensitive intelligence information. Second, and more crucially, experience shows that a plotter in one country could well be a relative of the ruler of another.[26] Thus, even in this realm of security, there are no common expectations concerning noninterference by the GCC governments in each other's domestic politics. For example, fellow GCC rulers extended their hospitality to Shaikh Khalifa al-Thani after he had been deposed by his son Shaikh Hamad in the summer of 1995. From the UAE Shaikh Khalifa organized an unsuccessful coup to regain the throne and, in reaction, Qatar refused to participate in joint military exercises planned for March 1996.[27] These and similar disputes were eventually patched up but, in general, when it comes to internal security, familiarity breeds suspicion as often as it facilitates cooperation.[28] While the GCC states can collaborate swiftly when faced with tampering and meddling by an external actor, there is always an underlying sense that old rivalries could reemerge quickly once an external threat dissipates. This clearly has an impact on which decisions are delegated to the GCC Secretariat. Security and intelligence officials from individual countries certainly do not coordinate their policies through that body.[29]

Some GCC-wide agreements have been formalized, however, and, in the past few years, rulers seem to be more concerned with Islamist opponents than with palace plotters. Furthermore, even if the GCC as an organization does not play a significant role in combating internal dissent, GCC forums and meetings have undeniably helped principal decisionmakers to coordinate the security policies of the member states informally. This is because the threats faced by the ruling families of the member states are of a similar nature.

As I noted above, the inaugural meeting of the GCC had deliberately underscored economic cooperation as the main focus of the nascent organization, but an attempted coup in Bahrain in December 1981, a few months after the GCC was established, sparked various attempts to formalize internal security cooperation among the member states. On December 13, 1981, the Bahraini government announced the arrest of seventy-three saboteurs allegedly involved with the coup. The prime minister, Shaikh Khalifa bin Salman Al-Khalifa placed responsibility squarely on the new Iranian revolutionary regime. He charged Iranian rulers with wanting to exploit Shi'ites in the GCC states to foment instability and chaos, although none of the arrested men was in fact of Iranian nationality.[30] This episode, and the fact that the Dubai authorities had provided crucial intelligence leading to the apprehension of the suspects, increased the appetite for multilateral cooperation in internal security.

The Saudis had wanted such an agreement for some time, even before the formation of the GCC, and Saudi Arabia took the lead in attempting to institutionalize informal cooperation on internal security. Four of the five smaller states, confronted with the prospect of successful meddling by Iran and despite earlier misgivings about Saudi aims, agreed to proceed along this path. Within a year, Saudi Arabia had signed bilateral security agreements first with Bahrain and then with the UAE, Qatar, and Oman. A draft multilateral agreement was prepared for the fourth Supreme Council conference in Doha, in November 1983. Both the bilateral agreements and the draft multilateral agreement provided for joint intelligence and training; extradition of suspected activists; and, crucially, border cooperation, including the right of hot pursuit into the territory of other member states.

Kuwait, however, refused to sign even a bilateral agreement with Saudi Arabia, let alone accede to the multilateral regime envisaged by Prince Nayif, the Saudi interior minister. The Kuwaiti parliament did not like the extradition clauses or the right of hot pursuit, feeling that the gap between the relatively liberal regime of Kuwait and the far stricter Saudi regime was too wide. The Kuwaiti cabinet concurred, noting additional concerns that signing a bilateral or multilateral internal security agreement would put Kuwait on a collision course with the new Iranian regime. Kuwait was still striving to establish a good relationship with Iran, despite a number of terrorist attacks for which the Iranian regime had been blamed by the local press and by international commentators.[31] It was only the dissolution of the Kuwaiti parliament in 1986 and the excision of the clause granting the right of hot pursuit from the draft multilateral agreement that allowed its eventual ratification by the Supreme Council in December 1987. The fact that the dissolution of the sole democratic body in the GCC states at the time was effectively a precondition for signing a multilateral security agreement shows the ambivalence with which the small states of the GCC regard security cooperation.

Any enthusiasm for cooperation and regionalization at the societal level is matched by a healthy distrust of possible Saudi hegemony. Abdullah Bishara elucidated this concern clearly and succinctly: "I can understand both points of view. On the one hand you want closer cooperation to face internal security threats. On the other hand, heads roll often in Saudi Arabia whereas the carrying out of a death sentence in Kuwait is a very rare event."[32] This attitude encapsulates well the ambivalence felt by many Kuwaiti citizens, whose attachment to a more liberal political discourse is remarkable given that Kuwait has made the target lists of several militant organizations such as Al-Qaida and local Islamist organizations such as the Peninsula Lions.[33] However, the spate of attacks in the GCC states that preceded and followed the US-led intervention in Iraq has induced them, particularly Saudi Arabia and Kuwait, to close ranks again.

The draft internal security agreement, with the exclusion of the right of hot pursuit, was ratified by the GCC Supreme Council in December 1987. It consists of thirty-nine articles divided into four chapters. In addition to general principles relating to collaboration among security services, the agreement tackles the issues of information exchange, extradition, and propaganda aimed against the regimes of any member country. The agreement has convenient loopholes; for example, individual governments can decide whether a particular crime is political and, therefore, not covered under the provisions of the agreement. Yet at the same time, the GCC states have a record of cooperating to limit internal dissent. In particular, information regarding the large number of expatriate workers, a constant preoccupation of GCC decisionmakers, is centrally stored in and shared via a Saudi data bank. Most collaboration happens through informal channels, however, so the formal agreement is rarely invoked.

Cooperation has proceeded smoothly and, until the wave of attacks in Kuwait and Saudi Arabia in 2003, it probably contributed to preventing violent attacks by domestic opponents in the GCC states. There were earlier incidents of terrorism; in addition to the attacks in Kuwait in the 1980s, there were prewar attacks on foreigners in Kuwait in 2002. But 2003 can be safely identified as the year when the GCC-wide perception changed and the GCC states, with Saudi Arabia at the forefront, decided that it would be in their interests to publicize their excellent collaboration in internal security matters.

In sum, GCC collaboration on internal security matters is far from symbolic but, unlike their stance toward external defense initiatives, member states did not, until fairly recently, have an interest in publicizing it. The internal security services that collaborated so closely were associated in the popular mind with the authoritarian nature of the regimes. They did not convey the same benign image associated with coordination in external defense matters. This began to change after September 11, 2001, and reached a height with the spate of related incidents that culminated in spectacular attacks on Saudi targets in May 2003. Then, suicide bombers attacked three Riyadh compounds housing foreigners. Thirty-five people were killed, including at least nine of the bombers. In February 2005, Saudi Arabia sponsored a major international conference on combating terrorism around the world. Massive publicity campaigns were launched throughout the GCC states highlighting the plight of those harmed in terrorist attacks. Meanwhile, the efficiency of internal security apparatuses has acquired a positive value in the international arena, where having an efficient *mukhabarat* is now seen as a sign of attention to homeland security. With regard to external security, the GCC states boast about their increased cooperation and coordination, which is seen as having a positive spillover in the realm of internal security and intelligence sharing. Even though the GCC states continue to be unable to attain independence in the military field, internal security cooperation against interference from external powers has been a mainstay of the members from the beginning. The fact that it is not channeled through the GCC itself is consistent with informal patterns of decisionmaking and the rules governing shaikhly decorum.

Internal and External Security Policies: An Assessment

In his study of subregional security cooperation, Tow identifies four criteria for evaluating what he calls subregional security organizations. These are a useful starting point in trying to assess how the GCC has performed in the first quarter-century of its existence and, crucially, in determining whether it could have accomplished more given the structural constraints under which it operates. Tow identifies the following tasks as integral to an organization like the GCC:

1. Broadening subregional economic and development cooperation and policy cooperation on sensitive political and security issues;
2. Converting shared ideological and political outlooks into a tangible mutual security approach to neutralize threats from both internal and external sources and to advance members' common security interests;
3. Balancing national security with region-wide and international security ties; and
4. Compelling major world powers to accept their collective security agenda.[34]

In relation to security matters, the GCC has fared well in perhaps one and one-half of these fields. The frequent meetings of interior ministers, foreign ministers, and security officials have certainly broadened cooperation on sensitive security issues. That this agenda has not been pursued through the formal procedures of the organization itself should not detract from the importance that frequent meetings and mid-level coordination have had in tackling collectively internal security challenges, such as the meddling by Iran that was so frequent during the 1980s and always dealt with swiftly.

On Tow's second point, although progress has been made in the internal security realm, results in the field of external security have been minimal. However, I argue that the much discussed disagreements between "lower" and "upper" Gulf states in identifying pressing threats are only part of the reason.[35] For example, while all of the GCC states agree on the need for a

US security umbrella, each seems to pursue a separate strategy when dealing with Iran. Because the GCC states believe that they cannot achieve self-sufficiency in external defense for the foreseeable future, they utilize arms procurement as a diplomatic tool. Their strategy is often mischaracterized as wasteful and counterproductive but, in fact, it constitutes a sort of insurance policy aimed at securing continued US military support and, more broadly, protection and diplomatic leverage they can use with other potential allies should the need arise.

As for the last two points, the GCC states have little chance of making major powers accept their collective security agenda, but they are fortunate in that their national interests broadly coincide with the regional interests of the great power of the day. The United States demonstrated its commitment to defending the territorial integrity of the Gulf shaikhdoms by coming to the rescue of Kuwait after it was invaded by Iraq in August 1990. The March 2003 US-led intervention in Iraq lessened considerably the menace posed by one of the two regional powers, despite its ambiguous results with regard to domestic security[36] and growing concerns about Iran's intentions and what in December 2004 Jordan's king Abdullah called an Iranian-created "Shi'ite crescent," envisioned as encircling and infiltrating Sunni Arab countries, including countries in the Gulf. The checkered history of GCC external defense cooperation must be assessed in light of these structural factors.

A tentative way forward for the GCC in the field of external security may be to take a more unified approach when dealing with the United States than it has on other issues. For example, in advance of the Iraq War, all six member states reached bilateral defense agreements with the United States regarding the prepositioning of military matériel and other measures to facilitate US intervention. However, unlike its position on free trade agreements, in this case the United States would have preferred a comprehensive multilateral pact.[37] An ability to speak with one voice on defense procurement matters could enhance the leverage of the GCC states without forgoing their traditional utilization of arms procurement as a foreign policy tool. But nothing apart from their frequent disagreements stops them from coordinating among themselves to present a united front in their dealings with the United States.

Conclusion

The GCC's security collaboration has evolved beyond symbolism in the field of internal security, but it has not done so in military matters. At a basic level, the risk that GCC regimes would incur in setting up effective standing armies clearly outweighs the benefits that could be gained in military efficiency. There is a long history in the Arab Middle East of monarchical regimes being overthrown in military coups. Consequently, the traditional separation between regular army, the national guard, and other units is bound to endure. Under these circumstances, little could be gained by closer military cooperation.

In the field of internal security, effective cooperation predates the founding of the GCC, mostly because all these regimes face similar internal threats. The fact that collaboration in this field has not been channeled formally through the GCC Secretariat comports with local bureaucratic culture and should not be seen as a sign that the organization is ineffective. Many meetings of security officials have been organized under the auspices of the organization and they clearly have yielded results. Intelligence is shared quickly among the GCC states and, at press conferences following the uncovering of various security threats, police officials routinely credit their counterparts in other GCC states.

More generally, collaboration in the external security sphere and increasingly in the realm of intelligence sharing has enhanced the image of the GCC on the world stage. It is at this discursive level that efforts in the realm of security cooperation should be judged. The fact that the GCC will increasingly be seen as speaking with one voice on security matters, whatever the reality on the ground, is in itself positive. In the wake of regime change in Iraq in 2003 and the problems the United States encountered there, multilateralism has acquired a greater value on the international stage. Multilateral processes are highly prized even if substance is lacking. From this point of view, the existence of the GCC is a definite asset to its member states because it confers on them an aura of legitimacy in the global arena.

In fact, geostrategic constraints allow little room for maneuver to the six member states, while the possibility of establishing a collective security system in the Gulf involving all eight littoral states seems quite remote. For now, the security of the Gulf depends on the willingness of the United States to intervene militarily and to maintain a large military force in theater despite local ambivalence. The situation is made more dangerous by conflicts over Iran's nuclear policy, especially if this should escalate to include military intervention from outside the region. While almost everyone endorses theoretically the desirability of a collective security system, the obstacles seem difficult to surmount. The triangular balance of power that has characterized the Gulf in the past decades is structurally determined. The best prospect for evolution is a change in the nature of the involvement of the United States.

Notes

1. For a useful analytical distinction between Gulf dynastic monarchies and other Middle East monarchies, see Michael Herb, *All in the Family: Absolutism,*

Revolution, and Democracy in the Middle Eastern Monarchies (Albany: SUNY Press, 1999). The differences are also highlighted in Joseph Kostiner, ed., *Middle East Monarchies: The Challenge of Modernity* (Boulder: Lynne Rienner, 2000). For traditional accounts of the rationale behind the creation of the GCC, see, for example, R. K. Ramazani, *The Gulf Cooperation Council: Record and Analysis* (Charlottesville: University Press of Virginia, 1988); or, more recently, Uzi Rabi, "The GCC: The Endless Quest for Regional Security," paper presented at the annual meeting of the Middle East Studies Association, San Francisco, November 2004. This view, though, is almost unanimous.

2. He develops his criteria in William T. Tow, *Subregional Security Cooperation in the Third World* (Boulder: Lynne Rienner, 1990). In spite of its many now-outdated references to the Cold War, this is still the most lucid theoretical treatment of subregional security organizations. The fact that the GCC is treated as such in this and in other works of international relations indicates how external observers always considered security to be the central focus of the organization.

3. The definition is found in Avi Shlaim, *War and Peace in the Middle East: A Concise History* (New York: Penguin, 1995).

4. See Frederick F. Anscombe, *The Ottoman Gulf: The Creation of Kuwait, Saudi Arabia, and Qatar* (New York: Columbia University Press, 1997).

5. I am indebted to Philip Robins for this image.

6. A different conceptualization is contained in James A. Bill, "The Geometry of Instability in the Gulf: The Rectangle of Tension," in *Iran and the Gulf: A Search for Stability*, ed. J. S. Al-Suwaidi (Abu Dhabi: Emirates Center for Strategic Studies and Research, 1996), pp. xi, 425. In my opinion, contra Bill, while the United States is an essential actor in the Gulf it cannot (yet) be considered a local actor. In spite of its intervention in Iraq, the United States does not interfere in the domestic politics of the GCC states and Iran as much as Britain used to do during its long spell as a hegemonic power.

7. The other two are Turkey and Egypt.

8. For a good overview of the military effects of the Iran-Iraq War on the GCC countries, see Lawrence G. Potter and Gary Sick, *Iran, Iraq, and the Legacies of War* (New York: Palgrave Macmillan, 2004).

9. The most recent and exhaustive account of this dispute is T. R. Mattair, *The Three Occupied UAE Islands: The Tunbs and Abu Musa* (Abu Dhabi: Emirates Center for Strategic Studies and Research, 2006). For an account more sympathetic to Iranian concerns, see H. Amirahmadi, ed., *Small Islands Big Politics: The Tonbs and Abu Musa in the Gulf* (London: Macmillan, 1996). Finally, the dispute will be tackled in my forthcoming book on the role of the GCC in the international relations of the Gulf.

10. For a review of the current dilemmas of Gulf security, see Matteo Legrenzi and E. El-Hokayem, *The Arab Gulf States in the Shadow of the Iranian Nuclear Challenge* (Washington, DC: Henry L. Stimson Center, 2006).

11. For a comprehensive treatment of the disputes surrounding the Shatt al-Arab, see Richard N. Schofield, "Position, Function, and Symbol: The Shatt Al-Arab Dispute in Perspective," in *Iran, Iraq, and the Legacies of War*, eds. Lawrence G. Potter and Gary Sick (New York: Palgrave Macmillan, 2004), p. 224.

12. Conferences and workshops on the possibility of establishing a collective security system abound, but technical discussions will be to no avail until the United States and Iran can sit at the same table.

13. See, for example, Anthony H. Cordesman, *The Gulf and the West: Strategic Relations and Military Realities* (London: Mansell, 1988); or Anthony H.

Cordesman, *Kuwait* (Boulder: Westview, 1997). For a European view, see Laura Guazzone, "Gulf Cooperation Council: The Security Policies," *Survival* 30, no. 2 (1988): 134–147. Colonel Giuseppe Di Miceli, Italian military attaché in Kuwait, colorfully described the situation as "trying to defend San Marino from an Italian attack," with reference to the microstate situated in central Italy; Giuseppe Di Miceli, Italian military attaché in Kuwait, interviewed by the author, Kuwait, November 12, 2000.

14. The establishment of the Eurogolfe network of scholars in 2002 was financed by two French arms manufacturers. In the United States, the National Council of US-Arab relations, active in the fields of elite networking and public diplomacy, is largely sponsored by US defense contractors.

15. For a rather impatient view of the GCC military achievements, see Anthony H. Cordesman, *Saudi Arabia Enters the Twenty-First Century: The Military and International Security Dimensions* (Westport: Praeger, 2003).

16. This issue was perceptively highlighted by Guazzone in the 1980s. The following twenty-plus years have fully validated her insight. See Guazzone, "Gulf Cooperation Council."

17. Di Miceli interview; also Anthony H. Cordesman, *Saudi Arabia Enters the Twenty-First Century.*

18. Cordesman, *Saudi Arabia Enters the Twenty-First Century.*

19. See Erik R. Peterson, *The Gulf Cooperation Council: Search for Unity in a Dynamic Region* (Boulder: Westview, 1988).

20. S. bin Khalid and P. Seale, *Desert Warrior: A Personal View of the Gulf War by the Joint Forces Commander* (New York: HarperCollins, 1995), pp. 248–249.

21. Guazzone, "Gulf Cooperation Council."

22. Quoted in Peterson, *The Gulf Cooperation Council.*

23. An examination of the final communiqués and statements of the meetings of the Supreme Council gives an idea of the insistence with which this notion is propounded by the organization.

24. For the reasons why the GCC does not constitute a security community, see Michael N. Barnett and F. Gregory Gause III, "Caravans in Opposite Directions: Society, State, and the Development of Community in the Gulf Cooperation Council," in *Security Communities*, eds. Emanuel Adler and Michael N. Barnett (Cambridge: Cambridge University Press, 1998), pp. 161–197. Karl Deutsch defines a pluralistic security community as one in which states become integrated to a point that they have a sense of community that, in turn, creates assurances that they will settle their differences short of war. See Karl Deutsch, *Political Community in the North Atlantic Area: International Organization in Light of Historical Experience* (Princeton: Princeton University Press, 1957).

25. One of the more amusing proofs of the success of these symbolic actions has been the call for a dissolution of the GCC on the part of a hostile author. Simon Henderson, who has written an account of Gulf security for the Washington Institute for Near East Policy, calls for the dissolution of the organization on the grounds that it provides a dangerous counterbalance to the US presence in the Gulf. See Simon Henderson, *The New Pillar: Conservative Arab Gulf States and U.S. Strategy* (Washington, DC: Washington Institute for Near East Policy, 2003).

26. Gulshan Dietl, *Through Two Wars and Beyond: A Study of the Gulf Cooperation Council* (New Delhi: Lancers, 1991).

27. See Barnett and Gause, "Caravans in Opposite Directions," for this and other factors that prevent the GCC from evolving into a full-fledged security community.

28. There is tension between the expeditiousness and convenience of collaborat-

ing with people known through informal channels and the need to be constantly aware of what these very same people might actually be doing. This tension marks not only internal security cooperation, but also societal relations. In Kuwait, the same professionals who expound the virtue of Gulf-wide cooperation will, in the next sentence, warn against the sneaky ways of the Saudis. It is a state of permanent, unresolved tension.

29. For example, I asked Prince Turki Al-Faisal Al-Saud, who headed Saudi intelligence for more than twenty years and is now ambassador to the United Kingdom and Ireland, to tell me his thoughts about the organization. He replied, "The GCC? You will have to tell me because I do not know anything about it." He then went on to emphasize how little interaction both of his offices had with the organization. Prince Turki Al-Faisal Al-Saud, ambassador to the United Kingdom and Ireland, interviewed by the author, Oxford, November 18, 2003.

30. Al-Mustaqbal, January 23, 1982.

31. For the Kuwaiti accommodationist policy toward Iran and the Soviet bloc during the 1980s, see Abdul Reda Assiri, *Kuwait's Foreign Policy: City-State in World Politics* (Boulder: Westview, 1990). At the time, Kuwait seemed to be the GCC state most mistrustful of Saudi hegemony, a role now played by Qatar.

32. Abdullah Yacoub Bishara, former secretary-general of the Arab Gulf Cooperation Council, interviewed by the author, Kuwait, November 17, 2000.

33. For the evolution of political discourse in Kuwait, see Mary Ann Tétreault, *Stories of Democracy: Politics and Society in Contemporary Kuwait* (New York: Columbia University Press, 2000).

34. Tow, *Subregional Security Cooperation.*

35. For the conventional wisdom about the difference in threat perception among the six GCC states, see Rabi, "The GCC"; or Ramazani, *The Gulf Cooperation Council*. In fact, GCC states all recognize that preserving their external security will necessitate in-area US support for the foreseeable future.

36. A note of caution is in order here. It is in fact remarkable how widespread the feeling that Kuwait is but an appendix of Iraq is among the Iraqi population, including notable members of the former opposition to Saddam Hussein. At the least, there is widespread consensus in Iraq that its access to the Gulf should be broadened. For a comprehensive treatment of Iraqi political culture giving rise to these feelings, see Charles Tripp, *A History of Iraq* (Cambridge: Cambridge University Press, 2000).

37. Robert Pelletreau, former US assistant secretary of state, interviewed by the author, Oxford, December 4, 1999.

PART 3
Conclusion

13

Juxtapositions and Sticking Points

Gwenn Okruhlik and Mary Ann Tétreault

IN CHAPTER 1 of this volume, we looked at three sources of pressure to liberalize the political economies of Arab Gulf states: external, internal, and regional. External sources refer not only to whether the international environment is permissive with regard to indigenous forces for liberalization, but also to whether foreign actors are active interveners who support or oppose it. Internal sources consist of large or influential domestic groups pressing for—or against—liberalization. Where do they appear? Are they supporters or opponents of existing regimes? That is, are they reformers with whom regimes might arrive at acceptable accommodations, or are they revolutionaries, whose threat to regime survival means they must be crushed? Regional sources are not quite external, although ideas and avenues might come from outside individual countries. Yet they are not quite internal either, even though, as several contributors to this volume emphasize (Christian Koch, Jill Crystal, and N. Janardhan, for example), they shape the goals and strategies of domestic political actors. All three sources were instrumental in the surprising liberalization that the Arab Gulf states experienced following the second Gulf war. Yet the transitions that seemed so promising even a few years ago appear to have stalled—they are stuck. Can we identify the causes of stuckness, and see where they are coming from?

The external environment for liberalization has changed markedly. The assertive unipolarity that marked the George W. Bush administration in the United States is gone, along with its reliance on military force as a means to achieve economic and political liberalization. President Barack Obama's foreign policy team is less engaged than its predecessor in the domestic politics of other states, and generally more interested in persuasion than sanctions as a way to further US interests. This new US stance leaves more space for energetic intervention in the Gulf by China and Russia. Neither supports political liberalization, but both are eager to develop ties with Gulf oil exporters. They offer strategic and economic options to the Arab Gulf states with regard to industrial cooperation, energy markets, and regional balancing with respect to Iran—and the United States. Although the European Union also appears less engaged than before in Gulf liberalization projects, France under Nicolas Sarkozy has embarked on an aggressive program to expand military ties and sell weapons to Gulf states, and has laid the groundwork for an eventual partnership in constructing nuclear power reactors. The United States and Britain also have strong interests in arms sales to the region, but the entry of a continental European power gives the Gulf states more room to maneuver among all of these contenders.[1] The accumulation of financial surpluses by the Gulf Cooperation Council (GCC) states also adds to their foreign policy autonomy and expands its choices of potential extraregional partners.

A renewed interest in substantial arms transfers to the Gulf, coupled with the rising influence of antidemocratic states from outside the region, reflects a permissive international environment. There appears to be no dominant outside power ready and willing to intervene against domestic actors working for systemic change. This does not mean, however, that the external environment favors liberalization. Strategic assets transferred to developing states are as likely to be used against domestic dissidents as against foreign challengers, and the marked decline in the willingness of Western states to intervene on human rights grounds—to exercise leverage—itself a reaction to the George W. Bush rationales for invading Iraq, effectively denies dissidents what could have been an important source of external restraint against harsh repression by their governments.[2]

Other systemic influences also tip the domestic balance of power further in the direction of the state. In addition to the loss of leverage, linkage among the Gulf states and the United States—which in the past has sometimes used its influence in the Gulf to favor opening—also is attenuating. Restrictions on visas for Muslim men have proliferated to the point of sacrificing the next generation of connections between the Gulf and the United States, forged in shared experiences at US universities. Not only students but also scholars have been denied entry into the United States thanks to such "antiterrorism" policies. At the same time, the rise in oil prices following the US-led invasion of Iraq in 2003 has brought large accumulations of financial assets into the hands of Gulf rulers. Insofar as the rentier state thesis holds, economic payoffs to regime allies are more likely both to happen and to incur fewer opportunity costs. Domestic constituencies looking for long-term development of human capital and infrastructure also see their needs and desires closer to fulfillment in the form of long-range planning and targeted investments that are easier for oil-rich states to supply.

Whether democracy would be one outcome of such development is an open question, and one we address further below.

The primary domestic source of pressures for and against liberalization lies in the relations between rulers and citizens. This is especially clear in the smaller GCC states, where customary expectations that rulers will be approachable personally and respond to citizens' problems and requests on a "retail" basis remain strong. Lisa Anderson argues that monarchy as a regime type is both institutionally flexible and inclusive,[3] and that monarchies in the Middle East rely on kinship and hierarchy to divide and rule vertically defined groupings that make their regimes both pluralistic and ambiguous.[4] As Jerzy Zdanowski and Eleanor Abdella Doumato show for Saudi Arabia in Chapters 7 and 9 of this volume, occupying what Benedict Anderson calls the "high center"[5] allows a ruler to appear to be the ally of more than one side in social conflicts. With respect to minority rights, the illusion that the king is a democrat at heart may encourage proponents of change to be patient and quiet, but both patience and quiet are increasingly in short supply. Doumato's comments on reactions to the fire at the Saudi girls' school are reinforced by a virtually unprecedented demonstration against corrupt admission policies by female university students in Riyadh in August 2009.[6] Violent protests against enforcement of the law banning tribal primaries shook urban Kuwaitis in 2008, and a less polite politics may also be in the future for one or two other Arab Gulf states, as Christian Koch suggests in Chapter 8 with regard to the United Arab Emirates (UAE). The illusions surrounding the high center are more difficult to maintain in a world connected by electronic media, which may be why repression of the press is growing throughout the Middle East.[7]

In Chapter 10, N. Janardhan shows how ambiguous the new media are with respect to the partly antagonistic processes of regime maintenance and liberalization. The accessibility of new media allows citizens to readily compare the situation in their country with what is going on elsewhere in the region and the world, and offers ways to vent dissatisfaction and find like-minded potential allies to work for political change. But new media offer advantages to regimes as well by providing means for tracking dissidents and monitoring their activities. States and citizens clash directly over the issue of censorship of news organizations, websites, and services like YouTube, but the state's ability to interdict entirely what it sees as subversive communication is limited. In 2006, Kuwaitis smuggled campaign videos out of the country so they could be beamed and streamed back to voters in Kuwait. Citizen reactions to the June 2009 election in Iran demonstrated the extent and utilization of mobile telephone and text-messaging networks, alongside the lasting power of very old media of communication such as praying aloud on rooftops. Reality TV has enlarged the media arena for state-society conflicts even further,[8] as it accelerates the regionalization of popular culture and the ownership of competing "satellite realms."[9]

Although religion as such remains strong and vibrant in the region, political Islam as an ideology framing electoral competition seems to have diminished in strength, especially in Iraq and Kuwait, where elections translate into significant political power for the winners. In Kuwait, candidates running for parliament as representatives of Islamist groups in the May 2009 election fared less well than they did in the election run the previous year.[10] Sectarianism also appears to have diminished in recent Iraqi elections, as Juan Cole indicates in Chapter 3. There it is overlain by struggles to control the state and lucrative ministries that may be articulated as religious and ethnic sentiments, but are significantly interest-based.[11] Yet sectarianism as religious identification is alive and well. In Chapter 7, Zdanowski shows how it galvanizes religious opposition with the potential to spill over into regime opposition even though Saudi Shi'a are nationalists and the potential regime opponents are conservative Sunnis. Gianluca Parolin shows in Chapter 2 how sectarianism can dilute criticism of the regime by deflecting attention toward what divides a population rather than what unites it.

Regional pressures for liberalization may be intensified by the new media, but the emulation noted by Jill Crystal in Chapter 6 and implied by Koch in Chapter 8 predates satellite television and texting and would persist without them. In Chapter 5 on Oman, J. E. Peterson argues for top-down emulation in the welfare policies of the sultan, whose efforts to raise living standards go back to the earliest days following his accession. The ruler of the newly constituted UAE was similarly dedicated to a high level of social welfare provision from his earliest days, and arguably improved upon the examples of Bahrain and Kuwait. Emulation has come full circle in the UAE as growing popular interest in politics reveals bottom-up emulation by Emiratis assessing the practical manifestations—or lack of them—of liberalization there. Emeratis looking for results from liberalization have Gulf neighbors whose experiences show that more can be expected than what they already have. These neighbors provide yardsticks or indications of the possible, but they are not imitated as such. Instead, perceptions of their experiences are used as raw materials for making arguments, invidious comparisons, and future plans.

Emulation is not the only mechanism generating regional trends. Population movements that may result from knowledge acquired via new media are sources of information in themselves.

> A few years ago the government of Abu Dhabi conducted a private study to examine the effect of the large number of Saudis moving to the country. There is some concern that hundreds of thousands of Saudi immigrants would produce a long-term ideological and security challenge. The UAE is now a haven for many Saudi artists, women, writers, businessmen, and others. They moved there for more freedoms, and to escape official and social restrictions.[12]

Ali al-Ahmed believes that a 2009 policy denying transit rights between Saudi Arabia and the UAE to citizens who show only their ID cards (rather than passports), justified as a reaction to an alleged incorrect map on UAE ID cards, is actually a reaction to the pressures arising from this migration in Saudi Arabia. Others believe that it is a continuation of the rift between the two neighbors over the location of a pan-Arab Gulf central bank.[13] Both are likely contributors to the discord between Saudi Arabia and the UAE and, as Matteo Legrenzi reminds us in Chapter 12, the smaller Gulf states routinely take a gingerly approach to relations with their far larger and more belligerent neighbor.

Limits to regional emulation, visible in conflicts over border transit and the location of a GCC central bank, reflect goals and concerns of a neighborhood of states vying with one another for status and authority in their region. Liberalization was an important dimension of this rivalry in the past. Indeed, we have argued in Chapters 4, 5, and 6 that such emulation pressed the democratization project forward in Qatar and Kuwait, and possibly also in Oman well before George W. Bush made it the rhetorical centerpiece of his Middle East strategy. Crystal argues in Chapter 6 that Bush's pressure was integral to pushing the liberalization agenda forward in Qatar, and that it proceeded no further than the United States was willing to press it. Yet Legrenzi points out in Chapter 12 that even the imperatives of strategic defense cannot overcome the state-based nationalism that makes calls for Arab unity a hallmark of aspiring hegemons.[14] As Iraq continues its efforts to reconstitute itself as an autonomous state among its Arab neighbors, regional pressures for liberalization are likely to touch off strategic conflicts that the GCC states have so far successfully eluded by relying on the United States to defend them against their larger neighbors, Iraq and Iran.

This brief survey indicates multiple sources of stuckness affecting liberalization among the Arab Gulf states. On the ground, many take the form of what we call juxtapositions, sets of situations and trends that embody these tensions. In the next section, we discuss several juxtapositions whose impact on transition could take it in a number of possible directions. All of them are rooted in domestic politics, but several incorporate international or regional dimensions.

Juxtapositions: Demographic Challenges and Cultural Struggles

Demographics and culture are intricately intertwined in all of the countries we have considered in this volume. The pressures of population growth in general, along with variations in the composition of the population in individual cases, often precipitate struggles over culture and development.

Tensions open small cracks into which citizens can pour their energies in the quest for reform. These cracks can be pushed wider apart by activists to force reforms or by the state to prevent cross-group coalitions. It is rare but not unheard of for social activists to build bridges over the cracks, such as those appearing between members of different sects or social classes, but they are more often closed by powerful state actors. Rulers apply a flexible caulk, creating a facade of structural integrity while allowing for some release of tension, but they seal the gap tightly if sharp criticism of their rule threatens to escape. Chapters 2, 3, 4, and 7 have focused on the struggles of minorities in the Arab Gulf. Here, we highlight other sites of demographic and cultural struggle.

Women are highly educated but less employed in the Gulf. Increasing numbers of women receive university degrees. Indeed, in Qatar and the UAE, female students outnumber male students by a ratio of 3:1.[15] For many years, a greater proportion of women in the Gulf earned doctoral degrees than their American counterparts. Yet while there is significant variation among the Arab Gulf countries, available opportunities for postgraduate employment of female citizens are limited in number and by field in all of them: women are a highly educated and underutilized resource.

In the Gulf states, employed women used to be concentrated in education and health care; now we see increasing numbers as business owners in finance, industry, and services. Women who stay in school long enough to acquire a PhD risk surpassing the prime marriageable age, although this "problem" tends to preoccupy social critics more than it does the women involved. Furthermore, women are largely responsible for domestic activities, and most have access to cheap unskilled household labor to assist them. They also are responsible for managing family obligations in the social sphere, tasks that rarely can be transferred to servants or even to other family members, and many participate in voluntary associations. As in the West, professional Arab women carry a double burden that cuts into the time they have available for nonfamily activities.[16]

Citizens are minorities in the labor force, and even in the general population, and there are concerted efforts to define what it means to be "local" in a cultural sense. Foreigners comprise a significant part of the total population of the Arab Gulf states (not just the labor force alone). They range from 20 percent to 25 percent of the total population in Oman to 30 percent in Saudi Arabia, over 50 percent in Bahrain, 68 percent in Kuwait, and a whopping 80 percent to 85 percent in Qatar and the UAE. Most of the foreign labor force is imported from Pakistan, India, Bangladesh, the Philippines, and other Arab countries; they bring along their own cuisine, dress, language, and social norms. Citizens feel threatened in their own countries, something that Anh Nga Longva calls "besieged empowerment" in her analysis of Kuwait.[17] Locals feel that their cultural integrity is under siege, prompting citizens and rulers to better define and protect their own cultural traditions. For example, a July 2009 proposal in the UAE would require foreign workers to pass a cultural awareness test in order to reside in the country.[18] In Saudi Arabia, there are calls to "protect our khusousiyyah," or unique traditions, in response to change and exposure to competing ideas.[19] In Bahrain, the labor minister spoke of an "Asian tsunami" and said he feared "the erosion of the national character of states in the Gulf."[20] The tone of these arguments exposes both the fear of Gulf societies that their own cultures are being diluted and their unwillingness to address the social and economic benefits to citizens of keeping this system just as it is.

There is significant unemployment among young local men, yet overwhelming dependence on an imported labor force. Local unemployment is a serious problem in the Arab Gulf states and reliable statistics are difficult to find. Official estimates are consistently lower than unofficial ones. The reasons for local unemployment include education and experience, salary expectations and other structural (dis)incentives, and the reluctance of the private sector to hire expensive locals, who are difficult to discharge for social reasons. The education gap occurs not only with regard to curriculum, but also because of pedagogy. Schools in the region historically favored memorization over creative problem solving; even though extensive educational modernization has taken place,[21] the old ways persist. They constitute a hindrance in economic decisionmaking and in other parts of the global economy. Throughout the Gulf, there are now myriad partnerships between local universities and institutions located abroad, including in the United States, Britain, Scotland, Australia, India, Canada, and Malaysia.[22] The most prominent among these "transplants" can be found in Qatar's Education City, where Virginia Commonwealth University, Cornell University, Georgetown School of Foreign Service, Carnegie Mellon University, Northwestern University, and Texas A&M University have branch campuses noted for the extent of the involvement of the foreign partner. The transplants tend to be more rigorous and more "American" than local counterparts, but among the criticisms of these institutions is that foreign students are more likely to meet entrance requirements than host country students.[23]

Dependence on foreign labor in the private sector, which reaches 88 percent in Saudi Arabia and 93 percent in the UAE,[24] is both a cause and an effect of a complex system of required sponsorship and supervision. Until recently the practice of workers surrendering their passports, thus leaving them at the mercy of sponsors with authority over them, was barely questioned.[25] Those in unskilled and semiskilled jobs are particularly vulnerable. Throughout the Gulf, extraregional expatriates are distinguished from the local population through their location in physical space, wage scales, costume, and social distance.[26]

Failure to deal honestly with deficiencies in the education and discipline of youth (and an excessive reliance on cheap unskilled labor to maintain a lavish lifestyle) impose a disproportionate burden on young people, who themselves represent a large burden in terms of demands on the public purse for infrastructure, housing, education and health care, and jobs. The youth bulge could be a window of opportunity if young nationals were trained adequately and if they could be productively absorbed into the labor force.[27] So far, that has proven to be an elusive goal.

In spite of their numbers, young people face constrained opportunities to express generational distinctiveness, and experience strong expectations that they will conform to traditional norms. These young populations, like youth everywhere, include rebels against long-standing and sometimes overwhelming expectations of behavioral conformity and cultural orthodoxy. They express generational difference through hip-hop music and social networking, in coffeehouses, and in their dress. In general, however, there are precious few outlets for such creative energies. In some Gulf countries, there are even prohibitions on the hours that youth can shop in malls. Familial standards of what constitutes proper behavior, especially for girls, are strict because the behavior of every family member reflects on the larger family unit.

Janardhan's discussion of blogging in Chapter 10 reveals an important outlet for rebellious youth—and other subalterns, like women. Other heavily utilized new media outlets include mobile phones, reality TV, and Internet social networking sites. Low-tech forms of rebellion also are evident. When Saudi Arabian youth expressed themselves through graffiti on buildings in the city of Jeddah, the government responded by erecting a "graffiti wall" on which their rebellious scrawls are legally permitted. The irony was lost on the officials. Kuwaiti youth have more freedom and are quietly pushing boundaries defining acceptable behavior, often with their parents' approval. Yet the boundary pushers also discover that some of their peers resent and disapprove of their behavior and, occasionally, express their hostile views through violence.[28]

Intergenerational gaps are another issue. The historical memories and worldviews of these young populations are radically different from those of their grandparents and, in later-developing Gulf countries such as Oman, Qatar, and the UAE, also from those of their parents. The oil-fueled transformations of all of these countries are relatively recent, and present affluence masks the hardships and sacrifices of earlier generations. New media, especially mobile telephones and television, are eliding some of these gaps. Parents feel reassured when they can check on their children regularly by phone, while reality TV has proven to be a surprising location for parent-child interactions as families discuss their favorites and run up their mobile phone bills voting for them.[29]

There are new social spaces and burgeoning artistic communities, yet new prohibitions and state intervention. Art galleries are thriving across the Gulf, along with literary societies, film festivals, book exhibits, and an increasing number and variety of spaces for social interaction. Women and men are active in artistic communities. All of this is welcome in historically staid and closed cultural spaces. It is unfortunate to say the least that state control of such creative expressions is increasing rather than decreasing. Prince Naif in Saudi Arabia simply closed a major film festival in Jeddah in the summer of 2009. There are new prohibitions on public behavior (kissing, dancing, and choice of clothing) in the UAE. Book festivals are raided and school plays have been the site of conservative confrontations. "Clubs," sans alcohol, music, or dancing, are raided.

Why are strong states concerned with social space and artistic expression? One reason is that they serve as substitute political spaces in the absence of access to real political spaces and rights. Poetry, novels, sculpture, music, and dance are all venues for disguised political criticism,[30] and are often targeted by entrenched authorities. Another reason for the closure of artistic and social spaces is to satisfy conservative political constituencies. Concerts in Kuwait have been a special target of parliamentary Islamists for years, and reality TV also has felt the heat generated by Islamist and tribalist forces that see it as violating "traditional" gender norms.[31] At the same time, on the state level, the UAE hosts branches of the Louvre and the Guggenheim Museums in Abu Dhabi. Qatar has opened the Museum of Islamic Art. Riyadh has a national museum and an annual cultural fair, and Kuwait's commitment to fine art has not diminished in spite of the loss of classical works during the Iraqi occupation. New social spaces also face opposition from social forces. The Al Jouf Literary Club in northern Saudi Arabia was set ablaze in 2009 because a woman poet had been scheduled to speak there. The director received a texted death threat.[32]

All media have become more widely used, yet are subject to increasing state censorship. Expanded access to more and more diverse information presents problems to governments interested in managing—limiting—information content and dissemination. The rapid increase in freedom of the press that was greeted hopefully just a few years ago seems to have slowed. Since then, laws to inhibit the flow of critical or investigative journalism have risen to the top of Gulf states' agendas. In Bahrain, the government continues to enforce the restrictive press law of 2002 even though there are constitutional guarantees of freedom of the press. Reporters have been harassed, detained, censored, and prosecuted. In June 2009, the country's oldest newspaper, *Akhbar Al Khaleej*, was temporarily suspended, apparently in response to an op-ed piece that was critical of the Iranian presidential election.[33] Qatar is the home of Al-Jazeera and a leader in opening regional television, yet Al-Jazeera must refrain from criticizing the Qatari state in its broadcasts. The staff of the new Doha-based Center for Media Freedom, intended to monitor freedom of the press worldwide, resigned in response to pressure from the government. In May 2010, five female anchors resigned from Al-Jazeera over the handling of a harassment case. They had been accused of "dressing immodestly." There are also charges of favoritism and corruption at the station.[34]

The print media in Kuwait are arguably the most free in the Gulf. But Kuwait's 2006 press law and a new law regulating electronic media permitting the establishment of new newspapers and television stations have imposed new constraints by opening the door to contending factions of the ruling family to buy media outlets to push their own agendas. These laws also instituted large fines and prison terms for violations that include blasphemy, calls for toppling the regime by illegitimate means, or insulting the amir. In 2009, two candidates for parliament were arrested for criticizing members of the ruling family—one critique was more than a year old at the time of the arrest (see also Chapter 4). Proposed "reforms" of the press laws in the UAE also seem to be a giant step backward. They call for draconian fines and harsh registration requirements. Human Rights Watch predicted that these press restrictions would undermine freedom of expression. They forbid the publication of any story deemed harmful to the national economy or insulting to members of the government or ruling family. As Koch noted in Chapter 8, Emiratis are fighting these attempts to limit their rights.

Saudi Arabia imposes the most restrictions on media in the Gulf. It is equally harsh with old and new media. It has the second highest number of bloggers in the Middle East after Egypt,[35] yet routinely censors and blocks websites and blogs, and occasionally arrests bloggers. In April 2009, the Interior Ministry imposed new regulations on Saudi Internet cafes that require owners to install secret surveillance cameras and register the names and identity numbers of all users. Similar regulations are about to go into effect in Iraq.[36] Saudi Arabia also prohibits unauthorized prepaid Internet cards, censors freedom of navigation, and requires that owners of Internet cafes be Saudi.[37] In the usually quiet state of Oman, there are strict new measures on use of the Internet. Prohibited content includes anything that can be construed as dishonoring the sultan and his family, threatening national security, or impairing public confidence in the government. In April 2009, an Internet moderator was imprisoned and fined for publishing a directive on the Web. All of this has resulted in self-censorship in both old and new media throughout the region.

The states of the Gulf are intimately tied to the global economy through oil, trade, and investment, yet all remain intensely protective of domestic jurisdiction and culture. The Arab Gulf states sign on to international conventions, but attach riders that express multiple reservations and claim exceptions to the conventions' applicability and enforcement. The tension between global economic and human rights imperatives, on the one hand, and national sovereignty, on the other, continues to play out on such vital issues as the treatment of foreign labor, the rights of women, the protection of children, and environmental sustainability. Further, the megaboom that these states experienced after 2003 has an underbelly. All of the Arab Gulf states have poor human rights records. Their industries and skyscrapers are being built in some instances by virtual slave labor. Dubai has been singled out for its dramatic, modern architectural skyline, which hides the world's worst environmental footprint.[38] All of the Gulf states are actively courting foreign investment even as they restrict citizen rights.

By several measures, Iraq fared significantly better than its GCC counterparts (e.g., in women's education and employment) prior to the three Gulf wars. Now it lags behind, scarred by the demographic and psychological effects of almost thirty years of war and domestic violence. The desire of Iraqis for autonomy and sovereignty is not matched by the ability of national police and military forces to maintain security for vulnerable groups in the population. The impact of war and insecurity is difficult to evaluate in Iraq because data on gender, age, income, and employment are scarce and probably inaccurate. In August 2009, Iraq postponed indefinitely its plans to conduct the first nationwide census in twenty-two years. Reminiscent of Lebanon, this seems to be a response to fears that census results could stoke religious and ethnic tension. Even without systematic data, however, we know that large proportions of Iraqi refugees are middle-class and professional. Iraqi literacy rates are reportedly lower than they were under Saddam Hussein.[39] Another tragic legacy of the three Gulf wars is that Iraq needs to develop all over again.

An Uncertain Future

Taking an optimistic view, these internal, international, and regional juxtapositions expose tensions that could be opportunities for reform. The reality, however, is that there has been far more technical and economic opening than substantive political reform in these states. Most of the political reforms discussed in this volume tend toward the cosmetic, and only rarely indicate a redistribution of power or rights. The Gulf states remain highly autocratic even though all of them now run elections for representative bodies of some sort. Elected representatives are counterbalanced by appointed chambers (Bahrain), and most councils have a merely advisory authority (Saudi Arabia, Oman, Qatar, and the UAE). The only parliament in the region with real legislative power has been hit with repeated legal dissolutions. Kuwait has seen the resignations of five governments and dismissals of three parliaments in less than four years, resulting in unscheduled elections in 2006, 2008, and 2009, and now faces increasingly open threats of unconstitutional closure in the future. The experience in Iraq provides ample evidence that democracy under conditions of war and occupation is tenuous at best.

Sociocultural reforms are today's hot potatoes, tossed to and fro in the struggle over political power and human rights. Debates over culture and tradition (the invocation to "protect our *khusousiyyah*!") inflame passions and deflect attention from demands for participation, accountability, and human rights. Despite early optimism about political openings in the Gulf, these regimes have quietly dropped the rhetoric of liberalization and reform. They have consolidated the authority of ruling families and appear, at best, stuck in transition. Yet as we show in this brief survey of juxtapositions, pressures for change either toward greater openness and citizen responsibility or in the direction of severe repression, perhaps in league with the conservative social forces that see themselves losing out to rivals, are increasing. Remaining on the table are sectarian unrest, particularly in Bahrain, Iraq, and Saudi Arabia, but also in Kuwait, where it is part of the arsenals of factions in the unruly ruling family; labor unrest, in all states but especially in the UAE; struggles for the rights of women, insufficiently represented in the public sphere and still repressed by political as well as social forces throughout the region; and protection of civil and political rights for all people of the Arab Gulf states.

Mehran Kamrava concludes in his analysis of Qatari politics that, "for now, meaningful steps toward liberalization . . . remain halted and tentative at best. The prospects for anything even remotely resembling democracy appear further [away] still." He ends on this pessimistic note after demonstrating the superior capacity of the state in relation to civil society. It has effectively penetrated the social domain, rendered civil society irrelevant, and tied itself to international capital.[40] All of these observations are true, but the last page has not yet been written on the washing of the third wave of democracy over the Gulf.

The chapters in this volume show that, however stuck these regimes appear to be, politics is dynamic and outcomes far from settled. As we have noted in Chapters 4 and 10 especially, so far the new media have managed to stay at least a half-step ahead of repressive responses from the state. Another reason not to abandon the idea of reform is the demonstrated inventiveness of activists with regard to the whole panoply of instruments at hand. This inventiveness is a combination of new media (Twitter, proxy servers, and mobile telephones) with very old media (cries of "Allahu Akbar!" from rooftops in cities) that is keeping the hope of citizens and regime dissidents alive in Iran. Quieting dissidents is a nastier and more public proposition today than it was a generation ago, both domestically and globally.

A characteristic of resistance in the Gulf, as elsewhere, is that dissidents also occupy the state. Like citizen activists, elite dissidents share similar aspirations for a more open system. Again, Iran is an excellent example of forces for and against liberalization among average citizens and within elites. Kuwait also features pro– and anti–status quo forces both inside and outside of government, as does the UAE. The reform impulse is evident among many Gulf elites, regardless of whether one believes that they see liberalization as a tactic for maintaining authority or as a strategy for change. Indeed, representative bodies are an institutional frame for containing dissent, and constitute a strong motive for autocratic rulers to establish them. One reason why rulers like the king of Bahrain have paid so much attention to crafting the rules governing representative institutions is precisely to limit dissent. Yet the very existence of even weak parliaments normalizes state-society conflict while election campaigns highlight regime critiques—the reason that Kuwaiti candidates were arrested during the 2009 parliamentary election campaign.

The effects of prior reform impulses require new state strategies for successful repression. One of the laudable projects of governments on both sides of the Gulf has been the attention paid to human development. An educated population has intellectual resources to apply to politics as well as to the everyday pursuit of economic development. Also, the technologies that further integration into a global economy have proven to be equally useful for the integration of political activists. This presents a dilemma to governments, now even more dependent on foreign investment and more closely linked to international capitalism than before they signed on to the World Trade Organization and accumulated piles of cash in their sovereign wealth funds: Can a state turn off mobile telephones to stop dissident communication without impeding international trade? Can a state apply violent repressive measures and not make potential investors uneasy about the security of their capital and the likely success of their operations on its territory?

We do not want to give the impression that activism and pressures for political change are uniformly benign. Many Gulf political activists seek to deliberalize their states and societies. Many salafi Islamists object to minority rights and women's rights. Although some tribalists seem ready to spread their wings and fly against the tribes that rule them, others ally themselves with Islamists, objecting to rights for women and young men, and also fighting economic rationalization, which they see as ending their preferential status as government workers. Choosing allies from a diversity of social groups, themselves as dynamic as the proliferation of interests they contain, is more difficult for rulers than it was before mass education and rising incomes generated social and economic pluralism, and before the appearance of technology that enables dissidents not only to coalesce but also to broadcast their existence across the world.

In spite of these arguments for optimism, however, we continue to be pessimistic with regard to how closely political liberalization tracks economic opening and other structural changes related to globalization. It may be that Arab Gulf regimes will be able to retain and even shore up their autocratic qualities without sacrificing the gains that globalization has brought to their region since oil income began to flow into their states. But it also may be that the scale of repression required to do so has become too large, its likely outcomes too destructive, and its exercise too public to guarantee restoration of the status quo ante with acceptable political costs. In that case, stuckness may persist for some years as a political dynamic, steps forward and back rather than a simple authoritarian consolidation of power. That the dance continues is, by itself, a cause for optimism—however cautious.

Notes

1. Paul Reynolds, "French Make Serious Move into Gulf," BBC News, January 15, 2008; "Bahrain Plans to Buy Air-to-Air Missiles," *Gulf Daily News*, August 9, 2009; AFP, "UAE Is World's Third-Biggest Arms Importer: Think-Tank," *Defence Talk*, April 28, 2009, www.defencetalk.com; Christopher M. Blanchard and Richard F. Grimmet, "The Gulf Security Dialogue and Related Arms Sales Proposals," Congressional Research Service, October 8, 2008; and Chapter 12 in this volume. President Obama's October 2010 proposal to sell between $50 and $60 billion worth of advance armaments to Saudi Arabia is the most recent bid by the United States to stay in the arms-sales game in the Gulf. For a detailed analysis of this proposal, see Joshua Teitlebaum, "Arms for the King and His Family: The US Arms Sale to Saudi Arabia," *Jerusalem Issue Briefs* 10, no. 11 (November 2, 2010), http://bit.ly/ai6em5.

2. The importance of linkage and leverage as external sources of support for democratization is analyzed at length in Steven Levitsky and Lucan A.Way, *Competitive Authoritarianism: Hybrid Regimes After the Cold War* (New York: Cambridge University Press, 2010), pp. 38–54. Mark J. Gasiorowski, *U.S. Foreign Policy and the Shah: Building a Client State in Iran* (Ithaca: Cornell University Press, 1991). Indeed, external intervention on human rights and liberties grounds, especially from the United States, became the kiss of death for prodemocracy activists following the Abu Ghraib revelations. One female candidate for parliament in Kuwait who had received campaign advice and training from the US National Endowment for Democracy was widely criticized during the 2006 election as the "American" candidate. During the years of the George W. Bush administration, opponents to liberal reformers tied them to the US democratization agenda as a way to marginalize their claims and undermine their credibility. Other than Iraq, the country where US intervention may have been most destructive is Iran, where its Bush-era "democratization" initiatives continue to fuel the government's harsh repression of dissidents. Well before the contested election of 2009, in reaction to what it said were US attempts to foster a "velvet revolution" in Iran, the Iranian government initiated crackdowns targeting students and academics. In the spring of 2007, it arrested a number of persons who held dual citizenship in Iran and a Western country, including several Americans. In July 2007, two of the incarcerated

Iranian Americans were shown on Iranian television "confessing" to having promoted contacts between Iranian and US citizens. The televised "confessions" of dissidents arrested in 2009—ironically, also charged with attempting a velvet revolution, make the 2007 events appear to be rehearsals of measures to be taken against actual activists.

3. Lisa Anderson, "Dynasts and Nationalists: Why Monarchies Survive," in *Middle East Monarchies: The Challenge of Modernity*, ed. Joseph Kostiner (Boulder: Lynne Rienner, 2000), p. 55.

4. Anderson, "Dynasts and Nationalists," p. 60.

5. Benedict Anderson, *Imagined Communities: Reflections on the Origin and Spread of Nationalism*, rev. ed. (London: Verso, 1991), p. 19.

6. AFP, "Saudi Women Stage Rare University Demo—Reports," *Daily Star* (Lebanon), August 4, 2009, www.dailystar.com.lb.

7. See, for example, the case of Mohammed Abd al-Qader al-Jasim, discussed in Chapter 4. Another troubling case in Kuwait involves the conviction of a young activist, Khaled al-Fadala, who is the secretary-general of the National Democratic Alliance, for a speech in which he criticized political corruption and also the prime minister's performance. See Arabic Network for Human Rights Information, "Political Activist Fined, Sentenced to Three Months in Jail," International Freedom of Expression Exchange, July 2, 2010, http://www.ifex.org. The situation in Bahrain is even more alarming, with hundreds arrested before the fall 2010 election, and repeated reports of torture in the prisons, including the torture of children. See the string of articles about these actions on the Bahrain Center for Human Rights website, http://www.bahrainrights.org/en.

8. Marwan M. Kraidy, *Reality Television and Arab Politics: Contention in Public Life* (New York: Cambridge University Press, 2010).

9. Naomi Sakr, *Satellite Realms: Transnational Television, Globalization and the Middle East* (London: I. B. Tauris, 2002).

10. Mary Ann Tétreault and Mohammed al-Ghanim, "The Day After 'Victory': Kuwait's 2009 Election and the Contentious Present," Merip Online, July 8, 2009, www.merip.org.

11. Also see Iraqi Crisis Report No. 300, part two, Institute for War & Peace Reporting, August 13, 2009, www.iwpr.net.

12. Ali al-Ahmed, director of the Gulf Institute in Washington, DC, personal communication with the author, August 20, 2009.

13. "Saudi Halts Recognition of UAE ID Cards over Map Issue," *Khaleej Times*, August 22, 2009, www.gulfinthemedia.com.

14. This is argued for the region as a whole in Fred Halliday, "The Middle East and Conceptions of 'International Society,'" in *International Society and the Middle East: English School Theory at the Regional Level*, eds. Barry Buzan and Ana Gonzalez-Pelaez (London: Palgrave Macmillan, 2009), pp. 1–23.

15. "Step by Step for Middle East Women," *Christian Science Monitor*, February 17, 2009.

16. See, for example, Mary Ann Tétreault, Katherine Meyer, and Helen Rizzo, "Women's Rights in the Middle East: A Longitudinal Study of Kuwait," *International Political Sociology* 3, no. 2 (2009): 218–237.

17. Anh Nga Longva, "Neither Autocracy nor Democracy but Ethnocracy: Citizens, Expatriates, and the Socio-Political System in Kuwait," in *Monarchies and Nations: Globalisation and Identity in the Arab States of the Gulf*, ed. Paul Dresch and James Piscatori (London: I. B. Tauris, 2005), p. 125.

18. "Culture Test for Residency Visa by UAE," *Emirates Update*, July 9, 2009,

http://emiratesupdate.wordpress.com. Elsewhere, immigrants wishing to settle in the Netherlands are also required to leap cultural hurdles before they are granted residency permits, a policy directed primarily against immigrants from Muslim countries. See "Film Exposes Immigrants to Dutch Liberalism," MSNBC, March 16, 2006, www.msnbc.msn.com. While the Dutch law is aimed at people who expect to live permanently in the Netherlands, it, like the UAE requirement, springs from similar cultural imperatives of besieged empowerment.

19. Saad Al-Sowayan, "Are We So Special or Do We Just Think We Are?" June 11, 2006, www.saadsowayan.com.

20. Majid Al Alawi, quoted in "Gulf States Suffer Erosion of Culture," *Gulf News*, October 1, 2007; and Majid Al Alawi, quoted in "Bahraini Labor Minister Warns of Asian Tsunami," *Asharq Al-Awsat*, January 27, 2008.

21. Eleanor Abdella Doumato and Gregory Starrett, eds., *Teaching Islam: Textbooks and Religion in the Middle East* (Boulder: Lynne Rienner, 2007). Also, Shafeeq Ghabra with Margreet Arnold, "Studying the American Way: An Assessment of American-Style Higher Education in Arab Countries," Policy Focus no. 71 (Washington, DC: Washington Institute for Near East Policy, June 2007).

22. John Willoughby, "Let a Thousand Models Bloom: Western Alliances and the Making of the Contemporary Higher Educational System in the Gulf Arab Countries," paper presented at the annual meeting of the Middle East Studies Association, Washington, DC, November 2008.

23. Tamar Lewin, "U.S. Universities Rush to Set Up Outposts Abroad," *New York Times*, February 10, 2008.

24. "Middle East: Saudi Arabia, Egypt, UAE," *Migration News* 12, no. 1 (2006), www.migration.ucdavis.edu.

25. Human Rights Watch, "'The Island of Happiness': Exploitation of Migrant Workers on Saadiyat Island, Abu Dhabi," May 2009, www.hrw.org.

26. See Anh Nga Longva, *Walls Built on Sand: Migration, Exclusion, and Society in Kuwait* (Boulder: Westview, 1997); Gwenn Okruhlik, "Dependence, Disdain and Distance: State, Labor and Citizenship in the Arab Gulf," in *Industrialization in the Arab Gulf*, eds. Jean Francois Seznec and Mimi Kirk (Boulder: Lynne Rienner, forthcoming); and Gwenn Okruhlik, "Excluded Essentials: Ethnicity, Oil and Citizenship in Saudi Arabia," in *The Global Color Line: Racial and Ethnic Inequality and Struggle from a Global Perspective*, eds. Pinar Batur-VanderLippe and Joe Feagin (Stamford: JAI Press, 1999), pp. 215–235.

27. Ragui Assad and Farzaneh Roudi-Fahimi, "Youth in the Middle East and North Africa: Demographic Opportunity or Challenge?" Population Reference Bureau, Washington, DC, April 2007. See also Ragui Assad, quoted in "The Middle East Youth Bulge," Population Reference Bureau, May 13, 2008, www.prb.org.

28. Mary Ann Tétreault, "Sex and Violence: Social Reactions to Economic Restructuring in Kuwait," *International Feminist Journal of Politics* 1, no. 2 (1999): 237–255.

29. Kraidy, *Reality Television.*

30. Lisa Wedeen, *Ambiguities of Domination: Politics, Rhetoric, and Symbols in Contemporary Syria* (Chicago: University of Chicago Press, 1999).

31. Kraidy, *Reality Television.*

32. Abdulaziz Abdulwahid, "Foul Play Suspected in Sakaka Club Fire," *Arab News*, January 15, 2009.

33. Habib Toumi, "Bahrain's Oldest Newspaper Indefinitely Suspended," *Gulf News*, June 23, 2009.

34. "Doha: Five Female Anchors Resign from Al Jazeera," *Los Angeles Times* blog, Babylon and Beyond, May 31, 2010, http://latimesblog.latimes.com.

35. Ian Black, "Saudi Arabia Leads the Arab Regimes in Internet Censorship," *The Guardian*, June 30, 2009.

36. "On the Media," National Public Radio, August 23, 2009.

37. Arabic Network for Human Rights Information (ANHRI), "New Security Measures Against Internet Cafes," April 19, 2009. See also "Saudi Arabia" on the Initiative for an Open Arab Internet at www.openarab.net.

38. "WWF Living Planet Report 2008," World Wildlife Fund, Gland, Switzerland, www.panda.org. See also Emmanuelle Landais, "UAE Tops World on per Capita Carbon Footprint," *Gulf News*, October 30, 2008.

39. USAID (US Agency for International Development, "Assistance for Iraq," April 9, 2007, www.usaid.gov.

40. Mehran Kamrava, "Royal Factionalism and Political Liberalization in Qatar," *Middle East Journal* 63, no. 3 (2009): 401–420.

Bibliography

Aarts, Paul. "Democracy, Oil, and the Gulf War." *Third World Quarterly* 13, no. 3 (1992): 525–538.

———. "Oil, Money, and Participation: Kuwait's *Sonderweg* as a Rentier State." *Orient* 32, no. 2 (1991): 205–216.

Abd al-Ghafour, P. K. "One-Third of Government Jobs for Women: Sultan." *Arab News*, May 27, 2007.

Abd al-Jabar, Faleh. "Why the Uprisings Failed." *Middle East Report*, no. 176 (1992): 2–14.

Abdelhadi, Magdi. "Hundreds of Saudi Clerics 'Dismissed.'" BBC News, May 30, 2003. news.bbc.co.uk.

Abdulwahid, Abdulaziz. "Foul Play Suspected in Sakaka Club Fire." *Arab News*, January 15, 2009.

Abdurredha, Sultan Kamal. "Effective Water Management Plan Needed." *Oman Daily Observer*, March 11, 1995.

Abedin, Mahan. "Dossier: Hezb al-Daawa al-Islamiyya (Islamic Call Party)." *Middle East Intelligence Bulletin,* June 2003.

Abou-Alsamh, Rasheed. "Saudi Women Unveil Opinions Online." *Christian Science Monitor*, June 19, 2006.

Abou El Fadl, Khaled. *Speaking in God's Name: Islamic Law, Authority and Women.* Oxford: One World, 2001.

Abrahamian, Ervand. *Khomeinism: Essays on the Islamic Republic*. Berkeley: University of California Press, 1993.

"Abu Dhabi Policy Agenda 2007–2008, Executive Summary." http://www.abudhabi.ae.

Abu Taleb, Hasan. "The Shi'ite Question in Saudi Arabia." Middle East Report, no. 45, September 19, 2005. http://merln.ndu.edu.

"Accountability Authority Set Up to Improve Government Efficiency in UAE." *Khaleej Times*, December 21, 2008.

"Achieving Middle East Stability Requires Inclusion and Solidarity Say Regional Leaders." World Economic Forum press release, May 19, 2007. www.weforum.org (October 25, 2007).

"Adapt or Die." *The Economist*, March 4, 2004.

Agence France Presse. "Bahrain Detains Moderator of Online Forum." March 5, 2001.

———. "Kuwait's Emir Blasts Parliament." *Maktoob*, April 26, 2010. http://business.maktoob.com.

———. "Online Forum Moderator Held in Bahrain." March 2, 2005.

———. "Saudi Ismailis Want Greater Say in Kingdom." *Daily Star* (Lebanon), September 22, 2005. www.dailystar.com.lb.

———. "Saudi Tribal Chief Urges Opposition in Security Forces." August 24, 2007.

———. "Saudi Women Stage Rare University Demo—Reports." *Daily Star* (Lebanon), August 4, 2009. www.dailystar.com.lb.

———. "UAE Is World's Third-Biggest Arms Importer: Think-Tank." *Defence Talk*, April 28, 2009. www.defencetalk.com.

———. "Watchdog Blasts Kuwait over Corruption Ranking." October 9, 2007. www.arabia.msn.com (October 16, 2007).

Akbar, Arifa. "Hello Boys: Lingerie Leads the Fight for Saudi Women's Rights." *Independent News*, April 27, 2006.

Akeel, Maha. "More Women Consultants Join Shura." *Arab News*, June 29, 2006.

———. "New Panel Disappoints Women." *Arab News*, January 1, 2006.

———. "Woman Appointed to Top Health Post in Jeddah." *Arab News*, July 12, 2004.

———. "Women Create History in JCCI Poll." *Arab News*, December 1, 2005.

———. "Women in JCCI Poll Fray." *Arab News*, October 3, 2005.

Akeel, Maha, and Hassan Adawi. "Abdullah Wins Applause for Assurance on Women Driving." *Arab News*, October 15, 2005.

Al'Abdallah. *Qirā'ah fī 'l-Marsūm bi-Qānūn raqam 56/2002*. September 2, 2002. www.aldemokrati.org (June 20, 2003).

Alhaj, Abdullah Juma. "The Political Elite and the Introduction of Political Participation in Oman." *Middle East Policy* 7, no. 3 (2000): 97–110.

———. "The Politics of Participation in the Gulf Cooperation Council States: The Omani Consultative Council." *Middle East Journal* 50, no. 4 (1996): 559–571.

Ali, Syed. *Dubai: Gilded Age*. New Haven: Yale University Press, 2010.

Ali, Tariq. *The Clash of Fundamentalisms: Crusades, Jihads and Modernity*. London: Verso, 2002.

Alkhereiji, Mohammed. "The Pros and Cons of Extremist Websites," *Daily Star* (Lebanon), June 4, 2004.

Allam, Abeer. "Riyadh Confronts Growing Shia Anger," *Financial Times*, March 25, 2009.

Allawi, Ali A. *The Occupation of Iraq: Winning the War, Losing the Peace.* New Haven: Yale University Press, 2007.

Allen, Calvin H., and W. Lynn Rigsbee II. *Oman Under Qaboos: From Coup to Constitution, 1970–1996*. London: Frank Cass, 2000.

Alshayeji, Abdullah. "Beyond Women's Suffrage in Kuwait." *Arab Reform Bulletin* 3, no. 6 (2005).

———. "Women's Suffrage Means Deep Change in Kuwaiti Politics." *Daily Star* (Lebanon), July 27, 2005.

Alterman, Jon B. *New Media, New Politics? From Satellite Television to the Internet in the Arab World.* Washington, DC: Washington Institute for Near East Policy, 1998.

Alturki, Noura. "Gender Analysis of the Eighth National Development Plan

(2005–2009).” Unpublished manuscript, Khadijah Bint Khuwailid Businesswomen Center, Jeddah, August 27, 2007.

Ambah, Faiza Selah. “Saudi Women Recall a Day of Driving: Women Who Protested in 1990 Reunite as Debate over Women Drivers Returns.” *Christian Science Monitor*, December 7, 2005.

Amirahmadi, H., ed. *Small Islands Big Politics: The Tonbs and Abu Musa in the Gulf.* London: Macmillan, 1996.

Amnesty International. “Saudi Arabia: Detention Without Trial of Suspected Political Opponents.” London, January 11, 1990.

———. “Shi‘a Men and Teenagers Held Incommunicado by Saudi Arabian Authorities.” London, March 23, 2009.

Anderson, Benedict. *Imagined Communities: Reflections on the Origin and Spread of Nationalism*, rev. ed. London: Verso, 1991.

Anderson, Irvine H. *Aramco, the United States, and Saudi Arabia: A Study of the Dynamics of Foreign Oil Policy, 1933–1950.* Princeton: Princeton University Press, 1981.

Anderson, Jon W. *Arabizing the Internet.* Abu Dhabi: Emirates Center for Strategic Studies and Research, 1998.

———. “New Media, New Publics: Reconfiguring the Public Sphere of Islam.” *Social Research* 70, no. 3 (2003): 887–906.

Anderson, Lisa. “Dynasts and Nationalists: Why Monarchies Survive.” In *Middle East Monarchies: The Challenge of Modernity*, ed. Joseph Kostiner (Boulder: Lynne Rienner, 2000), pp. 53–69.

———. “Searching Where the Light Shines: Studying Democratization in the Middle East.” *Annual Review of Political Science* 9 (February 7, 2006): 189–214.

Angrist, Michelle P. “The Outlook for Authoritarianism.” In *Authoritarianism in the Middle East: Regimes and Resistance*, eds. Marsha P. Posusney and Michelle P. Angrist (Boulder: Lynne Rienner, 2005), p. 227.

Anscombe, Frederick F. *The Ottoman Gulf: The Creation of Kuwait, Saudi Arabia, and Qatar.* New York: Columbia University Press, 1997.

“Apathy Reflects Women’s Mindset,” *Gulf News*, June 28, 2006.

“Arab Satellite Television: From the Periphery to Center.” Emirates Center for Strategic Studies and Research, August 11, 2004. www.ecssr.ac.ae.

“Arab Satellite Television—The World Through Their Eyes.” *The Economist*, February 24, 2005.

Arabic Network for Human Rights Information (ANHRI). “New Security Measures Against Internet Cafes.” Cairo, April 19, 2009.

al-Asadi, Mukhtar. *Al-Taqsir al-Kabir Bayna al-Salah wa al-Islah* [Mere Passive Goodness Falls Far Short of Active Reform]. Beirut: Dar al-Furat, 2001.

Assad, Ragui, and Farzaneh Roudi-Fahimi. “Youth in the Middle East and North Africa: Demographic Opportunity or Challenge?” Population Reference Bureau, Washington, DC, April 2007.

Assiri, Abdhul Ridha. *Kuwait’s Foreign Policy: City-State in World Politics.* Boulder: Westview, 1990.

Avebury, Eric. “Bahrain Seminar.” *Voice of Bahrain* 9, no. 140 (2003).

Ayoubi, Nazih N. *Over-Stating the Arab State: Politics and Society in the Middle East.* London: I. B. Tauris, 1999.

Azimi, Negar. “Bloggers Against Torture.” *The Nation*, February 19, 2007.

Aziz, Talib M. “An Islamic Perspective of Political Economy: The Views of (Late) Muhammad Baqir al-Sadr.” *Al-Tawhid Islamic Journal* (Qom) 10, no. 1 (1993). www.al-islam.org.

———. “The Political Theory of Muhammad Baqir Sadr in Shii Political Activism in Iraq from 1958 to 1980.” *International Journal of Middle East Studies* 25, no. 2 (1993): 207–222.

Baaklini, Abdo, Guilain Denoeux, and Robert Springborg. *Legislative Politics in the Arab World: The Resurgence of Democratic Institutions*. Boulder: Lynne Rienner, 1999.

“Bahrain Plans to Buy Air-to-Air Missiles.” *Gulf Daily News*, August 9, 2009.

“Bahraini Labor Minister Warns of Asian Tsunami,” *Asharq Al-Awsat*, January 27, 2008.

“al-Bahrayn tantasir li-l-dīmuqrātīyah: al-Mushārakah fāqat al-tawaqqu‘āt .. wa-haqqaqat 53.2 %.” *al-Ayyām* (Manama), October 25, 2002.

El-Baltaji, Dana. “Dubai: An Emerging Arab Media Hub.” *Arab Media and Society*, no. 3 (Fall 2007). www.arabmediasociety.org.

Barakat, Halim. *The Arab World: Society, Culture, and State*. Berkeley: University of California Press, 1993.

Barnett, Michael N., and F. Gregory Gause III. “Caravans in Opposite Directions: Society, State, and the Development of Community in the Gulf Cooperation Council.” In *Security Communities*, eds. Emanuel Adler and Michael N. Barnett (Cambridge: Cambridge University Press, 1998), pp. 161–197.

Barth, Fredrik. *Sohar: Culture and Society in an Omani Town*. Baltimore: Johns Hopkins University Press, 1983.

Batatu, Hanna. “Shi‘ite Organizations in Iraq: Al-Da’wah al-Islamiyah and al-Mujahidin.” In *Shi‘ism and Social Protest*, eds. Juan R. I. Cole and Nikki R. Keddie (New Haven: Yale University Press, 1986), pp. 179–200.

Beatty, Jack. “Fatal Vision.” *Atlantic Unbound*, May 1, 2003. www.theatlantic.com (August 4, 2006).

Beblawi, Hazem. “The Rentier State in the Arab World.” In *The Arab State*, ed. Giacomo Luciani (Berkeley: University of California Press, 1990), pp. 85–98.

Beeman, William O. *The “Great Satan” vs. the “Mad Mullahs”: How the United States and Iran Demonize Each Other*. Westport: Praeger, 2005.

Beinart, Peter. “The Rehabilitation of the Cold-War Liberal.” *New York Times Magazine*, April 30, 2006.

Benjamin, Daniel, and Gabriel Weimann. “What the Terrorists Have in Mind.” *New York Times*, October 27, 2004.

Bertelsmann Stiftung, ed. *Bertelsmann Transformation Index 2006: Toward Democracy and a Market Economy*. Bielefeld: Verlag Bertelsmann Stiftung, 2006.

———, ed. *Bertelsmann Transformation Index 2008: Political Management in International Comparison*. Bielefeld: Verlag Bertelsmann Stiftung, 2008.

———, ed. *Bertelsmann Transformation Index 2010*. Bielefeld: Verlag Bertelsmann Stiftung, forthcoming.

Bill, James A. “The Geometry of Instability in the Gulf: The Rectangle of Tension.” In *Iran and the Gulf: A Search for Stability*, ed. J. S. Al-Suwaidi (Abu Dhabi: Emirates Center for Strategic Studies and Research, 1996), pp. 99–117.

Bin Khalid, S., and P. Seale. *Desert Warrior: A Personal View of the Gulf War by the Joint Forces Commander*. New York: HarperCollins, 1995.

Bin Khalifa al-Thani, Emir Hamad. “Out of the Fog Through Arab Reform.” *Daily Star* (Lebanon), June 21, 2004. www.dailystar.com.lb.

“Bin Laden: An Apocalyptic Sect Severed from Political Islam.” *East European Constitutional Review* 10, no. 4 (2001): 108–114.

Bin Rashid Al Maktoum, His Highness Shaikh Mohammed. "Women in the UAE." 1999. www.sheikhmohammed.co.ae.

Bjornulund, Eric C. *Beyond Free and Fair: Monitoring Elections and Building Democracy.* Washington, DC: Woodrow Wilson Center Press, 2004.

Black, Ian. "Intellectuals Condemn Fatwa Against Writers." *The Guardian*, April 3, 2008.

———. "Saudi Arabia Leads the Arab Regimes in Internet Censorship." *The Guardian*, June 30, 2009.

Blanchard, Christopher M., and Richard F. Grimmet. "The Gulf Security Dialogue and Related Arms Sales Proposals." Congressional Research Service, October 8, 2008.

"Bloggers in Mideast Transforming Dialogue but Face Clampdowns by Authorities." Associated Press, February 9, 2007.

Boix, Carles, and Susan C. Stokes. "Endogenous Democratization." *World Politics* 55, no. 4 (2003): 517–549.

Bondoc, Jarius. "Veronica Pedrosa Joins 'Hated' Al-Jazeera TV." *Philippine Star,* December 7, 2005.

Boustany, Nora. "Al-Jazeera's Learning Curve." *Washington Post*, April 30, 2004.

———. "Shiite Muslims in Saudi Arabia Emboldened by Hussein's Fall." *Washington Post*, April 23, 2003.

Boyner, Mike. "Al-Jazeera's Brand Name News." *Foreign Policy*, April 18, 2005.

Bradley, John R. "Can Saudi Arabia Reform Itself?" *Daily Star* (Lebanon), September 5, 2003. www.dailystar.com.lb.

———. "Emboldened Shi'ites." *Al-Ahram Weekly*, May 15–21, 2003. http://weekly.ahram.org.eg.

Bromley, Simon. *Rethinking Middle East Politics*. Austin: University of Texas Press, 1994.

Brown, Nathan J. *Constitutions in a Non-constitutional World: Arab Basic Laws and the Prospects for Accountable Government*. Albany: SUNY Press, 2002.

———. "Kuwait's 2008 Parliamentary Elections: A Setback for Democratic Islamism?" Carnegie Endowment for International Peace, Web Commentary, May 2008. www.carnegieendowment.org.

———. "Pushing Toward Party Politics? Kuwait's Islamic Constitutional Movement." Carnegie Endowment for International Peace Democracy and Rule of Law Project, Carnegie Paper no. 79. Washington, DC, January 2007.

———. *The Rule of Law in the Arab World: Courts in Egypt and the Gulf.* Cambridge: Cambridge University Press, 1997.

———. "What's at Stake in Kuwait's Parliamentary Elections?" Carnegie Endowment for International Peace, Web Commentary, May 7, 2008. www.carnegieendowment.org.

Brumberg, Daniel. "The Trap of Liberalized Autocracy." *Journal of Democracy* 13, no. 4 (2002): 56–68.

Buchan, James. "Secular and Religious Opposition in Saudi Arabia." In *State, Society and Economy in Saudi Arabia*, ed. Tim Niblock (London: Croom Helm, 1982).

Bull-Berg, Hans Jacob. *American International Oil Policy: Causal Factors and Effects.* New York: Palgrave Macmillan, 1987.

Bunce, Valerie J., and Sharon L. Wolchik. "Defeating Dictators: Electoral Change and Stability in Competitive Authoritarian Regimes." *World Politics* 62, no. 1 (2010): 43–86.

Burnham, Gilbert, Riyadh Lafta, Shannon Doocy, and Les Roberts. "Mortality After the 2003 Invasion of Iraq: A Cross-Sectional Cluster Sample Survey." The Lancet Online, October 11, 2006. www.thelancet.com.

Bush, George W. "State of the Union Address," February 2, 2005. www.whitehouse.gov (April 27, 2006).

"Bush's Domino Theory." Editorial, *Christian Science Monitor*, January 28, 2003. www.csmonitor.com (August 3, 2006).

Butenshøn, Nila, Uri Davis, and M. Hassassian, eds. *Citizenship and the State in the Middle East: Approaches and Applications*. Syracuse: Syracuse University Press, 2000.

Caldicott, Helen, and Craig Eisendrath. *War in Heaven: Stopping the Arms Race in Outer Space Before It's Too Late*. New York: New Press, 2007.

Carothers, Thomas. "The End of the Transition Paradigm." *Journal of Democracy* 13, no. 1 (2002).

Carter, Jimmy. "State of the Union Address," January 23, 1980. www.jimmycarterlibrary.org (August 3, 2006).

CIA (Central Intelligence Agency). *World Factbook, 2010*. New York: CIA, 2009.

———. *World Factbook, Qatar, 2010*. New York: CIA. www.cia.gov.

Chalcraft, John. "Monarchy, Migration, and Hegemony in the Arabian Peninsula." Paper prepared for the Kuwait Programme in Globalization and Governance, London, June 2010.

Chandrasekaran, Rajiv. *Imperial Life in the Emerald City: Inside Iraq's Green Zone*. New York: Knopf, 2006.

Chapin Metz, Helen, ed. *Saudi Arabia: A Country Study*. Washington, DC: Government Printing Office for the Library of Congress, 1992. http://countrystudies.us.

Chatty, Dawn. *Mobile Pastoralists: Development Planning and Social Change in Oman*. New York: Columbia University Press, 1996.

———. "Women Working in Oman: Individual Choice and Cultural Constraints." *International Journal of Middle East Studies* 32, no. 2 (2000): 249–250.

Chatty, Dawn, and J. E. Peterson. "Oman." In *Countries and Their Cultures*, vol. 3, eds. Melvin Ember and Carol R. Ember (New York: Macmillan Reference USA, 2001), pp. 1681–1689.

Chaudhry, Kirin Aziz. *The Price of Wealth: Economies and Institutions in the Middle East*. Ithaca: Cornell University Press, 1997.

Chisholm, Archibald H. T. *The First Kuwait Oil Concession Agreement: A Record of the Negotiations, 1911–1934*. London: Frank Cass, 1975.

"Chronology." *Middle East Journal* 48, no. 2 (1994): 351.

———. *Middle East Journal* 57, no. 4 (2003): 656.

———. *Middle East Journal* 58, no. 3 (2004): 490.

Chubin, Shahram, and Charles Tripp. *Iran and Iraq at War*. Boulder: Westview, 1988.

"Civic Society." *Weekly Diwaniya*, July 3, 2007. www.moinfo.gov.kw.

Clarke, Richard A. *Against All Enemies: Inside America's War on Terror*. New York: Free Press, 2004.

Clinton, William Jefferson. "State of the Union, 1994," delivered version. January 25, 1994. www.let.rug.nl (February 22, 2006).

Cochrane, Paul. "Saudia Arabia's Energy Infrastructure Faces Terror Threat." *Daily Star* (Lebanon), December 2, 2004. www.dailystar.com.lb.

"Cohen Criticizes 'Wag the Dog' Characterization: Former Defense Secretary Testifies Before 9/11 Panel." CNN. www.cnn.com (February 22, 2006).

Cole, Juan. "The Iraqi Constitution DOA?" *Salon*, August 26, 2005. http://dir.salon.com.

———. "Marriage mal assorti entre les radicaux chiites irakiens et les États-Unis." *Le Monde diplomatique*, July 2003. www.monde-diplomatique.fr.

———. "The New and Improved Iraq." *In These Times*, June 22, 2004. www.in thesetimes.com.

———. "Portrait of a Rebellion: Shi'ite Insurgency in Iraq Bedevils U.S." *In These Times*, May 24, 2004. www.inthesetimes.com.

———. "Putin's War Enablers: Bush and Cheney." Salon.com, August 14, 2008. www.salon.com (August 14, 2008).

———. "The Rise of Religious and Ethnic Mass Politics in Iraq." In *Religion and Nationalism in Iraq: A Comparative Perspective*, eds. David Little and Donald K. Swearer (Cambridge, MA: Center for the Study of the World Religions/Harvard University Press, 2006), pp. 43–62.

———. *Sacred Space and Holy War: The Politics, Culture, and History of Shi'ite Islam*. London: I. B. Tauris, 2002.

———. "Saving Iraq: Mission Impossible." *Salon*, May 11, 2006. www.salon.com.

———. "Shi'a Militias in Iraqi Politics." In *Iraq: Preventing a New Generation of Conflict*, eds. Markus E. Bouillon, David M. Malone, and Ben Roswell (Boulder: Lynne Rienner, 2007), pp. 109–123.

———. "UIA Will Hold Secret Ballot." Informed Comment, February 22, 2005. www.juancole.com.

———. "The United States and Shi'ite Religious Factions in Post-Ba'athist Iraq." *Middle East Journal* 57, no. 4 (2003): 543–566.

Coll, Steve. *Ghost Wars: The Secret History of the CIA, Afghanistan, and Bin Laden, from the Soviet Invasion to September 10, 2001*. New York: Penguin, 2004.

———. "In the Gulf, Dissidence Goes Digital." *Washington Post*, March 29, 2005.

———. "Text Messaging Is New Tool of Political Underground." *Washington Post*, March 29, 2005.

Colley, Linda. *Captives: The Story of Britain's Pursuit of Empire and How Its Soldiers and Civilians Were Held Captive by the Dream of Global Supremacy, 1600–1850*. New York: Pantheon, 2002.

"Confidence Will Never Return to Dubai." *The Times* (London), December 5, 2009.

Connolly, Matthew. 2001. "Rethinking the Cold War and Decolonization: The Grand Strategy of the Algerian War for Independence." *International Journal of Middle East Studies* 33, no. 2 (2001): 221–245.

Conservative Caucus. "Wag the Dog? U.S. Policy on Iraq." Excerpted from *Howard Phillips Issues and Strategy Bulletin*, December 31, 1998. www.conservative usa.org (February 22, 2006).

Cordesman, Anthony H. *The Gulf and the West: Strategic Relations and Military Realities*. London: Mansell, 1988.

———. *The Gulf and the West: Strategic Relations and Military Realities*. London: Mansell, 1999.

———. *Kuwait*. Boulder: Westview, 1997.

———. *Saudi Arabia Enters the Twenty-First Century: The Military and International Security Dimensions*. Westport, CT: Praeger, 2003.

———. *Saudi Arabia: Guarding the Desert Kingdom*. Boulder: Westview, 1997.

Cordesman, Anthony H., and Abraham R. Wagner. *The Lessons of Modern War*, vol. 22, *The Iran-Iraq War*. Boulder: Westview, 1991.

Crane, Conrad C., and W. Andrew Terrill. "Reconstructing Iraq: Insights, Challenges, and Missions for Military Forces in a Post-Conflict Scenario." Carlisle, PA: US Army War College Strategic Studies Institute, February 2003.

Crystal, Jill. "Authoritarianism and Its Adversaries in the Arab World." *World Politics* 46, no. 2 (1994): 262–289.
———. *Oil and Politics in the Gulf: Rulers and Merchants in Kuwait and Qatar.* New York: Cambridge University Press, 1990.
"Culture Test for Residency Visa by UAE." *Emirates Update*, July 9, 2009. http://emiratesupdate.wordpress.com.
Dagher, Sam. "Gulf Bloggers: A New Breed of Arab Activists." Middle East Online, August 4, 2006. www.middle-east online.com (August 9, 2007).
Dahir, Ma'sud. *al-Istimrariyah wa-al-taghyir fi tajribat al-tahdith al-'Umaniyah, 1970–2005*. Beirut: Dar al-Farabi, 2008.
Al-Dakhil, Khalid. "Quiet Time." *New York Times*, November 27, 2004.
———. "2003: Saudi Arabia's Year of Reform." *Arab Reform Bulletin* 2, no. 3 (2004).
Daniels, John. *Kuwait Journey.* Luton, England: White Crescent, 1971.
Danner, Mark. "The Secret Way to War." *New York Review of Books*, June 9, 2005, pp. 70–74.
Daragahi, Borzou, and Noha El Hennawym. "Egypt's Dissidents Held Down by Law." *Los Angeles Times*, June 12, 2007. www.latimes.com (June 19, 2007).
"The Dark Side of Dubai." *The Independent*, April 7, 2009.
Davidson, Christopher M. *Dubai: The Vulnerability of Success.* New York: Columbia University Press, 2008.
———. *The United Arab Emirates: A Study in Survival.* Boulder: Lynne Rienner, 2005.
Deák, István. "Did the Revolution Have to Fail?" *New York Review*, March 1, 2007. www.nybooks.com (July 8, 2007).
De Borchgrave, Arnaud. "Tutwiler's Mission Impossible." *Washington Times*, May 7, 2004.
Deen, Thalif. "Is Al-Jazeera the New Symbol of Arab Nationalism?" Inter Press Service, October 12, 2004.
Dekmejian, Richard. "The Liberal Impulse in Saudi Arabia." *Middle East Journal* 57, no. 3 (2003): 400–413.
DePalma, Anthony. "Saudi Case Casting a Light on How Militants Infiltrate and Exploit Canada." *New York Times*, May 4, 1997.
Deutsch, Karl. *Political Community in the North Atlantic Area: International Organization in Light of Historical Experience.* Princeton: Princeton University Press, 1957.
Diamond, Larry. *Squandered Victory: The American Occupation and the Bungled Effort to Bring Democracy to Iraq*. New York: Holt, 2005.
———. "Thinking About Hybrid Regimes." *Journal of Democracy* 13, no. 2 (2002): 21–35.
Dickson, H. R. P. *Kuwait and Her Neighbours.* London: Allen & Unwin, 1956.
Dietl, Gulshan. *Through Two Wars and Beyond: A Study of the Gulf Cooperation Council*. New Delhi: Lancers, 1991.
Dinmore, Guy, and Roula Khala. "The US National Interest Is Caught Up with the Saudis in a Very Complex Way: They Are More Than a Gas Pump." *Financial Times*, November 19, 2003.
Donno, Hisham, Daniela Donno, and Bruce Russett. "Islam, Authoritarianism, and Female Empowerment: What Are the Linkages?" *World Politics* 56, no. 4 (2004): 582–607.
Doumato, Eleanor. "Separate and Unequal: Sex Segregation Is a Saudi National Obsession." Op-ed, Brown University News Service, March 2002.

Doumato, Eleanor Abdella, and Gregory Starrett. 2006. *Teaching Islam: Textbooks and Religion in the Middle East*. Boulder: Lynne Rienner, 2007.

Doyle, Michael. "Liberalism and World Politics." *American Political Science Review* 80, no. 4 (1986): 1151–1169.

Draper, Theodore. "Falling Dominoes." *New York Review of Books*, October 27, 1983. www.nybooks.com (February 13, 2006).

———. *A Very Thin Line: The Iran-Contra Affairs*. New York: Touchstone, 1991.

"Driving Ban Stays for Women." BBC, June 13, 2005.

Drysdale, Alasdair. "Population Dynamics and Birth Spacing in Oman." *International Journal of Middle East Studies* 42, no. 1 (2010): 123–144.

"Dubai Government Pledges War Against Corruption." Emirates News Agency (WAM), August 18, 2008.

"Echoes of Iraq Haunt U.S. Effort to Calm Russia-Georgia Fight." *Detroit Free Press*, August 12, 2008. www.freep.com (August 15, 2008).

Ehrenhaus, Peter, and A. Susan Owen. "Race Lynching and Christian Evangelicalism: Performances of Faith." *Text and Performance Quarterly* 24, nos. 3–4 (2005): 276–301.

Ehteshami, Anoushiravan, and Steven Wright, eds. *Reform in the Middle East Oil Monarchies* (Berkshire, UK: Ithaca Press, 2008), pp. 3–45.

Eickelman, Christine. *Women and Community in Oman*. New York: New York University Press, 1984.

Eickelman, Dale F. "From Theocracy to Monarchy: Authority and Legitimacy in Inner Oman, 1935–1957." *International Journal of Middle East Studies* 17, no. 1 (1985): 3–24.

———. "Kings and People: Oman's State Consultative Council." *Middle East Journal* 38, no. 1 (1984): 51–84.

al-Ekri, Abd al-Nabi. "Bahrain: al-Wefaq and the Challenges of Participation." *Arab Reform Bulletin* 5, no. 4 (2007).

Elias, Diana. "Kuwait Blocks Sites That Incite Violence." *USA Today*, February 8, 2005.

Eltahawy, Mona. "Happy Birthday, Saudi Arabia." Middle East Online, September 25, 2007.

Embassy of the Kingdom of Saudi Arabia. "Human Rights Commission to Open Women's Section in Riyadh." September 4, 2008. www.saudiembassy.net.

"Emirate Prince Ousted in Women's Rights Row." *Daily Telegraph*, June 15, 2003. www.telegraph.co.uk (March 11, 2008).

England, Andrew. "King Abdullah Seeks Stability by Reaching Out on Religion." *Financial Times*, June 24, 2008.

Englehart, Tom. "Permanent Bases the World Over: Behold the American Empire." Alternet. www.alternet.org (June 14, 2007).

Esposito, John. *The Islamic Threat: Myth or Reality*. Oxford: Oxford University Press, 1992.

Etheridge, Jamie. "Historic First: Kuwaiti Women Vote, Run." *Christian Science Monitor*, April 5, 2006. www.csmonitor.com (June 16, 2007).

"The Executive Council, Policy Agenda 2007–2008: The Emirate of Abu Dhabi." www.gulfnews.com (October 24, 2007).

Fakhro, Munīra. *Al-Mujtama' al-madanī wa-l-tahawwul al-dīmūqrātī fī 'l-Bahrayn*. Cairo: Markaz Ibn Khaldūn, 1995.

Fallows, James. "The Fifty-First State?" *Atlantic Monthly*, November 2002. www.theatlantic.com (March 4, 2003).

Fandy, Mamoun. *Saudi Arabia and the Politics of Dissent*. New York: Palgrave Macmillan, 2001.

———. "Where's the Arab Media's Sense of Outrage?" *Gulf News*, July 14, 2004.

Farrell, Stephen. "Election: Preliminary Results." *New York Times*, February 5, 2009.

al-Fassi, Hatun Ajwad. "Haqq al-nisa' fi al-salaat fi al-Haram al-Mecca." *al Iqtisadiah*, August 4, 2006.

Fattah, Hassan M. "Arab Media Focus on Voting, Not Violence." *New York Times*, January 31, 2005.

Fattah, Hassan M., and Rasheed Abou al-Samh. "Saudi Shiites Fear Gains Could Be Lost." *New York Times*, February 5, 2007.

"Fatwa for Anthony Shadid." [in Arabic] www.sistani.org; reported in Anthony Shadid and Rajiv Chandrasekaran, "Cleric Renews Call for Iraq Elections." *Washington Post*, November 29, 2003.

"Fawz al-Ja'fari . . ." *al-Zaman*, February 13, 2006.

Feigenbaum, Harvey B. *Politics of Public Enterprise: Oil and the French State*. Princeton: Princeton University Press, 1985.

Fergany, Nader. "Aspects of Labor Migration and Unemployment in the Arab Region." Almishkat Center for Research, Cairo, Egypt. www.mafhoum.com.

Feuilherade, Peter. "Al-Arabiya TV—Profile." BBC News, November 25, 2003.

"$15b. for Qatar Tourism." *Daily Star* (Lebanon), May 3, 2004.

"Film Exposes Immigrants to Dutch Liberalism." MSNBC, March 16, 2006. www.msnbc.msn.com.

Fischer, David Hackett. *Albion's Seed: Four British Folkways in America*. New York: Oxford University Press, 1989.

Fish, M. Steven. "Islam and Authoritarianism." *World Politics* 55, no. 1 (2002): 4–37.

Fisher, William. "Arab Internet Users Are Caught in a Terrible Web." *Daily Star* (Lebanon), December 7, 2004.

"Five Gulf States Threaten to Punish Al-Jazeera TV." Reuters, October 11, 2002.

Fleishman, Jeffrey. "Saudi Arabia's King Abdullah Appoints Moderates to Key Posts." *Los Angeles Times,* February 15, 2009.

Foran, John. *Fragile Resistance: Social Transformation in Iran from 1500 to the Revolution*. Boulder: Westview, 1993.

———. *The Future of Revolutions: Rethinking Radical Change in the Age of Globalization.* London: Zed, 2003.

———, ed. 1997. *Theorizing Revolutions*. New York: Routledge, 1997.

Franks, Thomas. 2005. *What's the Matter with Kansas*. New York: Holt, 2005.

Freedom House. *Freedom in the World—2009: Oman*. July 16, 2009. www.unhcr.org.

———. *Freedom in the World: Qatar.* 2003. www.freedomhouse.org.

Fromkin, David. 1978. *A Peace to End All Peace: The Fall of the Ottoman Empire and the Creation.* New York: Avon.

Fukuyama, Francis. *The End of History and the Last Man*. London: HarperPerennial, 1993.

"G-8 Greater Middle East Partnership Working Paper." *Middle East Intelligence Bulletin*, February 13, 2004. www.meib.org (July 14, 2006).

Gaddis, John Lewis. *Frontline*. January 16, 2003. www.pbs.org (July 14, 2006).

El Gamal, Rania. "God Save Nasrallah." *Kuwait Times*, August 3, 2006.

———. "Kuwait Curbs Tribal Primaries Ahead of Election." Reuters, March 27, 2008. www.reuters.com (July 27, 2008).

Gardner, Richard N. *Sterling-Dollar Diplomacy in Current Perspective: The Origins and the Prospects of Our International Economic Order*. New York: Columbia University Press, 1980.

Gasiorowski, Mark J. "The 1953 Coup d'État in Iran." *International Journal of Middle East Studies* 19, no. 3 (1987): 261–286.

———. *U.S. Foreign Policy and the Shah: Building a Client State in Iran.* Ithaca: Cornell University Press, 1991.

Gause, F. Gregory III. "Iraq's Decisions to Go to War, 1980 and 1990." *Middle East Journal* 56, no. 1 (2002): 47–70.

———. *Oil Monarchies: Domestic and Security Challenges in the Arab Gulf States.* New York: Council on Foreign Relations, 1994.

———. "Question Time." *National Newspaper* (UAE), June 18, 2009. www.thenational.ae.

———. "Saudi Islamists: Challenge or Support for Saudi Stability and Security?" Paper presented at the National Defense University conference, Washington, DC, April 2004.

Gavrielides, Nicolas. "Tribal Democracy: The Anatomy of Parliamentary Elections in Kuwait." In *Elections in the Middle East: Implications of Recent Trends*, ed. Lynda Layne (Boulder: Westview, 1987), pp. 153–223.

Gellman, Barton. *Angler: The Cheney Vice Presidency*. New York: Penguin, 2008.

Ghabra, Shafeeq. "Kuwait and the Dynamics of Socio-Economic Change." *Middle East Journal* 51, no. 3 (1997): 358–372.

Ghabra, Shafeeq, with Margreet Arnold. "Studying the American Way: An Assessment of American-Style Higher Education in Arab Countries." Policy Focus no. 71. Washington, DC: Washington Institute for Near East Policy, June 2007.

Ghafour, Abdul. "First Independent Human Rights Organization Established." *Arab News*, March 3, 2004.

———. "Qataris Stripped of Citizenship Cry Foul." *Arab News*, April 2, 2005.

Al-Ghanim, Mohammed. "Republicanism and the Failure of Elite-Pacted Transitions in Syria, 1961–1963." Unpublished manuscript, 2009.

———. "'Transitions to Nowhere?' Kuwait and the Challenge of Political Liberalization." Paper presented at the annual meeting of the Northeast Political Science Association, Philadelphia, November 2009.

Ghareeb, Edmund. "New Media and the Information Revolution in the Arab World: An Assessment." *Middle East Journal* 54, no. 3 (2000): 395–418.

Ghassan Salamé, ed. *Democracy Without Democrats: The Renewal of Politics in the Muslim World.* London: I. B. Tauris, 1994.

Ghazal, Rym. "New Saudi Law Ends Glaring Contradiction." *Daily Star* (Lebanon), September 19, 2007.

Ghazaleh, Dalal Abu. "Gulf States to Levy VAT from 2005." *Gulf News*, October 18, 2004.

Gilpin, Robert. *War and Change in World Politics.* New York: Cambridge University Press, 1981.

"Glacier in the Desert." *The Economist*, January 5, 2006.

Glosemeyer, Iris. "Checks, Balances and Transformation in the Saudi Political System." In *Saudi Arabia in the Balance: Political Economy, Society, Foreign Affairs*, eds. Paul Aarts and Gerd Nonneman (London: Hurst, 2005), pp. 214–233.

Goldberg, Ellis, Erik Wibbels, and Eric Mvukiyehe. "Lessons from Strange Cases: Democracy, Development, and the Resource Curse in the U.S. States." *Comparative Political Studies* 41, nos. 4–5 (2008): 477–514.

Goldberg, J. "The Sh'i Minority in Saudi Arabia." In *Shiism and Social Protest*, eds. J. Cole and N. Keddie (New York: Yale University Press, 1986), pp. 230–246.

Goldberg, Michelle. *Kingdom Coming: The Rise of Christian Nationalism*. New York: Norton, 2006.

Goldsmith, Jack. *The Terror Presidency: Law and Judgment Inside the Bush Administration*. New York: Norton, 2007.

Gordon, Michael R., and Bernard E. Trainor. *Cobra II: The Inside Story of the Invasion and Occupation of Iraq*. New York: Pantheon, 2006.

"Government of Kuwait Steps Down." BBC News, March 4, 2007. http://news.bbc.co.uk (August 8, 2007).

Greenwald, Glenn. *A Tragic Legacy: How a Good vs. Evil Mentality Destroyed the Bush Presidency*. New York: Crown Books, 2007.

Guazzone, Laura. "Gulf Cooperation Council: The Security Policies." *Survival* 30, no. 2 (1988): 134–148.

"Gulf States Suffer Erosion of Culture." *Gulf News*, October 1, 2007.

Habboush, Mahmoud. "FNC Members Ask for New Elections." *The National*, March 10, 2010.

Habermas, Jürgen. *The Structural Transformation of the Public Sphere: An Inquiry into a Category of Bourgeois Society*. Thomas Burger and Fredrick Lawrence, trans. Cambridge: MIT Press, 1991.

Hadid, Diaa. "National Women Demand Equal Rights as Men." *Gulf News*, January 25, 2006.

al-Haj, Abdullah Juma. "The Politics of Participation in the Gulf Cooperation Council States: The Omani Consultative Council." *Middle East Journal* 50, no. 4 (1996): 559–571.

Al Hakeem, Mariam. "Islamists Call on Saudi Leaders to Act Against 'Dangerous' Liberal Ideology." *Gulf News*, September 8, 2008.

"Al-Hakim: Yajib an yakun li al-Shi'ah Iqlimuhum fi Junub al-'Iraq." *al-Sharq al-Awsat*, August 12, 2005.

Halliday, Fred. "The Middle East and Conceptions of 'International Society.'" In *International Society and the Middle East: English School Theory at the Regional Level*, eds. Barry Buzan and Ana Gonzalez-Pelaez (London: Palgrave Macmillan, 2009), pp. 1–23.

Hammond, Andrew. "Saudi Cleric Says Shi'ites Loyal to Kingdom, Not Iran." Reuters, January 29, 2007. www.alertnet.or.

Al-Hamza, Hasan. *Shi'a fi al-Mamlaka al-Arabiyya al-Sa'udiyya*, part II. Beirut: Mu'assasa Baqi li-Ahya al-Turath, 1993, pp. 241–259.

Hardy, Roger. "Whatever Happened to Saudi Reform?" BBC News, February 6, 2008. http://news.bbc.co.uk.

Hasib, S. Waqar. "The Iranian Constitution: An Exercise in Contradictions." *Al-Nakhlah* (Spring 2004): 1–12. www.fletcher.tufts.edu.

Hassan, Oman. "First Woman Candidate Breaks Taboo in Kuwait." Middle East Online, March 22, 2006. www.middle-east-online.com (August 8, 2007).

———. "Young Kuwaitis Turn 'Orange.'" Middle East Online, May 29, 2006. www.middle-east-online.com (August 8, 2007).

Havel, Václav. "Kosovo and the End of the Nation-State." Paul Wilson, trans. *New York Review of Books*, June 10, 1999.

Heard-Bey, Frauke. "The United Arab Emirates: A Quarter Century of Federation." In *Middle East Dilemma: The Politics of Economics and Arab Integration*, ed. Michael Hudson (New York: Columbia University Press, 1999).

———. "The United Arab Emirates: Statehood and Nation-Building in a Traditional Society." *Middle East Journal* 59, no. 3 (July 2005): 357–375.

Hegghammer, Thomas, and Stephane Lacroix. "Rejectionist Islamism in Saudi

Arabia: The Story of Juhayman al-'Utaybi Revisited." *International Journal of Middle East Studies* 39, no. 1 (2007): 103–122.

Helman, Christopher. "Will Americans Tune to Al-Jazeera?" *Forbes*, July 13, 2009.

Henderson, Simon. *The New Pillar: Conservative Arab Gulf States and U.S. Strategy.* Washington, DC: Washington Institute for Near East Policy, 2003.

Herb, Michael. *All in the Family: Absolutism, Revolution, and Democracy in the Middle Eastern Monarchies*. Albany: SUNY Press, 1999.

———. "Princes and Parliaments in the Arab World." *Middle East Journal* 58, no. 3 (2004): 1–8.

———. "Taxation and Representation." *Studies in Comparative International Development* 38, no. 3 (2003): 3–31.

Hersh, Seymour. *Chain of Command: The Road from 9/11 to Abu Ghraib*. New York: HarperCollins, 2004.

———. "Preparing the Battlefield." *New Yorker*, July 9 and 16, 2007.

———. "The Redirection." *New Yorker*, March 5, 2007.

Hertog, Steffen. "Shaping the Saudi State: Human Agency's Shifting Role in Rentier State Formation." *International Journal of Middle East Studies* 39, no. 4 (2007): 539–563.

Heydemann, Steven. *Authoritarianism in Syria: Institutions and Social Conflict, 1946–1970.* Ithaca: Cornell University Press, 1999.

———. "Upgrading Authoritarianism in the Arab World." Analysis Paper no. 13. Washington, DC: Saban Center for Middle East Policy, October 2007.

"HH Sheikh Mohammad Bin Rashid Unveils the UAE Federal Government Strategy." AME Info, April 17, 2007. www.ameinfo.com (June 29, 2009).

Hicks, Neil, and Ghanim al-Najjar. "The Utility of Tradition: Civil Society in Kuwait." In *Civil Society in the Middle East*, ed. Augustus Richard Norton (New York: Brill, 1995), pp. 188–213.

"Highlights: Dubai Strategic Plan 2015: Dubai . . . Where the Future Begins." Dubai: Government of Dubai, n.d. http://egov.dubai.ae (October 24, 2007).

"Highlights of the UAE Government Strategy: Leadership . . . Integration . . . Excellence." www.wam.ae (October 24, 2007).

"Hilah Sayyarah Shabihah bi Sayyarat al-Hakim istukhdimat fi Ightiyalihi dakhil al-Masjid." *al-Sharq al-Awsat*, August 30, 2003.

"Hiring of Foreign Women in Lingerie Shops Ruled Out." *Gulf News*, April 11, 2006.

Hiro, Dilip. *The Longest War: The Iran-Iraq Military Conflict*. New York: Routledge, 1991.

Hoek, Corien. *Shifting Sands: Social-Economic Development in al-Sharqiyah Region, Oman*. Nijmegen: Nijmegen University Press, 1998.

Hofstadter, Richard. "The Paranoid Style in American Politics." *Harper's Magazine*, November 1964.

Hudson, Michael C. "After the Gulf War: Prospects for Democratization in the Arab World." *Middle East Journal* 45, no. 3 (1991): 407–426.

Hunter, Shireen T. "The Gulf Economic Crisis and Its Social and Political Consequences." *Middle East Journal* 40, no. 4 (1986): 593–613.

Human Rights Watch. *Denied Dignity: Systematic Discrimination and Hostility Toward Saudi Shi'a Citizens*. New York, September 3, 2009. www.hrw.org.

———. *Empty Reforms: Saudi Arabia's New Basic Laws.* New York: Human Rights Watch, May 1992.

———. "From Plebiscite to Contest: Egypt's Presidential Election." September 2, 2005. http://hrw.org (July 19, 2007).

———. "'The Island of Happiness': Exploitation of Migrant Workers on Saadiyat Island, Abu Dhabi." May 19. 2009. www.hrw.org.

———. "Just the Good News Please: New UAE Media Law Continues to Stifle Press." April 6, 2009. www.hrw.org.

———. "Kuwait: Free Jailed Activist." November 23, 2009. www.hrw.org.

———. "Saudi Arabia." 1996, p. 68. http://www.hrw.org.

———. "Saudi Arabia: Lift Travel Ban on Government Critics." February 14, 2007. http://hrw.org.

———. "Teachers Silenced on Blasphemy Charges." November 17, 2005. http://hrw.org.

———. "Torture Redux." February 2010. www.hrw.org (April 22, 2010).

———. "World Report 1997: Events 1996." New York: Human Rights Watch, 1996.

Huntington, Samuel P. "Democracy's Third Wave." *Journal of Democracy* 2, no. 2 (1991): 12–34.

———. *The Third Wave: Democratization in the Late Twentieth Century.* Norman: University of Oklahoma Press, 1991.

Hvidt, Martin. "The Dubai Model: An Outline of Key Development-Process Elements in Dubai." *International Journal of Middle Eastern Studies* 41 (2009): 397–418.

Ibrāhīm: Mā yahduth fī 'l-Bahrayn mazīj min al-idtihād al-tabaqī wa-l-tā'ifī [Ibrāhīm: What Happens in Bahrain Is a Combination of Class and Sectarian Oppression]. December 16, 2005. www.aldemokrati.com.

Ikenberry, G. John. *Reasons of State: Oil Politics and the Capacities of American Government.* Ithaca: Cornell University Press, 1988.

ILO (International Labour Organization). *Yearbook of Labour Statistics 2002.* Geneva: ILO, 2002.

IMF (International Monetary Fund). *World Economic Outlook: Crisis and Recovery.* Washington, DC: IMF, April 2009.

"In Defense of the Nation." Gwenn Okruhlik and Sara Youssef, trans. Gulf 2000, University of Texas, Austin. www.gulf2000.columbia.eclu.

India Office Records. R/15/7/706. "Bin Saud's Relations with Trucial Chiefs 18/3/1923–5/10/1939." British Library. http://indiafamly.bl.uk.

———. R/15/5/27. "British Relations with Ibn Sa'ud 18 March 1911–1 Oct 1920." British Library. http://indiafamly.bl.uk.

———. R/15/2/95. "Ibn Saud's Relations with Bahrain and Qatif, 19 Dec 1929–23 May 1930." British Library. http://indiafamly.bl.uk.

———. R/15/1/334. "Ibn Saud's Relations with Shaikhs: Najdis Agent's Activities 15 Apr 1923–31 Jul 1931." British Library. http://indiafamly.bl.uk.

———. R/5/2/1859. "Political Agency, Bahrain. Miscellaneous Correspondence with Amir and Notables of Najd, Hasa and Qatif." British Library. http://india famly.bl.uk.

"Inshiqaq fi Kutlat 'al-Tawafuq' . . . Hukumat al-Maliki ghayr al-Muktamalah tanal Thiqat al-Barlaman." *al-Hayat*, May 21, 2006.

International Crisis Group. "Saudi Arabia Backgrounder: Who Are the Islamists?" *Middle East Report*, no. 31 (2004): 8–11.

International Monetary Fund. *Regional Outlook Middle East and Central Asia.* Washington, DC, October 2009.

"Internet Filtering in the United Arab Emirates in 2004–2005: A Country Study." OpenNet Initiative. www.opennetinitiative.net.

"Internet Penetration in the UAE Increasing." *Emirates Business 24/7*, August 6, 2008.

"Internet Usage and Population Statistics." www.internetworldstats.com.
"Intikhabat al-'Iraq." *al-Sharq al-Awsat,* February 6, 2009. www.aawsat.com.
"Intisār li-l-irādah al-sha'bīyah." *al-Ayyām* (Manama), October 25, 2002.
"Iraq Tells Media to Toe the Line." Reuters, November 12, 2004.
"Iran, Bahrain Reject Newspaper's Province Claim." Reuters, July 15, 2007.
"Islamic Websites Call for Revenge After Iraqi Prisoner Abuse." Agence France Presse, May 5, 2004.
Izzak, B. "Islamists Make Strong Gains." *Kuwait Times*, May 19, 2008.
Jabarti, Somaya. "Engineers Council Poll: One More Step for Saudi Women." *Arab News*, December 28, 2005.
Jacobs, Jane. *Cities and the Wealth of Nations: Principles of Economic Life*. New York: Random House, 1984.
Janardhan, Meena. "UAE: Women's Participation Is the Norm." IPS News, February 25, 2009. http://ipsnews.net (June 29, 2009).
Janardhan, N. "Al-Jazeera TV Rubs Arab Governments the Wrong Way." Inter Press Service, August 13, 2002.
———. "Arabs Debate 'Misinformation' During War on Iraq." Inter Press Service, June 12, 2003.
———. "GCC Plans Media Campaign to Counter US Propaganda." Inter Press Service, November 9, 2001.
———. "In the Gulf, Women Are Not Women's Best Friends." *Daily Star* (Lebanon), June 20, 2005.
———. "Media Wage Their Own War." Inter Press Service, April 7, 2003.
———. "Media Widens Arab-West Differences." Inter Press Service, June 26, 2002.
Janzen, Jörg. *Nomads in the Sultanate of Oman: Tradition and Development in Dhofar*. Boulder: Westview, 1986.
"The Al-Jazeera Effect." Editorial, *Weekly Standard*, April 21, 2004.
"Al-Jazeera Iraq Coverage Clouds US-Qatar Ties." Agence France Presse, April 28, 2004.
"Al-Jazeera Most Popular in Saudi Arabia." *Arab News*, September 10, 2004.
"Al Jazeera Reports Affect US-Qatar Ties." Reuters, April 28, 2004.
"Al-Jazeera Targeted for Unbiased Reporting." *The Peninsula*, April 22, 2004.
"Al-Jazeera Unveils Ethics Code." *The Peninsula,* July 14, 2004.
"Al-Jazeera Will Not Bow to US Pressure." *The Peninsula*, April 29, 2004.
Jefferson, Thomas. Letter to James Monroe dated October 24, 1823. www.mtholyoke.edu (June 4, 2005).
Jones, Jeremy, and Nicholas Ridout. "Democratic Development in Oman." *Middle East Journal* 59, no. 3 (2005): 376–392.
Jones, Toby. "The Iraq Effect in Saudi Arabia." *Middle East Report*, no. 237 (2005).
———. "Rebellion on the Saudi Periphery: Modernity, Marginalization, and the Shi'a Uprising of 1979." *International Journal of Middle East Studies* 38, no. 2 (2006): 213–233.
———. "Seeking a 'Social Contract for Saudi Arabia.'" *Middle East Report*, no. 228 (2003): 42–48.
———. "Violence and the Illusion of Reform in Saudi Arabia." Middle East Report Online, November 13, 2003. www.merip.org/mero/mero111303.html (September 24, 2006).
Joseph, Suad. "Gendering Citizenship in the Middle East." In *Gender and Citizenship in the Middle East*, ed. Suad Joseph (Syracuse: Syracuse University Press, 2000).

Kamrava, Mehran. "Royal Factionalism and Political Liberalization in Qatar." *Middle East Journal* 63, no. 3 (2009): 401–420.

Kant, Immanuel. "Perpetual Peace." In *Kant: Political Writings*, ed. H. S. Reiss (Cambridge: Cambridge University Press, 2004), pp. 93–130.

Kapiszewski, Andrzej. "Elections and Parliamentary Activity in the GCC States: Broadening Political Participation in the Gulf Monarchies." In *Constitutional Reform and Political Participation in the Gulf*, eds. Abdulhada Khalaf and Giacomo Luciani (Dubai: Gulf Research Center, 2006), pp. 88–131.

———. "George Bush's Promotion of Democracy: Agenda in the Middle East." In *The Changing Middle East*, ed. Andrzej Kapiszewski (Kraków: Oficyna Wydawnicza AFM, 2006), pp. 13–54.

———. "Iran's Presidential Elections and Their Impact on the Republic's Politics." In *Iranian Challenges*, Chaillot Papers no. 89, ed. Walter Posch (Paris: Institute for Security Studies, 2006).

Karl, Terry Lynn. *The Paradox of Plenty: Oil Booms and Petro-States*. Berkeley: University of California Press, 1997.

———. "Petroleum and Political Pacts: The Transition to Democracy in Venezuela." *Latin American Research Review* 22, no. 1 (1987): 63–94.

Karsh, Efraim, ed. *The Iran-Iraq War: Impact and Implications*. London: Macmillan, 1989.

Katzman, Kenneth. "Iraq's Opposition Movements." Congressional Research Service Issue Brief, March 26, 1998. www.fas.org.

Kawach, Nadim. "Qatar Records Budget Surplus for Fourth Successive Year." *Gulf News*, February 21, 2004.

Keane, John, ed. *Civil Society and the State*. London: Verso, 1988.

Kechichian, Joseph A. *Oman and the World: The Emergence of an Independent Foreign Policy*. Santa Monica, CA: RAND, 1995.

Keddie, Nikki. *Modern Iran: Roots and Results of Revolution*. New Haven: Yale University Press, 2003.

———. *Roots of Revolution: An Interpretive History of Modern Iran*. New Haven: Yale University Press, 1981.

Kemp, Geoffrey. "The Impact of Iranian Foreign Policy on Regional Security: An External Perspective." In *Iran and the Gulf*, ed. J. S. al-Suwaidi (Abu Dhabi: Emirate Center for Strategic Studies and Research, 1996).

al-Ketbi, Ibitisam. "Women's Issues in the GCC Countries in 2004." In *Gulf Yearbook 2004*. Dubai: Gulf Research Center, 2005.

———. "Women's Political Status in the GCC States." *Arab Reform Bulletin* 2, no. 7 (2004).

Khalaf, 'Abdulhādī. "Bahrain's Election: Just What the King Ordered." *Voice of Bahrain*, no. 130, October 4, 2002.

———. *Binā' al-dawlah fī 'l-Bahrayn: al-Muhimmah ghayr al-munjazah*. Beirut: Dar al-Kunūz al-Adabīyah, 2000.

Khalaf, Roula. "There Is a Dangerous Period Coming: Between Reform and Repression, the House of Saud Faces Its Greatest Peril." *Financial Times*, November 18, 2003.

Al-Khaled, Ahmad. "Kuwaiti Shiite Cleric Calls for Jihad." *Kuwait Times*, July 19, 2006.

Khanfa, Wadah. *The Future of Al-Jazeera*. Adham Center for Television Journalism, American University, Cairo, August 2004.

Khouri, Rami G. "Arab Satellite Marriage: Osama bin Laden and Madonna." *Daily Star* (Lebanon), November 28, 2002.

Al-Khursan, Salah. *Hizb al-Da'wa al-Islamiyyah: Haqa'iq wa watha'iq* [The Islamic Da'wa Party: Facts and Documents]. Damascus: al-Mu'addadda al-'Arabiyya li'l-Dirasat wa'l Buhuth al-Istratijiyya, 1999.

El-Kikha, Mansour O. "Al-Jazeera—Filling the Void." *New York Times*, May 12, 2004.

"Kingdom Warns of Turmoil in Region After Iraq." *Arab News*, February 6, 2003.

Kinninmont, Jane. "Bahrain: Assessing al-Wefaq's Parliamentary Experiment." *Arab Reform Bulletin* 5, no. 8 (2007).

Kinzer, Stephen. *Overthrow: America's Century of Regime Change from Hawaii to Iraq*. New York: Times Books, 2006.

Koch, Christian. "The Societal Sources of Change in the Middle East." *International Politics and Society,* no. 4 (2004): 54–69.

Kohut, Andrew, Richard Wike, Erin Carriere-Kretschmer, Kathleen Wolzwart, and Jacob Poushter. "Confidence in Obama Lifts U.S. Image Around the World: Most Muslim Publics Not So Easily Moved." 25-Nation Pew Global Attitudes Survey, Washington, DC: Pew Research Center, July 23, 2009.

Kokushkin, Maksim. "New Institutionalism and New Alternatives to Normative Positivism." Paper presented at the annual meeting of the American Sociological Association, New York, August 2007.

Kostiner, Joseph, ed. *Middle East Monarchies: The Challenge of Modernity*. Boulder: Lynne Rienner, 2000.

Kraidy, Marwan M. *Reality Television and Arab Politics: Contention in Public Life.* New York: Cambridge University Press, 2010.

Krauss, Joseph. "US Troops Pact a Coup for Iraq's Maliki: Analysts." Agence France Presse, Zawya (UAE), November 27, 2008. www.zawya.com.

Kupperman, Karen Ordahl. *Indians and English: Facing Off in Early America*. Ithaca: Cornell University Press, 1998.

"Kurds Revive Civil War Grudges at Polls." Iraqi Crisis Report no. 300, part two. Institute for War & Peace Reporting, August 13, 2009. www.iwpr.net.

"Kuwait, a Moment of Great Promise: Four Elected Women Sworn in for First Time in Kuwaiti Parliamentary History." UNDP press release, May 31, 2009.

"Kuwait Parliament Asked to Lift Two Shia MPs' Immunity." Agence France Presse, Gulf in the Media, March 12, 2008. http://www.gulfinthemedia.com (March 18, 2008).

"Kuwait Police Disperse Protestors." Al-Jazeera.net, March 27, 2008. http://english.aljazeera.net (July 27, 2008).

"Kuwaiti Energy Minister Ousted to Appease Winners of Parliamentary Elections." CERA Reports Online, July 11, 2006. http://cera.ecnext.com (August 8, 2007).

"Kuwait's Prime Minister Survives Key Vote." Reuters, December 16, 2009. www.themalaysianinsider.com.

Kwarten, Leo. "Why the Saudi Shiites Won't Rise Up Easily." *Khitat Loubnaniya: A Lebanese Window on Shia Affairs*, January 6, 2009. www.khitat.info.

Lackner, Helen A. *House Built on Sand: A Political Economy of Saudi Arabia*. London: Ithaca, 1978.

La Guardia, Anton. "Muslim Clerics' Anger Delays Saudi Plan to Let Women Sell Lingerie." *The Telegraph*, May 16, 2006.

Landais, Emmanuelle. "UAE Tops World on per Capita Carbon Footprint." *Gulf News*, October 30, 2008.

Lando, Ben. "Iraq Gov't Oil Law in Limbo." UPI, July 19, 2007. www.upi.com (July 20, 2007).

Law, Bill. "Saudi Stories: Candidates." BBC News, July 4, 2005.

Lawson, Fred H. *Bahrain: The Modernization of Autocracy*. Boulder: Westview, 1989.
"Lawyers Welcome Unified Court System." *The Peninsula*, October 3, 2004.
Legrenzi, Matteo, and E. El-Hokayem. *The Arab Gulf States in the Shadow of the Iranian Nuclear Challenge*. Washington, DC: Henry L. Stimson Center, 2006.
Lemann, Nicholas. "The Quiet Man." *New Yorker*, May 7, 2001.
Lerner, Daniel. *The Passing of Traditional Society: Modernizing the Middle East*. New York: Free Press, 1958.
Levitsky, Steven, and Lucan A. Way. "Autocracy by Democratic Rules: The Dynamics of Competitive Authoritarianism in the Post–Cold War Era." Paper prepared for the conference "Mapping the Great Zone: Clientelism and the Boundary Between Democratic and Democratizing," New York, April 2003.
———. *Competitive Authoritarianism: Hybrid Regimes After the Cold War.* New York: Cambridge University Press, 2010, pp. 38–54.
Lewin, Tamar. "U.S. Universities Rush to Set Up Outposts Abroad." *New York Times*, February 10, 2008.
Lewis, Bernard. "Islam and Liberal Democracy." *Atlantic Monthly*, February 1993.
"The Limits of the Reform." *The Economist*, March 25, 2004.
Litvak, Meir. *Scholars of Nineteenth Century Iraq*. Cambridge: Cambridge University Press, 1998.
Lobe, Jim. "Gap Grows Between U.S., World Public Opinion." Inter Press Service, March 16, 2004. www.globalissues.org (August 5, 2006).
"Local News on Blackberry Banned in Bahrain." *Gulf News*, April 9, 2010.
Lombardi, Giorgio. *Premesse al corso di diritto pubblico comparato: Problemi di metodo.* Milan: Giuffré, 1986.
Long, Jerry M. *Saddam's War of Words: Politics, Religion, and the Iraqi Invasion of Kuwait.* Austin: University of Texas Press, 2004.
Longva, Anh Nga. "Citizenship in the Gulf States: Conceptualization and Practice." In *Citizenship and the State in the Middle East*, eds. Nils A. Butenschön, Uri Davis, and M. Hassassian (Syracuse: Syracuse University Press, 2000), pp. 179–197.
———. "Neither Autocracy nor Democracy but Ethnocracy: Citizens, Expatriates, and the Socio-Political System in Kuwait." In *Monarchies and Nations: Globalisation and Identity in the Arab States of the Gulf,* eds. Paul Dresch and James Piscatori (London: I. B. Tauris, 2005).
———. *Walls Built on Sand: Migration, Exclusion, and Society in Kuwait*. Boulder: Westview, 1997.
Louër, Laurence. *Transnational Shia Politics: Religious and Political Network in the Gulf,* s. 7. New York: Columbia University Press, 2008.
Lucas, Russell E. *Institutions and the Politics of Survival in Jordan: Domestic Responses to External Challenges, 1988–2001*. Albany: SUNY Press, 2006.
Luciani, Giacomo. "Allocation vs Production States: A Theoretical Framework." In *The Arab State*, ed. Giacomo Luciani (Berkeley: University of California Press, 1990), pp. 65–84.
———, ed. *The Arab State*. Austin: University of Texas Press, 1990.
Luke, Timothy W. 1985. "Dependent Development and the OPEC States: State Formation in Saudi Arabia and Iran Under the International Energy Regime." *Studies in Comparative International Development* 20, no. 1 (1985): 31–54.
Lynch, Marc. "Blogging the New Arab Public: Arab Blogs' Political Influence Will Grow." April 10, 2007. www.worldpoliticsreview.co.

———. "Not the Enemy: The Arab Media and American Reform Efforts." *Arab Reform Bulletin* 2, no. 4 (2004).
———. "Out of Tsunami, a Quiet Arab Media Revolution." *Christian Science Monitor*, January 31, 2005.
MacFarquhar, Neil. "Conflict Polarizes the Mideast, Leaving Little Middle Ground: Arab Reformers on the Defensive." *New York Times*, August 9, 2006.
———. "In Tiny Arab State, Web Takes on Ruling Elite." *New York Times*, January 15, 2006.
———. "Saudi Uneasy Balance Between Desires for Change and Stability." *New York Times*, May 4, 2004.
MacLeod, Scott. "How Al-Arabiya Got the Obama Interview." *Time*, January 28, 2009.
Al-Maeena, Khaled. "Media, Terrorism, and Reality." *Saudi-US Relations Information Service Newsletter*, October 19, 2004.
———. "Saudis Should Use the Power of the Internet to Stop Hate." *Gulf News*, July 5, 2004.
Mahdavy, Hossein. "The Patterns and Problems of Economic Development in Rentier States: The Case of Iran." In *Studies in the Economic History of the Middle East,* ed. M. A. Cook (London: Oxford University Press, 1970), pp. 255–267.
Mahfouz, Mohammad, ed. *Sectarian Dialogue in the Kingdom of Saudi Arabia*. Qatif, Saudi Arabia: Aafaz Center, 2007.
Mahnaimi, Uzi. "Qatar Buys Off Al-Qaeda Attacks with Oil Millions." *Sunday Times* (London), May 1, 2005.
Al Maktoum, Shaikh Mohammed bin Rashid. "Women in the UAE." www.sheikhmohammed.co.ae.
Mallat, Chibli. *The Renewal of Islamic Law: Muhammad Baqer al-Sadr, Najaf, and the Shi'i International*. Cambridge: Cambridge University Press, 1993.
Al Manie, Haya. "Paranoia in Society." *Al Riyadh*, reprinted in *Arab News*, January 9, 2008.
Mann, James. *Rise of the Vulcans: The History of Bush's War Cabinet*. New York: Free Press, 2004.
Marcel, Valérie. *Oil Titans: National Oil Companies in the Middle East.* London: Royal Institute of International Affairs, 2006.
Marquis, Christopher. "U.S. Protests Broadcasts by Arab Channels." *New York Times*, April 29, 2004.
Marr, Phoebe. *The Modern History of Iraq*. Boulder: Westview, 1995.
Al-Matrafi, Saad. "Scholars Frustrate Extremists on Women Driving Issue." *Arab News*, May 31, 2005.
Mattair, T. R. *The Three Occupied UAE Islands: The Tunbs and Abu Musa*. Abu Dhabi: UAE Emirates Center for Strategic Studies and Research, 2006.
Matveev, Konstantin. *Bahrain: The Drive for Democracy*. London: Prittle, 1997.
Mayer, Jane. *The Dark Side: The Inside Story of How the War on Terror Turned into a War on American Ideals*. New York: Doubleday, 2008.
———. "The Hidden Power." *New Yorker*, July 3, 2006.
Mazfar, Halima. "A King's Vision: Expanding the Role of the Saudi Women." *Asharq Al Awsat*, August 1, 2006.
McElroy, Damien. "Saudi Arabia to Lift Ban on Women Drivers." *The Telegraph* (UK), January 21, 2008.
Mead, Walter Russell. *Special Providence: American Foreign Policy and How It Changed the World*. New York: Routledge, 2002.

"Media Consumption in the Middle East—Examining the Data." InterMedia Surveys, September 2, 2003. www.zunia.org.

Melkumyan, Yelena. "Soviet Policy and the Gulf Crisis." In *The Gulf Crisis: Background and Consequences*, ed. Ibrahim Ibrahim (Washington, DC: Georgetown University Center for Contemporary Arab Studies, 1992), pp. 76–91.

Melvern, Linda. *The Ultimate Crime: Who Betrayed the UN and Why*. London: Allison & Busby, 1995.

MENA (Middle East and North Africa). *2008 Economic Developments and Prospects*. Washington, DC: International Bank for Reconstruction and Development/World Bank, 2009, p. 104. www.worldbank.org.

Menoret, Pascal. *The Municipal Election in Saudi Arabia 2005*. Arab Reform Initiative. December 27, 2005. http://arab-reform.net.

Mernissi, Fatma. *Scheherazade Goes West: Different Cultures, Different Harems*. New York: Washington Square, 2001.

Merom, Gil. *How Democracies Lose Small Wars: State, Society, and the Failures of France in Algeria, Israel in Lebanon, and the United States in Vietnam*. New York: Cambridge University Press, 2003.

"Message of President James Monroe to the US Congress," December 2, 1823. www.yale.edu (June 4, 2005).

"Message of President Theodore Roosevelt to the US Congress," December 6, 1904. www.uiowa.edu (June 5, 2005).

Meyer, Josh, and John Goetz. "Qatar's Security Chief Suspected of Having Ties to Al Qaeda." *Los Angeles Times*, March 28, 2003.

"Michael Rubin on the Sunni Vote in Iraq's Elections." National Public Radio, December 14, 2005.

"Middle East: Saudi Arabia, Egypt, UAE." *Migration News* 12, no. 1 (2006). www.migration.ucdavis.edu.

"The Middle East Youth Bulge." Population Reference Bureau. May 13, 2008. www.prb.org.

Milani, Mohsen M. "The Hostage Crisis." *Encyclopedia Iranica*, vol. 7, pp. 525–535.

———. "Iran's Active Neutrality During the Kuwaiti Crisis: Reasons and Ramifications." *New Political Science* 11, nos. 1–2 (1992): 41–60.

———. "Iran's Ambivalent World Role." In *Comparative Foreign Policy*, ed. Steven W. Hook (Upper Saddle River, NJ: Prentice Hall, 2003), pp. 219–244.

———. "Iran's Gulf Policy: From Idealism and Confrontation to Pragmatism and Moderation." In *Iran and the Gulf*, ed. J. S. al-Suwaidi (Abu Dhabi: Emirate Center for Strategic Studies and Research, 1996), pp. 83–98.

———. "Iran's Policy Toward Afghanistan." *Middle East Journal* 60, no. 2 (2006): 235–256.

———. "Iran's Relations with Iraq Under the Pahlavis, 1921–79." *Encyclopedia Iranica,* 2006.

Miles, Hugh. *Al-Jazeera: The Inside Story of the Arab News Channel That Is Challenging the West*. New York: Grove, 2005.

Mofid, Kamran. *The Economic Consequences of the Gulf War*. New York: Routledge, 1990.

Moghadam, Valentine, and Fatima Sadiqi, eds. "Women's Activism and the Public Sphere." Special issue, *Journal of Middle East Women's Studies* 2, no. 2 (2006): 1–7.

Monten, Jonathan. "The Roots of the Bush Doctrine: Power, Nationalism, and

Democracy Promotion in U.S. Strategy." *International Security* 29, no. 4 (2005): 112–156.

Moore, Pete W., and Andrew Schrank. "Commerce and Conflict: U.S. Effort to Counter Terrorism with Trade May Backfire." *Middle East Policy* 10, no. 3 (2003): 112–120.

Moran, Theodore H. "Managing an Oligopoly of Would-Be Sovereigns: The Dynamics of Joint Control and Self-Control in the International Oil Industry Past, Present, and Future." *International Organization* 41, no. 4 (1987): 575–607.

"Most Kuwaiti MPs Involved in Corruption." Middle East Online, June 23, 2007. www.middle-east-online.com (August 8, 2007).

Mubarak, Ebtihal. "Abdullah Pardons 'Qatif Girl.'" *Arab News*, December 18, 2007.

Al-Mughni, Haya. *Women in Kuwait: The Politics of Gender*, 2nd ed. London: Saqi, 2001.

———. "Women's Movements and the Autonomy of Civil Society in Kuwait." In *Conscious Acts and the Politics of Social Change*, eds. Robin L. Teske and Mary Ann Tétreault (Columbia: University of South Carolina Press, 2000), pp. 170–187.

Al-Mughni, Haya, and Mary Ann Tétreault. "Engagement in the Public Sphere: Women and the Press in Kuwait." In *Women and the Media in the Middle East*, ed. Naomi Sakr (London: I. B. Tauris, 2004), pp. 120–137.

———. "Gender, Citizenship, and Nationalism in Kuwait." *British Journal of Middle Eastern Studies* 22, nos. 1–2 (1995): 64–80.

———. "Political Actors Without the Franchise: Women and Politics in Kuwait." In *Monarchies and Nations: Globalization and Identity in the Arab States of the Gulf*, eds. Paul Dresch and James Piscatori (London: I. B. Tauris, 2005), pp. 203–221.

Munck, Geraldo, and Carol Leff. "Modes of Transition and Democratization: South America and Eastern Europe in Comparative Perspective." *Comparative Politics* 29. no. 3 (1997): 343–362.

Murphy, Carlyle. "Saudis Slowly Opening Dialogue About Rights." *Christian Science Monitor*, March 28, 2008.

———. "With Shi'ites Rising Across the Region, Saudi Arabia's Grow Impatient." *Christian Science Monitor*, April 27, 2009.

Mūsā, Hussayn. *Masīrat al-qam' fī 'l-Bahrayn*. Al-Manāma: NCLB, 1984.

Mushaime, Hassan. "On Political Naturalization." Speech delivered in the House of Lords on August 22, 2003. *Voice of Bahrain* 140, no. 4 (October 2003).

Al-Musnad, Muhammad bin Abd al-Aziz. *Islamic Fatwa Regarding Women*. Riyadh: Darussalam, 1996.

Mustafa, Ahmed. "Al-Jazeera Can't Strike a Balance Between Politics and Media." *Gulf News*, July 23, 2004.

"Mutahaddith bi Ism al-Sistani: al-Marja' al-A'la yad'amu la'ihat al-I'tilaf al-'Iraqi al-Muwahhid." *Al-Sharq al-Awsat*, January 17, 2005.

"Najah al-istifta' 'ala Muswadat al-Dustur al-'Iraqi." Middle East Online, October 25, 2005. www.middle-east-online.com.

Al-Najjar, Ghanim Hamid. "Decision-Making Process in Kuwait: The Land Acquisition Policy as a Case Study." PhD diss., University of Exeter, 1984.

———. "Human Rights in a Crisis Situation: The Case of Kuwait After Occupation." *Human Rights Quarterly* 23, no. 1 (2001): 188–209.

Nakash, Yitzhak. "The Conversion of Iraq's Tribes to Shiism." *International Journal of Middle East Studies* 26, no. 3 (1994): 443–463.

———. *The Shi'is of Iraq*. Princeton: Princeton University Press, 1994.

Nakhleh, Emile A. *Bahrain: Political Development and Stability*. Lanham, MD: Lexington Books, 1976.

———. "Political Participation and the Constitutional Experiments in the Arab Gulf: Bahrain and Qatar." In *Social and Economic Development in the Arab Gulf*, ed. Tim Niblock (London: Croom Helm, 1980), pp. 135–160.

"Nation in Danger of 'Losing a Generation.'" *The National*, February 10, 2010.

"Nationals Push for Polls to Elect FNC Members." *Gulf News*, February 23, 2005.

El-Nawawy, Mohammad, and Adel Iskandar. *Al-Jazeera: How the Free Arab News Network Scooped the World and Changed the Middle East*. Boulder: Westview, 2002.

Al-Nayyan, Shaikh Zayid Bin Sultan. *The Leader and the Nation*. Abu Dhabi: The Emirates Center for Strategic Studies and Research, 2004.

Neep, Daniel. "Dilemmas of Democratization in the Middle East: The 'Forward Strategy of Freedom.'" *Middle East Policy* 11, no. 3 (2004): 73–84.

"New Explanatory Statement by the Ministry of Justice on Qatif Girl." Saudi Press Agency, November 24, 2007. www.spa.gov.sa.

Niblock, Tim. *Saudi Arabia: Power, Legitimacy and Survival*. London: Routledge, 2006.

Nitzan, Jonathan. "Differential Accumulation: Toward a New Political Economy of Capital." *Review of International Political Economy* 2, no. 3 (1995): 446–515.

Nitzan, Jonathan, and Shimshon Bichler. *The Global Political Economy of Israel*. London: Pluto, 2002.

"No Time to Lose." *The Economist*, February 19, 2009.

"No Women Win Office in Kuwait." Associated Press, July 1, 2006.

Norris, Pippa, and Ronald Inglehart. "Islamic Culture and Democracy: Testing the 'Clash of Civilizations' Thesis." In *Human Values and Social Change: Findings from the Values Surveys*, ed. Ronald Inglehart. Leiden: Brill, 2002.

Norton, Augustus Richard. 2005. *Civil Society in the Middle East*. Boston: Brill Academic, 2005.

"Number of Women in UAE Cabinet Doubled." Agence France Presse, February 18, 2008. www.grc.ae (March 11, 2008).

Al-Nuwaysir, Muwaffaq. "Terrorists Exploit Easy Access to Arabic Websites to Post Images of US Victim." *Al-Sharq Al-Awsat* (London), June 21, 2004. www.aawsat.com.

The Oasis of Al-Hasa. Dammam: ARAMCO, Arabian Research Division, 1955.

Obaid, Nawaf. "Clerical Hurdles to Saudi Reform." *Washington Post*, March 9, 2004.

———. "What the Saudi Public Really Thinks." *Daily Star* (Lebanon), June 24, 2004. www.dailystar.com.

O'Donnell, Guillermo, and Phillippe C. Schmitter. *Transitions from Authoritarian Rule: Tentative Conclusions About Uncertain Democracies*. Baltimore: Johns Hopkins University Press, 1986.

Okruhlik, Gwenn."Dependence, Disdain and Distance: State, Labor and Citizenship in the Arab Gulf." In *Industrialization in the Arab Gulf*, eds. Jean Francois Seznec and Mimi Kirk (Boulder: Lynne Rienner, forthcoming).

———. "Excluded Essentials: Ethnicity, Oil and Citizenship in Saudi Arabia." In *The Global Color Line: Racial and Ethnic Inequality and Struggle from a Global Perspective*, eds. Pinar Batur-VanderLippe and Joe Feagin (Stamford: JAI, 1999), pp. 215–235.

———. "The Irony of Islah (Reform)." *Washington Quarterly* 28, no. 4 (2005): 153–170.

———. "Making Conversation Permissible: Islamism and Reform in Saudi Arabia." In *Islamic Activism: A Social Movement Theory Approach*, ed. Quintan Wiktorowicz (Bloomington: Indiana University Press, 2004), pp. 250–269.

———. "Networks of Dissent: Islamism and Reform in Saudi Arabia." *Current History*, January 2002.

———. "Religious Revivalism and Its Challenge to the Saudi Regime." In *Religion and Politics in Saudi Arabia*, eds. Mohammed Ayoob and Hasan Kosebalaban (Boulder: Lynne Rienner, 2009), pp. 109–123.

———. "Rentier Wealth, Unruly Law and the Rise of Opposition: The Political Economy of Oil States." *Comparative Politics* 31, no. 3 (1999): 295–315.

———. "State Power, Religious Privilege, and Myths About Political Reform." In *Religion and Politics in Saudi Arabia: Wahhabism and the State*, eds. Mohammed Ayoob and Hasan Koselbalaban (Boulder: Lynne Rienner, 2009), pp. 91–107.

"On the Media." National Public Radio, August 23, 2009.

"Opposition MPs Want Kuwait Oil Minister Sacked." Middle East Online, June 25, 2007. www.middle-east-online.com (August 8, 2007).

Oren, Ido. *Our Enemies and US: America's Rivalries and the Making of Political Science.* Ithaca: Cornell University Press, 2003.

———. "The Subjectivity of the 'Democratic' Peace: Changing U.S. Perceptions of Imperial Germany." *International Security* 20, no. 2 (1995): 147–184.

Ottoway, David B. "Pressure Builds on Key Pillar Supporting Saudi Royal House." *Wall Street Journal Europe*, June 9, 2004.

Ottaway, Marina, and Thomas Carothers. "The Greater Middle East Initiative: Off to a False Start." Policy Brief no. 29, Carnegie Endowment for International Peace, March 2004. www.carnegieendowment.org (July 14, 2006).

Owtram, Francis. *A Modern History of Oman: Formation of the State Since 1920.* London: I. B. Tauris, 2004.

Packer, George. *The Assassin's Gate: America in Iraq.* New York: Farrar, Straus & Giroux, 2005.

———. "Fighting Faiths." *New Yorker*, July 10 and 17, 2006.

Parolin, Gianluca P. *Citizenship in the Arab World.* Amsterdam: Amsterdam University Press, 2009.

———. "Generations of Gulf Constitutions: Paths and Perspectives." In *Constitutional Reform and Political Participation in the Gulf*, eds. Abdulhadi Khalaf and Giacomo Luciani (Dubai: Gulf Research Center, 2006), pp. 51–87.

———. "L'evoluzione istituzionale delle monarchie del Golfo tra modernità e tradizione: Il caso del Bahrein." *Diritto Pubblico Comparato ed Europeo* 1 (2003): 59–80.

Patterson, Orlando. *Rituals of Blood: Consequences of Slavery in Two American Centuries*. New York: Basic Books, 1998.

Paul, James A. "Oil Companies in Iraq: A Century of Rivalry and War." Paper presented at the Global Policy Forum Conference on Corporate Accountability, Berlin, November 2003. www.globalpolicy.org (July 19, 2007).

"PEN American Center Hails Release of Saudi Reformers." International Freedom of Expression Exchange, n.d. www.ifex.org.

Penketh, Anne. "Succession at House of Saud: The Men Who Would Be King." *The Independent*, June 17, 2008. www.independent.co.uk.

Penrose, Edith T. *The Large International Firm in Developing Countries: The International Petroleum Industry*. Cambridge, MA: MIT Press, 1968.

Peterson, Erik R. *The Gulf Cooperation Council: Search for Unity in a Dynamic Region*. Boulder: Westview, 1988.

Peterson, John E. *The Arab Gulf States: Further Steps Towards Political Participation*. Gulf Papers. Dubai: Gulf Research Center, 2006.

———. *The Arab Gulf States: Steps Towards Political Participation*. New York: Praeger, 1988.

———. "Oman's Diverse Society: Northern Oman." *Middle East Journal* 58, no. 1 (2004): 32–51.

———. "Oman's Diverse Society: Southern Oman." *Middle East Journal* 58, no. 2 (2004): 254–269.

———. "Oman: Three and a Half Decades of Change and Development." *Middle East Policy* 6, no. 2 (2004): 125–137.

———. "Succession in the States of the Gulf Cooperation Council." *Washington Quarterly* 24, no. 4 (2001): 173–186.

Pew Global Attitudes Project. *Global Unease with Major World Powers*. Pew Research Center, Washington, DC, June 27, 2007. http://pewglobal.org (July 17, 2007).

Phillips, Kevin. *American Theocracy: The Peril and Politics of Radical Religion, Oil, and Borrowed Money in the 21st Century*. New York: Viking, 2006.

"Poll Claims Support for Allowing Women to Drive." *The Guardian*, December 28, 2005.

"Poll Opens for First UAE Elections." Al-Jazeera English website, December 16, 2006. http://english.aljazeera.net (October 23, 2007).

Potter, Lawrence G., and Gary Sick. *Iran, Iraq, and the Legacies of War*. New York: Macmillan, 2004.

Prindle, David F. *Petroleum Politics and the Texas Railroad Commission*. Austin: University of Texas Press, 1981.

Pripstein Posusney, Marsha. "Behind the Ballot Box: Electoral Engineering in the Arab World." *Middle East Report*, no. 209 (1999): 12–15.

Pripstein Posusney, Marsha, and Michele Penner Angrist, eds. *Authoritarianism in the Middle East: Regimes and Resistance*. Boulder: Lynne Rienner, 2005.

"Profile: Saudi Political Opposition." BBC, February 10, 2005.

"Putin Says Missile Test Is Response to U.S." Radio Free Europe/Radio Liberty. www.rferl.org (July 17, 2007).

"Al-Qaeda Online Journal Resumes Publication." Associated Press, April 28, 2005.

"Qatar, Playing All Sides, Is a Nonstop Mediator." *New York Times*, July 9, 2008.

"Qatar Fears Civil War in Iraq." Reuters, April 6, 2004.

"Qatar: Five Female Anchors Resign from Al-Jazeera." *Los Angeles Times* blog, Babylon and Beyond, May 31, 2010. http://latimesblogs.latimes.org.

"Qatar Hires Regulator Dismissed by Dubai." *Financial Times*, March 2, 2005.

"Qatar Is Now a Global Gas Powerhouse." *The Economist*, January 6, 2005.

"Qatar's Personal Law Aims to Strengthen Family Stability." *Gulf News*, May 14, 2005.

"Qatar to Probe Al-Jazeera After US Complaints." *Arab News*, April 30, 2004.

"Qatar Unveils $5.5bn Airport Development." Agence France Presse, January 13, 2005.

"Qatar: US Reform Plan Should Be Considered." Reuters, April 5, 2004.

Al-Qazwini, Jawdat. "The School of Najaf." In *Ayatollahs, Sufis and Ideologues:*

State, Religion and Social Movements in Iraq, ed. Faleh Abdul-Jabar (London: Saqi, 2002), pp. 245–264.

Al-Qudaihi, Anees. "Saudi Arabia's Shi'a Press for Rights." BBC Arabic Service, March 24, 2009. http://news.bbc.co.uk.

Qusti, Raid. "Reforms in Kingdom Are Under Study, Sultan Says." *Arab News*, July 21, 2003.

———. "Saudi Men and Women Petition Rights Body on Women Driving." *Arab News*, June 28, 2005.

———. "Scholars Urge Moderation and Dialogue." *Arab News*, June 21, 2003.

———. "Tash Ma Tash: A Barometer of Self-Criticism." *Arab News*, November 3, 2004.

Qusti, Raid, and Somayya Jabarti. "New Identity Cards: Saudi Women Find Their Feet and Face Too." *Arab News*, March 13, 2005.

Rabi, Uzi. "The GCC: The Endless Quest for Regional Security." Paper presented at the annual meeting of Middle East Studies Association, San Francisco, 2004.

Rabī'ah, 'Alī. "The Constitutional Crisis in Bahrain." Speech delivered in the House of Lords on August 22, 2003. *Voice of Bahrain* 140, no. 4 (October 2003).

Rahman, Asad Abdul. "The Sky Is the Limit." *Gulf News*, May 28, 2004.

Ramazani, R. K. *The Gulf Corporation Council: Record and Analysis.* Charlottesville: University Press of Virginia, 1988.

Rand-Qatar Policy Institute. "Education for a New Era: Design and Implementation of K–12 Education Reform in Qatar." 2007.

———. *Revolutionary Iran: Challenge and Response in the Middle East.* Baltimore: Johns Hopkins University Press, 1986.

"The Ras al-Khaima Succession Crisis." *The Estimate*, July 4, 2003. www.theestimate.com (March 11, 2008).

Al-Rasheed, Madawi. *Contesting the Saudi State: Islamic Voices from a New Generation.* Cambridge: Cambridge University Press, 2007.

———. *Politics in an Arabian Oasis: The Rashidis of Saudi Arabia.* London: I. B. Tauris, 1991.

———. *al-Saudiyyah wa ma'zaq al-islah al-siyasi fi al-qarn al-hadi wa-al-'ishrin.* London: Saqi, 2005.

———. "The Shi'a of Saudi Arabia: A Minority in Search of Cultural Authenticity." *British Journal of Middle Eastern Studies* 25 (1998).

Rashid, Ahmed. *Taliban.* New Haven: Yale University Press, 2000.

Al-Rashid, M., and L. al-Rashid. "The Politics of Encapsulation: Saudi Policy Towards Tribal and Religious Opposition." *Middle Eastern Studies* 32, no. 1 (1996): 96–119.

Rasooldeen, Mohammed. "HRC Opens Women's Wing in Riyadh." *Arab News,* September 4, 2008.

Recknagel, Charles. "U.S.: Washington's 'Greater Middle East Initiative' Stumbles amid Charges It Imposes Change." Radio Free Europe, March 23, 2004. www.rferl.org (July 14, 2006).

"Reform Debate Rages in Saudi Arabia." *Gulf News*, March 4, 2003.

"Reformists in Free, Frank Talks with Abdullah." *Arab News*, February 2, 2003.

Regan, Tom. "US in Iraq Greatest Threat to World Peace?" *Christian Science Monitor*, June 15, 2006. www.csmonitor.com (November 5, 2006).

"Religious Freedom in the Kingdom of Saudi Arabia—Focus on Citizens." Shi'a News Agency, October 15, 2001. www.Shi'anews.com.

"Religious Freedom in Saudi Arabia: Incitement for Hatred Is Still Ongoing." *Saudi*

Shi'a: The Affairs of the Shi'ites in Saudi Arabia. May 16, 2009 www.saudiShi'a.com.
Remnick, David. "Letter from Cairo: Going Nowhere." *New Yorker*, July 12 and 19, 2004.
Reynolds, Paul. "The 'Democratic Domino' Theory." BBC News Online, April 10, 2003. http://news.bbc.co.uk (August 5, 2006).
———. "French Make Serious Move into Gulf." BBC News, January 15, 2008.
Richards, Alan. "Testimony Before the U.S. Senate Foreign Relations Committee." June 2, 2004. www.senate.gov (July 14, 2006).
Richards, Alan, and John Waterbury. *A Political Economy of the Middle East*. Boulder: Westview, 1990.
Ricks, Thomas E. *Fiasco: The American Military Adventure in Iraq*. New York: Penguin, 2006.
Riphenburg, C. J. *Oman: Political Development in a Changing World*. Westport: Praeger, 1998.
Risen, James. *State of War: The Secret History of the CIA and the Bush Administration*. New York: Free Press, 2006.
Ritter, Scott. *Iraq Confidential: The Untold Story of America's Intelligence Conspiracy*. London: I. B. Tauris, 2005.
Rogin, Michael. *Ronald Reagan, the Movie, and Other Episodes in Political Demonology*. Berkeley: University of California Press, 1987.
Rose, Gideon. "Neoclassical Realism and Theories of Foreign Policy." *World Politics* 51, no. 1 (1998).
Rosen, Nir. *In the Belly of the Green Bird*. New York: Free Press, 2006.
Rosman-Stollman, Elisheva. "Qatar's Road to Democracy: Truth or Dare?" In *Economic and Political Liberalization in the Gulf*, ed. Josh Teitelbaum (New York: Columbia University Press, 2009).
Ross, Michael L. "Does Oil Hinder Democracy?" *World Politics* 53, no. 2 (2001): 325–361.
Ruggie, John. "Continuity and Transformation in the World Polity: Toward a Neorealist Synthesis." In *Neorealism and Its Critics*, ed. Robert O. Keohane. New York: Columbia University Press, 1986, pp. 131–157.
Rugh, William A., ed. *Engaging the Arab and Islamic Worlds Through Public Diplomacy: A Report and Action Recommendations*. Washington, DC: George Washington University, 2004.
———. "The United Arab Emirates: What Are the Sources of Its Stability?" *Middle East Journal* 5, no. 3 (1997): 14–24.
Ruhaimi, Abdul Halim. 2002. "The Da'wa Islamic Party." In *Ayatollahs, Sufis, and Ideologues*, ed. Faleh 'Abd al-Jabar (London: Saqi, 2002), pp. 149–161.
Rumaihi, Muhammad G. *Bahrain: Social and Political Change Since the First World War*. London: Bowker, 1976.
"Rumsfeld's War." *Frontline*, October 26, 2004. www.pbs.org (August 4, 2006).
Russett, Bruce. *Grasping the Democratic Peace: Principles for a Post–Cold War World*. Princeton: Princeton University Press, 1993.
Rutherford, Paul. *Weapons of Mass Persuasion: Marketing the War Against Iraq*. Toronto: University of Toronto Press, 2004.
Sabbah, Haitam. "Weblogs Soar in Gulf States." Agence France Presse, June 14, 2006.
Saberi, Mahmood. "Isn't It Time to Stop Kidding?" *Gulf News*, February 12, 2005.
Sakai, Keiko. "Modernity and Tradition in the Islamic Movements in Iraq." *Arab Studies Quarterly* 23, no. 1 (2001): 37–52.

Sakr, Naomi. *Arab Media and Political Renewal: Community, Legitimacy and Public Life.* London: I. B. Tauris, 2007.

———. *Satellite Realms: Transnational Television, Globalization and the Middle East.* London: I. B. Tauris, 2002.

———. "Seen and Starting to Be Heard: Women and the Arab Media in a Decade of Change." *Social Research* 69 (2002): 821–850.

———, ed. *Women and Media in the Middle East: Power Through Self-Expression.* London: I. B. Tauris, 2004.

Salama, Samir. "More Than 1,000 Women Eligible to Vote." Gulf News.com, September 13, 2006. http://archive.gulfnews.com.

Salamé, Ghassan, ed. *Democracy Without Democrats: The Renewal of Politics in the Muslim World.* London: I. B. Tauris, 1994.

Saleh, Heba. "Iraq Conflict Leaves Saudi Shi'a Anxious of Backlash." *Financial Times*, May 4, 2006.

———. "Saudi Arabian King Approves Selected Human Rights Group." *Financial Times*, March 11, 2004.

———. "Saudi Warning to Critical Civil Servants Dents Hopes of Reform." *Financial Times*, September 16, 2004.

Al-Saleh, Hudah. "Saudi Clerics Seek Dialogue Among Various Sects." *Asharq Alawsat*, January 5, 2007. www.aawsat.com.

Salih, Roshan Muhammed. "No Role for Women in Saudi Council." Al-Jazeera, October 27, 2003.

Samara, Abdel Karim. "The Arab Media and the Iraq War." *Open Democracy,* April 12, 2003. www.opendemocracy.net.

Sampson, Anthony. *The Seven Sisters: The Great Oil Companies and the World They Shaped.* New York: Viking, 1975.

Sankari, Farouk. "The Character and Impact of Arab Oil Embargoes." In *Arab Oil: Impact on the Arab Countries and Global Implications*, eds. Naiem A. Sherbiny and Mark A. Tessler (New York: Praeger, 1976), pp. 265–278.

Saudi Arabia, Ministry of Justice. "Explanatory Statement by the Ministry of Justice About Qatif Girl." November 21, 2007. www.mofa.gov.sa.

"Saudi Arabia Backgrounder: Who Are the Islamists?" *Middle East Report*, no. 31 (2004).

"Saudi Arabia Gives Mixed Signals About Reforms." Reuters, June 26, 2009. Gulf in the Media. www.gulfinthemedia.com.

"Saudi Arabia Mulls Allowing Women to Vote." *Khaleej Times*, April 26, 2009.

"Saudi Arabia's Prince Nayef: A Rising but Enigmatic Prince." *The Economist*, April 2, 2009.

"Saudi Arabia's Promised Reforms: King Abdullah of Saudi Arabia." *New York Times*, January 4, 2008.

"Saudi Clerics Backtrack on Female Prayer Ban Near Kaaba." Reuters, September 12, 2006.

"Saudi Clerics Reform Extremists Through Online Dialogue." *Arab News*, February 7, 2005.

"Saudi Election Delayed; Government Employees Silenced." *Reform Bulletin* 2, no. 9 (October 20, 2004).

"Saudi Halts Recognition of UAE ID Cards over Map Issue." *Khaleej Times*, August 22, 2009. www.gulfinthemedia.com.

"Saudi Ministry of Interior Considers Special Police Unit for Domestic Violence." *Asharq Al-Awsat*, January 26, 2009.

"Saudi Municipal Polls Put Off Two Years." Agence France Presse, May 19, 2009.

"Saudi Restrictions on Women Questioned." *Los Angeles Times*, January 18, 2008.
"Saudi Shi'ite Call for Fairness." *Arab News*, April 24, 2003.
"Saudi Shi'ite Held After Meeting King." *Kuwait Times*, May 19, 2008.
"Saudi Shi'ites Won't Exploit Power Gains in Iraq." *Gulf News*, February 8, 2004.
"Saudi Women Petition for Right to Drive." Agence France Presse, January 3, 2008.
"Saudis Block Liberal Internet Forum, Says Activist." Reuters, August 9, 2007.
"Saudi Woman Killed for Chatting on Facebook." *The Telegraph*, March 31, 2008.
Savage, Charlie. *Takeover: The Return of the Imperial Presidency and the Subversion of American Democracy*. New York: Little, Brown, 2007.
Al-Sayegh, Fatma. "Arab Media Must Try to Meet Its Social Responsibility." *Gulf News*, July 23, 2004.
Schlesinger, Arthur M., Jr. *The Cycles of American History*. New York: Mariner, 1999.
Schlumberger, Oliver. "Arab Authoritarianism: Debating the Dynamics and Durability of Nondemocratic Regimes." In *Debating Arab Authoritarianism: Dynamics and Durability in Nondemocratic Regimes*, ed. Oliver Schlumberger (Palo Alto, CA: Stanford University Press, 2007), pp. 1–20.
———, ed. *Debating Arab Authoritarianism: Dynamics and Durability in Nondemocratic Regimes*. Palo Alto, CA: Stanford University Press, 2007.
Schmitter, Phillippe C. "Twenty-Five Years, Fifteen Findings." *Journal of Democracy* 21, no. 1 (2010): 17–28.
Schofield, Richard N. "Position, Function, and Symbol: The Shatt Al-Arab Dispute in Perspective." In *Iran, Iraq, and the Legacies of War*, eds. Lawrence G. Potter and Gary Sick (New York: Palgrave Macmillan, 2004), pp. 29–70.
Scollon, Michael. "Putin Says Missile Test Is Response to U.S." Radio Free Europe/Radio Liberty, May 31, 2007. www.rferl.org (July 17, 2007).
———. "Russia: A New MIRV Emerges." Radio Free Europe/Radio Liberty, May 31, 2007. www.rferl.org (July 17, 2007).
Sen, Amartya. *Development as Freedom*. New York: Anchor Books, 1999.
"Seven New Faces as Cabinet Reshuffled." *Khaleej Times*, February 18, 2008. www.grc.ae (March 11, 2008).
"75 pc of Labour Force in UAE Belongs to Asian Countries." *Khaleej Times*, February 25, 2008. www.khaleejtimes.com (March 11, 2008).
Seznec, Jean-Francois. "The Gulf Sovereign Wealth Funds: Myths and Reality." *Middle East Policy* 15, no. 2 (2008): 97–110.
Shaikh Zayid Bin Sultan Al-Nahyan. *The Leader and the Nation*. Abu Dhabi: Emirates Center for Strategic Studies and Research, 2004.
Shapiro, Samantha M. "The War Inside the Arab Newsroom." *New York Times*, January 2, 2005.
Sharabi, Hisham. *No Patriarchy: A Theory of Distorted Change in Arab Societies*. New York: Oxford University Press, 1988.
"Sheikh Mohammed Joins Facebook." *The National*, June 26, 2009.
"Shia Crackdown Fuels Tensions in Kuwait." Khaleej Times Online, March 13, 2008. http://www.khaleejtimes.com (July 28, 2008).
"Shi'a Men and Teenagers Held Incommunicado by Saudi Arabian Authorities." Amnesty International, March 23, 2009.
Shlaim, Avi. 1995. *War and Peace in the Middle East: A Concise History*. New York: Penguin, 1995.
Shultziner, Doron. "Struggles of Recognition: The Psychological Causes of Democratization." PhD diss., University of Oxford, 2007, chap. 8.

Shultziner, Doron, and Mary Ann Tétreault. "How Democratization Is Won Under Non-democratic Regimes: Emotion, Psychology, and Agency in the Kuwaiti Women's Rights Movement." Paper presented at the annual meeting of the American Political Science Association, Washington, DC, August 2008.

Sick, Gary. "Trial by Error: Reflections on the Iran-Iraq War." *Middle East Journal* 43 (1989): 230–245.

SIPRI (Stockholm International Peace Research Institute). "World Military Expenditures, 1988–2005." *SIPRI Yearbook 2006*, table 8A,1m. www.sipri.org (November 5, 2006).

Skeet, Ian. *Oman: Politics and Development*. London: Macmillan, 1992.

Skocpol, Theda. *States and Social Revolutions*. New York: Cambridge University Press, 1979.

Slackman, Michael, and Mona el-Naggar. "Police Beat Crowds Backing Egypt's Judges." *New York Times*, May 12, 2006.

Smith, Jean Edward. *George Bush's War.* New York: Holt, 1992.

Smith, Lee. "The Road to Tech Mecca." *Wired* 12, no. 7 (July 12, 2004).

Snyder, Alvin. "Al-Jazeera and Al-Hurra Contend with TV Ratings Problems." March 27, 2007. www. uscpublicdiplomacy.org.

Al-Sowayan, Saad. "Are We So Special or Do We Just Think We Are?" June 11, 2006. www.saadsowayan.com.

"Spotlight on Qatar's Human Rights Record." *Financial Times*, May 18, 2005.

Steinberg, Guido. 2001. "The Shi'ites in the Eastern Province of Saudi Arabia (al-Ahsa'), 1913–1953." In *The Twelver Shi'a in Modern Time: Religious Culture and Political History*, eds. Reiner Brunner and Werber Ende (Leiden: Brill, 2001), pp. 239–240.

"Step by Step for Middle East Women." *Christian Science Monitor*, February 17, 2009.

Stoda, Kevin Anthony. "Tribe, Tribalism, and Cultural Change." Kuwait, April 12, 2008. opednews.com.

Stork, Joe. "Violence and Political Change in Saudi Arabia." *ISIM Review* 19 (2007): 54–55.

"The Suffocating Limits of Reforms." *The Economist*, May 19, 2005.

Sultanate of Oman, Ministry of National Economy. *Final Results of 2003 National Census*. Muscat, 2004. www.moneoman.gov.om.

———. *Statistical Yearbook 2003*. Muscat, 2004. www.moneoman.gov.om.

———. *Statistical Yearbook 2005*. Muscat, 2005. www.moneoman.gov.om.

———. *Statistical Yearbook 2008*. Muscat, 2008. www.moneoman.gov.om.

"Sunnis Rejoin Iraqi Cabinet." Al-Jazeera, July 19, 2008. http://english.aljazeera .net.

Surowiecki, James. "Unsafe at Any Price." *New Yorker*, August 7 and 14, 2006.

Suskind, Ron. *The Price of Loyalty: George W. Bush, the White House, and the Education of Paul O'Neill*. New York: Simon & Schuster, 2004.

———. "Without a Doubt." *New York Times Magazine*, October 17, 2004.

Taheri, Amir. "Doesn't the Gulf Suffer from Hope Deficit?" *Gulf News*, May 21, 2004.

"Tahran tudhakkir washington bi 'ta'awun' fi al-Iraq." *al-Hayat*, February 18, 2005.

Taqi, Ali. "Kuwaiti Women Voters Have the Upper Hand." *Gulf News*, May 22, 2005.

Tatham, Steve. *Losing Arab Hearts and Minds: The Coalition, Al-Jazeera and Muslim Public Opinion*. London: Hurst, 2006.

Tavits, Margit. "The Development of Stable Party Support: Electoral Dynamics in

Post Communist Europe." *American Journal of Political Science* 49, no. 2 (2005): 283–298.
Taylor, Catherine. "Saudi Arabia's Quiet Voices of Reform Start to Speak Up." *Christian Science Monitor*, January 15, 2003.
Teitelbaum, Joshua. "Arms for the King and His Family: The US Arms Sale to Saudi Arabia." *Jerusalem Issue Briefs* 10, no. 11 (November 2, 2010). http://bit.ly/ai6em5.
———. *Holier Than Thou: Saudi Arabia's Islamic Opposition*. Washington, DC: Washington Institute for Near East Policy, 2000.
"Terrorism Has Saudi Television Talking." United Press International, February 7, 2005.
Tétreault, Mary Ann. "Civil Society in Kuwait: Protected Spaces and Women's Rights." *Middle East Journal* 47, no. 2 (1993): 275–291.
———. "Complex Consequences: Hydrocarbon Production as a Route to Economic Health." In *Rebuilding Devastated Economies in the Middle East*, ed. Leonard Binder (New York: Palgrave Macmillan, 2007), pp. 77–94.
———. "Divided Communities of Memory: Diasporas Come Home." In *The Muslim Diaspora: Gender, Culture, and Identity*, ed. Haideh Moghissi (London: Routledge, 2006), pp. 81–98.
———. "Economics and Security: Ronald Reagan's Energy Policy." *Forum* 3, no. 4 (1988): 70–79.
———. *The Kuwait Petroleum Corporation and the Economics of the New World Order.* Westport: Quorum, 1995.
———. "Kuwait's *Annus Mirabilis*." Middle East Report Online, September 7, 2006. www.merip.org (September 11, 2007).
———. "Kuwait's Parliament Considers Women's Rights, Again." Middle East Report Online, September 2, 2004. www.merip.org (October 20, 2005).
———. "Pleasant Dreams: The WTO as Kuwait's Holy Grail." *Critique: Critical Middle Eastern Studies* 12, no. 1 (2003): 75–93.
———. *Revolution in the World Petroleum Market*. Westport: Quorum, 1985.
———. "Sex and Violence: Social Reactions to Economic Restructuring in Kuwait." *International Feminist Journal of Politics* 1, no. 2 (1999): 237–255.
———. "A State of Two Minds: State Cultures, Women, and Politics in Kuwait." *International Journal of Middle East Studies* 33, no. 2 (2001): 203–220.
———. *Stories of Democracy: Politics and Society in Contemporary Kuwait*. New York: Columbia University Press, 2000.
———. "Women's Rights and the Meaning of Citizenship in Kuwait." Middle East Report Online, February 10, 2005. www.merip.org (July 4, 2007).
Tétreault, Mary Ann, and Robert A. Denemark, eds. *Gods, Guns, and Globalization: Religious Resurgence and International Political Economy*. Boulder: Lynne Rienner, 2004.
Tétreault, Mary Ann, and Mohammed al-Ghanim. "The Day After 'Victory': Kuwait's 2009 Election and the Contentious Present." Merip Online, July 8, 2009. www.merip.org.
———. "Transitions in Authoritarianism: Political Reform in the Persian Gulf Reconsidered." Paper presented at the annual meeting of the International Studies Association, Montreal, March 2011.
Tétreault, Mary Ann, Katherine Meyer, and Helen Rizzo. "Women's Rights in the Middle East: A Longitudinal Study of Kuwait." *International Political Sociology* 3 (2009): 218–237.
al-Thani, Emir Hamad Bin Khalifa. "Out of the Fog Through Arab Reform." *Daily Star* (Lebanon), June 21, 2004. www.dailystar.com.

"Thousands of Saudi Shi'ites Observe Ashura." *Gulf News*, March 3, 2004.
Tilly, Charles. 1985. "War Making and State Making as Organized Crime." In *Bringing the State Back In*, eds. Peter B. Evans, Dietrich Rueschemeyer, and Theda Skocpol (New York: Cambridge University Press, 1985), pp. 169–191.
"Tiptoeing Towards Reform." *The Economist*, February 19, 2009.
Tow, William T. *Subregional Security Cooperation in the Third World*. Boulder: Lynne Rienner, 1990.
Trabelsi, Habib. "Bahraini Opposition Turns Against King's 'Imposed' Reforms." Agence France Press, February 24, 2006.
———. "Saudis Learn to Protest." *Saudi Wave*, May 26, 2009. www.saudiwave.com.
———. "Sheikh Kalbani: All Shi'ite Clerics Are Heretics." *Saudi Wave*, May 6, 2009. www.saudiwave.com.
Transparency International. Corruption Perceptions Index, 2008. www.transparency.org.
Tripp, Charles. *A History of Iraq*. Cambridge: Cambridge University Press, 2000.
Trofimov, Yaroslav. "Saudi Arabia Switches Its Policies, Letting Some Dissidents Speak Out." *Wall Street Journal*, May 9, 2002.
———. "Saudi Shi'ites See Hope in an Invasion of Iraq." *Wall Street Journal*, February 3, 2003.
"Tuning in to the Middle East." Inter Press Service, January 2, 2003.
Toumi, Habib. "Bahrain Allows Female Diplomats to Work Abroad." *Gulf News*, August 16, 2005.
———. "Bahraini MPs Reject Motion to Boost Number of Female Diplomats." *Gulf News*, April 13, 2006.
———. "Bahrain's Oldest Newspaper Indefinitely Suspended." *Gulf News*, June 23, 2009.
———. "Kuwait Human Rights Association Calls for Immediate Release of Mohammad Al Jassem." *Gulf News*, May 23, 2010.
———. "Liberals Seek Law to Grant Citizenship to Children of Non-Bahraini Fathers." *Gulf News*, March 9, 2007.
———. "Six Women to Be Named in Bahrain's Council." *Gulf News*, August 6, 2006.
Tyler, Patrick E. "U.S. Strategy Plan Calls for Insuring No Rivals, Develop a One-Superpower World: Pentagon's Document Outlines Ways to Thwart Challenges to Primacy of America." *New York Times*, March 8, 1992.
"UAE Economy Soars 7.4 pc in 2007." *Khaleej Times*, March 10, 2008. www.grc.ae (March 11, 2008).
"UAE Fares Well in World Press Freedom Index." *Khaleej Times*, October 17, 2007.
"UAE to Have Women Judges Soon." *Arab News*, January 7, 2008.
"UAE Head Announces First Election." BBC News, December 1, 2005.
"UAE Leads Gulf Region with Most Twitter Users." *The National*, March 9, 2009.
"UAE Temporarily Shuts Down Saudi Dissident Website." Associated Press, June 22, 2004.
UAE (United Arab Emirates) Ministry of Information. *United Arab Emirates Yearbook 2007*. Abu Dhabi, 2007. www.uaeinteract.com.
———. *United Arab Emirates Yearbook 2008*. Abu Dhabi, 2008. www.uaeinteract.com.
"UN Questions Saudi Rules for Women." *Los Angeles Times*, January 18, 2008.
UNDP (United Nations Development Programme). *Arab Human Development Report 2002*. New York: UNDP, 2002. www.undp.org.
———. *Arab Human Development Report 2003*. New York: UNDP, 2003. www.undp.org.
———. *Human Development Report 2005*. New York: UNDP, 2005. www.undp.org.

———. *Human Development Report 2009, Overcoming Barriers: Human Mobility and Development*. New York: UNDP, 2009. www.undp.org.

UNDP Programme on Governance in the Arab Region. "The Gender and Citizenship Initiative; Country Profiles: Saudi Arabia." 2007. http://gender.pogar.org.

"The United Arab Emirates: Statehood and Nation-Building in a Traditional Society." Middle East Institute Policy Brief, November 30, 2004. www.mideasti.org.

Urquhart, Brian. "How Not to Fight a Dictator." *New York Review of Books*, May 6, 1999. www.nybooks.com (August 3, 2006).

US Central Intelligence Agency. "UAE." *The World Factbook*, December 13, 2007.

US Congress, US Senate, Committee on International Relations, Special Subcommittee on Investigations. "Oil Fields as Military Objectives: A Feasibility Study." Report prepared by the Congressional Research Service, 94th Cong., 1st sess., August 21, 1975 (Washington, DC: US Government Printing Office, 1975), parts I and II, pp. 1–39. www.mtholyoke.edu (July 19, 2007).

US Department of State. "Human Rights Report." March 11, 2010. www.state.gov.

US Department of State, Bureau of Democracy, Human Rights, and Labor. *Country Reports on Human Rights Practices B 2005: Oman*. Washington, DC, March 8, 2006. www.state.gov.

———. *Qatar: Country Reports on Human Rights Practices, 2003*. Washington, DC, February 25, 2004.

US Federal Trade Commission. *The International Petroleum Cartel*. US Senate Select Committee on Small Business, Staff Report to the Federal Trade Commission, 82nd Cong., Committee Print no. 6. Washington, DC: US Government Printing Office, 1952.

US House of Representatives, Committee on Foreign Affairs, Subcommittee on Europe and Subcommittee on Terrorism, Nonproliferation, and Trade. "Do the United States and Europe Need a Missile Defense System?" Joint Hearing, May 3, 2007. http://foreignaffairs.house.gov (July 17, 2007).

"The US National Interest Is Caught Up with the Saudis in a Very Complex Way. They Are More Than a Gas Pump." *Financial Times*, November 19, 2003.

USAID (US Agency for International Development). "Assistance for Iraq." April 9, 2007. www.usaid.gov.

Van der Ploeg, Irma. "Biometrics and the Body as Information: Normative Issues of the Socio-Technical Coding of the Body." In *Surveillance as Social Sorting: Privacy, Risk and Digital Discrimination*, ed. David Lyon (New York: Routledge, 2003), pp. 57–73.

———. "'Only Angels Can Do Without Skin': On Reproductive Technology's Hybrids and the Politics of Body Boundaries." *Body and Society* 10, nos. 2–3 (2004): 153–181.

"Veil Protest Dogs Kuwait Minister." BBC, April 2, 2007.

Vidal, F. S. *The Oasis of Al-Hasa*. Dammam: ARAMCO, Arabian Research Division, 1955.

Vissar, Reidar. "Sistani, the United States and Politics in Iraq: From Quietism to Machiavellianism?" NUPI Paper no. 700. Oslo: Norwegian Institute of International Affairs, March 2006. http://historiae.org.

Vitalis, Robert. *America's Kingdom: Mythmaking on the Saudi Oil Frontier*. Palo Alto, CA: Stanford University Press, 2006.

"Wa-jahdī khārij al-majlis yumkin an yakūn akthar fa'idah." *al-Wasat* (Manama), October 8, 2007.

Walbridge, Linda. "The Counterreformation: Becoming a Marja' in the Modern

World." In *The Most Learned of the Shi'a: The Institution of the Marja' Taqlid*, ed. L. Walbridge (New York: Oxford University Press, 2001), pp. 237–244.

"Wāshintun: al-Intikhābāt hurrah wa-nazīhah wa-nad'am al-islāhāt." *al-Ayyām* (Manama), October 25, 2002.

Waterbury, John. "Democracy Without Democrats? The Potential for Political Liberalization in the Middle East." In *Democracy Without Democrats? The Renewal of Politics in the Muslim World*, ed. Ghassan Salamé (London: I. B. Tauris, 1994).

———. *A Political Economy of the Middle East*. Boulder: Westview, 1990.

"Weblogs Soar in Gulf States." Agence France Presse, June 14, 2006.

Wedeen, Lisa. *Ambiguities of Domination: Politics, Rhetoric, and Symbols in Contemporary Syria*. Chicago: University of Chicago Press, 1999.

Wehrey, Fred. "Shi'a Pessimistic About Reform, but Seek Reconciliation." *Arab Reform Bulletin*, June 19, 2007.

Weisberg, Richard C. *The Politics of Crude Oil Pricing in the Middle East, 1970–1975*. Research Series no. 31. Berkeley: University of California Press, 1977.

Weisman, Steven. "Under Pressure, Qatar May Sell Jazeera Station." *New York Times*, January 30, 2005.

Werth, Barry. *31 Days: The Crisis That Gave Us the Government We Have Today*. New York: Nan A. Talese, 2006.

Wheeler, Deborah L. "The Internet and Youth Subculture in Kuwait." *Journal of Computer-Mediated Communication* 8, no. 2 (2003).

———. *The Internet in the Middle East: Global Expectations/Local Imaginations in Kuwait*. Albany: SUNY Press, 2005.

Whitaker, Brian. "More Women Win Vote in Kuwait." *The Guardian*, January 6, 2006.

Whitehead Consulting Group. *Economic Survey of Oman 1972*. London: Harold Whitehead, 1972.

"al-Wifāq wa-l-'Amal: Sanata'āwun ma'a nuwwāb al-barlamān." *al-Ayyām* (Manama), October 25, 2002.

Wikan, Unni. *Behind the Veil in Arabia: Women in Oman*. Baltimore: Johns Hopkins University Press, 1982.

Wiley, Joyce N. *The Islamic Movement of Iraqi Shi'ites*. Boulder: Lynne Rienner, 1992.

Wilkinson, John C. *The Imamate Tradition of Oman*. Cambridge Middle East Library. Cambridge: Cambridge University Press, 1987.

Willoughby, John. "Let a Thousand Models Bloom: Western Alliances and the Making of the Contemporary Higher Educational System in the Gulf Arab Countries." Paper presented at the annual meeting of the Middle East Studies Association, Washington, DC, November 2008.

Wills, Garry. *Lincoln at Gettysburg: The Words That Remade America*. New York: Simon & Schuster, 1993.

———. *"Negro President": Jefferson and the Slave Power*. Boston: Houghton Mifflin, 2003.

Woertz, Eckhart. "Implications of Dubai's Debt Troubles." Gulf Research Center, December 2009.

"Women Can Issue Fatwas, Be Muftis: Shaikh Abdullah Al-Manea." *Saudi Gazette*, August 2, 2008.

"Women Shut Out of Upcoming Saudi Vote." Associated Press, October 12, 2004.

Woodward, Bob. *Bush at War*. New York: Simon & Schuster, 2002.

World Bank. "MENA Flagship Report on Education: The Road Not Traveled—

Education Reform in the MENA." Preliminary findings as presented at Georgetown University, March 24, 2005.

World Bank. *World Development Indicators*. Washington, DC, April 2007. http://ddp-ext.worldbank.org.

World Bank, Technical Cooperation Unit, Country Department IV, Middle East and North Africa Region. *Sultanate of Oman: Sustainable Growth and Economic Diversification*. Report no. 12199-OM. Washington, DC, May 31, 1994.

Wright, Robin. "Al-Jazeera Puts Focus on Reform." *Washington Post*, May 8, 2005.

"WWF Living Planet Report 2008." World Wildlife Fund. Gland, Switzerland. www.panda.org.

Yao, Joanne. "Kuwait: The Italy of the Gulf?" *Middle East Times*, April 14, 2008. www.metimes.com (July 27, 2008).

Yergin, Daniel. *The Prize: The Epic Quest for Oil, Money and Power*. New York: Simon & Schuster, 1991.

Yousef, Raed, Ayed al-Enezi, Hadi al-Ajmi, and Ben Arfaj al-Mutairi. "Arrest in Death Threat to MP on Co-education." *Arab Times*, February 7, 2008. www.zawya.com (July 27, 2008).

Zayani, Mohamed. *Arab Satellite Television and Politics in the Middle East*. Abu Dhabi: Emirates Center for Strategic Studies and Research, 2004.

Zednick, Rick. "Perspectives on War: Inside Al Jazeera." *Columbia Journalism Review* (2002).

Zeller, Tom, Jr. "On the Open Internet, a Web of Dark Alleys." *New York Times*, December 20, 2004.

The Contributors

Juan R. I. Cole is Richard P. Mitchell Collegiate Professor of History at the University of Michigan. His most recent books are *Engaging the Muslim World* and *Napoleon's Egypt: Invading the Middle East*. He is seen and heard frequently on radio and television news and commentary programs and has a regular column at Salon.com. He speaks and reads Arabic, Persian, and Urdu as well as some Turkish. He has lived in various parts of the Muslim world for nearly ten years, and continues to travel widely there.

Jill Crystal is professor in the Department of Political Science at Auburn University. She is the author of several journal articles, book chapters, and two books on the Gulf, *Oil and Politics in the Gulf: Rulers and Merchants in Kuwait and Qatar* and *Kuwait: The Transformation of an Oil State*. Her research interests include Gulf politics, authoritarianism and democratization, and police and law.

Eleanor Abdella Doumato is a historian who specializes in gender, Islamic education, and social change in the Gulf region. Her recent publications include *Teaching Islam: Religion and Textbooks in the Middle East* (coedited with Greg Starrett), "Manning the Barricades: Islam According to Saudi Arabia's School Texts," *Middle East Journal* 57, no. 2 (2003), and "Saudi Expansion in the United States: Half-Hearted Missionary Work Meets Rock-Solid Resistance," in *Kingdom Without Borders: Saudi Arabia's Political, Religious, and Media Frontiers,* edited by Madawi al-Rasheed (2008). She is currently writing a creative nonfiction account of the misadventures of young New England missionaries in northern Iraq in the 1840s.

N. Janardhan is a political analyst based in the United Arab Emirates. He was formerly editor of Gulf in the Media and program manager of Gulf-Asia relations at the Gulf Research Center in Dubai. Current research interests include democracy, media, labor, and international relations in the Gulf Cooperation Council. His forthcoming book is titled *Boom amid Gloom: The Spirit of Possibility in the 21st Century Gulf.*

The late **Andrzej Kapiszewski** was professor of sociology and chair of the Department of Middle East and Far East Studies at Jagiellonian University, Kraków. During the 1990s, he served in the Polish diplomatic service as ambassador of Poland to the United Arab Emirates and Qatar. He wrote numerous books and articles devoted to ethnic and national issues and development in the Arab world. His most recent publication is *Conflicts Across the Atlantic: Essays on Polish-Jewish Relations in the United States During WWI and in the Interwar Years*.

Christian Koch is director of international studies at the Gulf Research Center in Dubai, United Arab Emirates. Previously, he worked for eight years in the Strategic Studies Department at the Emirates Center for Strategic Studies and Research in Abu Dhabi. He has studied at the University of Erlangen-Nürnberg in Germany, the American University in Washington, DC, and the University of South Carolina.

Matteo Legrenzi is assistant professor at the Graduate School of Public and International Affairs of the University of Ottawa. He has published articles on the Gulf Cooperation Council and on the international relations of the Gulf. He is coeditor (with Bessma Momani) of *Beyond Regionalism? Regional Cooperation, Regionalism, and Regionalization in the Middle East*; editor of *Security in the Gulf: Historical Legacies and Future Prospects*; and author of the forthcoming *The GCC and the International Relations of the Gulf: Diplomacy, Security and Economy Co-ordination in a Changing Middle East.*

Gwenn Okruhlik is a visiting scholar in political science at Trinity University. Her research specializes in the politics of the Arabian Peninsula with a focus on Saudi Arabia, where she has conducted extensive fieldwork. Her research is largely at the intersection of political economy and social movements. She has written on Islamist dissent, oil wealth and the rise of opposition, labor migration, regional border disputes, tourism and narrative, struggles over citizenship, and government–private sector relations. Her work appears in *Comparative Politics*, *Middle East Journal*, *Middle East Policy,* and the *Middle East Report* as well as numerous edited volumes.

Gianluca P. Parolin is assistant professor of law at the American University in Cairo, Egypt. He has closely followed the constitutional transition in Bahrain, and in 2002 was invited to monitor the first general elections after the dissolution of parliament in 1975. Beyond Bahrain, his main research interests are plural legal systems and, from a slightly different angle, citizenship in the region. His publications include *Citizenship in the Arab World.*

J. E. Peterson is a historian and political analyst specializing in the Arabian Peninsula and Gulf. He has taught at several universities in the United States, published some sixty scholarly articles and book chapters, and served in the Office of the Deputy Prime Minister for Security and Defence in Muscat. His most recent books are *Defense and Regional Security in the Arabian Peninsula and Gulf, 1973–2004: An Annotated Bibliography*; *Historical Muscat: An Illustrated Guide and Gazetteer*; and *Oman's Insurgencies: The Sultanate's Struggle for Supremacy.*

Mary Ann Tétreault is the Una Chapman Cox Distinguished Professor of International Affairs at Trinity University in San Antonio, Texas. Her publications include books and articles about social movements, gender, oil markets, war crimes, international political economy, world politics, US foreign policy, and the Middle East. She has published two books on Kuwait, *The Kuwait Petroleum Corporation and the Economics of the New World Order* and *Stories of Democracy: Politics and Society in Contemporary Kuwait.*

Jerzy Zdanowski is director of the Centre for Studies on Non-European Countries at the Polish Academy of Sciences in Warsaw. He teaches at Jagiellonian University in Kraków and at Kraków College. He also spent a Fulbright year at Princeton and Rutgers. A historian and Arabist who concentrates on the nineteenth and twentieth centuries, his recent research has focused on slavery in the Gulf states, and on the development of Saudi Arabia as a regional power. His most recent book is *Slavery in the Persian Gulf in the First Half of the 20th Century.*

Index

About the Book

ALTHOUGH REFORM MOVEMENTS have been prominent in varying degrees in most Middle Eastern countries for some time, the cascade of events following the overthrow of Saddam Hussein has generated new pressures for democratization throughout the Arab world. *Political Change in the Arab Gulf States: Stuck in Transition* explores the politics influencing the volatile situation in the region as well as specific measures devised by regimes in power to adjust to the challenges of the current environment.

The authors first focus on the politics of seven Gulf states: Bahrain, Iraq, Kuwait, Oman, Qatar, Saudi Arabia, and the United Arab Emirates. They then consider four forces that are shaping current political attitudes and behavior across the region: movements to broaden women's political participation, the media, current US national security policy, and regional defense cooperation. The result is an up-to-date assessment of the prospects for political reform in the Gulf—and an important corrective to a simplistic domino theory of democratization.

Mary Ann Tétreault is Distinguished Professor of International Affairs at Trinity University. Her recent publications include *Stories of Democracy: Politics and Society in Contemporary Kuwait* and *World Politics as If People Mattered*. **Gwenn Okruhlik** is visiting scholar in the Department of Political Science at Trinity University. She has published widely on a range of issues related to Saudi Arabia. The late **Andrzej Kapiszewski** was professor of sociology at Jagiellonian University in Kraków. Among his many publications is *Nationals and Expatriates: Population and Labor Dilemmas of the GCC States*.